Many books have been published about the life of our Savior, but *The Crises of the Christ*, first published in 1903, stands out among the rest – a book offering a rare insight into the pivotal events in Christ's life.

In examining Christ's life as the accomplishment of a divine work, the author divides it into seven turning points – the "crises":

- The Birth
- The Baptism
- The Temptation
- The Transfiguration
- The Death
- The Resurrection
- The Ascension

Let this renowned classic inspire you as it has thousands of others over the years.

The Crises of the Christ

G. Campbell Morgan

Power Books

Fleming H. Revell Company
Old Tappan, New Jersey

Printed in the United States of America

Library of Congress Cataloging-in-Publication Data

Morgan, G. Campbell (George Campbell), 1863–1945.
  The crises of the Christ / by G. Campbell Morgan.
     p.   cm.
  Reprint. Originally published: New York : F.H. Revell, 1903.
  Includes indexes.
  ISBN 0-8007-5307-0
  1. Jesus Christ—Biography.   2. Christian biography—Palestine.
I. Title.
BT301.M7   1989b
232.9′01—dc20   89-8429
  [B]   CIP

TO

MY FATHER AND MOTHER

Who forty years ago gave me to CHRIST, *and who, never doubting
the acceptance by* HIM *of their child, did from infancy,
and through youth, train me as* HIS; *from whom I
received my first knowledge of* HIM, *so that when
the necessity came for my personal choosing,
so did I recognize the claims of* HIS
*love, that without revulsion, and
hardly knowing when,*

I YIELDED TO HIM

*my allegiance and my
love, devoting spirit, soul, and body
to* HIS *sweet will, and glad service; in
thankfulness to them for their earliest teaching,
and continuance of revelation of* HIM *by example, in
many differing circumstances, in which their loyalty to* HIM
was a perpetual witness to my heart, of the perfection of HIS *love;
in thankfulness that they still are with me labouring together in prayer,*

I DEDICATE THE BOOK.

"*You have had various 'lives of Christ,' German and other, lately provided among your other severely historical studies. Some, critical; and some, sentimental. But there is only one light by which you can read the life of Christ,—the light of the life you now lead in the flesh; and that not the natural, but the won life. 'Nevertheless, I live; yet not I, but Christ liveth in me.'*"—JOHN RUSKIN.

"*St. Mark's Rest.*"

PREFACE

Professor Osler some years ago was reputed to have said what he certainly did not say, namely that a man's work was done at forty. The spirit of what he did say was that a man's original work was completed by that time; and with perhaps some rare exceptions, there is no doubt that he was correct. By the time a man is forty, he has come to certain clear visions and definite conclusions. Unless that is so, it is probable that he will never have either clear visions or definite conclusions. This fact, however, does not militate against the value of work done after that time. The added years are years of riper consideration, fuller examination, and varied application of the things already done.

These opening sentences are the result of the fact that my publishers tell me that they are about to issue the sixteenth edition of this work. At forty years of age I wrote this book, in which I attempted to put in form the vision which possessed me of Christ in His relation to God and His purpose, and to man in his need.

Thirty-three years have gone since that time. In other words, a full generation has passed. During its passing I have been very fully occupied in varied places, witnessing to this self-same Christ. I look back across the years, and then I take up my book again, and go through it. As I do so, I find that Christ is today seen in greater clearness and more amazing glory. I feel, however, that nothing new has given me any reason for any alteration in the statement I made when I wrote this book of the elemental, essential, eternal things concerning Him as I then saw them.

In the happy nature of things it cannot be long ere I see Him, whether He come for me, or I go to Him; and if this presentation of Him may still serve to help others to apprehend some of His ineffable glory, the remaining years of my life and service will be greatly gladdened.

I may add that I am profoundly thankful to God, and constantly surprised, at the continuous messages which have come to me from all parts of the world these three and thirty years, speaking of real help received by this presentation.

No one could possibly be more conscious than I am of the comparative unworthiness of this attempt to deal with the majesty and mystery of the Person and the Mission of Christ.

In the midst of world confusion, and the break-down of so many things on which the human heart was set hopefully, this Christ of God is ever seen moving on, by His own way of the Cross, to the ultimate crowning and glory. In the ages of God we now wait the ultimate Crisis, when He returns again. It is good when our hearts are maintained in a patient waiting for that hour.

G. Campbell Morgan

Westminster Chapel,
   London, S.W.1.
    April, 1936.

Contents

INTRODUCTORY—THE SUBJECT AND THE SCHEME

PRELIMINARY—THE CALL FOR CHRIST—MAN FALLEN

I.	MAN DISTANCED FROM GOD BY SIN	23
II.	MAN IGNORANT OF GOD THROUGH SIN	36
III.	MAN UNLIKE GOD IN SIN	48

BOOK I—THE BIRTH

IV.	THE GREAT MYSTERY—THE GOD-MAN	67
V.	THE MEANING—GOD WAS IN CHRIST	84
VI.	SIGNS TO THE SONS OF MEN	95

BOOK II—THE BAPTISM

VII.	THE PARTING OF THE WAYS	107
VIII.	LIGHT ON THE HIDDEN YEARS	123
IX.	THE VISION OF JOHN	137

BOOK III—THE TEMPTATION

X.	INTRODUCTORY	153
XI.	THE FIRST TEMPTATION	162
XII.	THE SECOND TEMPTATION	174
XIII.	THE THIRD TEMPTATION	186
XIV.	FINAL	200

9

BOOK IV—THE TRANSFIGURATION

XV. INTRODUCTORY 215
XVI. THE MASTER HIMSELF 224
XVII. THE CELESTIAL VISITORS 235
XVIII. THE DAZED DISCIPLES 246
XIX. THE THINGS THAT REMAINED 257

BOOK V—THE CRUCIFIXION

XX. THE APPROACH 275
XXI. THE SUFFERINGS OF CHRIST 290
XXII. SIN UNVEILED, GRACE OUTSHINING 304
XXIII. THE KINGLY EXODUS 317
XXIV. THE REPRESENTATIVE CROWDS 329

BOOK VI—THE RESURRECTION

XXV. PERFECT VICTORY 350
XXVI. THE DIVINE SEAL 361
XXVII. FAITH'S ANCHORAGE 371

BOOK VII—THE ASCENSION

XXVIII. GOD'S PERFECT MAN 389
XXIX. MAN'S WOUNDED GOD 398
XXX. THE NEW UNION 405

RESULTANT—THE ANSWER OF CHRIST—MAN
REDEEMED

XXXI. MAN RESTORED TO GOD BY CHRIST 421
XXXII. MAN KNOWING GOD THROUGH CHRIST . . . 428
XXXIII. MAN LIKE GOD IN CHRIST 439

INDEXES

SCRIPTURES REFERRED TO 451
POETRY 456
WRITERS QUOTED OR REFERRED TO 458
SUBJECT INDEX 459

INTRODUCTORY

THE SUBJECT AND THE SCHEME

" *Christ has come, the Light of the world. Long ages may yet elapse before His beams have reduced the world to order and beauty, and clothed a purified humanity with light as with a garment. But He has come: the Revealer of the snares and chasms that lurk in darkness, the Rebuker of every evil thing that prowls by night, the Stiller of the storm-winds of passion; the Quickener of all that is wholesome, the Adorner of all that is beautiful, the Reconciler of contradictions, the Harmonizer of discords, the Healer of diseases, the Saviour from sin. He has come: the Torch of truth, the Anchor of hope, the Pillar of faith, the Rock for strength, the Refuge for security, the Fountain for refreshment, the Vine for gladness, the Rose for beauty, the Lamb for tenderness, the Friend for counsel, the Brother for love. Jesus Christ has trod the world. The trace of the Divine footsteps will never be obliterated. And the Divine footsteps were the footsteps of a Man. The example of Christ is such as men can follow. On! until mankind wears His image. On! towards yon summit on which stands, not an angel, not a disembodied spirit, not an abstract of ideal and unattainable virtues, but THE MAN JESUS CHRIST.*"
—PETER BAYNE, A. M.
" *The Testimony of Christ to Christianity.*"

INTRODUCTORY

THE SUBJECT AND THE SCHEME

THE authoritative literature concerning the history of the Lord Jesus Christ is contained within the New Testament. He is the supreme subject of the whole library. Every several book gathers its value from its testimony to His person, His teaching, or His work. The perfection of the whole is created by its unification in Him. The first four of its books chronicle His deeds, and His words, during the brief span of a lifetime lasting for a generation. The rest of the book is occupied with the subject of His deeds and His words through all subsequent generations. The book of Acts is the first chapter in that history of the Church, which is the history of the deeds of Christ by the Holy Spirit through His people. The epistles contain the teaching of Christ by the Spirit, through chosen men, for the guidance of His Church until His second advent. The last book contains a prophetic vision of the final movements, which shall firmly establish His reign over the whole earth.

The Old Testament foretells His coming, and chronicles for these days the methods by which the hope of His advent was kept alive; and, indeed, burned ever more brightly through the processes of the past. The New is the history of that advent; and the new message of hope, under the inspiration of which men move through the confusion of conflict towards the certainty of ultimate victory.

The history of the New Testament is at once the story of the life of Jesus of Nazareth, and the account of the accomplishment of the mission of the Christ. These are phases forming the one perfect story. The life of Jesus was the carrying out of the mission of the Christ. The work of the Messiah was accomplished in the orderliness of the life of Jesus.

In this connection it is interesting to notice the opening and closing verses of the New Testament. Matthew the evangelist, places Jesus in His relation to the race. " The book of the generation of Jesus Christ, the Son of David, the son of Abraham." [1] The reference is not to the whole of the New Testament, nor even to the whole of the Gospel, but to the genealogy which immediately follows. The use here of the word " Christ" declares the appoint ment of this Man to definite service. It is rather a title than a name. By His name " Jesus" He is indicated as united to the race, coming through the chosen people. By the title " Christ" He is identified as the One Who comes to fulfil the promises of the past, by the accomplishment of Divine purposes.

The last verse of the New Testament reads, " The grace of the Lord Jesus Christ be with the saints. Amen." [2] Here there is prefixed to the name "Jesus," the title " Lord." The Revised Versions both English and American have relegated the word " Christ" to the margin. Some ancient authorities, however, include it. The essential value of this comparison of verses is not interfered with, whichever view may be taken. The New Testament opens with a declaration, introducing the Man Jesus, and declaring His appointment to service. It closes with a benediction, which announces the crowning of Jesus as Lord, consequent upon

[1] Matt. 1 : 1.   [2] Rev. 22 : 21.

His accomplishment of the purpose appointed; and the use of the word "grace" as the portion of the saints, reveals the glorious issue of that work.

He came for a purpose. The purpose is realized. He was anointed of God for the doing of a work. The work is accomplished, and He is now the Lord through Whom the grace of God is expressed towards, and becomes operative in, such as are subject to Him. Thus between the opening words of Matthew, and the closing statement of John, there lies the story of His life and the account of His mission.

The literature of the Church has been enriched by many lives of Jesus. Some of these have emphasized the facts of His humanity, while others have emphasized the truth of His Deity. All have been of value. They have however been largely devoted to the contemplation of the Person of Jesus, rather than to a consideration of the accomplishment of a Divine work. It is to this particular aspect of the life of Jesus Christ that the present volume is devoted. Interest in Jesus Himself is of preeminent importance. The mystery of His Person, the graciousness of His teaching, the beauty of His character, the wonder of His deeds, all these are of such value that it is impossible to attend to them too closely, or to write too much concerning them. It is, however, of equal importance that this wonderful life should be seen as that of the anointed Servant of God, the Christ, Who in all the details of the passing days, was working a larger work, and towards a mightier issue than a mere contemplation of the human life might seem to suggest. Indeed, the beauty of the life itself is only fully appreciated when it is seen as related in its every part to this mighty movement of God towards the redemption of man.

Here therefore attention is to be fixed, not so much upon the words of His lips, or His working of wonders and signs, as upon His uttering of a Divine word, and His accomplishment of a Divine work.

It is for this reason that the volume is entitled "The Crises of the Christ." In all the works of God there is to be discovered an unvarying method of process and crisis. The process is slow, and difficult to watch in its progress. The crisis is sudden, and flames with a light, which flashing back upon the process, explains it; and forward, indicates a new line of action, which after all is the continuity of that which has preceded it. This might certainly be illustrated by reference to the observation of all natural phenomena. The story of the earth, as read by scientists, is the story of slow movements, and of mighty upheavals. The history of the butterfly of many hues, is that of the pupa, dormant to all appearance, which through crisis emerges into the flower of the air. The crisis is not an accident, not a catastrophe, in the sense of disaster, but a stage in an orderly method. This method, it may be said in passing, is also to be seen in God's revelation of Himself to men, the history of which is recorded in the Divine Library.

In the great song of Isaiah,[1] which assuredly is Messianic in value, there is an indication of this method, and perhaps the key to the interpretation of the whole Scripture, as a Divine revelation. The first lessons concerning God that men had to learn were of Him as the "Wonderful Counsellor." Then through long centuries there was unfolded the fact that He is the "Mighty God." Then in the mission of Christ, in which are included the days of His earthly life, and these years of the application of His work,

Isa. 9: 6.

men are learning that God is the "Everlasting Father." And yet again, in an age that has not yet dawned upon the world, but which must surely come, men will know Him as the "Prince of Peace." In each case the process has been slow, but the lesson once learned, the crisis has initiated a new movement, and commenced a new process.

This same method obtains in the work of the Christ, and in that method, the crises rather than the processes form the subject of the present consideration. Of these there are seven. The initial, that of the birth of Jesus, then secondly, the baptism; thirdly, the temptation; fourthly, the transfiguration; fifthly, the crucifixion; sixthly, the resurrection; and seventhly, the ascension. These are not at equal distances as to time, but they follow in orderly sequence, and in their entirety contain the whole story of that work by which redemption has been wrought for the race.

Each of them ushered in a new order of things in the work of Christ, crowning that of the past, and creating the force for that which was to come.

All these lie between two facts, which must be considered. The first is that of the ruin of the race, which created the necessity for the work of the Christ. The second is that of the redemption of the race, which issues from the work of the Christ. A preliminary section of this volume will be devoted to the ruin which called for Christ, and a final section to the statement of that redemption which constitutes His answer to the call. Thus with reverence, and a deep sense of its transcendent wonder, let the great subject be approached.

PRELIMINARY

THE CALL FOR CHRIST—MAN FALLEN

I. Man Distanced From God by Sin
II. Man Ignorant of God through Sin
III. Man Unlike God in Sin

" This, we say, is man, the fallen principality. In these tragic desolations of intelligence and genius, of passion, pride, and sorrow, behold the import of his eternity. Be no mere spectator, turn the glass we give you round upon yourself, look into the ruin of your own conscious spirit, and see how much it signifies, both that you are a sinner and a man. Here, within the soul's gloomy chamber, the loosened passions rage and chafe, impatient of their law; here huddle on the wild and desultory thoughts; here the imagination crowds in shapes of glory and disgust, tokens both and mockeries of its own creative power, no longer in the keeping of reason; here sits remorse scowling and biting her chain; here creep out the fears, a meagre and pale multitude; here drives on the will in his chariot of war; here lie trampled the great aspirations, groaning in immortal thirst; here the blasted affections weeping out their life in silent injury; all that you see without, in the wars, revenges, and the crazed religions of the world, is faithfully represented in the appalling disorders of your own spirit."

—HORACE BUSHNELL.
" The New Life."

"Now the serpent was more subtle than any beast of the field which Jehovah God had made. And he said unto the woman, Yea, hath God said, Ye shall not eat of any tree of the garden? And the woman said unto the serpent, Of the fruit of the trees of the garden we may eat : but of the fruit of the tree which is in the midst of the garden, God hath said, Ye shall not eat of it, neither shall ye touch it, lest ye die. And the serpent said unto the woman, Ye shall not surely die : for God doth know that in the day ye eat thereof, then your eyes shall be opened, and ye shall be as God, knowing good and evil. And when the woman saw that the tree was good for food, and that it was a delight to the eyes, and that the tree was to be desired to make one wise, she took of the fruit thereof, and did eat ; and she gave also unto her husband with her, and he did eat. And the eyes of them both were opened, and they knew that they were naked ; and they sewed fig-leaves together, and made themselves aprons. And they heard the voice of Jehovah God walking in the garden in the cool of the day : and the man and his wife hid themselves from the presence of Jehovah God amongst the trees of the garden.

"And Jehovah God called unto the man, and said unto him, Where art thou ? And he said, I heard Thy voice in the garden, and I was afraid, because I was naked ; and I hid myself. And He said, Who told thee that thou wast naked ? Hast thou eaten of the tree, whereof I commanded thee that thou shouldest not eat ? And the man said, The woman whom Thou gavest to be with me, she gave me of the tree, and I did eat. And Jehovah God said unto the woman, What is this thou hast done ? And the woman said, The serpent beguiled me, and I did eat. And Jehovah God said unto the serpent, Because thou hast done this, cursed art thou above all cattle, and above every beast of the field ; upon thy belly shalt thou go, and dust shalt thou eat all the days of thy life : and I will put enmity between thee and the woman, and between thy seed and her seed : he shall bruise thy head, and thou shalt bruise his heel. Unto the woman He said, I will greatly multiply thy pain and thy conception ; in pain thou shalt bring forth children ; and thy desire shall be to thy husband, and he shall rule over thee. And unto Adam He said, Because thou hast hearkened unto the voice of thy wife, and hast eaten of the tree, of which I commanded thee, saying, Thou shalt not eat of it : cursed is the ground for thy sake ; in toil shalt thou eat of it all the days of thy life ; thorns also and thistles shall it bring forth to thee ; and thou shalt eat the herb of the field ; in the sweat of thy face shalt thou eat bread, till thou return unto the ground ; for out of it wast thou taken : for dust thou art, and unto dust shalt thou return. And the man called his wife's name Eve ; because she was the mother of all living. And Jehovah God made for Adam and for his wife coats of skins, and clothed them.

"And Jehovah God said, Behold, the man is become as one of us to know good and evil ; and now, lest he put forth his hand, and take also of the tree of life, and eat, and live forever—therefore Jehovah God sent him forth from the garden of Eden, to till the ground from whence he was taken. So He drove out the man ; and He placed at the east of the garden of Eden the Cherubim, and the flame of a sword which turned every way, to keep the way of the tree of life."—*Genesis 3.*

*   *   *   *   *   *   *

"Therefore, as through one man sin entered into the world, and death through sin ; and so death passed unto all men, for that all sinned."—*Romans 5 : 12.*

I

MAN DISTANCED FROM GOD BY SIN

In the mission of Christ, that wisdom of God was manifested, and that power of God operated, through which it became possible for ruined man to be redeemed and reconciled. The marvel of that wisdom, and the light of that power, can only be fully appreciated, in the measure in which the extent and nature of the calamity which called for Christ is understood. The whole subject is indicated in the titles of the three chapters, forming this preliminary section. The first deals with the initial act of sin, and its result, man distanced from God by sin. The second deals with the relative result of sin, man ignorant of God through sin. While the third has to do with the effect of sin upon man, man unlike God in sin.

In dealing with the first of these phases of the one fact, it is necessary first to consider man according to the Divine ideal in his unfallen condition; secondly, to consider the fall, as to man's action; and thirdly, to contemplate the resulting fact, man's alienation from God.

I. The essential truth concerning the nature of man is contained in a descriptive expression found in the book of Genesis, and in New Testament Scriptures. He is spoken of as being "created in the image and likeness of God." In order to understand the significance of this expression, it will be well to read the whole of the Scriptures where it occurs.

"And God said, Let Us make man in Our image, after Our likeness: and let them have dominion over the fish of the sea, and over the birds of the heavens, and over the cattle, and over all the earth, and over every creeping thing that creepeth upon the earth. And God created man in His own image, in the image of God created He him; male and female created He them." [1]

"This is the book of the generations of Adam. In the day that God created man, in the likeness of God made He him." [2]

"Whoso sheddeth man's blood, by man shall his blood be shed: for in the image of God made He man." [3]

"For a man indeed ought not to have his head veiled, forasmuch as he is the image and glory of God: but the woman is the glory of the man." [4]

"In whom the god of this world hath blinded the minds of the unbelieving, that the light of the Gospel of the glory of Christ, Who is the Image of God, should not dawn upon them." [5]

"Who is the Image of the invisible God, the First-born of all creation." [6]

"And have put on the new man, that is being renewed unto knowledge after the image of Him that created him." [7]

"Who being the effulgence of His glory, and the very Image of His substance, and upholding all things by the word of His power, when He had made purification of sins, sat down on the right hand of the Majesty on high." [8]

These are the only passages in which the fact of man's being created in the image and likeness of God is definitely declared. What is intended by the expression may be

[1] Gen. 1 : 26, 27.   [2] Gen. 5 : 1.   [3] Gen. 9 : 6.   [4] 1 Cor. 11 : 7.
[5] 2 Cor. 4 : 4.   [6] Col. 1 : 15.   [7] Col. 3 : 10.   [8] Heb. 1 : 3.

elucidated by an examination of the actual words used. The root idea of the Hebrew word translated " image " is that of a shadow. Of the other word there can be no better translation than the one adopted, that namely, of likeness.

Turning to the New Testament, the word translated " image " in the first four Scriptures quoted, is the word εἰκών, which suggests the idea of an outline resemblance, very literally a profile. The word translated " image " in the passage from Hebrews is the word χαρακτήρ, which simply means an exact copy, or an engraving. Thus it will be seen that both in Old and New Testaments, the expression suggests a definite resemblance, rather than an exact representation, except where, as already indicated in ᵗhe letter to the Hebrews, the language is descriptive of Christ in such aspect of His Person as is peculiar to Himself, and in which men by original creation have no participation.

Passing over these Scriptures again, let the progression of thought be noted carefully. In the account of creation, it is affirmed that man was in some respect a shadow or manifestation of God. Here are two ideas, arresting thought, and not to be forgotten in the subsequent discussion. First, man is but a faint representation, a shadow merely ; and secondly, the very dignity of his being lies in the fact that he is even so much as that. Perhaps the simplest exposition of the thought would be gained by a contemplation of the shadow of a man cast upon some white background, by the shining of a great light. What the shadow would be to the man, the man would be to God. Like and unlike, suggesting an idea, but by no means explaining the mystery, impossible apart from the substance, and yet infinitely less in essence than the substance. Man no more perfectly expresses all the facts concerning God, than does the shadow those concerning man. Nevertheless the shadow is the image of the man, and indicates truth concerning him.

This expression never occurs in the Old Testament after the account of creation, save when in the ninth chapter of the book of Genesis, man is safeguarded from murder, the reason given being that no man has a right to destroy that which was made in the Divine image. By the act of sin, the image and likeness of God in man was not destroyed but defaced, and in all the history, contained in Old Testament Scripture, is seen a degraded ideal.

Turning to the New Testament, after the completion of the work of Christ, the expression is restored in the writings of the apostle. In the Scripture first quoted, he is evidently referring to man as to the original Divine intention concerning him, and he speaks of him as the "image and glory of God." In the second reference he uses the expression of Christ, as the One Who has realized that primal Divine intention, and in Colossians he declares that the original Divine ideal may be restored through the work of Christ. In Hebrews, where it has been shown, the word is a far stronger one, it is used of Christ, Who is infinitely more than a shadow of God, seeing that He is "the effulgence of His glory, and the very image of His substance." [1]

Having thus examined the Scriptures, and the use of the phrase therein, it may be enquired, In what sense was man created in the image of God? The answer to the enquiry may be found, by suggesting another question. What is man essentially, for it is in his essential nature that he is in the image of God? Man essentially is spirit, his

[1] Heb. 1: 3.

present body being his probational dwelling place, that through which he receives impressions, and that through which he expresses the fact of his own being. In his letter to the Romans the apostle says, "I beseech you therefore, brethren, by the mercies of God, to present your bodies a living sacrifice, holy, acceptable to God, which is your spiritual service."[1] The marginal reading of the Revised Version changes the word "service" into "worship," and therein lies a revelation of the true relation of the spirit of man to his body. Through the medium of the body, the truth concerning the spirit expresses itself. Where the body is presented, it is presented by the spirit, and through this devotion of the body, the spirit expresses its worship. The essential fact in man therefore is his spirit, and it is in spiritual essence that man is made in the image of God. There are secondary senses in which even in bodily form, man is a shadow of Deity. As the body of man is the expression of his spirit, and the spirit is the image of God, so through the tabernacle of man's spirit there are made certain suggestions concerning God Himself.

The present study however, is confined to the essential fact. Within the spiritual fact of man's being there are three constituents. These have been variously described. Perhaps at once the simplest and most lucid analysis is that of Kant. He speaks of intelligence, emotion, and will. It is in the possession of these things that man is in the image of God. God is a Spirit, having intelligence, having emotion, having will. Man is in the shadow of God. He also is a spirit, having intelligence, having emotion, having will. In all these things he is but a shadow, that is to say, there are limitations upon these

[1] Rom. 12 : 1.

facts in human nature, which in the Divine are illimitable and consequently not to be perfectly understood of men It has been objected to the doctrine of the personality of God that the thought of personality implies limitation. This, however, is to argue from a false hypothesis. Perfect personality is unlimited, so that personality is only perfect in God, and is imperfect in man. In God intelligence is unlimited, emotion is unlimited, will is unlimited. In man all these facts are found, but in each case within limitations. He does not know all things, his intelligence being limited, his emotional nature also can only act within comparatively narrow limitations, and the exercise of his will is limited by the demand for a cause, which is never perfectly found within himself.

Man as originally created, was not only in the image of God. He was also made to live in union with God, so that all his limitation might find its complement in the unlimited life of the Eternal. It is a great mistake to think of man as made, and then put into some position, where he might rise or fall, according to the capacity of his own personality. It is rather to be remembered that he was created in the image of God, and then put in the probationary position through which he was to pass unharmed to some larger form of existence, if his life were lived in union with the God Who had created him. If however he chose a separate existence, and cut himself off from union, in that act, he would encompass his own ruin, he would fall.

This intended life of union with God may be described in two ways, as personal fellowship, which is holiness of character; and as cooperative activity, which is righteousness of conduct. For a full understanding of what this meant, it is useless to tarry in the garden of Eden. There, in the account of creation, a faint suggestion is given of the Divine intention. It is necessary, however, to come to the last Adam, the Man Jesus, for a full appreciation of this Divine intention. In Him unbroken fellowship with the Father manifested itself in holiness of character, and unceasing cooperation with God expressed itself in absolute righteousness of conduct.

In order to an appreciation of the meaning of fellowship with God there must be remembered the analysis of personality already referred to, intelligence, emotion, and will. In unfallen man the limited intelligence was nevertheless enlightened, and was able to understand the things of God. Limited emotion was nevertheless enkindled towards the things thus known, and man loved God and all He loved. The limited will was yet energized by the superior and Infinite Will of God, and so chose ever the things that were in harmony with that Will. Thus in unfallen man there was to be found enlightened intelligence, enkindled emotion, energized will, wholly within the realm of the Divine Sovereignty.

Then beyond that personal fellowship, there was cooperative activity, which is righteousness of conduct. And again the analysis of personality may be taken as the basis of consideration. All activity is the outward expression of an inward intelligence. The enlightened intelligence of unfallen man, appreciating the things of God, the deeds of the life of such a being were in perfect harmony with the purposes of God. The emotional nature of such a being, appreciating and loving the things of God, became the spring from which streams of action emerged, which were all moving in the Divine direction. In such a being the will exercised its highest function in choosing the things of God, and the activities of the life were therefore always those of partnership with the enterprises of God. The old word spoken to the father of the race was "have dominion." In the midst of a wondrous creation God set man. The creation in which man found himself had not yet realized all the possibilities of its own being. It waited the touch of man in cooperation with God for that realization. God put man into a garden to dress it, and to keep it. The preparation of man's work was of God, the creation of the worker was of God, there was perfect fitness between the work to be done, and the workman prepared, and while man lived in fellowship with God, and co-operated with God, all creation recognized his leadership, yielded to his dominion, and moved along the line of a new progress towards a yet more wondrous beauty and perfection.

These truths are yet evidenced by the power of man even in a fallen condition. All the cultivation of flowers, all the inventions of science, are in the last analysis, but man's cooperation with God, issuing in new forms of beauty, and fresh forces of utility. A very simple illustration in floral culture is that of the chrysanthemum. But a very few years ago it was looked upon as an old-fashioned garden flower, very sweet, but very simple. To-day it is one of the most gorgeous and marvellous of decorative blossoms, so beautiful in the length and delicacy of its petals, so poetic in its restless waviness of beauty, and so splendid in its possibility of colour, that it has well been described as "a rose gone wild with joy."[1] The possibility of this beauty always lay within the modest garden flower, and the development thereof has been wholly due to man's discovery of certain laws of Nature, which laws are ever the thoughts of God.

[1] Dr. Joseph Parker.

So also in the realm of scientific discovery. Let a map of the world be taken, and let the hand be placed upon the centres where such discoveries have been made, and it will invariably be found that the hand is resting on a land where the light of the Christian revelation has most brightly shined. These things but go to prove that it is in cooperation with God that man is capable of highest activity, because in cooperation with God he realizes the perfection of character. Unfallen man, then, was a being like God, in the essentials of his nature, in that he was a spirit having intelligence, emotion, and will. Unfallen man realized the highest possibility of his being in a life of personal fellowship and cooperative activity with God.

There yet remains one other fact to remember, concerning the unfallen condition of man. He was placed in circumstances of probation. That is to say, the citadel of his nature was his will. It was for him to choose whether he would abide in that relation to God, which would ensure his fullest realization of possibility, or whether he would by severance from God encompass his own ruin. It was a terrible and awful alternative. Yet unless it were offered to man, the highest fact of his being would be atrophied, for will power, having no choice, ceases to be of value. Thus in the garden of his activity God marked the limit of his possibility by two sacramental symbols. Both were trees. The one was the tree of life, of which he was commanded to eat. The other was the tree of the knowledge of good and evil, which was forbidden. Between these lay an endless variety of which he might or might not eat, as pleased himself. Of the tree of life he must eat, and thus he was reminded, in a positive symbol, of his dependence for the sustenance of his being upon God. Of the tree of the knowledge of good and evil he was forbidden to eat, and thus he was reminded of the limitation of his freedom within the government of God. Finite will is to be tested, and it will stand or fall as it submits to, or rebels against the Infinite Will of the Infinite God. Thus unfallen man was a being created in the image of God, living in union with God, cooperating in activity with God, having the points of the limitation of his being marked by simple and definite commands laid upon him, gracious promises luring him to that which was highest on the one hand, and a solemn sentence warning him from that which was lowest on the other. He was a sovereign under a Sovereignty, independent, but dependent. He had the right of will, but this could only be perfectly exercised in perpetual submission to the higher will of his God. The whole fact is summarized concerning essential human nature in the exquisite couplet,

> " Our wills are ours, we know not how ;
> Our wills are ours to make them Thine." [1]

II. In considering the Bible account of the fall of man, it is necessary first to note carefully the process of his temptation. In the story of Genesis is clearly revealed the great distinction between testing and tempting. Man's position in the economy of God was one in which he was in the place of testing. That testing became definite enticement towards evil through the agency of evil already existing, and expressing itself through its prince, the devil. The method of the enemy was full of all subtlety. He first asked a question which was calculated to create the sense of restricted liberty, and so cast an aspersion on the goodness of God. To paraphrase the question, he said, In this garden is there some tree forbidden to you ? Are you

[1] Tennyson.

at any point of your will limited and restricted? The
answer of the woman admitted the limitation, a limitation
which certainly existed. Then the very essence of evil is
seen in the interpretation of that limitation. Whereas the
limitation in the purpose of God was wholly beneficent,
and intended to hold man within the only sphere in which
he could make progress towards the largest and fullest possibility of his being; the enemy suggested that it was imposed by a desire on the part of God to keep man from
progress and enlargement of capacity. Thus it is seen that
at the back of the method of the devil is an aspersion cast
upon the character of God. Man was made to question
the goodness of law. Appealing to the intelligence of
man, the enemy created an aspersion, which was calculated
to change the attitude of his emotion, and so capture the
final citadel, that namely, of his will. He declared that
man's intellectual nature was prevented from development
by this limitation. By this declaration he created in the
mind of man a question as to the goodness of the God Who
had made the law, and thus imperilled the relation of the
will to God, as he called it into a place of activity outside,
and contrary to, the will of God.

Then came the actual fall, and its essential characteristic
was that of independent action. The wisdom and the love
of God having been called into question, man instead of
taking counsel with Him, concerning this suggestion of evil,
acted independently, and in that act of self-separation from
God, he fell from the sphere in which it was possible to realize all the infinite meaning of his being, into that of utter
and irremedial ruin. All the rivers that have made sad tnt
life of man, had their source in this turning of the will of man
from its proper channel, that of community of action with
the will of God, into the channelless rush of undetermined

and ungoverned activity. By taking of the fruit of the for-bidden tree, man desecrated the sacramental symbol, be-cause he had departed from that sphere of life of which the non-partaking tree was the confine. By the assertion of his own will he dethroned God and enthroned himself. Man as to spiritual essence sinned when listening to the tempter, he doubted the love, and decided to act as against the will of God. That inward and spiritual fall of man found its expression in the overt act of taking that which God had forbidden.

III. The issue of the act is revealed in the words " so He drove out the man." [1]   Man by his own decision and deed has separated himself from God. God by the necessity of the being created, judicially separates man from Himself. Having violated the covenant man is put outside its bene-fits. The life of dependence upon God was the life of union and cooperation with God. Man having chosen the position of independence, is now cut off from union and cooperation. To say this, is to declare that by his own act, man has become separated from that fellowship with God which constitutes his holiness of character; and from that cooperation with God, which is the condition of righteous-ness of conduct. He has passed into a region where the essential powers of his being can find no fitting field of op-eration. He retains the essential facts of his being, but they cannot be perfected, because they have lost their true sphere. Henceforward his intelligence must be bounded by its own limitation, as it is severed from the Infinite Knowledge. So also his emotion must become dwarfed as to capacity, because it has lost its perfect object in the loss of God. His will, a magnificent ruin, will perpetually at-

[1] Gen. 3 : 24.

tempt to secure mastership, and yet will never succeed, because it has lost its own true spring of action, and its own Master. Man distanced from God has not lost the powers of his original creation; he has lost the true sphere of their exercise. His intelligence is darkened, his emotion is deadened, his will is degraded. Darkened intelligence henceforth will see only the things that are near. The spaciousness of the spiritual condition has ceased, and man will look at material things in a semi-blindness, which is at once tragic and pathetic. Deadened emotion, a heaven-born capacity, will attempt to satisfy itself wholly within the realm of the earth, and love being set wholly upon the things material, will forever be wounded in their loss. Degraded will, ever attempting to be authoritative, masterful, will always be thwarted, beaten, overcome. Out of this dire and desolate ruin, God hears the call for a Deliverer.

II

MAN IGNORANT OF GOD THROUGH SIN

WHILE the attack of evil was directed finally towards the capture of human will, the method of approach was that of suggesting the possibility of a development of the intellect. By the assertion of the right to exercise the will outside all limitation, it was declared that man should know. In his attempt to grasp knowledge, man alienated himself from the light of fellowship with God, and thus his intelligence was darkened and dwarfed, rather than enlightened and enlarged. The result of this is so far reaching in the being of man, that it is important to devote a chapter to the discussion of the fact of man's ignorance of God, resulting from sin. In order to a proper understanding of this, there must be a correct conception of man's original capacity for the knowledge of God; and secondly, an understanding of the injury that happened to this capacity; in order that thirdly, there may be an explanation of the idolatry which resulted.

I. In dealing with man's capacity for God, the thought again gathers round the threefold fact of his personality, that as to spiritual essence, man has intelligence, emotion, and will, these being but a shadowing forth of the Divine personality. These three facts in man are interrelated, so that the appreciation of the intelligence will determine the action of the emotion, and finally also the attitude of the will. In the first Divine intention the intelligence of man is capacity for the knowledge of God. It would seem as though in the whole creation, man is the only being to whom God could perfectly reveal Himself, and this fact defines the dignity of human nature. In this connection a statement in the beginning of the Gospel of John has to be carefully noted. " In the beginning was the Word, and the Word was with God, and the Word was God. The same was in the beginning with God. All things were made through Him; and without Him was not anything made that hath been made. In Him was life; and the life was the light of men." [1] The declaration, " in Him was life," is a general and comprehensive one, declaring that all forms of life are related to the living Word. The announcement that " the life was the light of men," is a particular declaration revealing an essential truth concerning the nature of man. This cannot be said concerning the life of any plant, nor of animal life, until in the scale of being man is reached. In man life became consciousness of God, and capacity for the understanding of Him. This statement of John of course has far wider application. It certainly indicates the truth that perfect light concerning manhood has shined in the Word Incarnate, but as Jesus was the fulfillment of an original purpose, it becomes evident that according to that purpose, man is capable of intelligent appreciation of, and communion with, God. The whole process of creation was carried forward through the Word of the Eternal, and every form of life exists and subsists through the energy of that Word. In man however, life was first of such a nature as to comprehend the Creator. In the writings of the apostle Paul it is evident how he perpetually recognizes as one of the most glorious results of the redemption of man, the fact

[1] John 1 : 1–4.

that there is restored to him the knowledge of God. Especially in the epistles of the imprisonment, when writing to the churches of his love, he thanks God for their faith, for their hope, for their love, but still is labouring for them in prayer; and the overmastering desire that he has for them is that they may come to the full knowledge of God. In the creation of man, God originated a being capable of knowing Him. For the comprehension of wisdom there must be intelligence, and in man God created an intellect equal to such wonderful knowledge.

To know God is to know love, and to know love is to love. Hence man is created with an emotional nature, ready to act in response to knowledge. The apostle of love declares, "we love, because He first loved us."[1] Herein is a declaration of the origin of love in the consciousness of man. Man knowing God is conscious of His love, and that love of God is the generator of the love of man. The accurate knowledge of unclouded intelligence, inevitably issues in the perfect love of undegraded emotion. Such knowledge issuing in such love, creates the true governing principle for the action of the supreme fact of human life, that namely of the will.

The doctrine of the freedom of the will is itself only true within certain limitations. There is a sense in which in the very nature of will it cannot be free. Only in lack of reason, or madness, is there perfect freedom of the will. Man never wills save under the impulse of a conviction. Behind every decision of the will there must of necessity be a governing principle. Man constantly asserts, I will. He never does this, but that he might add to the statement something more. He might, that is to say, declare the reason why he wills, so that the full statement is always, I

[1] I John 4: 19.

will because ——. That which follows the because, is the authority that commands the will. In unfallen man the authority behind will is the love of God, which is the outcome of a perfect knowledge of God. Thus the perfect activity of the will of man is always conditioned by submission to the will of God. Herein is a revelation of the meaning of much that Jesus said concerning His relation to His Father, and an explanation of all that He was in perfection of character, in wisdom of teaching, and in beauty of activity.

To this it may be objected that while this is true of human will, it cannot be said that the Divine will is under authority; and yet, that the very will of God is acting under an authority, is precisely the truth. The principle governing the movements of the will of God, is that of the perfect communion of Infinite Love and Infinite Light. In the very essential of His being, God is Love. It is equally true that He is Light, so that every action of the will is determined by Love, and by the unerring wisdom of Light. Thus let it be definitely stated that God is limited in every action of His will by unlimited Love and that unclouded Light, in which no darkness is. Thus unfallen man wills in response to love, which is the result of knowledge.

II. In this consideration lies an explanation of the method of the enemy. When man, listening to his suggestion of evil, asserted his will, it was upon the basis of a doubt of the Divine Love, which he had allowed himself to entertain. By that act of self separation from God, man lost the knowledge of God, which issues in love to God, and creates the true governing principle behind the action of will. Distance from God means the clouding of the intelligence, and therefore the debasement of the emotion, and therefore the degradation of the will. The fact that man's intelligence is clouded is by no means a popular doctrine, and yet human history, equally with inspired revelation, attest the truth of the declaration. Through all the ages, and through all the schools of human thought, man has been engaged in a fruitless search after a final knowledge. Too often man is utterly unconscious of what that knowledge is after which he seeks, and yet the restlessness of human intellect, and its passionate striving, indicate its incompleteness, and its deep consciousness of that incompleteness. Zophar the Naamathite, speaking to Job said,

> " Canst thou by searching find out God ?
> Canst thou find out the Almighty unto perfection ? " [1]

A most remarkable question in perhaps the oldest book in the Divine Library, indicating the consciousness of incompleteness existing among the meditative men of a far gone age. Yet take that question and ask it in the midst of the vaunted culture of this century, and the implied answer of the age in which Zophar asked, is the actual answer of the present age. Man does not know, nor can he discover God by the unaided working of his intellect, and that because his intellect is clouded, having lost its action with the true light. The hardest thinking of the nineteenth century was done in its latter half, by men, who, in comparison with other men, were intellectual giants. Let it be granted, as it is almost certainly true, that they were honest in their searching, and the names of them will be sufficient guarantee, Darwin, Huxley, Tyndal, and Spencer. They observed, they collected, they compared, they laboured to

[1] Job. 11 : 7.

discover the deepest secrets, and yet what were the conclusions at which they arrived? They claimed to have
found, and declared, a certain method discoverable through
all natural phenomena. They were not able perfectly to
explain the very method which they discovered, much less
were they able to account for the method as to its origin.

Spencer speaks of being " in the presence of an infinite
and eternal energy from which all things proceed." That
n itself is a very remarkable discovery, and yet how
vague, and inadequate for the satisfaction of the passion of
the human intellect for definiteness and absolute truth.

What then have these men found, if these things be true.
They have found certain evidences of the working of God,
have discovered it may be, certain attributes of Deity, but
they have not by searching found out God. So that the
most remarkable activity of the human intellect in the most
enlightened century of the human race, stops short exactly
where man's clouded intellect stopped short in those dim
and distant times of Zophar the Naamathite. Man
watches still, and in his searching tracks the footprints of
Deity, sees something of the methods of the Divine, but
utterly fails to find God. And yet for an intimate and
immediate knowledge of God the intellect of man was
created.

III. Man is a ruined instrument. He nevertheless retains, though in impaired form, the natural elements which
constitute the Divine image. There is therefore a constant
demand in his nature for that for which he was created.
Intelligence is still demanding light. Emotion continues
to seek for objects upon which to fasten. Will requires a
governing principle, in brief, man demands God. Having
lost his knowledge of God, he proceeded to substitute in

the place of the dethroned One, other deities. It is unthinkable and impossible that human nature should exist
without a god in some form. The most blatant infidel,
denying the existence of a Supreme Being, yet worships;
and where there is no other object, then man enshrines his
own intellect, bows down before that, declaring that he
will receive and yield to the things he can comprehend,
thus making his understanding the very deity that receives
his worship. As a bird cannot fly except in air, and a fish
cannot swim save in water, so man cannot exercise the
necessary functions of his life save in relation to God.

When man is thus driven to the dire necessity of creating his own deity, there is but one way in which he can do
it. The only conception of God that man has, is gathered
from an understanding of his own personality. This is
true even in the case of the most devout believer. It is
almost impossible to think of God save by projecting the
lines of human personality into infinitude, and this is the
true method. The last and highest fact of Divine creation
is the spiritual in man, and that is in the image of God.
Therefore it is possible to argue back from the final creative movement to the originating Creator. If man is the
image of God, he is like God; and that is at once to say
that God is like man. The intelligence of Deity is argued
from the intelligence of man, so that man, projecting the
lines of his own intelligence into immensity, thinks of God.
This is true also with regard to emotion, and with regard
to will.

This creation of a god upon the basis of man's knowledge
of himself, lies at the back of the whole story of idolatry.
From whence then has come all the ignorance and brutality, and vindictiveness of false gods ? Evidently from the
fact that the lines projected were in themselves imperfect.

Project the ruined man into immensity, and a ruined god is the result, only the ruin is worse than the ruined man. In the magnified man there is magnified evil and intensified failure. That is the history of all idolatry. Man having fallen, demanded a god, and having lost the knowledge of the true God, has projected into immensity the lines of his own personality, and thus has created as objects of worship, the awful monsters, the service of which, in process of time, has reacted in the still deeper degradation of the worshipper. All false deities are distortions of the one true God, and the distorted idea is the result of the ruin of the image of God in man.

Referring to the idolatry of Ephraim, the prophet Hosea declared, "And now they sin more and more, and have made them molten images of their silver, even idols according to their own understanding, all of them the work of the craftsman."[1] "Idols according to their own understanding." That understanding being darkened, the idol resulting was a libel upon God.

With regard to idolatry, it may broadly be stated that the Old Testament reveals three great ideas of God embodied within the false systems of religion, all of them based upon a truth, but in the distortion of truth resulting most disastrously. These three ideas may be indicated by the three words, Baal, Moloch, and Mammon. All false ideas of Deity gather around those words. Other gods are mentioned, but they are all subsidiary, and stand for some aspect or attitude of these essential misconceptions.

These ideas moreover, have by no means ceased to be the gods which men worship. The form of the worship may have changed, and the garb of the idol may be different, but all else remains the same. Every human being

[1] Hosea 13: 2.

who is not worshipping the One living God, is worshipping Baal, or Moloch, or Mammon, or all three.

The worship of Baal was essentially the deification of Nature, and in that deification there comes at last to be necessary the worship of the central and most marvellous fact in Nature. That fact is the reproductive faculty. All Nature worship which may seem to begin in the innocent and harmless adoration of the beauty and the order of Nature, issues at last in all uncleanness and lasciviousness, and the highest forms of worship come to be acts so foul as to be nameless.

The worship of Baal is the groping of the intelligence after God in Nature, and its search is futile; so that at last the darkened understanding touching the last mystery of power, without being able to discover the final truth, there results the degradation of the whole being.

The worship of Moloch expressed itself in all cruelty, its chief expression being the sacrifice of little children. This is the prostitution of the emotional nature. Hate always lives next door to love. Man magnifying his own emotional nature finds a god who will be appeased by acts of cruelty. As in the worship of Nature there is finally committed all manner of sins and sensualism through the debasement of the intelligence, so necessarily the degraded affectional nature will express itself in lack of love, and therefore in deeds of brutality towards the offspring of man.

The worship of Moloch has by no means ceased. As man to-day has deified, and worships in fearful form at the shrine of, the central mystery of life, he does so with callous heart and absolute indifference to the ruin wrought. Here are suggested lines of thought which must be followed without the expression of words to aid. Let it only be said that as love is the fairest word in all the vocabulary of human speech, the foulest is lust. Yet both these words are the result of the operation of one capacity. Its operation within the realm of a perfectly informed understanding is indicated by the word love. Its operation within the realm of a degraded intelligence is indicated by the word lust.

Yet there remains the third of these—Mammon. Schleusner has asserted that Mammon was the name of a Syrian deity. Of this however there seems to be no positive proof. The word was one in common use in the East among the Phœnicians, the Syrians, and others, and it stood for wealth, and the power of wealth. Jesus made a most significant and remarkable use of the word. He said, "Ye cannot serve God and Mammon."[1] In that statement there is evidence of His intimate understanding of fallen human nature, and of His far-seeing appreciation of all the facts resulting from sin. He did not say, Ye cannot serve God and the devil. If He had, for purposes of practical application His word would be almost pointless in this particular age. As it is, with every movement of material progressiveness, His word becomes still more searching, more arresting. The method of the evil one has ever been that of obscuring himself behind some other object of worship. In the dark ages men had a very weird and terrible consciousness of the personality of Satan, and the art of the time depicts him as a monster with hoofs and horns, and all ugliness of countenance. For the purposes of those dark ages, when men were superstitious, because ignorant, such method of appeal proved the subtlety of the foe. In the case of more cultured mental capacity, the foe always hides the ugliness of his being, and to-day as never before he asks for the submission of man to his sway, by presenting before the vision of man the fascinations of wealth, and

[1] Matt. 6: 24.

the power which wealth commands. The worship of Mammon is the rendering to wealth for the sake of its power, of all that man ought to render to God. In the dethronement of God and the enthronement of man's personal desire as the governing principle behind the activity of his will, man has come to think of greatness as consisting in ability to govern and master other people. There is no way by which man may secure more power over other men than by the possession of wealth, and therefore man worships Mammon with all his soul, with all his mind, with all his heart, because Mammon represents unlimited power.

Thus in the last analysis Mammon is the deification of human will. In projecting himself into immensity, man has magnified a will that insists upon the subservience of others, and so has come to worship a deity whose expression of godhead is mastery, and whose sceptre of power is the possession of wealth.

May it not thus be said in brief, that the worship of Baal is the adoration of imperfect knowledge, resulting from the darkening of the intelligence; that the worship of Moloch is the adoration of prostituted emotion, resulting from the degradation of the affectional nature; that the worship of Mammon is the adoration of a degraded will, resulting from the loss of the true governing principle behind the will of man. All this in its thousand manifestations in the idolatries of the race, and in its continued manifestation in the godlessness of the vast multitudes of the most civilized people, has issued from the fact that man being distanced from God by sin, has become ignorant of God through sin.

Thus all unconsciously out of a terrible ignorance, and, indeed, by that very ignorance, man calls for Christ; calls, that is, for the shining of the true Light, in which there shall be the restoration of the true and only God, by which knowledge there shall come a destruction of the false gods, the worship of which has resulted so terribly in the history of the race.

III

MAN UNLIKE GOD IN SIN

IF it be true that man having lost his vision of God, creates gods for himself, by projecting into immensity his own distorted being, it follows therefore that there must be reaction on the character of man himself.

In describing the idols of the nations, the Psalmist makes use of remarkable and suggestive words.

> "Their idols are silver and gold,
> The work of men's hands.
> They have mouths, but they speak not;
> Eyes have they, but they see not;
> They have ears, but they hear not;
> Noses have they, but they smell not;
> They have hands, but they handle not;
> Feet have they, but they walk not;
> Neither speak they through their throat.
> They that make them shall be like unto them;
> Yea, every one that trusteth in them."[1]

This is the declaration of a great principle, that a man is always like his God. Having created a god upon the pattern of himself, man becomes governed by that idea, and so the process of deterioration goes forward.

The whole fact may be indicated by bringing together a group of Scriptures.

First, the statement of Genesis, "So He drove out the man."[2]

[1] Psa. 115: 4–8.　　　　　　[2] Gen. 3: 24.

Next the statement from the prophecy of Hosea, "They . . . have made them molten images of their silver, even idols according to their own understanding." [1]

Third, a declaration of the Psalmist, "they that make them shall be like unto them; Yea, every one that trusteth in them."

Fourth, Paul's description of the condition of the people, who have become idolaters, "having no hope and without God in the world." [2] Man alienated from God throug' sin, answered the craving of his nature for God by creating one. He became degraded by his own false conception, and the final fact is, that being without God, he is also without hope.

The present study will be devoted to a consideration, first, of the fact that separation from God issues in unlikeness; secondly, of the unlikeness resulting from separation; concluding with a summing up of the position as indicating the call for Christ.

I. In the fact of his alienation from God, man has lost his own spiritual life. As material death is the separation of the spirit from the body, so spiritual death is the separation of the spirit from God. The Scripture thought concerning the death of the spirit is nowhere that of cessation of the spirit's existence. Death means cessation of existence only with regard to that which is perishable. The body is but the temporary and probationary dwelling-place of man's spirit. Death for that means the end of its existence. The death of the spirit consists in its existence, but in separation from that Spirit of God, in fellowship with Whom it is alone equal to the fulfillment of all its essential functions. Separated from God, the spirit of man

[1] Hosea 13: 2.   [2] Eph. 2: 12.

retains its consciousness of great possibilities, without being able to realize and fulfill them. Eyes which do not see, ears which do not hear, the only consciousness of God is that of an intellectual conviction of His existence, not that of a personal acquaintance with Him.

This statement comes as more than a declaration of a doctrine. It is the expression of an experience. Apart from the miracle of regeneration no man has a true vision of God. Sometimes in boastfulness, and in the attitude of ridicule, men will declare that they do not believe in the existence of God, because they have never seen God. God is present in the orderliness of Nature, in the magnificent and minute beauty of the infinitely great and the infinitely small. Man cannot see Him. To those whose hearts are pure and whose eyes are open, He is to be seen in the face of a little child, and in all the movements of the times. But man, alienated from the Divine life, though dwelling in the place of vision sees nothing. The light shines, but the darkened eye perceives it not. The voice speaks, but the heavy ear hears it not. God is near to every man, but the dead spirit is unconscious of His nearness.

In that wonderful address of Paul to the men of Athens, he said, " Ye men of Athens, in all things I perceive that ye are very religious. For as I passed along, and observed the objects of your worship, I found also an altar with this inscription, TO AN UNKNOWN GOD. What therefore ye worship in ignorance, this I set forth unto you. The God that made the world and all things therein, He, being Lord of heaven and earth, dwelleth not in temples made with hands ; neither is He served by men's hands, as though He needed anything, seeing He Himself giveth to all life, and breath, and all things ; and He made of one every nation of men to dwell on all the face of the earth, having determined their appointed seasons, and the bounds of their habitation ; that they should seek God, if haply they might feel after Him, and find Him, though He is not far from each one of us : for in Him we live, and move, and have our being ; as certain even of your own poets have said,

" For we are also His offspring." [1]

The great statement that He " is not far away from each one of us : for in Him we live, and move, and have our being " has reference not merely to the company of the saints, but to all men. Human life is sustained within the fact of the Divine and all its energy. All human force exerted is of God. The very strength in which man rebels against Him, and hinders the coming of His Kingdom, and walks along the way of his pilgrimage, is Divine strength, though prostituted to base uses by the perversion of the will of God. Thus man, walking in the midst of a great light, stumbles and falls in darkness, because he is blind. Man alienated from God is in the place of vision, but sees it not ; passes along his pathway surrounded by the infinite music of the voice of God, and yet has no hearing thereof. He is spiritually dead. In the light, but sightless ; spoken to, but deaf.

The result of this with regard to man's conception of God is, as has been shown, that he creates the false deities upon the basis of a magnificent but false humanity. Its result in the case of his spiritual nature is inevitably that of deterioration. Having no pattern, and therefore no true understanding of his own being as to its possibility and goal, he appropriates the very energies that were supplied for his progress in such way as to ensure his degradation. Man who does not know God, does not know himself, and is therefore not able to realize the true ideal of life. The

[1] Acts 17 : 22–28.

final word in the system of Greek thought, was expressed in the oft-quoted sentence, "man know thyself." That which is remarkable about the injunction is that these men had discovered the supreme necessity. What they failed to discover was the way in which men should be able to obey their injunction, and know themselves. No man can know himself who does not know God. Just as man, having lost the vision of God, creates a false deity upon the basis of his own distorted intelligence, so thereafter, he attempts to bring himself into conformity with the false deity, and thus perpetuates the ruin, and ensures the final degradation. In the Divine economy man is a perfect union of spirit and body, which union issues in a mind or consciousness truly balanced, having comprehension of spiritual things, and therefore true understanding of things material. Through sin and the death of the spirit, there has entered into human life discord between spirit and flesh, and the mind is unbalanced in appreciation of values, and clouded in its outlook upon all facts. Discord tends to discord. The instrument created for fellowship with God, in order to the representation of God, itself being out of order, because out of communion with God, is now only capable of expressing distorted truth concerning God, which is the most terrible form of heresy.

II. In dwelling more particularly upon the unlikeness resulting, the two facts in human nature already referred to must be remembered. Essentially man is spirit. Apparently man is body. That is to say the unseen but essential fact in human life is that of the spirit. The body is at once a medium through which the spirit receives its impressions, and its knowledge concerning material things, and expresses to others spiritual truths. In both of these man has become unlike God. As unfallen man is like

God, the essential likeness being in the fact of the spirit, but the revelation of that fact being through the medium of the body ; so fallen man, distanced from God, and ignorant of God, is unlike God in the essential fact of his spiritual nature, and therefore fails to give any expression of God through the medium of his physical being.

As to the first, spirit. Falling back upon the analysis of human personality already considered, that namely of intelligence, emotion, and will; man is, in the whole fact, unlike God. Think first of the intellectual side of a man's nature. All are possessed of this, and yet apart from restoration to God, the intellect in its working, and in its achievements, is utterly unlike the working and the achievements of the wisdom of God. For illustration, instead of thinking of an ignorant man, whose intellectual capacity is dwarfed, let the mind contemplate the finest product of education and culture that can possibly be produced, and even then, at its best it is utterly unlike God. This statement does not undervalue the culture of the intellect. It simply asserts that an intellect cultured to all refinement, is nevertheless the degradation of intellect, unless the spirit of man is in harmony and actual intercourse with the Spirit of God. The operation of the human intellect apart from the life of fellowship with God is an operation wholly within the realm of material things. Intellect divorced from Deity, deals only with dust. Take all scientific investigation, and it is but the investigation and tabulation of material things. Indeed science is ever urgent in her declaration that she has nothing to do with subjects that lie beyond this limit of investigation and tabulation of the facts of material life. With splendid daring, and with a most remarkable accuracy, the intellect of man has forced its way back through all the movements of material order, until at last it has come to the protoplasmic germ. Here science stands still, and honestly declares it has no more to say. That is perfectly true, and it is admirably honest that men should confess its limitation. And yet there is infinitely more to say. No man by searching can find out God, but the intellect of man in harmony with God, is instructed by the higher intelligence of God Himself, as to the supreme fact which lies behind the dead wall, that prevents further investigation, of intellect unilluminated by spiritual communion. Had there been no break with God, no death, no darkening of the intelligence, man would never have stood still at the point indicated. Men, in communion with the spiritual, have declared what lies behind the limit of investigation possible to intellect acting apart from God.

The opening sentence of Genesis, at which man's proud intellect smiles, because it contains a statement too profound for his comprehension, is a revelation of the enlargement of intellect in communion with God. Behind the mighty movements and orderly sequences, which clouded intelligence has been able to observe, intellect inspired discovers the fact which illuminates the mystery, and satisfies the reason, as none other can. "In the beginning God created." [1]

Or to take the statement of Job. "He . . . hangeth the earth upon nothing," [2] is again to hear a most profound statement, resulting from spiritual insight. The scientist will declare that to be unthinkable, and in his declaration he confesses the truth of the argument. There are things unthinkable to human intellect until it is illumined. And yet the scientist objects because he does not rightly understand. He leads back, and back, and back, until he comes

[1] Gen. 1: 1.   [2] Job 26: 7.

to the simplest form of things material, of which it is possible for his mind to conceive. The spiritually enlightened man then says to him, " In the beginning God created." " He hangeth the earth upon nothing." To this the scientist objects that he cannot find foothold on nothing, and by that statement shows his utter ignorance of the declaration of these inspired intellects. In the first declaration the scientist lays his emphasis upon the apparent vacuum or nothingness, which precedes the things which had their beginning. The spiritually-instructed intelligence lays its emphasis upon God Who filled the void, and through the working of Whose energy the new became.

So also with the second. Man's intelligence unillumined, lays its emphasis upon the " nothing." Intellect inspired by communion with the spiritual lays its emphasis upon the " He." It is this God, this " He " that human intellect in its degradation is wearying itself to find, and He never can be found by the unaided working of a degraded intelligence, whose operations are wholly limited within the facts material. The intellect of man, created by God for largest purposes, has become imprisoned within the material realm. God is a Spirit, and the secret at back of all material phenomena is that God has spiritual personality. The mighty wisdom of the eternal God is spiritual. The intellect of man has become materialized, and thus as to intelligence he is unlike God.

It is equally true that man is unlike God in his emotional nature. The action of man's affection at its highest, apart from fellowship with God is selfish. Traced back to the final fact, human love is self-centred in its choice of an object, and in its expression of itself towards that object. Said Jesus to His disciples, " If ye love them that love you, what reward have ye? do not even the

publicans the same?"[1] In that question there is revealed
the very inwardness of depraved human emotion. Man
loves such as love him. That fact alone is sufficient to
demonstrate man's unlikeness to God. He loves in the
very necessity of His Being, and in such way as forever to
make impossible the thought of selfishness as a motive.
The deepest emotion of man acts finally along the line
that will tend to the gratification of desires that are
purely selfish. Invariably and inevitably when the capacity
for love operates from this centre of self, love itself becomes selfish, self-centred, self-inspired, self-considering,
and thus destroys itself. God's love is spiritual and
sacrificing, and is set upon objects utterly unworthy of
love, upon such as have given no reason for love, in that
they have hated Him. The love of God is self-emptying,
self-sacrificing. Not first for self-enrichment does He
bestow gifts, but for the enrichment of those upon whom
He bestows them. The highest culture of the emotional
nature of man, apart from the moving love of God, is
debased, in that it is self-centred; and thus in the fact of
his emotional nature also, man is unlike God.

Moreover, in the realm of the will as to its governing
principle, and activity, man has become utterly unlike God.
The motive power behind the action of human will, apart
from its relation to the Divine will, is that of desire for
mastery. The motive power behind the will of God, dominating its action, is always that of a love which is set upon
the well-being of others, and which urges God Himself
towards such ministry as shall encompass that well-being.
A strong-willed man, as the phrase goes, is one who means
to have his own way. Whether he is a saint or a sinner,
that is equally true. He is masterful, and is determined

[1] Matt. 5 : 46.

that the wills of others shall yield to his. This, apart from the operation of the grace of God, tends to tyranny. The highest exercises of human will, those which have lifted certain men above the plane of their fellows, have made them conspicuous in human history, and have created the reason why vast multitudes of their fellows have done them homage, have been those of determination to drive a highway through opposing difficulties, in order that men and movements may submit to the dominating desire of such men. How utterly and absolutely unlike the action of the will of God. That will is simple and beneficent, and its very strength lies in the fact that it is set determinately upon the well-being of others. The will of God for man is that he should be the best, and have the best; and that determination creates the mighty force thereof. And yet how little this is really understood. Here again man libels God, by thinking of His will in its determinings and doings, as an enlargement of the will of man. How constantly men think and speak of the will of God as being the determination of an Autocrat, Who insists upon the keeping of His laws. That is perfectly true, but the reason behind the insistence is the reason which creates the will, that namely, of His infinite and unwearying love. The force behind man's will is the passion for mastery. The force behind God's will is the passion of an Infinite Love which impels to service.

In the story of the fall there is the account of the genesis of that which is evil in the will of man. When the enemy said, "Ye shall be as God," [1] he suggested a false conception of God. Then for the first time there was held before man the possibility of being master, and therein lay a scandal upon God. In effect the enemy said, God has His way

[1] Gen. 3: 5.

and masters you.   Take the mastery out of His hands, and
be masters yourselves.   When Jesus came He said, "the
Son of Man came not to be ministered unto, but to minister, and to give His life a ransom for many."[1]   In that
great statement is a revelation of the truth concerning God.
God's mastery is the channel of His service.   By insistence
on authority He serves all highest interests in human life.
Of this man has lost all consciousness.   He has but one
conception of greatness, that of authority over others, one
understanding of the operation of the human will, that of
determination to be obeyed.   When the soldier returns from
battle, men still sing

> "See the conquering hero comes,"
>   Sound the trumpet, beat the drums;
>   Sports prepare, the laurel bring,
>   Songs of triumph to him sing.
>   See the godlike youth advance,
>   Breathe the flutes and lead the dance;
>   Myrtle wreaths and roses twine
>   To deck the hero's brow divine."

Is that conquering hero godlike?   That is the moment
in which man is far more like the devil than like God,
Men do not sing

> "See the conquering hero comes"

of such as in some obscure place quietly wait and serve,
and yet they are the truly godlike.   All this, however,
men of darkened intelligence, and prostituted emotion will
not believe.   There can be no acceptance of such teaching as this, save by those who are restored to relationship with God, and see things from the standpoint of the
spiritual.

Thus in the spiritual fact of his nature, man by the fall

[1] Matt. 20 : 28.

has become unlike God, in that his intelligence operates wholly within the material realm, whereas the Divine wisdom is spiritual, and therefore explanatory of all material facts; his emotion acts from wrong principle of self-love, whereas the Divine love ever operates upon the principle of love for others; and his will asserts itself upon the basis of the passion for mastery, whereas the Divine will insists upon obedience, through determination to serve the highest interests of others.

What bearing has this then upon the physical fact in human nature? This question may be briefly answered by declaring that the body has become the prison of the spirit. It deadens the spirit's consciousness, silences its voice, and practically treats it as non-existent. Man provides for physical food, and neglects the sustenance of the spirit. He builds and furnishes a house for his body, while he pays no attention to the ultimate homelessness of his spirit. He takes great care as to the air in which his physical life exists, but provides no atmosphere for the invigoration of his spirit. Wherever this is so, the body itself becomes vulgarized. Man's physical nature can never realize its highest possibilities of beauty, by divorcing it from that which is spiritual.

The sense of spiritual beauty lost, man seeks only the attractiveness of the flesh, and thereby ministers to its own decay and vulgarization. Illustrations from the methods of fashionable women might be quoted, were it not a subject too nauseous. The highest perfection of beauty can only be realized where there is a recognition of the supremacy of the spiritual, and the body consequently becomes, not the prison house of the spirit, but its temple. It follows therefore that the image of God lost in the spiritual, cannot be expressed in the physical.

III.   In this threefold consideration it has been seen that man is out of harmony with God as to motive, method, and manifestation of life.   Character being at variance, conduct is antagonistic.   Fallen man is a lie.   Man was made the shadow of God, for the manifestation of God.   Having departed from the true line of light, being separated from the forces of life, instead of shadowing God forth, he has cast the shadow of his depraved personality back upon God, and therefore instead of revealing, hides.

All this serves to demonstrate the fact that there is now no further use for man in the economy of God, no reason for his continuity.   There can be no reflection upon the infinite wisdom and justice of God, if so terrible a failure were cast out hopelessly from His presence.   The very reason for the existence of humanity is rendered impossible of realization.   Broken lenses can but reveal broken lights. The ruined camera can but distort images, and man who was created an instrument for the forthshadowing of God, is now incapable of doing his work, in that it is impossible for a ruined instrument to reveal, its very ruin consisting in its unfitness for the work of revelation.

There can be no reconstruction within the realm of destruction.   If ever this ruined instrument is to be reconstructed, it must be by a process from without.   Now let the question solemnly be asked at this point.   Is there any reason why man should be redeemed, why the wreckage should be restored, why the instrument should be renewed?   If it be declared that the reason is that God still needs an instrument of illumination, it may be fairly averred that He can create a new instrument, abandoning the one that has been a failure. The plain fact which must be faced is this, that there is no reason in the realm of righteousness, or of justice merely, why there should be any redemption provided for lost man.

And yet there is a reason, so powerful, so conclusive, and inclusive, that it may be reverently, and yet unhesitatingly affirmed that God is bound to find a way of redemption, and answer the call of a ruined race. That reason lies within the nature of God. It is that He is Love. Because He is Love, He must; and the "must" has in it nothing of the declaration of human claim, but it is the affirmation of faith, based upon profound conviction. The reason of redemption lies in the heart of God.

This is not a statement calculated to create satisfaction in the mind of man with himself. It is hardly a popular doctrine. It cuts from underneath the feet all ground for human boasting. God is not bound to do anything for man. Man has forfeited his whole claim upon God by sin. There is absolutely no reason why the distorted and ruined image should be redeemed or reconstructed. And yet there is a reason, and that so powerful, that there can be no escape from it.

> "He saw me ruined in the fall,
> Yet loved me notwithstanding all." [1]

If God had been other than Love, man must have remained endlessly in the realm of ruin. But the very ruin of man included within it man's spoiling, and man's sorrow, creating a great cry which appealed to the Infinite Love of the Infinite Heart. The call of man in his ruin Love heard, and Love answered, in the gift of Christ, Who is Himself, to traverse the path of pain and suffering, to the final and absolute limit, that out of all this, man might be lifted into the realm where it will be possible to fulfill the initial purpose of his creation, and thus satisfy the purpose of God, which is the purpose of Love.

[1] Medley.

BOOK I

THE BIRTH

IV. The Great Mystery—The God-Man
 V. The Meaning—God Was in Christ
VI. Signs to the Sons of Men

" *We need not wonder, that mist and all its phenomena have been made delightful to us, since our happiness as thinking beings must depend on our being content to accept only partial knowledge, even in those matters which chiefly concern us. If we insist upon perfect intelligibility and complete declaration in every moral subject, we shall instantly fall into misery of unbelief. Our whole happiness and power of energetic action depend upon our being able to breathe and live in the cloud; content to see it opening here and closing there; rejoicing to catch, through the thinnest films of it, glimpses of stable and substantial things; but yet perceiving a nobleness even in the concealment, and rejoicing that the kindly veil is spread where the untempered light might have scorched us, or the infinite clearness wearied.*

     *   *   *   *   *   *

" *I know there are an evil mystery and a deathful dimness,—the mystery of the great Babylon—the dimness of the sealed eye and soul; but do not let us confuse these with the glorious mystery of the things which the angels ' desire to look into,' or with the dimness which, even before the clear eye and open soul, still rests on sealed pages of the eternal volume.*"

—JOHN RUSKIN.
" Modern Painters."

Now when Jesus was born in Bethlehem of Judæa in the days of Herod the king, behold, Wise-men from the east came to Jerusalem, saying, Where is He that is born King of the Jews? for we saw His star in the east, and are come to worship Him. And when Herod the king heard it, he was troubled, and all Jerusalem with him. And gathering together all the chief priests and scribes of the people, he inquired of them where the Christ should be born. And they said unto him, In Bethlehem of Judæa: for thus it is written through the prophet,

> And thou Bethlehem, land of Judah,
> Art in no wise least among the princes of Judah:
> For out of thee shall come forth a governor,
> Who shall be Shepherd of My people Israel.

Then Herod privily called the Wise-men, and learned of them exactly what time the star appeared. And he sent them to Bethlehem, and said, Go and search out exactly concerning the young child; and when ye have found Him, bring me word, that I also may come and worship Him. And they, having heard the king, went their way; and lo, the star, which they saw in the east, went before them, till it came and stood over where the young child was. And when they saw the star, they rejoiced with exceeding great joy. And they came into the house and saw the young child with Mary His mother; and they fell down and worshipped Him; and opening their treasures they offered unto Him gifts, gold and frankincense and myrrh. And being warned of God in a dream that they should not return to Herod, they departed into their own country another way."—*Matt. 2 : 1–12.*

*   *   *   *   *   *   *

And it came to pass, while they were there, the days were fulfilled that she should be delivered. And she brought forth her firstborn son; and she wrapped Him in swaddling clothes, and laid Him in a manger, because there was no room for them in the inn.

And there were shepherds in the same country abiding in the field, and keeping watch by night over their flock. And an angel of the Lord stood by them, and the glory of the Lord shone round about them: and they were sore afraid. And the angel said unto them, Be not afraid; for behold, I bring you good tidings of great joy which shall be to all the people: for there is born to you this day in the city of David a Saviour, Who is Christ the Lord. And this is the sign unto you : Ye shall find a babe wrapped in swaddling

65

clothes, and lying in a manger. And suddenly there was with the
angel a multitude of the heavenly host praising God, and saying,

Glory to God in the highest,
And on earth peace among men in
whom He is well pleased.

And it came to pass, when the angels went away from them into
heaven, the shepherds said one to another, Let us now go even
unto Bethlehem, and see this thing that is come to pass, which the
Lord hath made known unto us. And they came with haste, and
found both Mary and Joseph, and the babe lying in the manger.
And when they saw it, they made known concerning the saying
which was spoken to them about this child.—*Luke 2 : 6–17*.

*   *   *   *   *   *   *

And the Word became flesh, and dwelt among us (and we beheld His glory, glory as of the only begotten from the Father), full
of grace and truth.—*John 1 : 14*.

IV

THE GREAT MYSTERY—THE GOD-MAN

THE subject of the Incarnation is at once initial and fundamental. All the significance of the crises that follow, grows out of this first, and most marvellous mystery. The Lord Jesus Christ is a Person infinitely transcending the possibility of perfect human comprehension. Nevertheless the Scripture declares certain facts concerning Him, which account for His glory and His grace, and without which He remains an unsolved problem, defying every successive age in its attempts to account for Him. It should at once be admitted that no final words of explanation can be written concerning Him. And yet it is of the utmost importance that so much as has been revealed should be recognized, in order to a comprehension of the true meaning of His mission.

In the later letters of the apostle Paul, notably that to the Colossians, it is evident that he is supremely anxious that Christian people should know Christ. In declaring this he expresses the thought in the words, " That they may know the mystery of God, even Christ." [1] He speaks of Christ as " the mystery of God." It will be of value to understand, through all these studies, the New Testament use and meaning of the word " mystery." That has been most lucidly stated to be " a truth undiscoverable except by revelation; never necessarily (as our popular use of the word may suggest) a thing unintelligible, or perplexing in

[1] Col. 2 : 2.

itself.   In Scripture a mystery may be a fact which, when revealed we cannot understand in detail, though we can know it, and act upon it.   .   .   .   It is a thing only to be known when revealed." [1]

In this sense Christ is the mystery of God.   Perfect analysis and explanation of His Person is impossible.   The fact thereof is declared as to origin, and essential characteristics.   These must be recognized, in order to a right understanding of the great subject of human redemption.

Having seen, that reconstruction in the region of destruction was utterly impossible, that there was no way, in the wisdom or power of man, for the encompassing of his own restoration, it was to be expected that the Divine method of redemption would be beyond perfect explanation to the sons of men.   That which human wisdom cannot plan must necessarily be beyond its power perfectly to understand.   Human intelligence is capable of appreciating anything that lies within the range of the working of human wisdom.   The intelligence of one man may not be equal to the discovery of the method of transmitting words by electricity without use of wires.   When, however, another human intelligence has thought the matter out, this man is able to comprehend the explanation given.   It may therefore be argued that while man was not equal in his own wisdom to devising a plan of redemption, he ought to be able perfectly to comprehend the plan of God.   Yet this does not follow.   In the first case, the whole movement is within the compass of human intelligence.   In the second, all human wisdom had been utterly exhausted in its attempt to think of, or to discover a method of salvation, and had failed.   The failure, moreover, must have continued through all the ages, for the Person of

[1] Bishop Handley Moule.

Christ, and the whole scheme of human redemption, are so transcendently marvellous as to demand for their explanation the recognition of their Divine origin. All this is to emphasize a fact that must not be lost sight of in approaching the contemplation of this initial movement of God towards man, that while the great facts are declared, they cannot be perfectly comprehended by human reason; and it is necessary therefore to approach them in the attitude of faith.

These statements apply with equal force to the whole mystery of the life, and death, and resurrection of Jesus. The subject is therefore to be approached with holy and submissive reverence. The attitude of the mind in its approach, is defined in words spoken long centuries ago for the children of Israel, by Moses the servant of God. "The secret things belong unto Jehovah our God; but the things that are revealed belong unto us and to our children forever, that we may do all the words of this law."[1] There are secret things which belong unto the Lord. There are revealed things, which God has made so plain that they may be comprehended, these "belong unto us and to our children." It is the solemn duty of all who desire to know the Christ, that they should diligently study the things revealed, and reverently rest with regard to the secret things.

The present study is devoted chiefly to the birth of Christ, as the crisis of Incarnation. There is always the danger of dwelling more upon the birth of the human, than of contemplating that birth as the crisis through which God became incarnate. It is in the latter way however, that the subject is now to be approached, and in the following order. First, the testimony of Scripture; secondly, the

[1] Deut. 29: 29.

mystery as to the secret things; third, the mystery revealed.

I. From the great mass of declaration in the New Testament concerning this subject, it will be sufficient to take four principal passages. These will again be divided into, first, annunciations to be reverently read, and received without attempted explanation; and secondly doctrinal declarations to be reverently considered.

The annunciations are those of the angel to Joseph and to Mary. In connection with the latter it will be necessary also to read the brief historic statement concerning the fulfillment of the angelic message.

The annunciation to Joseph was uttered in these words, " Joseph, thou son of David, fear not to take unto thee Mary thy wife: for that which is conceived in her is of the Holy Spirit. And she shall bring forth a son; and thou shalt call His name JESUS; for it is He that shall save His people from their sins. Now all this is come to pass, that it might be fulfilled which was spoken by the Lord through the prophet, saying,

> Behold, the virgin shall be with child,
>   and shall bring forth a son,
> And they shall call His name Immanuel;

which is, being interpreted, God with us." [1]

In the presence of this mysterious announcement, there can be no fitting attitude of the human intellect save that of acceptance of the truth, without any attempt to explain the absolute mystery. The annunciation reveals the fact that in the origin of the Person of Jesus there was the co-operation of Deity and humanity, each making its own contribution.

[1] Matt. 1: 20-23.

The annunciation to Mary should be read in close connection with the statement of its fulfillment in history. "And the angel answered and said unto her, The Holy Spirit shall come upon thee, and the power of the Most High shall overshadow thee: wherefore also the holy thing which is begotten shall be called the Son of God." . . . "And she brought forth her first-born son; and she wrapped Him in swaddling clothes, and laid Him in a manger, because there was no room for them in the inn."[1] This annunciation and declaration concerned one Person, spoken of in the former as the Son of God, in the latter as "her son." Here are not two Persons, but one.

These annunciations are to be read and received without any attempt to explain the central mystery contained within them, which absolutely transcends all human understanding. They must be received, or else the whole superstructure of Christianity totters and falls. It is only by the way of the fact here declared, that it is at all possible to comprehend the great facts which are evident in the whole subsequent work of this Person. To deny the truth of this account of the initial crisis, is to be left to the contemplation of effects, for which no sufficient cause can be found. The stupendous and ever manifest combination in the Personality of Jesus of essential Deity, and proper humanity, is totally without sufficient cause, the moment men have ceased to have faith in the Scripture account of the miraculous conception. That initial miracle cannot be finally explained, but neither can the origin of any form of life be finally explained in the last analysis.

The doctrinal declarations to be considered are those of John and of Paul. That of John is in the introduction to his Gospel. "And the Word became flesh, and dwelt

[1] Luke 1: 35; 2: 7.

among us . . . full of grace and truth." [1] For the sake of the present consideration, the parenthetical declaration " and we beheld His glory, glory as of the only begotten from the Father," is omitted. To rightly appreciate the meaning of this statement it is necessary to connect it with the opening words of the Gospel. " In the beginning was the Word, and the Word was with God, and the Word was God." [2] The passage from the second to the thirteenth verse inclusive, is a statement giving parenthetically the history of the Word from the beginning of the first creation to the beginning of the second.

Omitting this passage, verses one and fourteen, read in immediate connection, contain a declaration of the sublimest facts concerning the Person of Christ, and a statement of His coming into relation with the human race in the mystery of Incarnation. In each of these passages there is a threefold statement, and they answer to each other.

" In the beginning was the Word."   " And the Word became flesh."

" And the Word was with God."   " And tabernacled among us."

" And the Word was God."   " Full of grace and truth."

This is a statement of the mystery of the Incarnation, a setting in doctrinal form of that fact, announced by heavenly messengers to Joseph and to Mary.

The first statement is full of a majesty and sublimity which flings its light about the pathway, but which cannot be penetrated or perfectly comprehended. " In the beginning was the Word." The phrase " in the beginning " in this connection antedates any other reference to the ages to be found in the sacred volume. By it man is borne back into the infinite and unfathomable reaches of the unmeasur-

[1] John 1 : 14.   [2] John 1 : 1.

able. The phrase with which the book of Genesis opens takes man to the beginning of the history of the present order, to those original movements of the Divine mind and power, by which material things originated. The phrase as John uses it, in these opening words, carries the mind yet again beyond those original movements of creation. By its aid the mind of man is introduced to the presence of the Self-existent God. Contemplating the unutterable splendour, whose very light darkens the understanding of the finite mind, the Word is found existing. A word is a means of expression. The word of man is man's method of self-expression. The Word of God is the name here used for that Person in the Trinity, Who is the Divine method of self-expression.

"The Word became flesh." The statement is appalling, overwhelming. Out of the infinite distances, into the finite nearness; from the unknowable, to the knowable; from the method of self-expression appreciable by Deity alone, to a method of self-expression understandable of the human.

In the inscrutable mystery of the Trinity the Son is ever the Medium of self-expression. By this awe-inspiring fact of Incarnation, the office of the Son is not changed. Its method is changed for the sake of man. The movement of the change no human intelligence can follow. It is darkly mysterious with the darkness of a blinding splendour. The conception is too mighty ever to have been born in the intelligence of man. "The Word which was in the beginning . . . became flesh."

"The Word was with God." The natural home of the Eternal Son Who was the Medium of self-revelation of Deity was in close fellowship with the Eternal Father. "The Word tabernacled among us," that is, took up His manifest dwelling-place in proximity to the human race, as close as that which characterized His relation to the Eternal Father. He stooped into an actual identification with human nature, and by that stoop lifted human nature into the spaciousness of fellowship with God.

This, however, let it be stated in advance, is not the doctrine of Atonement. In the Person of Jesus, God has come into new and mystic relationship with unfallen humanity; and in the life of Jesus, God in relation with unfallen humanity, tabernacles among fallen man. Something more will be necessary to make possible union between the members of a fallen race, and this new Head of an unfallen race. That something more will be accomplished by the way of the Cross to be considered in due course.

"And the Word was God." The final declaration is that of the supreme Deity of the Word, and thus the Person of Christ is safe-guarded from any interpretation which would place Him in infinite superiority to the human race, and yet in inferiority to essential Deity. He was God, and yet in His Person there was not all the truth concerning God, for He was with God. He was with God, and yet by no means inferior to the Eternal Father, for He was God. The unity of Deity is marked by the word " God." The diversity is marked by " the Word." The God Who created, the Word was with. In the revelation of Incarnation, the phrase answering this final sentence is " full of grace and truth." This teaches that in the grace or loveliness, and truth or righteousness of the Man seen of John and the rest, there was an outshining of the essential facts of the love and the light of Deity.

In the statement of Paul the same great truths are affirmed in other language. From the passage in Philip-

pians, in which the humiliation and exaltation of Christ
are so splendidly set forth, let the words be taken which
deal immediately with this fact. "Who, existing in the
form of God, counted not the being on an equality with
God a thing to be grasped, but emptied Himself, taking the
form of a Servant, being made in the likeness of men." [1]
In this passage there is first stated the eternal fact concerning Christ, "existing in the form of God." Then follows
the attitude of the mind of the Eternal Word, in the presence of the call for redemption. He "counted not the
being on an equality with God a thing to be grasped."
Then follows the sublime act, through which He came to
the level of those needing succour. He "emptied Himself taking the form of a Servant, being made in the likeness of men." Carefully note three facts in the compass
of this brief passage. First it declares the eternal verity
concerning Christ. He existed in the form of God, on an
equality with God. Second, it reveals the position He
took, when He came for the redemption of man. He
took the form of a Servant in the likeness of men.

In these two there is a contrast. Take the extreme
statements, and He is seen as passing from the form of
God to the likeness of men; and taking the nearer contrast, He is seen as passing from the Sovereignty of equality
to the submission of subservience.

The third fact is the revelation of the attitude of mind,
and the act of will, by which this change was wrought.
In the presence of a great need He did not hold to, or
grasp His right of equality, but for the accomplishment of
an Infinite purpose, abandoned this. The action of the
will is declared in the sublime and all-inclusive declaration
that He emptied Himself. The Eternal Word stooped

[1] Phil. 2: 6, 7.

from the position of an Infinite expression to the limitations of human life.

It is now of the utmost importance to understand what
is involved in the declaration that He emptied Himself.
There is no warrant for imagining that He emptied Himself
of His essential Deity.   The emptying indicates the setting
aside of one form of manifestation, in which all the facts
of equality with God were evidently revealed, for another
form of manifestation, in which the fact of equality with
God must for a time be hidden, by the necessary submiss--
iveness of the human to the Divine.   That which the
Eternal Word set aside was a form, and this in order that
another form might be taken.   It is evident, therefore, that
a very great deal depends upon the meaning of the word
form.

The Greek word μορφή, only occurs in one other place
in the whole of the New Testament.   In speaking of an
appearance of Christ after resurrection, Mark says, "After
these things He was manifested in another form unto two
of them, as they walked, on their way into the country."[1]
Taking this use of the word for the sake of illustration, it
is evident that the change was not in the essential nature
or personality, but in the method of manifestation.   To
the men who walked to Emmaus the same One came, but
in a changed form, so that they did not recognize Him,
until He willed to reveal His identity.   This of course
by comparison with the subject now under consideration
was but a small change, and yet it serves to illustrate the
larger fact.

In the coming of the Eternal Word to the earth for the
purposes of redemption, He did not lay aside the essential
fact of His Deity.   He simply changed the form of mani-

[1] Mark 16: 12.

festation. It would seem clearly evident that the Son of God had forever been the One in Whom God took form, and therefore the One through Whom God was revealed. The Son is always the manifestation of the Father. What the form, what the manifestation was in the past, it is impossible to declare, for it is beyond the comprehension of the finite and the limited. This alone is certain that He was the Word, the Speech, the Method of communication of the Eternal God. For the redemption of man He laid aside that form, whatever it may have been, and took a new form for manifesting the same God, a form upon which men might look, and through which, in the process of time, they might come to know the Eternal God. If it were possible for a moment to penetrate the mysteries of the past, the Son would be seen within the mystery of the Trinity, as the perpetual Medium of Divine expression, just as the Spirit is the perpetual Medium of Divine consciousness. In the coming to the level of man, and in the taking of a form possible of comprehension by man, it was necessary to bring the illimitable into the range of the limited. He passed from the heavenly to the earthly, from the infinite to the finite, that is, as to the form of expression. This is impossible of final explanation. It is however a mystery revealed, upon which the whole superstructure of Christianity depends. It would seem as though the eternal heavens were for a period emptied of the manifestation of God, though never of His presence, while for the work of redemption, God was manifest in the flesh.

The Word passed from government to obedience, from independent cooperation in the equality of Deity, to dependent submission to the will of God. By the way of the Incarnation there came into existence a Person in all points human, in all essentials Divine. In all points human, that is to say, fulfilling the Divine ideal of human nature, not descending to the level of the degradation of humanity, resulting from sin. The Man of Nazareth was perfect as Man. He was moreover perfect as God, lacking nothing of the powers of essential Deity, save only the heavenly form of manifestation.

II. At this point the temptation is to ask questions. These may be asked, but they cannot be answered. Here is the sphere in which faith becomes operative, for here the mystery is seen as to its secret things which belong to God. How can there be united in one Person, perfect and complete Deity, and perfect and complete humanity? It is impossible to reply to the "how." Will not these things, however, so contradict each other as to make both impossible? The only answer is that they did not, and that through all the life of Jesus, there were constantly manifested the essential and absolute nature of Deity, and the undoubted facts of humanity. There are no essentials of human nature that cannot be discovered in the story of this Person. His spiritual nature is evidenced by His unceasing recognition of God. His mental capacity is manifest in the marvellous majesty of His dealing with all problems. His physical life is seen moving along the line of the purely human in its hunger, its weariness, its method of sustenance, and its seasons of rest. The human will is seen, but always choosing, as the principle of activity, the Divine will. The emotional nature is manifest in the tears and the tenderness, the rebuke and the anger, gleaming with soft light, flaming as the lightning. The intellectual nature is seen so perfectly balanced, and so wonderfully equipped, that men marvelled at His wisdom, seeing, as they said, that He had never learned.

Yet moreover, the essentials of Deity are seen. Such wisdom, that the ages have failed to understand perfectly the deep meaning of His teaching. Such power, that through weakness He operated towards the accomplishment of works that were only possible to God. Such love, that attempts to describe it, but rob it of its fairest glory.

And yet again, in this Person, is seen the merging of the Divine and the human, until one wonders where is the ending of the one and the beginning of the other. Denouncing and proclaiming doom upon guilty Jerusalem, the voice is yet choked with emotion, and the face is wet with tears. That is surely human. And yet it is essentially Divine, for while the expression of the emotion is human as all tears are, the emotion expressed is Divine, for none but God can mingle the doom of the guilty with the tears of a great pity.

It would seem as though there were no adequate naming of this Personality, but that created by the combination of the two names in one. He was the God-man. Not God indwelling a man. Of such there have been many. Not a man Deified. Of such there have been none save in the myths of pagan systems of thought; but God and man, combining in one Personality the two natures, a perpetual enigma and mystery, baffling the possibility of explanation. It may be asked how if indeed He were God He could be tempted in the realm of humanity, as other men are tempted? It may be objected that had He been God, He could not have spoken of the limitation of His own knowledge concerning things to come. When asked to explain these things, the only possible answer is that they do not admit of explanation, but they remain facts, proving His essential humanity; while on the other hand are the incontrovertible proofs of His Deity, in the activity of raising the dead, and in the matchless wisdom of His teaching, and supremely in the revelation of God, which has taken hold of, and influenced the whole conception of Deity during the passing of the centuries since His life upon earth.

This mystery and revelation uniting God and man in a Person is the centre of Christianity, and is without parallel, and without possibility of explanation by analogy.

It has been objected that this is the creation of the imagination of man. This however is to presuppose the possibility of an exercise of the imagination, to which it is wholly unequal. Imagination can only rearrange known facts. The poems of the poet may be new, and the picture of the artist also, but in each case upon examination they will be found to be new, in their combination and representation of old facts. The union in a Person of God and man is something undreamed of, unknown, until it broke upon the world as a fact in human history.

III. In the Gospels there are three expressions descriptive of Jesus Christ, which are suggestive of the double fact in His Personality, a contemplation of which will aid in the study of the revealed mystery. The first of them, the Son of God, indicates the Deity of Jesus, and yet perfectly describes His humanity. The second, the Son of Man, indicates His relation to the race, and yet ever suggests that separateness from it, which was created by the fact of His Deity. The third, the Son, always suggests the union of these facts in the unity of His Person. An examination of the four Gospels, and a selection from them of the passages in which these titles occur, reveal certain facts of interest concerning them.

Taking them in order, the term, the Son of God, occurs

ın Matthew, nine times; in Mark, four times; in Luke, six times; and in John eleven times. The title in Matthew is never used by Christ Himself, six times it is the language of men, and three times that of devils. In the Gospel of Mark it is never used by Christ, but by men twice, by devils twice. In the Gospel of Luke it is never used by Christ, but by an angel once, by a man once, and by devils four times. In the Gospel of John the title is on five occasions used by Jesus, and six times by men. It is interesting to note that in the three Gospels dealing principally with the humanity of Jesus, He is never recorded as having spoken of Himself as the Son of God. In the one Gospel of His Deity, He is recorded as having used the expression five times. About one of these there is a doubt, for it is not at all certain whether the words " He that believeth on Him is not judged: he that believeth not hath been judged already, because he hath not believed on the name of the only begotten Son of God," [1] do not form part of John's commentary, rather than of the actual discourse of Jesus. Four times that are certain, indicate a method and a reason. Twice He so described Himself in answering His critics,[2] once when He brought comfort and light to an excommunicated man,[3] and once when He would succour two broken-hearted women, whose brother Lazarus He was about to raise from the dead.[4]

The term, Son of Man, occurs in Matthew thirty-two times, in Mark fifteen times, in Luke twenty-six times, and in John twelve times. In the first three Gospels, the title is always recorded as having been used by Christ of Himself, and never by angel, by man, or by demon. Of the twelve occasions in John, ten are from the lips of Christ, twice only was the expression used by men, and then in

[1] John 3: 18.   [2] John 5: 25; 10: 36.   [3] John 9: 35.   [4] John 11: 4.

the spirit of criticism and unbelief, " We have heard out of the law that the Christ abideth forever: and how sayest Thou, the Son of Man must be lifted up? Who is this Son of Man?"[1]

The last of these expressions, the Son, the greatest of the three, without either qualifying phrase, and therefore suggesting both relationships, occurs in Matthew four times, in Mārk once, in Luke three times, and in John fifteen times. Without a single exception the phrase is used by Christ Himself, never by angel, or man, or demon.

This rapid survey shows that Christ's favourite expression for describing Himself is the one which veiled His glory, the Son of Man. He most often described Himself in a way in which men never describe Him, save when repeating His own language, they in doubt ask what He meant. He also used, and He alone, the expression, the Son, suggesting in the light of the other two expressions, His relation to the Divine, and His relation to the human. The expression which declared His essential glory only passed His lips, in all probability, four times.

The value of this examination of the use of the descriptive phrases may thus be stated. He was the Son of God, but that great fact never passed His lips, save when some pressing circumstance made it necessary that for rebuke or comfort He should declare the Eternal relationship which He bore to God. The title which He seems to have loved best, was that which marked His humanity, and His relationship to the race, the Son of Man. Occasionally, and always under circumstances of special need, He spoke of Himself as the Son.

These very titles suggest the essential fact concerning Him. At the birth of Jesus of Nazareth there came into

[1] John 12: 34.

existence One Personality, such as, with reference to the duality of its nature, had never had existence before. The Son of God came from the eternities. The Son of Man began His Being. The Son combining the two facts, in one Personality, commenced that mighty work which He alone could accomplish, bringing to its carrying out all the forces of Deity, in union with the capacities of humanity.

V

THE MEANING—GOD WAS IN CHRIST

HAVING endeavoured to consider the sublime fact of the Incarnation, without attempting to fathom the infinite mystery, it is now competent to enquire what was the purpose of the Incarnation. The question may immediately be answered in the brief statement of Paul, " God was in Christ reconciling the world unto Himself." [1] All the ful' ness of this declaration cannot be comprehended until the final movements in the mission of Jesus have been considered, those namely of His passion, and resurrection, and ascension. It is by these that God reconciles the world to Himself in Christ. The first fact however, rendering these possible of accomplishment, is that of the Incarnation, and in it there is the great first movement towards the reconciling of man to God.

By Incarnation God has revealed Himself anew to the intelligence of man, in such way as to appeal to his emotion, and call for the submission of his will. All this however could only be completed by the completion of the work of Incarnation, for it was only through the death of Jesus that the perfect revelation of God came to the intelligence, as it was only through that death that a reconciliation could be accomplished, which should have as its foundation fact, the forgiveness of sin, and the communication of a new life principle. All this is most clearly contained

[1] 2 Cor. 5 : 19.

within the word of the apostle, who in writing to the Colossians declares that they " being in time past alienated and enemies in your mind in your evil works " were " now . . . reconciled in the body of His flesh through death." [1] Thus the reconciling work is only completed through the death of Jesus, but that final work is made possible in the fact of " the body of His flesh." That is to say that Incarnation prepares for Atonement. The present subject is wholly that of the revelation God has given man of Himself in the Person of the Christ.

In previous studies it has been shown that man distanced from God by sin became ignorant of Him, and unlike Him. Notwithstanding this fact, the capacity, and indeed the necessity for God remains, even though man has lost his knowledge of Him, his love for Him, and his likeness to Him. It has been seen, moreover, that the only conception of God that man has, is what he finds within himself, and in attempting to think of God, he has consciously or unconsciously always projected his own personality into immensity. This would have been a true thing for him to do, had man remained true to the Divine ideal, for he was created in the image of God. Seeing that the shadow had become blurred, and the image defaced, in the projection of himself man has emphasized the defects, and intensified the ruin. To correct that, God became incarnate, stooped to the level of man's power to comprehend Him, gave him a perfect Man in order that the lines projected from the perfect Personality into immensity might be true lines, and so reveal correctly the facts concerning Himself.

The present study is an attempt to examine that broad statement, first by noticing how the Incarnation has corrected false ideas; and secondly, by examining the Incarna-

[1] Col. I : 21, 22.

tion as the fulfillment of all that was highest in the thinking of the past, and the beginning of a new understanding.

I.   Man's ideas of God are necessarily anthropomorphic.
Eliminating for the moment from the discussion the fact
of the fall, it still remains true that man's comprehension
of the Eternal God must necessarily be based upon the
facts of his own personality.   When man stood erect in
full possession of the facts of his own being, he was in
very deed in the shadow and image of God.   Essentially a
spirit, possessed of an intellectual, an affectional, and a
volitional nature, he was a medium through which these essential facts should be expressed along the line of force or
power.   The body of man was the medium of the spirit's
expression.   Such was the Divine ideal of humanity, spirit
and body; the spirit crowned, the body subservient; the
spiritual nature dominant, the physical submissive thereto.
Therein lay a suggestion, and indeed a revelation concerning the essential facts of Deity.   God is a Spirit, intelligent, emotional, volitional.   These essential facts of His
being govern all the forces of His nature, and so find expression in a thousand different ways, through created
things.   What man's body is to his spirit, all the created
universe is to God.   The Old Testament literature is full
of this thought, and so God is described as clothing Himself with light, as riding upon the wings of the wind, as
making the clouds His chariot.   Thus unfallen man, reverently projecting the facts of his own being into immensity, would have a true conception of God.   It follows by
a sequence from which there can be no escape, that when
man has fallen, if he still continue the same process he
will create a deity, but it must be false, a contradiction of
the truth, because man himself is a failure, and a contra-

vention of the Divine purpose. In man, out of harmony
with God, the spiritual fact has been neglected, with the
result that the intelligence operates wholly within the realm
of the material, the affection is warped, and prostituted;
the will has lost its true principle of action. Project these things into immensity, and there will result gods,
or a god, sensuous, cruel, tyrannical. It is the story of the
religions of the human race.

This has also been dealt with in a previous chapter as
revealed in Baal, in Moloch, in Mammon. New emphasis
is added to the fact by a consideration of the gods of Rome
and of Greece. In each case the deities worshipped were
so many, that no man pretended to know their number,
and the character of them may be described in very few
words, vindictive, lazy, trivial, always seeking their own,
treating men in such way that the only reason why men
still feared or served them was that they would buy off from
vengeance, and prevent their cruelty. In the presence of
this universal incapacity to discover God, what can be
done ? The answer did not come, as it could not come,
from man. It came from God.

II. In Jesus of Nazareth, God gave to the world again
a Man, perfect in His humanity, and therefore perfect in
His revelation of the facts concerning Himself. In Jesus
there was a fulfillment of all that was highest and best in
the ideas of God, which had come to men by the revelations of the past. The continuous work of God from the
moment when man fell from his high dignity, by the act
of his rebellion, and so obscured his vision of God, was
that of self-revelation. Through processes that were long
and tedious, judged from the standpoint of human lives,
God with infinite patience spoke in simple sentences, shone

forth in gleams of light, and so kept enshrined within the heart of man, facts concerning Himself, which man was unable to discover for himself. So degraded was human intelligence, that speaking after the manner of men only, it may be said that it took whole centuries for God to enshrine in the consciousness of the race, some of the simple and most fundamental facts concerning Himself. Man's ruin was so terrible, and so profound, as witness the darkened intelligence, the deadened emotion, and the degraded will, that there was but one alternative open to the Eternal God. Either He must sweep out and destroy utterly the race, or else in infinite patience, and through long processes, lead it back to Himself. He chose the pathway of reconciliation in His infinite grace, at what cost the story of the Christ alone perfectly reveals.

It may be objected that Christ might have been immediately sent, and yet this is utterly to fail to comprehend the depth of the degradation of man. There were many lessons which the race must learn, before it was ready to receive the light that should shine in the Person of the Christ. For instance, man had lost his conception of the unity of God, and was making to himself thousands upon thousands of deities. The history of Israel is the history of the enshrining within the race of the great truth of the unity of God. "Hear, O Israel: Jehovah our God is one Jehovah." [1] That was the initial lesson, and yet Israel never learned it fully until she had passed into Babylonish captivity, and returning therefrom, abandoned for evermore every form of idolatry.

The slowness of the work was due entirely to the ruin of the only instrument through which a perfect revelation could be made. God cannot be as perfectly expressed

[1] Deut. 6:4.

through any symbol as through a man. Not through a system of ethics could God make Himself known, as through one who lives wholly within His law. In the fullness of time there came into human history the Revealer. Man everywhere had been attempting to discover God by the projection into infinitude of his own personality, and had utterly, and absolutely, and necessarily failed. By the coming of Christ, God gave man One Who, perfectly realizing His ideal of humanity, made a perfect instrument through which God should reveal Himself to the heart of the race. Jesus was the express Image of God. From every fact in the Personality of the Man Jesus, lines may be projected into infinity, and the infinite enlargement of the Person of Christ correctly reveals the fact of God. In Incarnation God accepts the human standpoint of appreciation of Himself, which was also His own standpoint, and enshrining Himself in human life, He thinks, He speaks, He acts through human channels.

Think then for a moment of the Personality of Christ, in order that it may be seen how within the compass of that which is knowable to man, lies a revelation of that which otherwise is utterly unknowable. In that perfect Personality there is found perfect humanity, humanity which in itself harmonizes the spiritual and the material, humanity in which the spirit is dominant, and the body subservient and expressive. In Jesus the physical is not scourged, and bruised, but governed and glorified. In Him the Spirit is not imprisoned and degraded, but enthroned and dominant. He is a perfect human Personality.

When these lines of perfect humanity are flung out into the infinitudes, there is presented to the mind the perfect Deity, the spiritual essence dominant, while all force, as expressed through creation, is subservient to spirit. Every

fact of the clear shining of the wisdom of the Christ, as
Man, reveals the infinite wisdom of the Eternal God.
Every manifestation of the unselfish and unwearying love of
the heart of Jesus, is an outshining of the Eternal and undying love of God Himself.   Every movement and decision
of the will of Jesus, under the constraint of the Divine will,
is a revelation of the action and method of the will of God,
under the constraint of the Infinite and Eternal Love.

The God-man then is the gateway between God and
man.   Through Him God has found His way back to
man, from whom He had been excluded by his rebellion.
In Him man finds his way back to God from Whom he
had been alienated by the darkening of his intelligence, the
death of his love, and the disobedience of his will.   God
finds Himself in this Person and is with men.   Man finds
himself in this Person, and is with God.

Through the God-man, Deity takes hold upon humanity.
Through the God-man, humanity takes hold upon Deity.

This revelation of God in Jesus may be illustrated both
by His teaching, and His deeds.   Let there be selected any
word that fell from His lips, any incident of His wonderful life, and when carefully considered, it will be discovered
that there is sounding in the air the very Word of God, and
appearing before the mind His activity.   The simplest
simplicity of humanity to be found in Jesus of Nazareth is
the gateway through which the reverent and submissive
soul passes into the sublimest sublimity of Deity.

His teaching was the sum of all wisdom.   The sweet and
tender words that come like music still, to all who in the
stress and strain of life hear them, " Come unto Me, all
ye that labour and are heavy laden, and I will give you
rest.   Take My yoke upon you, and learn of Me; for I
am meek and lowly in heart: and ye shall find rest unto

your souls. For My yoke is easy, and My burden is light," [1] are yet the words that none but God could have uttered in the hearing of the restless feverishness of a fallen race. How human the utterance. Take out the words that arrest attention, " Come . . . labour . . . heavy laden . . . rest . . . yoke . . . burden." Is there one of them that sounds at first like the language of the infinite God, or the speech of the perfect heaven? The whole passage thrills and throbs with a common consciousness of human life. Yet sit down in front of it, and take time to think. Press the ear closely to these little words of earthly value, and there will be heard sounding through them the deep organ notes of the Eternal Wisdom. The tender call of the man is the putting into such words as may be heard and understood by the heavy laden masses, all the deepest philosophies of life. Surely never man spake like this Man. The speech of this Man is the speech of God.

Or take His deeds, any of them. Take them almost at haphazard. The cleansing of the temple, the nursing of little children, the human interest that watched people as they gave at the treasury, the tears which chased each other down the face, the white hot anger that flamed and burned and scorched. And yet behind all is the evident going of Deity, not one of them have explanation apart therefrom. Let any man who imagines that the cleansing of the temple was a purely human act, possess himself of a whip of small cords, and attempt to drive out the vested interests and the hoary superstitions, which gather around and spoil the temple which should be a place of prayer. It is simply absurd to suppose that the men who fled from His presence were frightened of a Galilean peasant. That

[1] Matt. 11 : 28–30

anger at the desecrated house of God, which flamed from His eye, and made His whole demeanour terrifying, was the flashing forth of the outraged God, Whose house of succour had been made a den of thieves. It is not conceivable that a mob of Jews would yield their money tables to the claim of a peasant fresh from Galilee. They were conscious for once of the anger of Deity.

It was indeed a Man Who took the children in His arms and blessed them. The picture is so human, so suggestive of all that is finest and most beautiful in true manhood; and yet listen, for He is speaking, and the word is revolutionary and yet authoritative. "Suffer the little children, and forbid them not, to come unto Me : for to such belongeth the Kingdom of Heaven." [1] If this Man be Man alone, He is an ignorant fanatic. The children were never counted as in the Kingdom of God, until from the sacred rite of confirmation, they became themselves sons of the law. Yet this Man, holding in His arms young children, babes, says that they are the true type of the character of such as are in His Kingdom. The centuries have vindicated the declaration, and have proved that it was the voice of God, rebuking false conceptions of human greatness, which cured human thinking, and announced the supremacy of simplicity.

And yet again, it was a great human heart that shook with emotion, and cast forth tears when from the mountain He beheld the city of His love, corrupt, and hastening to her doom. And yet it is unthinkable that that is all, for in the tears is caught the flash and glory of that Divine compassion, which pronounces doom, not with the note of exultant triumph, but with the pathos of wounded love.

The teaching of Jesus, considered and followed to its

[1] Matt. 19 : 14.

final conclusions, brings the mind into contact with the infinite wisdom of the Eternal God. The deeds of Jesus, correctly appreciated, reveal the activities of God as to purpose and method.

The Incarnation is first a revelation to man of man as to first Divine intention. It is therefore also a revelation of God, for perfect man is the image of God. In Jesus there has been revealed to the race God's purpose for every human being, a mind of royal and loyal love, and the activity of self-emptying service, as expressive of that loyalty. The greatest injunction laid upon Christian men by the writers of the New Testament is that of the apostle, " Have this mind in you, which was also in Christ Jesus." [1] His mind was the mind wholly actuated by the principle of love. It was submissive and regnant, submissive to the dominion of love, reigning in the power of love.

From this consideration of ideal man, there breaks upon the consciousness the truth concerning God. In Jesus, man finds Him for Whom he has been searching, and being unable to find, has created the false deities that have cursed his whole life. According to this revelation, God's knowledge is the knowledge of personal interest in all His creation. His affection joys in the joy of His people, and sorrows in the midst of their sorrows. His will is ever impulsed by this perfect affection, and operates within this intimate knowledge. These truths, too large for perfect comprehension, are yet recognized as the lines project from the unique Personality of Jesus into immensity. Through the Man Jesus, man has found God. He had built upon his ruined nature a false conception of God, but now upon the perfect nature of the last Adam, man forms a correct idea of the infinite God. Jesus of Nazareth is

[1] Phil. 2 : 5.

perfect in His humanity. That humanity is the corner-stone, and if its lines are all carried forth, as in the case of the corner-stone of the pyramid, the whole fact will be included.

The value of the Incarnation then at once becomes apparent. Human misconceptions of God have created human hatred of God. The hatred of the human heart therefore is not hatred of the true God, for He is not known. In Christ He is revealed, and when men know Him as the Revealer, they love Him.

Much more of course needs to be said, as in the mission of Christ much more needed to be done, for though the light of Deity has perfectly shone in the Person of the Christ, man does not see it. Something must be done to quicken his intelligence, to open his eye. That, the Incarnation does not do. It provides the true view of God for the quickened intelligence. In the present study the subject is merely that of the Divine self-revelation, contained within the Incarnation. When man through the mystery of Atonement, is reconciled, and the miracle of regeneration is completed, then in the vision of God granted in Christ, he will also be reconciled in intelligence, in emotion, in will.

Thus the Incarnation has made provision for the reconciliation of the whole man, but into this reconciliation man will only pass as he becomes reconciled through the death of Jesus. When so reconciled, his full salvation will proceed through the harmonizing of the facts of his being, with the revelation of the possibilities thereof in the Man Jesus, under the constraint of the infinite love of God revealed also in Him. " If while we were enemies, we were reconciled to God through the death of His Son, much more, being reconciled, shall we be saved by His life." [1]

[1] Romans 5 : 10.

VI

SIGNS TO THE SONS OF MEN

So far as man was concerned there was a marked un-preparedness for the advent of Jesus. Yet He came in the fullness of time. Everything was ready in the purpose and economy of God. But while there was a general spirit of unrest and undefined expectation abroad in the world, neither His own nation nor the Gentile world were prepared for the appearing of the Messiah.

With regard to Israel it was true that " He came unto His own, and they that were His own received Him not." [1] They did not receive Him, because partial blindness had fallen upon them even in regard to their own prophecies. It is remarkable that these people who possessed, and were supposed to be instructed in, the prophecies concerning the Messiah, had almost altogether lost sight of one side of the prophetic message concerning Him.

Isaiah had portrayed, in unmistakable lines, and with detailed definiteness, the picture of the suffering Servant of God. How wonderfully the fifty-third chapter of Isaiah was realized in the Person of Jesus Christ. But these people had not begun to understand the fact of the suffering of Messiah; they had no conception of a lowly, despised, and rejected Deliverer. They expected One Who should set up a kingdom of earthly power. And when He came from lowly and despised Nazareth, and took the position of the Son of God, they were incredulous, unbeliev-

[1] John 1 : 11.

ing, simply because they had not understood their own Scriptures.

The same prophet had announced the fact of the incarnation. "Behold, a virgin shall conceive, and bear a son, and shall call His name Immanuel."[1] To the Hebrew that was a descriptive name, and the simple meaning of Immanuel was "God with us." It was the distinct foretelling of the stupendous fact that He should be the God-man, but they had never realized it. The people had largely lost their spiritual sense, and were looking only for the advent of a great prince who should deliver them from the bondage of Roman tyranny, unmindful of the more awful slavery of materialism. They had no conception of the Servant of God as lowly and suffering, neither of that deeper and sublimer truth that God would be manifest in the flesh; consequently there was no preparation for His coming, no official national recognition of the advent.

Turning from His own people to the Gentile world, what was the condition of affairs? The three great world-forces when He came were the Roman, the Greek, and the Hebrew. The Roman was the nation of government, the Greek of culture, and the Hebrew of religion. The militarism of Rome utterly despised Judæa, looking down upon it as one of the small and turbulent provinces, always to be kept in subjection. The Roman was certainly not waiting for a new king to be born in Judæa.

And what was the attitude of Greece? The cultured men of Greece held in contempt the religion of the Hebrews. Hellenism and Hebraism were utterly opposed as ideals of life. The Greek would have treated with the utterest scorn the idea that a new teacher could arise out of Hebraism. All this serves to show that there was not,

[1] Isa. 7 : 14.

neither could there be, any welcome to the Saviour from the world as it was when He came. He was neither expected nor desired. All the known world was in a spirit of unrest, but men had no conception of the character of the deliverance really needed, and therefore Jesus came unrecognized and unknown. There was no welcome for Him.

But the time was now ripe in the economy of God for His advent, for man in sin had sunk to deepest depths. The world has never had a more powerful government than the Roman, and in many respects Greek culture has never been surpassed; but in spite of all this, sin was rampant. While there still exists terrible corruption in the world today, there is nothing to compare with the pollution of life when Jesus Christ came. Corruption was everywhere, and that in spite of the best that men could do in government, in culture, and in religion.

But though there was no human welcome to Christ, God granted to the men of that day certain signs that were wholly supernatural and remarkable.

These were of two kinds,—direct and indirect. Of the first there were three,—the star that led the wise men to Christ; the angelic ministry renewed at the time of the advent, and the fulfilling and renewal of the voices of prophecy. All these were definite signs, pointing to Him, directing attention to Him, in a world where men were not prepared to accept Him, and did not welcome Him, as the One sent from God for the fulfillment of the Divine purpose.

I. Of the sign of the star in the East [1] a great many explanations have been attempted, with a view to accounting

[1] Matt. 2: 1, 2.

for it in other than a supernatural way, which if they were not sad, would be amusing. Men have attempted to prove that it was simply the ordinary movement of some star which attracted the attention of these men. The evident sense of Scripture leads to the conclusion that it was a special Divine arrangement. There was in the shining of that star a signification which led these men from their country to the place where Jesus was born. It was an extraordinary and special movement in the stellar spaces, designed to lead these men to Christ. One of the most poetic thoughts about that star fell from the lips of a Welsh preacher. He suggested that it may have been the embodying of the Shekinah glory of old, which had been homeless since the infidelity of God's people, and now went outside the covenant to bring men back to the true ark of the covenant, its abiding home henceforth. This star shone in an unexpected place, outside of the covenant, to attract men to the privileges of the covenant.

It has been often said that the magi were kings. There seems to be no warrant for the statement. More probably they were priests in their own country. The word is of Aryan derivation. These men in all likelihood came from Persia, and had devoted their life to the study of the stars. They were astrologers. In these times men smile at astrology; but it should never be forgotten that astrology preceded astronomy, as alchemy preceded chemistry. Israel had been under Persian rule, and there is no doubt that the men of Persia had become acquainted with much of the religion and hope of the Hebrew; and they would in all likelihood be specially attracted by such predictions as coincided with their own religious habits. In all probability they knew the prophecy about the star out of Jacob,

the sceptre out of Judah.[1] They knew that this star indicated the birth of a king, so that when they came they
said, "Where is He that is born king of the Jews, for we
saw His star in the east, and are come to worship Him."[2]
This sign within the radius of their own observation led
them to the fulfillment of what was best in their thought
and service. That has always been the way with devout
seekers after truth. God reveals Himself to them at the
point where they are sincere seekers. The first sign of the
advent of Christ was the star which shone in the darkness
of an outside nation.

Next there was the sign of the angelic ministry,—the
message to Zacharias;[3] the message to Mary;[4] the word to
Joseph;[5] the first solo of the advent over the plains of
Bethlehem.[6] An angel announced the coming of the forerunner to Zacharias; an angel announced to Mary that
she should bring forth a son; an angel warned Joseph, and
led him out of peril; an angel sang the song of the advent
to the shepherds, and was joined by a multitude of the
heavenly chorus. So that the angels who had so long been
silent, came again to announce the advent on earth of their
King.

But perhaps the most remarkable sign was that of the
voices of prophecy. They had been silent from the time
of Malachi until the advent of Messiah. In dealing with
the voices of prophecy, there is first the fulfillment of
prophecy in the coming of Jesus; and secondly the uttering of the new prophecies in connection therewith. Matthew deals only with the old voices. In Luke, on the contrary, the voices of the old prophets are not referred to; all

---

[1] Num. 24: 17.   [3] Matt. 2: 2.   [8] Luke 1: 11.
[4] Luke 1: 26.   [5] Matt. 1: 20.   [6] Luke 2: 10-12.

are new.[1]   In Luke are found the new voices to Zacharias, to Mary, and Elizabeth in the first chapter; to Simeon, and Anna in the second chapter.   Christ was coming unrecognized and unwelcome, but all the voices of prophecy of the past were being fulfilled in Him, and in Elizabeth, Mary, and Anna, Simeon and Zacharias, new powers of prophecy gained inspiration from His advent.   Add to these the voice of the forerunner which, in the period immediately preceding the opening of the public ministry of Christ, attracted crowds to the valley of the Jordan, and moved the nation to its very centre.   This new prophetic manifestation centring in Jesus was an unmistakable sign to the sons of men of the Divine nature of His mission.

II.   Beyond these there were indirect signs.   In connection with the visit of the magi, remember their testimony to Herod and to Jerusalem, the splendour of their gifts, and their attitude to the Child.   These all constituted signs to men.   They brought gifts for a monarch, and the significance of their visit is seen in Herod's terror.   He knew what it meant.   It was a sign to royalty, this bringing of rich gifts.

Then again there was the story that the shepherds told, at which the people wondered,—a strange story that spread over that whole district.[2]

There was also the sign of the slaughter of the innocents.   All these were such as to arrest the attention of the people.   The star in the East, the visit of the magi, the story of the shepherds, the slaughter of the innocents, the

[1] The Scriptures which speak of the old voices are Matt. 1: 23; 2: 6, 15, 17, 23.
The Prophecies to which they refer are Isa. 7: 14; Micah 5: 2; Hosea 11: 1; Jer. 31: 15, and Isa. 53: 3.
[2] Luke 2: 18.

songs of the angels, all directed attention to the advent of Jesus. The heavens gave their testimony, and became luminous with a new light at night. The stellar spaces spoke by the appearance of a new star, which arrested the attention of the men who watched the heavens. Heaven as well as earth was moved at the advent, and hell itself was moved, as is shown by the stirring up of the hatred of Herod's heart, and the awful slaughter of the innocents.

These signs were sufficient to attract attention, and point to the advent of Christ, but there were few to read the signs of the times, and not until long after, did men begin to understand the deep significance of these signals of the advent. To-day men understand them in part, and every day are coming to realize more and more their deep significance.

BOOK II

THE BAPTISM

VII. The Parting of the Ways
VIII. Light on the Hidden Years
IX. The Vision of John

"   .   .   .   .   .   My Lord at home
Bright in the full face of the dawning day
Stood at His carpentry, and azure air
Inarched Him, scattered with the glittering green:
I saw Him standing, I saw His face, I saw
His even eyebrows over eyes grey-blue,
From whence with smiling there looked out on me
A welcome and a wonder,—' Mine so soon?'
Ah, me, how sweet and unendurable
Was that confronting beauty of the boy!

*   *   *   *   *   *

And once again I saw Him, in latter days
Fraught with a deeper meaning, for He came
To my baptizing, and the infinite air
Blushed on His coming, and all the earth was still;
Gentle He spake; I answered; God from heaven
Called, and I hardly heard Him, such a love
Streamed in that orison from man to man.
Then shining from His shoulders either-way
Fell the flood Jordan, and His kingly eyes
Looked in the east, and star-like met the sun.
Once in no manner of similitude,
And twice in thunderings and thrice in flame,
The Highest ere now hath shown Him secretly;
But when from heaven the visible Spirit in air
Came verily, lighted on Him, was alone,
Then knew I, then I said it, then I saw
God in the voice and glory of a man."
                    —FREDERICK W. H. MYERS.
                    "Saint John the Baptist."

Then cometh Jesus from Galilee to the Jordan unto John, to be baptized of him. But John would have hindered Him, saying, I have need to be baptized of Thee, and comest Thou to me? But Jesus answering said unto him, Suffer it now : for thus it becometh us to fulfill all righteousness. Then he suffereth Him. And Jesus, when He was baptized, went up straightway from the water : and lo, the heavens were opened unto Him, and He saw the Spirit of God descending as a dove, and coming upon Him ; and lo, a voice out of the heavens, saying, This is My beloved Son, in Whom I am well pleased.—*Matt. 3 : 13–17.*

And it came to pass in those days, that Jesus came from Nazareth of Galilee, and was baptized of John in the Jordan. And straightway coming up out of the water, He saw the heavens rent asunder, and the Spirit as a dove descending upon Him : and a voice came out of the heavens, Thou art My beloved Son, in Thee I am well pleased.—*Mark 1 : 9–11.*

Now it came to pass, when all the people were baptized, that, Jesus also having been baptized and praying, the heaven was opened, and the Holy Spirit descended in a bodily form, as a dove, upon Him, and a voice came out of heaven, Thou art My beloved Son ; in Thee I am well pleased.—*Luke 3 : 21, 22.*

VII

THE PARTING OF THE WAYS

THE second crisis in the mission of the Christ was reached when, emerging from the long silence and seclusion of Nazareth, He faced the brief period of speech and service, culminating in His Cross. That crisis is marked by His baptism in the river of Jordan. Concerning the thirty years, practically no details are given. A few brief statements constitute the record of this period. These statements reveal the principles of His life, and a bare statement of facts, quite sufficient for an understanding of all that is of value. They were years of seclusion and privacy.

The Gospel narratives give a much fuller account of the three years of public ministry.

Between these periods, the baptism in Jordan stands, at once dividing and uniting them. An understanding of the meaning of that ceremony, in the case of Jesus, will be gained by a contemplation of the thirty years and of the three. The order of the present study then is that of considering, first, the thirty years of private life; secondly, the three years of public ministry; and lastly, the ceremony coming between the two periods.

I.   With regard to the thirty years, it will be well first to gather the statements of Scripture concerning them, thus coming into possession of the facts, and then to consider the characteristics of those years, as therein revealed.

The facts chronicled concern the infancy, the childhood, the youth, and the manhood of Jesus.

Concerning the infancy, the following facts are recorded.

" And when eight days were fulfilled for circumcizing Him, His name was called JESUS, which was so called by the angel before He was conceived in the womb." [1]

" And when the days of their purification according to the law of Moses were fulfilled, they brought Him up to Jerusalem, to present Him to the Lord." [2]

"Now when they were departed, behold, an angel of the Lord appeareth to Joseph in a dream, saying, Arise and take the young child and His mother, and flee into Egypt, and be thou there until I tell thee: for Herod will seek the young child to destroy Him. And he arose and took the young child and His mother by night, and departed into Egypt; and was there until the death of Herod: that it might be fulfilled which was spoken by the Lord through the prophet. saying, Out of Egypt did I call My Son." [3]

" But when Herod was dead, behold, an angel of the Lord appeareth in a dream to Joseph in Egypt, saying, Arise, and take the young child and His mother, and go into the land of Israel: for they are dead that sought the young child's life. And he arose and took the young child and His mother, and came into the land of Israel. But when he heard that Archelaus was reigning over Judæa in the room of his father Herod, he was afraid to go thither; and being warned of God in a dream, he withdrew into the parts of Galilee, and came and dwelt in a city called Nazareth; that it might be fulfilled which was spoken through the prophets, that He should be called a Nazarene." [4]

[1] Luke 2: 21.   [2] Luke 2: 22.   [3] Matt. 2: 13–15.   [4] Matt. 2: 19–23.

In exact fulfillment of the requirements of the Hebrew aw Jesus was circumcized at the age of eight days. He was thus brought into the outward and visible manifestation of His relationship to the covenant of God with Israel.

The second fact is that of His presentation in the temple, and dedication as the first-born child of His mother, to the purpose and service of God.

The third fact chronicles the flight into Egypt, and the fourth the return from thence to His own land and people.

Thus in connection with the infancy there is a record of suggestive facts, the identification of Jesus with the covenant people of God, by the symbol of separation and purity, His dedication to special and specific work by His presentation in the temple, the carrying into Egypt, as part of a Divine programme of protection for One set apart to Himself, and the return to Nazareth for the entry upon that life of obscurity, in which the human is to make its progress from innocence to holiness, in the place of such ordinary testing as comes to man, and which is necessary for His development.

Concerning the childhood of Jesus, all the recorded facts are in the Gospel of Luke, and are as follows:

" And the child grew, and waxed strong, filled with wisdom: and the grace of God was upon Him." [1]

" And His parents went every year to Jerusalem at the feast of the passover. And when He was twelve years old, they went up after the custom of the feast; and when they had fulfilled the days, as they were returning, the boy Jesus tarried behind in Jerusalem; and His parents knew it not; but supposing Him to be in the company, they went a day's journey; and they sought for Him among their

[1] Luke 2: 40.

kinsfolk and acquaintance: and when they found Him not, they returned to Jerusalem, seeking for Him. And it came to pass, after three days they found Him in the temple, sitting in the midst of the teachers, both hearing them, and asking them questions: and all that heard Him were amazed at His understanding and His answers. And when they saw Him, they were astonished; and His mother said unto Him, Son, why hast Thou thus dealt with us? behold, Thy father and I sought Thee sorrowing. And He said unto them, How is it that ye sought Me? knew ye not that I must be in My Father's house? And they understood not the saying which He spake unto them. And He went down with them, and came to Nazareth; and He was subject unto them: and His mother kept all these sayings in her heart." [1]

The whole story of the childhood of Jesus from infancy to His religious coming of age, is contained in one verse The main statement of the verse is, "the child grew." Then follows an explanation of the statement, in what may be spoken of as an analysis of the lines of His growth. The whole fact of His human nature, physical, mental, and spiritual is recognized; the physical development in the words, He "waxed strong"; the mental development in the words, "becoming full of wisdom" (see margin); the spiritual development in the words, "the grace of God was upon Him." Thus the development of Jesus was not one-sided. Under the careful training of His mother, the advancement was a perfect harmony of progress in the whole fact of His life.

The other fact of His childhood recorded, is that of His religious coming of age. It is altogether to miss the importance of this story to think of it as accidental. The

[1] Luke 2: 41-51.

purpose of the coming to Jerusalem on the part of Mary, was undoubtedly primarily that of fulfilling the requirements of the law, the bringing of Jesus to His confirmation. At this point the boy was supposed to enter upon that period of life when He should have immediate dealings with the law, receiving it no longer through the instruction of His parents; but having been brought by them into a knowledge of its requirements, He would now take upon Himself the responsibility. The rite which is still in existence, consists in the preparation by the candidate of certain passages of the law, which are to be recited, and his presentation to the rulers and doctors, that in conversation with him, they may ask him questions, testing his knowledge, and he may submit to them questions arising out of his training. It was to this ceremony of confirmation that Jesus was brought at the age of twelve.

The picture of Christ here is very full of beauty, although too often the natural fact is obscured, by false ideas concerning the attitude of Jesus towards the teachers. A very popular conception of His action here is that of a boy delighting to ask questions that will show His own wisdom, and puzzle the doctors. This would seem to be utterly contrary to the facts. Jesus, a pure, beautiful boy, physically strong, mentally alert, spiritually full of grace, moving into new and larger experiences of His life, answered the questions of the doctors with a lucidity that astonished them, and submitted problems to them which showed how remarkable was the calibre of His mind, and how intense the fact of His spiritual nature. So great an opportunity was this to Him, that He tarried behind, still talking with these men.

Supposing Him to have been with the company, His parents had started on the homeward journey, and missing

Him, returned. Here again violence has been done to the character of Christ by the tone in which His question has been repeated. There was no touch of rebuke in what He said to His mother. It is far more probable that there was a tender expression of surprise that she from whom He had received His training, and under whose direction His mind had developed, and His spiritual nature been nurtured, should not know how "the things of His Father" were to Him the chief things.

So far of course Jesus is seen in the development of His human nature along the ordinary lines. The difficulty suggested in a previous chapter, how there could be growth and advancement, or why training was necessary if He was indeed God, admits of no explanation save that of repeating the fact that while He was very God, He was actual Man. His human life was lived wholly within the realm of humanity. The Son of God in His Deity refrained from giving to the human fact in its testing and development, any assistance other than was originally at the disposal of unfallen man. It cannot be over-emphasized or too often repeated, that this is a mystery defying explanation. Yet to deny it is to create a new mystery on either of the sides of the Personality of Jesus, involving the rout of the reason, in that there is discovered a marvellous effect, of which the only possible cause is denied.

The conclusion of the story of the confirmation is that He went down with His parents, and was subject unto them.

Concerning the youth of Jesus, that is, the period from His confirmation to His young manhood, there is one statement.

"And Jesus advanced in wisdom and stature, and in favour with God and men." [1]

[1] Luke 2 : 52.

Here again there is no detail, but the bare declaration of His advancement, and that advancement is revealed as being balanced, and including the whole of His nature, " in wisdom, in stature, in favour with God and men." The application of this statement, very often lost sight of, is that He grew in favour not only with God, but with men.   It is not a sign of being in the grace of God when one is out of favour with men.   It was not the Personality and character of Jesus that alienated the crowds from Him, but the teaching which rebuked their sin, and called them to repentance.   It is very beautiful to read that in those long years at Nazareth Jesus was a favourite.   No details are given, and yet it is quite possible to sit down in front of the statement, and imagine various facts included within it.   One could almost picture the children going to Him, taking perhaps their toys for Him to mend; and the young men, visiting Him to talk out some of the problems that were vexing their hearts.   And the old people, bent with sorrow, and loving to hear the tones of some strong and yet tender voice, sitting while He talked to them. Let this never be forgotten " He grew in favour with God and men."   Jesus was a favourite in His own village until the days came when, in fulfillment of His Father's will, He had to speak such words as alienated them from friendship, and made the very men of Nazareth attempt His murder, long before it was accomplished by the priests of the nation.

There yet remains one fact chronicled concerning the years, that namely, of the occupation of His Manhood.

" Is not this the carpenter, the son of Mary, and brother of James, and Joses, and Judas, and Simon ? and are not His sisters here with us ? And they were offended in Him." [1]

[1] Mark 6 : 3.

The question was asked in the days when the enmity of the men of Nazareth was stirred against Him, because of His superior wisdom, and authoritative teaching. And yet it lights up facts of those past years. He was the village carpenter. The Greek word τέκτων, here translated carpenter, etymologically means a producer, but specifically, and in its use in that country, it indicated a craftsman in wood. The declaration reveals Him to us as One Who learned a trade, becoming Master of the tools of His craft. All this is to be dealt with more fully in the next chapter.

These facts, brief as is the chronicle of them, reveal the characteristics of the life of Jesus. Through the process of training, He lived in dependence upon the guidance of other human wills. He trod the path of a daily duty. Toil was not to Him merely the taking up of work for the sake of amusement. It was His response to stern necessity. He laboured for the bread which was to sustain physical life. Through all the years, His life was conditioned within human limitations. These limitations were of course, such as were part of an original Divine plan. There was a difference throughout between the experience of the Man Jesus, and the experience of fallen men. Their intelligence is darkened. His shone clearly, and yet in ever increasing capacity. Their emotion is prostituted. His was ever set upon highest things, and responsive to the most perfect. Their will is degraded, because under the dominion of a false governing principle. His was exercised within the true realm of submission to the highest of all. The thirty years were the years of the long silence, in which the Son of God is seen stripped and emptied of all royalty, save that of a victorious manhood.

II.   Turning to the three years, there may again be con-

sidered the facts and the characteristics. Here everything
is different. Silence has given way to speech, privacy to
publicity; submission to human authority has been changed
into authoritative teaching and deeds, in the midst of
human affairs. His induction to public ministry is recorded by Luke. Returning to the synagogue, with which
He was so familiar, and taking up the book of the prophet,
He read Himself into His sacred office. From the prophecy
of Isaiah He read the marvellous description of the mission of the Servant of God, and then in sublime and quiet
majesty announced that " to-day hath this Scripture been
fulfilled in your ears." [1]   There was no one to introduce
Him, for no one appreciated the meaning of His mission.
Passing from the life of privacy to the days of publicity,
He definitely and positively claimed that He was the One,
anointed of God, for the fulfillment of the dreams, and the
realization of the hopes, of the ancient people.

The description of the following years is all crowded
into the brief descriptive statement, with which Luke
opens his second treatise. " Jesus began both to do and
to teach." [2]   For the purposes then of gathering the
general impression of the facts of the three years, they
may be considered under that twofold heading, of His doing and His teaching.

There is no necessity here to attempt to chronicle the
deeds. It will be sufficient to state concisely their
character again in the words of Luke. " Jesus of
Nazareth . . . went about doing good, and healing
all that were oppressed of the devil; for God was with
Him." [3]   That covers the whole fact concerning the deeds
of Jesus in the three years of public ministry. Doing
good means infinitely more than being good, or doing good

[1] Luke 4: 16–21.   [2] Acts 1: 1.   [3] Acts 10: 38.

things that are right. The phrase indicates active beneficence. He was, in the richest and fullest sense of the
word, a Benefactor. He lived a life in which there was
the constant activity of deeds of goodness and kindness towards other people. The goodness referred to is positive
and relative, assuredly the goodness of character, but also
that manifested in conduct, not merely the rightness of
inward attitude, but the beneficence of outward act. His
vocation during the hidden years had been that of a carpenter. When He laid that calling aside, He entered upon the
vocation of doing good, serving others, scattering blessing.
All life now was an opportunity for benefiting some one.
His journeyings, His ordinary deeds, the miracles of His
power, are all contained within the phrase " doing good."
He was pouring out of His own rich treasury upon other
people, scattering gifts, bestowing benefits. He went about
doing good.

Then as to the teaching. This consisted in the announcement of the principles of human life, and was a
revelation of the convictions and conditions lying behind true
conduct. It is almost impossible to summarize the teaching of Jesus, and yet the attempt must be made, though
the result will of necessity be imperfect.

As in the Gospels four facts are revealed concerning
the Personality of Christ, so also these Gospels reveal four
phases of His teaching ; and the whole system of the
teaching of Jesus can only be understood, as these phases
are all present to the mind, and their harmony and balance
are discovered.

The teaching of Matthew has to do with the government
of God. It is teaching concerning the Kingdom. In it
lies that most matchless document, the Manifesto of the
King. Afterwards there occurs His commissioning of His

first messengers, with yet fuller revelation of the true meaning of the Kingdom. Then in perfect harmony of deed with word, illustrations and explanations of the benefits and values of the Kingdom are given. Then incidentally scattered through the Gospel there are illuminative illustrations, and ever broadening teaching, concerning the powers and perfections of the kingly authority. The people who have listened, have become antagonized, and as in the beginning of the teaching, there were the Beatitudes, so towards its closing, so far as the crowd is concerned, the woes are pronounced, the stern and awful denunciations of such as reject the Kingdom of God. Towards the close of the three years, the programme concerning the final movements of the Divine economy, in the casting out of evil, and the establishment of the Kingdom is announced. Along all the pathway incidental teaching, great parables, and revealing deeds, unite in making clear the great facts concerning the Kingdom of God, yet to be set up on the earth, and spoken of almost invariably, therefore, through Matthew, as the Kingdom of heaven.

In the Gospel of Mark, the teaching is of a different character. There is very little of it. He is revealed as to His Person, as the Servant, always girded, always busy, stripped of royalty, and consecrated to duty. Incidental accounts which had to do largely with that aspect of truth, fall from His lips. A special section is devoted to the charge He delivers to His servants, concerning their work, and in which He speaks of the final things.

In Luke again the character of the teaching is different, harmonizing as it does with the Person of Jesus as therein presented. In this Gospel there is no consecutive body of teaching. The Son of Man, the universal Saviour, speaks as occasion demands, of the great subjects that are ever on

His heart. First the Gospel contains in condensed form some of the mighty sayings contained within the Manifesto of the King, as recorded by Matthew. Then there are general instructions, and solemn warnings uttered to His apostles, as He equips them for their work. That however which is peculiar to Luke is His wonderful teaching concerning publicans and sinners, their lost condition, and the redemption He has come to accomplish for them. In Luke there is the parable concerning the lost sheep, the lost silver, and the lost son. It is a parable of the lost. It is a parable of the lost sought. It is a parable of the lost found. And that parable of Jesus may be said to reveal His teaching concerning humanity in the light of His mission more perfectly than it is revealed in any other of His recorded words. In this Gospel moreover, is contained the denunciation of the Pharisees, the parables of service, of the talents, and yet again, words concerning the final things.

Coming to the Gospel of John, in some senses the greatest of all, because presenting Jesus as to His Deity, there is the most wonderful teaching of all. From first to last the teaching of Jesus in John may be spoken of as the speech of heaven to earth. There are the wonderful conversations with Nicodemus, and the woman at the well; the remarkable discourses, delivered in the hearing of the crowds, concerning His unity with the Father; His discourse on the sustenance of the life of the spirit, as being of infinitely greater importance than the feeding of the physical; a declaration of the meaning of His mission, as being that of providing life for those who need it, by the liberation of His own, through the mystery of death. Finally, the great Paschal discourses, in which He promises to His Church the coming of the Spirit, and declares the meaning and the method of that great advent.

It is in John that there is the repetition so constantly of
the Divine title, " I am," linked to simple symbols of
things human, and in that very fact is a key to the whole
teaching of Jesus, as contained in the Gospel of John.   It
is the speech of heaven to earth, of God to men.   It is
but to pass through the Gospel reading His " I am's," and
their setting, to discover this key.   " I am the bread." [1]
" I am the Light." [2]   " I am." [3]   " I am the door." [4]   " I
am the good Shepherd." [5]   " I am the resurrection." [6]   " I
am the way, and the truth, and the life." [7]   " I am the
true vine." [8]   Here is a growing revelation.   Here is a
declaration of the whole meaning of His gracious mission.
The human symbols are simple.   The Divine title ever
thrills with the infinite music unfathomable.   Yet in their
combination is heard the voice from heaven, the Logos,
the Word of God.

How different these three years from the thirty.   The
characteristics of the thirty, and those of the three, make a
striking contrast.   In the thirty, depending on human will.
In the three, uttering authoritative speech, and performing
deeds of power.   In the thirty years, the commonplace
duty a daily call   In the three, manifesting Himself as the
Lord of duty, demonstrating the dignity of the Son of Man
by the miracles of His power, and the glory of the Son of
God in the matchless magnificence of His Person, and the
infinite wisdom of His teaching.   In the thirty years, a life
lived strictly within human limitations, a life in which there
was constant relation to the Divine, but the relation of dependence, submission, fellowship.   In the three years while
this continued, yet the life was evidently broadening out into
a spacious and conspicuous cooperation with the Divine,

[1] John 6: 35.   [2] John 8: 12.   [3] John 8: 58.   [4] John 10: 7.
[5] John 10: 11.   [6] John 11: 25.   [7] John 14: 6.   [8] John 15: 1.

until the supreme consciousness left upon the mind is that of the movements of God through the deeds and words of man. The thirty years were those of the long silence in which the Son of God was seen stripped and emptied of all royalty, save that of His perfect Manhood. The three years are the years of the brief speech, in which the Son of Man is seen clothed in authority, filled with power, speaking in the tone and accent of the Son of God.

III.   Between these periods there came the solemn and significant ceremony of the baptism.   As Jesus left that in His life which was preparatory, and entered upon the actual work of the ministry, He devoted Himself to the ultimate issue of His work, that namely, of an identification with men even to death. His being baptized was an act by which He consented to take His place among sinners. John's baptism was that of repentance. There was no room for repentance in Jesus, and yet because of His devotion to their redemption, He took His place with them. This will be referred to again in subsequent considerations. It is named here as helping to explain the value of the supernatural manifestations accompanying the baptism. As in the act of baptism He yielded Himself, a sacrifice and an offering; the opened heavens, the descending dove, the living voice, each having its own significance, unite in the attestation of the perfection of the One so yielding Himself, to the mightiest phase in the purpose of God, that of redemption by the way of sacrifice. The significance of this threefold fact may be considered briefly.

The opened heavens suggest the perfections of the thirty years, and declare in sacred sign and symbol that no act of His has excluded Him from the fellowship of the perfect. Heaven which must forever exclude whatsoever is imperfect, could have enfolded Him without the violation of any principle of the Eternal Holiness.

The descending Spirit in the form of a dove was a recognition of the character, the Spirit, the disposition, of this Man, which lay behind the outward expression in conduct. Never anywhere else, is it recorded that the Spirit descended in the form of a dove. It rested upon Christ as the symbol of purity and of meekness. And yet it was also His anointing for the work of the three years. Seeing that the Spirit of anointing, which was preparation for the future, came in the form of a dove, which sealed the past ; the fact was signified that the ministry in public would be exercised in the strength of, and carried forward in the Spirit of, the purity and the meekness which had characterized the past.

Superadded to these signs there was the sound of the living voice. First in identification of this Person as the One Who was referred to in the prophetic writings, and in the words of the Psalmist,

> " I will tell of the decree :
> Jehovah said unto Me, Thou art My Son ;
> This day have I begotten Thee . . .
> Kiss the Son, lest He be angry, and ye perish in the way." [1]

The great word coming out of the old economy is " the Son." Now at the baptism God says, " Thou art My beloved Son." [2]

Thus the description has reference to His office, and appointment and anointing for service. The second part of the Divine pronouncement declares that God is well pleased in Him. This sets the seal of the Divine approbation upon the thirty years, and declares therefore the

---

[1] Psalm 2 : 7, 12. [2] Luke 3 : 22.

perfect fitness of the approved One for the carrying out of the work of the three.

Thus the thirty years of privacy merge into the three years of publicity, by the way of solemn and significant ceremony.

By this study the baptism is placed in its relation to these two periods in the ministry of Jesus. The next study will deal more fully with the perfections of the thirty, and the following one will indicate more fully the true meaning and value of the three.

VIII

LIGHT ON THE HIDDEN YEARS AT NAZARETH

THE baptism of Jesus separated between His private and public life. At that baptism the opened heavens, the descending Spirit, and the voice of the Father alike bore testimony to the perfection of the Son.

The Divine voice had special significance as a declaration concerning the character of Christ as He emerged from the seclusion of the hidden years. Thrice during the period of public ministry did this Divine voice break the silence of the heavens, announcing the Father's approval of the Son of His love. On each occasion the silence was so broken for the bearing of testimony to the perfection of Jesus.

The first occasion was the one now under consideration, when the voice declared, " This is My beloved Son, in Whom I am well pleased." [1]

The second was when upon the mount of transfiguration, the same voice was heard saying, " This is My beloved Son, in Whom I am well pleased ; hear ye Him." [2]

The third was when Jesus, drawing near to His Cross, the shadow and sorrow thereof falling over His life, prayed, " Father, glorify Thy name," and the answer came, " I have both glorified it, and will glorify it again." [3]

In each case the breaking of the silence of the heavens was for the announcement of God's approbation of Christ, as in some fresh crisis of life He set His face towards the

[1] Matt. 3 : 17.   [2] Matt. 17 : 5.   [3] John 12: 28.

123

death, which was to culminate the work of redemption, according to the purposes of God. He went into the waters of Jordan, and was numbered with the transgressors in the baptism of repentance, taking His place with them in that symbol of death, as He would finally associate Himself with them in actual death. So far as the Person and character of Christ were concerned, He had no need of the baptism of John. The prophet was perfectly right when he said, " I have need to be baptized of Thee, and comest Thou to me ? " [1]   By His action He signified His consent to identification with sinners, even to death. Here then, at once becomes evident the value of the Divine statement. It was a declaration of the perfection of Jesus, and consequently of the value of that sacrifice which He would ultimately offer.

This indeed was the signification in each of the three cases quoted, for on the mount of transfiguration, He spoke with the heavenly visitors of His coming exodus, thus in the light of that wondrous glory facing His death for men. And on the third occasion it was when He, troubled in Spirit, at the prospect of death, yet deliberately declared that for death He had come unto that hour, and prayed only for the glorification of the Divine name. In three crises He faced and consented to death, and on each occasion heaven sealed the sacrifice as being perfect, and therefore of infinite value.

This statement of the perfection of Jesus made at His baptism is a window through which light falls upon His Person and character in the years that had been spent at Nazareth.

In the account of the creation in Genesis, it is declared that man, created in the image of God was appointed

[1] Matt. 3 : 14.

master of all created things, the fish of the sea, the fowl of the air, and the beasts of the field.   He was, moreover, placed in the garden of Eden to dress it and to keep it, that fact indicating that all the wonderful possibilities lying within the new creation were to be realized by the attention and work of man.   The psalmist, overwhelmed by the majesty of the heavens, asks in astonishment,

> " What is man, that Thou art mindful of him ? "

and then answers his question in words that recall the Divine intention as revealed in Genesis :

> " For Thou hast made him but little lower than God,
> And crownest him with glory and honour.
> Thou makest him to have dominion over the works of Thy
>   hands ;
> Thou hast put all things under his feet :
> All sheep and oxen,
> Yea, and the beasts of the field,
> The birds of the heavens, and the fish of the sea,
> Whatsoever passeth through the paths of the seas." [1]

Man, in the first Divine intention, is master of creation. He is born to have dominion.   This psalm is quoted by the writer of the letter to the Hebrews :

But one hath somewhere testified, saying,

> What is man, that Thou art mindful of him ?
> Or the son of man, that Thou visitest him ?
> Thou madest him a little lower than the angels ;
> Thou crownedst him with glory and honour,
> And didst set him over the works of Thy hands :
> Thou didst put all things in subjection under his feet.

For in that he subjected all things unto him, he left nothing that is not subject to him. [2]   That is a declaration of the original purpose of God.   The writer then proceeds, " But now we see not yet all things subjected

[1] Psa. 8 : 4–8.   [2] Heb. 2 : 6–9.

to him. But we behold . . . Jesus." Without dealing with the full purpose or intention of the writer's
argument, it is evident that he intends to declare, that
while man as he is to-day has failed to realize the Divine intention, this Man was an exception to the general
failure, in that He perfectly realized it. To Him all things
were in subjection. He was Master of the fish of the
sea, and knew where to find them, when the disciples had
been baffled in their all-night fishing. He understood the
habits of the birds of the heavens, and drew some of His
sweetest lessons from them. The very beasts of the field
recognized His Lordship. Of this there is a glimpse in
the account of the temptation as chronicled by Mark,
" He was with the wild beasts ; " [1] the preposition used indicating close contact, and therefore also suggesting that He
was unharmed by them. He was indeed God's perfect Man,
having dominion over the things of His Father's creation.

To facilitate the meditation on the perfections of Jesus
as Man, fall back upon the simplest analysis of human
personality, that of spirit and body, dealing with the mind
as the consciousness of this compound personality. Inferentially the New Testament has much to say concerning the perfection of Jesus in spirit and body during those
years of seclusion in Nazareth.

I. We commence with spirit, for that is the essential
fact in man. For an understanding of the perfection of
His Spirit again let the analysis of intelligence, emotion, and
will be accepted. In all of these, and in their combination,
Jesus of Nazareth realized the Divine thought, and therefore was absolutely perfect.

In Him intelligence was unclouded. In the Divine

[1] Mark 1 : 13.

economy there are three ways in which men may know God,—through creation, through revelation, and through direct communication.

All these avenues were open to Jesus, and through them He saw all that was to be seen. To Him creation was an open book, revelation was radiant, and communication with God was immediate and uninterrupted. These things can be said of none other. Creation is not an open book to man. God is allowing him by the slow and tedious processes of the centuries to learn to read its secrets. To Jesus all these secrets were apparent.

The revelation of the Scriptures, while perfect in themselves, are not perfectly understood because of the clouding of man's intelligence, and it is out of his limitation that all the misinterpretation and misunderstanding of the centuries have risen. To Jesus all the words of revelation rang with the meanings of God, and He knew Him, and understood His message in the holy writings.

The communication of men with God, even of the saints, is intermittent and partial, interfered with often by moods and frames. His was perpetual, the Divine voice sounding in the deepest consciousness of His soul, and He, answering with the naturalness of a child, in the immediate presence of the Father.

In this connection hear the testimony of the men of Nazareth. To this hamlet on the hills He had been taken as an infant on the return from Egypt, and there for the next twenty-eight years the greater part of His life was spent. At the age of twelve He had been taken to Jerusalem, and in all probability had visited the Holy City each subsequent year; but most likely all the remaining months of the years were passed in Nazareth. The people of Nazareth would know Him perfectly. It was a little town

standing out of the run of the ordinary traffic of the country. So far is it removed from the ordinary course of
events that it seems as though no invading army has ever
touched it; and there is great probability that the synagogue standing to-day is the very one in which the Lord
read the words of the law. It was a small and unimportant place, where in all likelihood every one knew every one
else, and would be perfectly familiar with the boy who had
grown up in the shop of the village carpenter, and had
finally Himself succeeded His reputed father in the work
of that shop.

At about thirty years of age, He had turned His back
upon the village. After an absence of a few months He
returned, and as His custom was, visited the synagogue on
the Sabbath day. But now what He did was unusual and
unexpected—He opened His mouth and began to speak to
them, and as they listened to Him they were astonished;
and presently some one asked the question, " Whence hath
this Man these things? and, What is the wisdom that is
given unto this Man?"[1]

To gather the full force of the question it is necessary
to understand what they meant by wisdom. According to
Trench the word σοφία, signifies clearness of understanding, and is a word used only "as expressing the highest
and noblest." As these men of Nazareth listened to Him,
what surprised them was that they heard in His teaching,
such wisdom as was proof at once of great intellect, and
great goodness.

There is a yet more remarkable statement recorded about
Him in the Gospel of John. Coming from Galilee to
Jerusalem He taught in the temple. Speaking here was a
very different thing from speaking in the synagogue at

[1] Mark 6: 2.

Nazareth. Here were gathered and centred the light and scholarship of the day. Here a false accent, or a misquotation of ignorance, would immediately have been detected. When Savonarola came to Florence for the first time, his magnificent eloquence of conviction was counted nothing, because of the objectionable Lombardy accent. When Jesus passed from the villages to the metropolis, and opened His mouth to teach, surrounded by the most critical ears of His day, " the Jews therefore marvelled, saying, How knoweth this Man letters, having never learned ? " [1] Now this word γράμματα, translated " letters," is a most significant one. It only occurs in one other place in the New Testament. " And as he thus made his defence, Festus saith with a loud voice, Paul, thou art mad; thy much learning is turning thee mad." [2] Festus meant by the word " learning " exactly what these men meant by " letters." Festus detected in the speech of Paul, all that he had gained from his careful training. There was the accent of the school of Gamaliel, and it was this tone of erudition that the Jews were astonished at in Jesus when they spoke of His knowing letters. " When they said, ' How knoweth this Man letters, having never learned,' they meant that He had never studied in the schools, and yet possessed all that the schools could give Him." [3] The remarkable thing was that Jesus showed Himself familiar with the literary methods of His time, which were confined to the disciples of the popular teachers. He did not speak amongst them as an earnest and yet ignorant Man ; but by His use of language, and His evident familiarity with the philosophies of the schools, He impressed the Jerusalem crowds, and in astonishment they exclaimed, " How knoweth this Man letters, having never learned ? "

[1] John 7 : 15.   [2] Acts 26 : 24.   [3] Bishop Westcott.

Men have to learn, to study, to go through processes of training, to obtain what He possessed without these processes. To return to the Gospel of John, notice that He answered their question : " My teaching is not Mine, but His that sent Me. If any man willeth to do His will, he shall know of the teaching, whether it is of God, or whether I speak from Myself." [1] While that passage is generally quoted as declaring a philosophy of Christian discipleship, and while it has that application, it should never be forgotten that the first intention of the words is that of an answer to a question of the Jews, and is our Lord's account of His knowledge of the things that astonished His hearers. The Man Who perfectly does the will of God is the Man Who understands all mysteries ; and is familiar with facts which ordinary men only understand by long effort and study. The secrets that lie hidden in Nature, fallen man with clouded intelligence must search after; but God's unfallen Man will read them upon the open page of Nature, discovering immediately the deepest philosophie of life. Never let Christ be robbed of the royalty of inte' lectual kingship. He was in no sense ignorant or illiterate He never learned, for there was no necessity for learning Learning is a process made necessary by the fall of man, and the sin of the race. God's perfect and unfallen Man needed no such process ; being sinless, He knew letters without having learned. In Him was most perfectly fulfilled the wonderful words " The secret of Jehovah is with them that fear Him." [2]

This intelligence operated not only in the realm of Nature, but in keen and marvellous accuracy of understanding of the inner secrets of other human lives. As John declares, " He needed not that any one should bear witness

[1] John 7 : 16, 17.   [2] Psa. 25 : 14 (margin).

concerning man; for He Himself knew what was in man."[1] Telepathy and thought-reading are great mysteries to the mind of men to-day, mysteries towards the solution of which a few are bending all their mental power, while the rest watch, and smilingly imagine that they are either playing tricks, or are themselves being tricked. And yet this whole realm of the communication of the mind of man with the mind of man, is part of the estate lost through sin. In it Jesus was at home. He knew the thought of sin, and the lustful desire, and the hidden malice, and the trembling aspiration after God; and to watch carefully His dealings with the varied men and women, who crossed His pathway, is to see the method of an intelligence the calibre of which cannot be understood, for He read the inner thought of the heart of each as an open book.

Let workers for God in dealing with individual souls ever bear this in mind. He knows the secret of the heart of the one to whom the worker is talking. There are times when in dealing with men of intellectual mold there has come the temptation of imagining that Jesus of Nazareth was not able perfectly to satisfy the capacity of their great minds. Shame on all such unworthy doubt. Be it ever remembered that Jesus, the Son of Mary, was Prince of scholars, Master of learning, King of wisdom, His enemies being His witnesses. He had the γράμματα, the wisdom of letters, which they so coveted, though He never passed through human process to reach the human result.

He was moreover perfect in His emotional nature. His affection was undivided. Unclouded intelligence issued in perfect consciousness of God. Seeing God perfectly in the ways and works of God, He loved God perfectly. Herein is the deepest meaning of His own words, " Blessed

[1] John 2 : 25.

are the pure in heart : for they shall see God." [1]   Himself pure in heart, He saw God perfectly, and this was to realize the Divine unity.   Let this sequence be carefully noted.   First, unclouded intelligence producing perfect consciousness of God ; secondly, perfect consciousness of God revealing the unity of God and of all things in God ; thirdly, this discovery capturing the whole heart and necessitating perfect love.

This unity of God was the central fact for the understanding of which the Hebrew nation had been created. " Hear, O Israel : Jehovah our God is one Jehovah." [2] To see and know God as Jesus saw and knew Him is to discover this unity, and therein to discover the unity of all the purposes of Deity,—that

". . . through the ages one increasing purpose runs,
And the thoughts of men are widened with the process of the suns." [3]

This vision of the unity of God captures the heart of man.   The consciousness of the One Who creates and maintains unity, is the perfection of love in the soul of man.   Thus the passage already quoted in Deuteronomy concerning the unity of Jehovah is immediately followed by the command, " And thou shalt love Jehovah thy God with all thy heart, and with all thy soul, and with all thy might." Jesus knowing with unclouded intelligence was perfectly conscious of the character of God, and the unity of His purpose, and loved Him with all His heart.   The Man of unclouded intelligence was the Man of undivided affection.

Then follows the fact of the unopposing will.   The will is the citadel against which all the forces of temptation are directed, and within this citadel Jesus repelled these tempta-

[1] Matt. 5 : 8.   [2] Deut. 6 : 4.   [3] Tennyson.

tions in the light of unclouded intelligence, and the power of undivided affection. He saw God perfectly, and therefore He loved God perfectly, and therefore He obeyed God perfectly, and was able to say, " I do always the things that are pleasing to Him." [1]

In this analysis of the spiritual perfection of Jesus, there must ever be borne in mind the interaction of these three facts within the spiritual nature. Love, through light, appealed to will. Will, responding, strengthened love and increased light. That is the perpetual process in human life. Yielding to God, light falls upon the pathway, and creates love. Love suggests obedience. The will, impulsed by love, yields to light. The experience that follows obedience increases love and light, and thus there is perpetual progress, growth, development in the grace that makes men grow in favour with God and man.

II. Turn now to the physical perfection of Jesus. When will some inspired artist give us a true picture of this glorious Man? He is almost always depicted as frail in physical form, and lacking in bodily beauty. Perhaps the German artist, Hoffmann, has come nearest to the true ideal. It may be argued that the prophet Isaiah declared, " There is no beauty that we should desire Him; " [2] but surely the prophet did not mean that He would be devoid of beauty, but rather that men would be blind and would not recognize the true type of Divine beauty. I strenuously hold that He was perfect in physical form and proportion. The body is the outward and visible sign of the inward and invisible spirit, and the perfect spirit of Jesus would form a perfect physical tabernacle in which He passed the probationary life.

[1] John 8: 29. [2] Isa. 53: 2.

In the letter to the Romans the apostle urges the saints "to present your bodies a living sacrifice, holy, acceptable to God, which is your spiritual worship." [1] That is the marginal reading, and catches the real thought of the writer. The spirit worships through the presentation of the body. The spirit expresses itself through the body. It will readily be conceded that the most plain and commonplace faces become transfused with light, when the spirit is in communion with God; and to grant the spiritual perfection of Jesus is of necessity to admit bodily perfection likewise. Marred with the furrows of sorrow and of pain His sacred face most surely was, yet in form and feature and fashion it was the fairest face of man the world has ever seen. Perhaps bent, and even at the last faltering with weariness, that sacred tabernacle of His spirit, and yet the boasted perfections of Greek gods were but human abortions by the side of the perfectly balanced physique of Jesus. In Him spirit was dominant, and all bodily powers were perfectly under control, within the sphere appointed in the Divine economy.

It follows that every piece of work that Jesus did in physical strength under the control of spiritual intelligence, was perfect work, and this because He perfectly understood His work, was perfectly able to do it, and rendered it in the perfect love of His heart to God. How delightful it is to meditate upon Him as He bent over His bench and made yokes and ploughs for the cultivation of the fields He so dearly loved, which stretched around the hamlet where He lived. It is worthy of remembrance that He used both plough and yoke as illustrations in His preaching. Think for a moment of the wonderful skill with which He would carry out His work. His knowledge of nature was

[1] Rom. 12: 1.

such that He knew exactly the best wood to use for any given piece of work; and in the tree lying before Him, He read all the story of its growth, and knew the precision of its method, and so understood just how to cut it so as not to spoil it in the process. He knew, moreover, how to join it, so that in the joint the strength of each part should minister to the new strength of union. He was a perfect Workman, doing perfect work.

Perhaps apart from the Master, one of the most wonderful illustrations the world has ever had of perfection of spirit producing perfection of work was that of Stradivarius, the great, and may it not be said, the only, maker of the violin. Certain it is that his instruments have never been improved upon. When he was at work on them, he would pass into the woods, and placing his hands upon the trees would know by the very touch, which wood was best for each part of the musical mechanism. He discovered the tones of music in the fibre of the wood, with the result that he made a perfect instrument. In him there was the development of spirit on the side of music.

Now lift the thought, and remember that Jesus of Nazareth was not developed upon one side only, but was perfect in His understanding of all the methods of God in creation. See then how His work would be most perfect. Every piece of carpentry passing from His shop, if men had but been able to appreciate it, thrilled with the energy of perfect manhood.

In Him there was an utter absence of disease. He had strength enough for the accomplishment of the Divinely ordained work of the day. No more than that, for He was Man. Tired was He when the day was over, because His strength had been used for the day for which it was given. Tiredness is God's call to sleep which is Nature's sweet restorer. O perfect Man, perfect in spirit, having learning, loving always, obeying ever; perfect in body, with face of rarest beauty, and form of finest mold, expressing in common daily tasks the thoughts of God and the perfections of eternity!

Then finally, and in a word, let it be remembered that He passed from those thirty years of privacy, perfect in spite of temptation. His had not been a life free from temptation. The old question asked in Eden was surely asked of Jesus, " Has God imposed limitations? " and the suggestions, listening to which the first of the race was ruined, were made to Him also, " This limitation of the carpenter's bench is cruel bondage." And yet there He remained while days multiplied into weeks, and weeks grew into months, and months passed on, until years had multiplied themselves to thirty. And even when perhaps the subtlest temptation of all came, the temptation to hurry on His own greatest work, the temptation which coming to Moses and mastering him postponed deliverance for so long, He still remained, there also learning obedience by the things which He suffered, and growing in favour with God and men; until, responsive to the inward call, He left the seclusion and the privacy, and standing on the threshold of public work, with the waters of a death baptism, which He had shared in the grace of His heart with man, still clinging about Him, the silent heavens broke into the language of a great music, as the Almighty Father declared, " This is My beloved Son in Whom I am well pleased."

IX

THE VISION OF JOHN

ONE of the supreme glories of the Hebrew nation was its long line of prophets. The function of the prophet may be gathered from the varied names by which these men were called. One or two instances will suffice. The prophet was called "a seer,"[1] that is, simply, one who sees. He was also called "man of God,"[2] that is, a man wholly devoted to God, and therefore speaking with authority the messages of God. And yet again, he was called "man of the Spirit,"[3] that is, one through whom the Spirit declared the will and purpose of Jehovah. The prophetical order commenced with Samuel, and in the marvellous succession were such men as Elijah, and Elisha, Isaiah, and Ezekiel. Splendid as was this succession, none among them was greater than the last of the long line, John the Baptist, who was also the immediate forerunner of Jesus.

In common with all his predecessors in the prophetic office, John's message resulted from his vision. He saw clearly, and therefore spoke with authority. The message which aroused the whole nation was the outcome of the clear seeing of this man, wholly devoted to the will of God. Undeceived by the accidental and external in the condition of his nation, his vision was of the true moral condition, and gave birth to his message. When his work was approaching its termination, a new vision, that of the

[1] 1 Sam. 9: 9.   [2] 1 Sam. 9: 6.   [3] Hosea 9: 7 (A. V. Margin).

Saviour, was granted to him, and his last and mightiest utterances were concerning the Christ. It is of deep interest and undoubted value to consider his view of Christ, at this crisis in his work.

How important this vision is, may be argued from the manner in which Luke introduces him. "Now in the fifteenth year of the reign of Tiberius Cæsar, Pontius Pilate being governor of Judæa, and Herod being tetrarch of Galilee, and his brother Philip tetrarch of the region of Ituræa and Trachonitis, and Lysanias tetrarch of Abilene, in the high-priesthood of Annas and Caiaphas, the word of God came unto John." [1]   One Roman emperor, one Roman governor, three tetrarchs, and two high priests are all made use of, to mark the hour in which the word came to John.

Incidentally this is an illuminative illustration of the Divine perspective in human history. To the men of the day, any one of the great men named would have counted for far more than the man of the wilderness; but in the economy of God, they are simply used to mark the hour in which the most important event of the period happened, that namely of the coming to a man of the word of God, which announced the advent of His Son. The greatness of John in the estimate of heaven, is revealed by the fact that the word of God passed emperor, governor, tetrarchs, and high priests, and came to him; and the mention of these facts proves how important was the message of this man, to whom was given the high honour of uttering the word which announced the fulfillment of the aspirations of the past, and the merging of one dispensation of government into a new and a better.

The subject is divided into two parts, first, John's pre-

[1] Luke 3 : 1, 2.

liminary vision and burden; and secondly, the greater vision that broke upon him and closed his work.

I. The preliminary vision was a twofold one. First a great consciousness of the sin of the people, and secondly an overwhelming sense of an approaching crisis. These were the two great facts that made the ministry of John powerful, his sense of sin, and his sense of the imminence of Divine interposition. His vision of the people as they really were, instead of as they thought they were, and his understanding of the signs of the times were so perfect, that he knew that he stood on the eve of a new departure.

His consciousness of the sin of the people is evidenced first by the words addressed to them, especially by that stinging and terrible description, "Ye offspring of vipers." [1] Perhaps the best way to have any correct idea of how these words sounded in the ears of the listeners is to imagine that a prophet to-day should use them in addressing a promiscuous congregation. John looked into the faces of the multitudes and deliberately called them "offspring of vipers." These multitudes were not made up exclusively of one class of people. All Judæa went out to hear him. Among the rest there is very little doubt that Herod at times was an attentive listener. Royalty mingled with the masses, all sorts and conditions of men stood together, and listened to the burning words that fell from the lips of the prophet; and looking out over the sea of upturned faces, and knowing their true moral condition, he called them "offspring of vipers." Matthew says that these words were specially addressed to the Pharisees and Sadducees. Luke tells us that they were spoken to the whole of the multitudes, and undoubtedly both are correct. Luke gives his declamation

[1] Luke 3: 7.

against the nation, while Matthew records the special address of John, in which he puts his finger upon the heart of the sore, showing that he understood the process of the nation's corruption. Said he to the Pharisees and Sadducees, "Ye offspring of vipers, who warned you to flee from the wrath to come?"[1] These men were the ritualists and the rationalists of the day, the men under whose influence religion was evaporating in mere outward form and ceremony, and men who were sapping the very life essence of religion by denying the spiritual realm. The Pharisees were ritualists, having form without power. The Sadducees were rationalists, denying power, and holding even the form in contempt. Between them, they had undermined the whole religious fabric, which still stood, a vast and gaudy pile, covering untold corruption, and liable at any moment to fall in utter ruin.

John looking at these men and at the people whom they had influenced said, "Ye offspring of vipers." It was forceful and terrible language, indicative of the prophet's righteous indignation, born of his keen understanding of the true condition of affairs.

His sense of sin is also proved by the varied answers he gave to different people who questioned him. To the common multitudes he cried, "Bring forth therefore fruits worthy of repentance, and begin not to say within yourselves, We have Abraham to our father."[2] In these last words he indicated the characteristic sin of the people, that namely, of satisfaction in blood relationship to Abraham, despite the fact that the material corruption of their life contradicted the first essential greatness of Abraham, that of his faith in God and obedience to the Divine will.

[1] Matt. 3: 7.   [2] Luke 3: 8.

When the publicans came to him, and asked him what they were to do, he replied, "Extort no more than that which is appointed you."[1] From this answer is seen how accurately he understood the dishonesty of these men, who under the ægis of their influential position were robbing the people, and enriching themselves.

When the soldiers came to him and asked, What are we to do, he replied, "Extort from no man by violence, neither accuse any one wrongfully; and be content with your wages."[2]

Here again is seen how keen was his consciousness of the sin of the alien armies, the tyranny of the conquerors. These men were exacting that which was not their due, and this by violence, creating false charges against men, in order that they might enrich themselves by the fines imposed. All these replies show how accurate a knowledge the prophet had of the true condition of affairs, and that was the first part of his burden.

This sense of sin had given birth to another, that of an approaching crisis. Listen to his words, "And even now the axe also lieth at the root of the trees: every tree therefore that bringeth not forth good fruit is hewn down, and cast into the fire."[3] The axe is laid at the root of the trees. That is a figure of coming and swift destruction, not the pruning of the knife, but the destruction of the axe. It is not an occasional branch in which the signs of decay are manifest. The tree is diseased, and the axe is laid at its root. Outwardly fair, but inwardly decayed, the tree is doomed to an immediate destruction.

But the vision was clearer than this alone would indicate. It was not an undefined crisis that was approaching, but the definite coming of One, for hear his language,

[1] Luke 3: 13.   [2] Luke 3: 14.   [3] Luke 3: 9.

"He that cometh after me is mightier than I, Whose shoes I am not worthy to bear: He shall baptize you in the Holy Spirit and in fire." [1] This One was to be active, and mark well the characteristics of His activity as John foresaw them, "Whose fan is in His hand, and He will thoroughly cleanse His threshing floor; and He will gather His wheat into the garner, but the chaff He will burn up with unquenchable fire." [2] Note the twofold fact, the destructive side as symbolized by the fan and the fire; and the constructive aspect, as seen in the cleansing by fire and the gathering into the garner of precious things.

John had a sense of the sin of the people, a consciousness of a coming crisis, a clear vision of the Deliverer, Whose work was to be destructive and constructive. With this double consciousness, he preached with overwhelming force to the vast multitudes that flocked to the valley of the Jordan to hear him.

II.   It is probable that John had never seen Jesus, or if they had known each other in boyhood's days, long years had elapsed since their last meeting. John having turned his back upon the priesthood, had gone to the splendid isolation of the wilderness in preparation for the great work that lay before him; while Jesus had remained in the midst of the commonplaces of every-day life, in the carpenter's shop at Nazareth. At last the moment came when the forerunner was to look upon the face of the King, and it was a wonderful vision that broke upon this stern and burdened soul, when for the first time he looked into the face of Him, Whose advent he had so magnificently foretold.

The story is chronicled in detail by the apostle John,

[1] Matt. 3: 11.   [2] Matt. 3: 12.

and in eleven verses are the doings of three distinct days, the vision of the 'first day;[1] that of the second, beginning with the words, " On the morrow,"[2] and that of the third commencing " Again on the morrow."[3]

On the first day there is the speech of John declaring the presence of Christ in the crowd, but in all probability he did not point Him out to the people. Said he, " In the midst of you standeth One Whom ye know not."[4] The emphasis is on the "*ye*," for John certainly knew Him. Let it be borne in mind that about six weeks had passed since the day of the baptism of Jesus. He had been hidden in the wilderness, passing through the forty days of temptation, and had now returned, and was mingling with the crowds just upon the eve of commencing His own public ministry.[5]

Mark the prophet's sense of the dignity of the One Who as yet had not chosen to manifest Himself openly to men. " He that cometh after me is become before me: for He was before me . . . the latchet of Whose shoe I am not worthy to unloose."[6] That was the statement of the first day.

It would appear as though on the second day Jesus no longer merely stood among the crowd as a spectator, but approached John. As He approached, John made his greatest pronouncement, " Behold, the Lamb of God, that taketh away the sin of the world."[7] First his vision of

---

[1] John 1 : 26-28.　　[2] John 1 : 29-34.　　[3] John 1 : 35, 36.　　[4] John 1 : 26.

[5] A careful study of the context will prove that this statement of John was made after the baptism, for immediately after the three days' events here recorded, Jesus began the gathering of His disciples, and His public work. It would seem therefore as if this study of the vision of John should come after the chapters on the temptation. It is taken here, however, as the pronouncement which John made, as the one direct outcome of the vision of Christ, which he had received on the occasion of the baptism, as he himself distinctly declared (John 1 : 33, 34).

[6] John 1 : 15, 27.　　　　　　　　　　　　[7] John 1 : 29.

the Person; secondly, a declaration concerning His work. The phrase which describes the Person as John saw Him, at once arrests attention. It declares the character of the Christ, and suggests, moreover, the character of His work. "The Lamb of God" indicates meekness, gentleness, forbearance. May it not have been that John was surprised, when first he looked into the face of Him Whose coming he had foretold. All the language in which he had predicted the advent of the Deliverer suggested strength, force, authority and administration, "One mightier than I, Whose shoes I am not worthy to bear . . . Whose fan is in His hand, and He will thoroughly cleanse His threshing-floor; and He will gather the wheat, but shall burn the chaff." This Man was of quiet demeanour, and restful eyes, and calm countenance, with no lurking suspicion of vindictiveness, nothing of the lion in His fair face. Purity even to innocence was the impression produced by the presence of the King, "Behold, the Lamb of God."

And yet there was more than this in the phrase as it fell from the lips of John, and that which was more, was emphasized by this first impression. "The Lamb of God" suggests the thought of sacrifice, and this very meekness of demeanour, and purity of impression, but adds weight to this conception of the meaning of the phrase. Had John, looking into the face of Jesus had to say, "Behold, the Lion of the tribe of Judah," no thought of sacrifice could have been connected therewith, but the very submissive beauty, so evident in the personality of Christ, merged the thought of the forerunner from the majesty of the work soon to be accomplished, into the mercy of the method.

We are in great danger to-day of losing sight of that second suggestion of the great phrase. To interpret Scripture aright, it is necessary to find the way back into the temper and tone, into the habit of thought of the people to whom the words were addressed. To the Jewish mind there was no other meaning in this phrase than that of sacrifice. The season at which these words were spoken lent weight to this view of the meaning. The Passover was approaching, and along that very highway droves of sheep and cattle were in all probability being driven towards Jerusalem for sacrifice. The thought of sacrifice was sub-consciously present amid the crowds, and the prophet, who had seen the sin of the people, now looking into the face of this strange new King, beholds in Him God's perfect Lamb, the One final Sacrifice for sin. The first time in the Bible where the word " Lamb " occurs is in connection with the sacrifice of Isaac. Coming up from the long gone centuries is heard the plaintive cry of the lad, about to be bound upon the altar, " My father . . . behold, the fire and the wood: but where is the lamb for a burnt offer-ing?"[1] The first time that the word occurs in the New Testament, is where the last messenger of the great nation that had sprung from the loins of Abraham through Isaac, announced to the multitudes of the children of Abraham, " Behold, the Lamb of God."[2] This is no mere accident. It is a part of the great proof of the unity of the Book. The Old Testament asks the question, " Where is the lamb?" The New Testament answers, " Behold the Lamb of God." The old economy was able to produce the fire and the wood, symbols of judgment, but nothing more. The new produces the perfect sacrifice by the offering of which Isaac and his seed in faith might go free.

No one will dispute that the question asked by Isaac concerning the lamb, is a question having reference to sacrifice. All through the Old Testament, the lamb is dis-

[1] Gen. 22: 7.　　　　　　　　[2] John 1: 29.

tinctly connected with the thought of sacrifice,—the lamb of the atonement, the morning and evening lambs of sacrifice. John, knowing the meaning that gathered around the word in the mind of the people he addressed, declared that here at last had appeared upon the scene of human action the Lamb of God, that is, One Who should fulfill all the promises and suggestions concerning sacrifice in the old economy.

To dwell for a moment longer upon this aspect, let it be remembered that the word " lamb " only occurs four times in the New Testament, until the book of Revelation is reached, twice in the passage now under consideration, once in the Acts, where Philip reads from the prophecy of Isaiah,

> " He was led as a sheep to the slaughter ;
> And as a lamb before his shearer is dumb," [1]

and once in the first epistle of Peter, where the apostle speaks of " the precious blood, as of a lamb without blemish and without spot, even the blood of Christ." [2]   These are the only occasions where the word " lamb " is used, and they all refer to Christ.   The last two most evidently have reference to His sacrificial and atoning work, and so also without any doubt have the statements of John. The language of Scripture is not contradictory, but unified in its symbolism, in both these cases, as it ever is.

The words following place this beyond the possibility of contradiction, " the Lamb of God that taketh away the sin of the world."   The meaning of the phrase " taketh away " is that of bearing or carrying.   That is to say, the prophet declared that there stood before them the Lamb of God Who had become responsible for the sin of the world.

[1] Acts 8 : 32.   [2] 1 Pet. 1 : 19

He taketh it away, He carries it, He bears it, He has made it His own, He has become responsible for it. What a radiant vision of love ineffable was this that broke upon the soul of John, and what a vision for the world! The spotless Lamb of God laden with the sin of the race. Men had been asking for Him from the days of Isaac. Behold Him! He stands before the crowds in quiet, submissive splendour, and yet He is burdened, as man was never burdened. He carries the sin of the world. Not the sins, but the principle of sin. He has gathered into His own perfect personality, and has made Himself responsible for all that sin means as to guilt and penalty. That is the very heart of the atonement, " Behold the Lamb of God."

Thus John who had been heavily burdened with a sense of sin, and out of that sense had spoken words that had scorched the consciences of the listening multitudes, at last found the burden lifted from his shoulders, and carried in a way he never could have carried it, by the meek and gentle Lamb of God.

He then proceeded to tell the crowds that his knowledge of Jesus was the result of the Divine sign, of which he had received previous notice, the sign of the descending Spirit; ending his whole declaration with the words, " I have seen, and have borne witness that this is the Son of God." [1] What a thrill of satisfaction there seems to be in the words " I have seen." The eyes of men had wearied looking, and the hearts of a few faithful souls had almost sickened with hope deferred; but at last the prophet had seen.

And then notice how carefully he announces another fact concerning this Person, this Lamb of God. He is

[1] John 1 : 34.

the Son of God.　John recognized the mystery of the personality of Jesus.　He was the God-man, the Lamb of God, the Son of God.　Two facts in one personality, and in the union of these two facts, in the one Person lay the possibility of His doing the mighty work of bearing away the sin of the world.

Now lastly, there is the account of the vision of the third day.　Jesus is leaving John and the crowds.　He is going to His work, and as He leaves, John points his disciples towards Him, and cries, " Behold, the Lamb of God ! " [1]　These were in reality the final words of John's message.　They have in them the tone of a great conviction.　It is the crowning climax of all his marvellous message.　The herald of the King, the forerunner of the Christ, one of the greatest born of women outside the Kingdom of God, had carried on his heart, as perhaps no other man apart from Jesus, the burden of human sin.　This is proven by the force and solemnity of his preaching.　But at last he has looked into the face of the Saviour, and when presently men came to him, and told him of the successful preaching of Jesus, and of His growing fame, this great soul was able to say, " This my joy therefore is made full.　He must increase, but I must decrease." [2]　Mark well the quiet calm dignity of the satisfied heart, able to say with perfect acquiescence, " He must increase, but I must decrease."

[1] John 1 : 36.　　　　[2] John 3 : 29, 30.

BOOK III

THE TEMPTATION

X. Introductory
XI. The First Temptation
XII. The Second Temptation
XIII. The Third Temptation
XIV. Final

" *The subject of our Lord's temptation is mysterious, and therefore difficult. Lying in part within the domain of human consciousness and experience, it stretches far beyond our sight, throwing its dark projections into the realm of spirit, that realm, 'dusk with horrid shade,' which Reason may not traverse, and which Revelation itself has not illumined, save by occasional lines of light, thrown into, rather than across it. We cannot, perhaps, hope to have a perfect understanding of it, for in a subject so wide and deep there is room for the play of many hypotheses ; but inspiration would not have recorded the event so minutely had it not a direct bearing upon the whole of the Divine Life, and were it not full of pregnant lessons for all times. To Him who suffered within it, it was a wilderness indeed ; but to us ' the wilderness and the solitary place' have become 'glad, and the desert . . . blossoms as the rose.' Let us, then, seek the wilderness reverently yet hopefully, and in doing so let us carry in our minds these two guiding thoughts— they will prove a silken thread for the labyrinth—first, that Jesus was tempted as Man ; and second, that Jesus was tempted as the Son of Man."*—HENRY BURTON.

" *The Gospel of Luke.*"

Then was Jesus led up of the Spirit into the wilderness to be tempted of the devil. And when He had fasted forty days and forty nights, He afterward hungered. And the tempter came and said unto Him, If Thou art the Son of God, command that these stones become bread. But He answered and said, It is written, Man shall not live by bread alone, but by every word that proceedeth out of the mouth of God. Then the devil taketh Him into the holy city; and he set Him on the pinnacle of the temple, and saith unto Him, If Thou art the Son of God, cast Thyself down: for it is written,

He shall give His angels charge concerning Thee:

and,

On their hands they shall bear Thee up,
Lest haply Thou dash Thy foot against a stone.

Jesus said unto him, Again it is written, Thou shalt not make trial of the Lord thy God. Again, the devil taketh Him unto an exceeding high mountain, and sheweth Him all the kingdoms of the world, and the glory of them; and he said unto Him, All these things will I give Thee, if Thou wilt fall down and worship me. Then saith Jesus unto him, Get thee hence, Satan: for it is written, Thou shalt worship the Lord thy God, and Him only shalt thou serve. Then the devil leaveth Him; and behold, angels came and ministered unto Him.—*Matt. 4: 1–11.*

And straightway the Spirit driveth Him forth into the wilderness. And He was in the wilderness forty days tempted of Satan; and He was with the wild beasts; and the angels ministered unto Him. —*Mark 1: 12, 13.*

And Jesus, full of the Holy Spirit, returned from the Jordan, and was led in the Spirit in the wilderness during forty days, being tempted of the devil. And He did eat nothing in those days: and when they were completed, He hungered. And the devil said unto Him, If Thou art the Son of God, command this stone that it become bread. And Jesus answered unto him, It is written, Man shall not live by bread alone. And he led Him up, and shewed Him all the kingdoms of the world in a moment of time. And the devil said unto Him, To Thee will I give all this authority, and the glory of them: for it hath been delivered unto me; and to whomsoever I will I give it. If Thou therefore wilt worship before me, it shall all be Thine. And Jesus answered and said unto him, It is written, Thou shalt worship the Lord thy God, and Him only shalt thou serve. And he led Him to Jerusalem, and set Him on the pinnacle of the temple, and said unto Him, If Thou art the Son of God, cast Thyself down from hence: for it is written,

He shall give His angels charge concerning Thee, to guard Thee:

and,

On their hands they shall bear Thee up,
Lest haply Thou dash Thy foot against a stone.

And Jesus answering said unto him, It is said, Thou shalt not make trial of the Lord thy God.

And when the devil had completed every temptation, he departed from Him for a season.—*Luke 4: 1-13.*

X

INTRODUCTORY

THE third crisis in the mission of Christ followed the second almost immediately. On the threshold of the second period in His work—the three years of public ministry—He met in conflict the arch-enemy of the race. Not that this was by any means the first encounter. All the thirty years had been years of conflict. There is no room for doubt that questions intended to cast reflections upon the motives of God had been asked in Nazareth, similar to those asked in the Garden of Eden. The last Adam was familiar by the experience of the years with the method of attack which had issued in the ruin of the first Adam. The suggestion had certainly been made to Him that the will of God was capricious and unkind. No day had passed in which He had not been subject to temptation. To think of the tempting of Jesus as beginning and being exhausted in that special season in the wilderness which is the subject of present consideration, is to misunderstand utterly the years at Nazareth, and the full meaning of the wilderness experience. During those thirty years He had been unceasingly victorious. At His baptism, the opened heavens, the descending Dove, the Divine voice are each and all significant of the perfections of the thirty years, that is, of the absolute victory Jesus had won over all the attacks of the enemy. The Master had met and triumphed over all the temptations incidental to private life.

He is now entering upon the three years of public ministry, and He meets the foe of the race in the supreme conflict of all His testing,—supreme, that is, in the fact that now evil appears before Him in all its tremendous strength and naked horror in the personality of the devil. In all likelihood never had there been such an attack before, and certain it is that it never occurred again. After this experience His attitude towards Satan and all his emissaries is that of the Victor towards the vanquished. Never again is He seen in the place of temptation in the same specific way. Suggestions which as to their inner meaning are identical, are made to Him by Satan through Peter, and yet once more in the Garden of Gethsemane, but the victory won in the wilderness is most evidently the source of strength in subsequent experiences.

The attack of the foe is directed against Him in view of His coming work. Its subtlety is manifest in that it is directed against three aspects of triumphant service. To serve God there must be manhood strong in the realization of Divine ideals. Against this the first attack was made. There must also be such implicit trust in God as expresses itself in contentment with the Divine arrangement, and refusal to tempt God by false heroics. The second temptation was craftily aimed at the breaking down of this confidence. And yet again, the servant of God must accept the methods of God at whatever cost to himself. The final temptation was a suggestion that a Divine end should be reached by other than the Divine method.

In this preliminary study the subject is that of the setting of the temptation, reserving for future chapters the temptations themselves. In thus viewing the temptation in its relation to the whole mission of Christ, there are four matters to be considered,—The time of the temptation. The place of the temptation. The agent of the temptation. The significance of the temptation. For the purpose of this study, reference will have to be made to the three accounts by Matthew, Mark, and Luke. John has no chronicle of the temptation, his Gospel being essentially that of the Deity of Jesus, and God cannot be tempted.

I. In dealing with the *time of the temptation* there are three significant words. Matthew opens the story with the word " then." [1] Mark uses in this connection a characteristic word of the Gospel, " straightway." [2] Luke opens with the word " and." [3] These words " Then," " Straightway," " And " show the connection of the temptation with what had preceded it, and thus mark with great distinctness its time. " Then was Jesus led up of the Spirit." When ? Immediately after the baptism, with its Divine attestation of satisfaction. " And straightway the Spirit driveth Him forth." [4] Here the emphasis is yet greater upon the fact that the temptation followed immediately upon the baptism. " And Jesus . . . was led by the Spirit in the wilderness during forty days." [5] The " and " here marks continuity. Thus the first act of the new phase of service was that of the testing of the Servant, and His perfect victory over the foe. God had sealed, as approved, the first phase of the work. The anointing Spirit had indicated His preparedness for the future. His forerunner had recognized in Him the King, of Whose coming he had spoken to the gathered crowds, on the banks of the river. The whole circumstances of the baptism must have been full of satisfaction to the heart of Christ, and now in

[1] Matt. 4 : 1.   [2] Mark 1 : 12.   [3] Luke 4 : 1.
[4] Mark 1 : 12.   [5] Luke 4 : 1.

the conscious strength of victory already achieved, He passes into the gloom and loneliness of the wilderness, that He may be tested, and through the testing prove His strength.

II. Then as to the *place of the temptation*, again notice the threefold description. Matthew says, "Into the wilderness;"[1] Mark, "forth into the wilderness;"[2] Luke says, "In the wilderness."[3] The common thought is that the temptation was experienced in the wilderness. The meaning of this in relation to the mission of Christ deserves special attention. Jesus now stands as the second Man, the last Adam. Here let this Scriptural statement be specially noted and remembered. Too often He is spoken of as the second Adam. Scripture does not use the expression. It speaks of the "last Adam."[4] The first Adam was the head of a race. The last Adam is the Head of a race, and He is the last, because there will be no new departure, no other federal headship, and no other race. The last Adam, then, passing into temptation, went to the wilderness, into single and lonely combat with the enemy. No foe other than the captain of the hosts of evil is opposed to Him there, and no friend other than the God in Whose hand His breath is, and Whose are all His ways, is with Him. The wilderness is the place of immediate dealing with evil. All secondary things are swept aside.

It is interesting to contrast the circumstances under which the second Man, the last Adam, meets temptation, with those under which the first man and first Adam met them. Jesus stood among circumstances far more disadvantageous than did Adam. In each case there was a perfect man,—in Eden a man God-made ; in the wilderness a Man God-begotten. The first, however, was in Eden,

[1] Matt. 4 : 1.   [2] Mark 1 : 12.   [3] Luke 4 : 2.   [4] 1 Cor. 15 : 45.

amid circumstances of beauty and plenty, a place where
there was no lack, and all man's God-made nature was
satisfied. The second was in the wilderness, in surroundings of barrenness, and poverty, and hunger for the bread
that perishes.

And yet note one graphic touch of Mark, " He was with
the wild beasts." [1] There are those who seem to think
that the statement reveals the horror of the situation, that
the prowling wild beasts in the neighbourhood made the
situation still more fearful. But the word " with " suggests
not that they were in His neighbourhood or He in theirs
merely, but that there was companionship between them.
The fact is, that even these wild beasts recognized God's
millennial Man, and lost their ferocity, as has been already
seen in a previous study. Thus in the very place of conflict was a glorious shadowing forth of the day when the
lamb shall lie down with the lion, and when all the wonderful prophecies that foretell man's communion with, and
dominion over, the lower forms of creation shall be realized.
He made even the wilderness to blossom with millennial
glory.

III. Next as to *the agent of the temptation.* Matthew
says, " To be tempted of the devil " ; [2] Mark, " Tempted
of Satan " ; [3] Luke, " Tempted of the devil." [4] The emphasis here is upon the fact that in the wilderness experience Jesus came face to face with the prince of the power
of the air, with the god of this world, with Lucifer, son of
the morning, fallen from his high estate of the first rank of
heaven, and now leader of the hosts of darkness.

There have been many attempts to account for the
temptation in other ways. It has been suggested that some
man or company of men visited Him in the wilderness, and

[1] Mark 1 : 13.   [2] Matt. 4 : 1.   [3] Mark 1 : 13.   [4] Luke 4 : 2.

voiced the suggestions of evil ; some even holding that the tempter was a member of His own family, who followed Him into the wilderness, and, with motives not unmixed with concern for Him, yet became the voice of evil. As all this is pure imagination, and has not the slightest warrant in Scripture, it must be dismissed at once as false.

The more serious error is that the temptation arose from the natural operations of the mind of Christ. This is as unwarranted as is the other. As evil was presented to the first man from without, so also was it to the second. But no time need be taken with these futile attempts to discount the actual accuracy of the scripture narrative. One of the chief values of this account of the temptation lies in the fact that Jesus here dragged Satan into the light, and revealed to all His followers the fact of his personality, and the method of his operations.

To deny the personality of Satan is to deny Scripture. It is moreover to reflect upon humanity in a way that is unwarranted by the whole scheme of revelation. If there be no personal devil, then all the evil things that blot the page of human history are the outcome of human nature. This is not possible of belief. Evil is not a natural product of God's humanity. It is not a process of evolution. To hold that, in the last analysis, is to make God the Author of sin. It is evident therefore that to deny the personality of Satan is not to escape the problem of evil. If the Bible account of the fall of man is not correct, there yet remains the unsolved problem. While freely granting the mystery, man refuses to believe that the genesis of evil lies within the fact of human nature, accepting the teaching of Scripture that the problem lies further back, evil having originated prior to the creation of man. Revelation takes man no further back than the fall of the angels, which is declared and not explained. From that fall came the first movement of evil in human life, and the ruin of a race. The Head of the new race goes back to the point of the origin of evil in man, and confronts the personality, who is the head and front of the offending.

IV. With regard to the *significance of the temptation*, again refer to the three narratives. Matthew writes, " Then was Jesus led up of the Spirit ; "[1] Mark expresses it, " The Spirit driveth Him,"[2] while Luke declares He " was led by the Spirit."[3] The one fact announced in these varied ways is of supreme importance to keep in mind, if the true significance of this temptation is to be understood. A Divine plan was being wrought out. It did not—to use a common expression—" happen " that Jesus met Satan and was tried. Neither is it true to say that the devil arranged the temptation. Temptation here is in the Divine plan and purpose. Jesus went into the wilderness under the guidance of the Holy Spirit to find the devil. My own conviction is that if the devil could have escaped that day, he would have done so. It is a very popular fallacy that the enemy drove Christ into a corner and tempted Him. But the whole Divine story reveals that the facts were quite otherwise. God's perfect Man, led by the Spirit, or as Mark in his own characteristic and forceful way expresses it, driven by the Spirit, passes down into the wilderness, and compels the adversary to stand out clear from all secondary causes, and to enter into direct combat. This is not the devil's method. He ever puts something between himself and the man he would tempt. He hides his own personality wherever possible. To our first parents he did not suggest that they should serve him, but that they should please themselves. Jesus dragged him from behind

[1] Matt. 4: 1. [2] Mark 1; 12. [3] Luke 4.

everything, and put him in front, that for once, not through the subtlety of a second cause, but directly, he might do his worst against a pure soul.

Nothing can be more clear than the simple and full statement. Matthew does not assert that being led of the Spirit into the wilderness He was tempted of the devil; but that He was " led up into the wilderness to be tempted of the devil." Mark adds some further light, by declaring, He was " in the wilderness forty days, tempted of Satan; "[1] while Luke declares the same thing with even greater detail, " He was led by the Spirit in the wilderness during forty days, being tempted of the devil." [2]

To gather up these different side lights, the case thus be stated. Jesus was led by the Spirit into the wilderness to be tempted of the devil. He was tempted of the devil during forty days, during the whole of which period He was still led by the Spirit. The Spirit took Him to the place of temptation, and was with Him through the process of temptation. Not in His Deity did He resist, but in His perfect Manhood. Manhood is however never able to successfully resist temptations of the devil save when fulfilling a first Divine intention, that, namely, of depending upon God, and thus being guided by the Spirit of God. Thus the Man Jesus was led by the Spirit into the wilderness, and was led by the Spirit through all the process of temptation.

Herein lay the deep significance of this temptation. The second Man, acting under the guidance of the Spirit, passed into the wilderness, and by His coming challenged evil, and, acting simply under the guidance of that Spirit, overcame.

In conclusion, the significance of the temptation may be

[1] Mark 1 : 13.   [2] Luke 4 : 1, 2.

seen by placing the whole of the facts in contrast with the account of the temptation of Adam. The devil challenged the first man. The second Man challenged the devil. The devil ruined the first Adam. The last Adam spoiled the devil. The first Adam involved the race in his defeat. The last Adam included the race in His victory. The first Adam stood as the head of the race, and falling, dragged the race down with him. The last Adam stood as the Head of the new race, and being victorious, lifted that race with Him.

This is not a picture of the last Adam doing merely what the first Adam did, going into the place of passive life, and then when temptation came, resisting it. The second Man had not only to resist temptation when it assailed Him for His own sake, but He had to lay hold of the tempter, and defeat him and punish him for the wrong he did in the ruin of the first man.

XI

THE FIRST TEMPTATION

The order of the temptations is different in Matthew and Luke. In both the suggestion that stones be turned into bread is first. Matthew then records the experience on the pinnacle of the temple, and lastly the invitation to worship Satan for the possession of the kingdoms of the world. Luke reverses the order of the last two. It is almost certain that the order in Matthew was the actual order, for Christ's word at the close of the last of the temptations as there chronicled marks the end of the proc ess. "Thou shalt worship the Lord thy God, and Him only shalt thou serve. Then the devil leaveth Him; and behold, angels came and ministered unto Him."[1]

There is no detailed account of the forty days spent in the wilderness prior to the temptations which are now to be considered in detail. Mark and Luke record the fact that through that period He was the subject of temptation. He moreover declares that it was a period of fasting, "He did eat nothing in those days."[2] It is most likely that the temptation of the forty days was presented by the foe unrevealed to human sight. Having been foiled through the thirty years and the forty days, at last he took shape, and as Matthew puts it, "The tempter came and said unto Him."[3]

In examining the first temptation, as also in the remain-

[1] Matt. 4: 10, 11. [2] Luke 4: 2. [3] Matt. 4: 3.

ing two, consider first the attack; and secondly, the repulse. And yet further, under each of these divisions the same method will be followed. In considering the attack of the enemy notice, first, the objective point; second, the avenue of approach; and third, the argument used. In considering the repulse notice, first, the weapon employed; second, the argument rebutted; and third, the citadel held.

I.   In *the first attack* of Satan upon Christ, the objective point is His loyalty to the will of God. This does not appear on the surface, and in that fact there is marked the method of the enemy. He never foreannounces the point against which his attack is to be directed, but an examination of the whole situation will reveal the truth of the position. As has been already emphasized, Jesus was led by the Spirit, driven by the Spirit, to and in the wilderness, and in that fact there was great significance. In the life of every being wholly devoted to the will of God, there is nothing accidental. Every detail of arrangement is in the Divine plan, and cannot be interfered with without changing the result, and interfering with the purpose. The circumstance of hunger was not only within the Divine knowledge, it was part of the Divine plan. The circumstance of hunger was incidental, but not accidental. It was not an unexpected contingency. It was part of the Divine programme. Led by the Spirit into the wilderness He was taken to physical hunger, and that hunger was a necessary process in the economy of God, a circumstance within His will.

This is emphasized by the very fact of His being taken to the wilderness. If there had been no necessity for hunger, the temptation might have taken place in quite other surroundings; or, to put the matter from the other side, the very fact of His being led to and through forty days in a place barren of sustenance for physical life, indicates the need for hunger, and at last suggests its meaning, the suggested meaning being, that man even in his weakness, leaning wholly upon God, is stronger than man in strength standing alone, stronger moreover than the forces that are against him. When God leads a man, every last detail is always taken into account. This fact should come in comfort as well as in searching power to every one. There are no accidents to those who abide wholly within the will of God. There may be events which men outside will look upon as accidents, but when life is lived in the centre of the circle of the Divine will, nothing can approach it save those things which are foreordained, and which are therefore integral parts of the Divine plan, and the Divine programme.

The hunger of Jesus therefore was within the purpose of God for Him. Now if He might be persuaded to cancel this circumstance, small and unimportant though it appear, He would nevertheless throw out of perfect working order, that whole Divine plan. If He could only be persuaded to minister to His physical need by the use of a Divinely-bestowed power, outside the Divinely-indicated line, and so satisfy His hunger, while yet in the place where God had put Him, and intended that He should suffer it, then that act of personal choice against the choice of God would controvert the whole plan, and the citadel towards which the enemy moves, His loyalty to the will of God, would be taken.

Thus it is seen that the point towards which this first temptation was directed was the quiet, peaceful strength of Jesus as He rested in the will of God in triumph over all circumstances. That is the objective point.

Now consider the avenue of approach. The enem,
appealed to the sense of hunger. Hunger was natural,
and therefore sinless. Perhaps that statement needs some
word of explanation. In evangelical teaching and thinking to speak of a thing as natural, is often to associate w⸱⸱⸱
it the idea of depravity. For instance, to speak ot tne
natural man is to think of that which is in opposition to
the spiritual man. This is due to the fact that Paul uses
the term " natural " invariably in reference to man in his
fallen nature. It must however never be forgotten that
behind the fallen is the unfallen. God's archetypal Man
is the truly natural man. This is not to quarrel with the
apostle's use of the word, but to indicate the meaning
when it it said that hunger was natural. If man had neve
sinned he would still have grown hungry. Hunger is noư
a result of sin. It is a consciousness Divinely implanted,
which suggests the need for food. It is a part of the wonderful economy of God for the sustenance of the physical
need of man. In the use of the body there is a waste of
tissue, and for its reconstruction there must be a reception
of food. Whenever that food is necessary there is a sense
of need, that sense being hunger. Hunger, then, is within
God's gracious economy in the creation of man.

Notice carefully that it was after the lapse of the forty
days that Jesus was hungry. It would seem as though
during their passing, He was unconscious of His physical
need. His thoughts had been of things within the spiritual realm, and the demands of the physical had been unrecognized. At the close of forty days the sense of need
swept over Him. He was hungry. That sense of hunger
was perfectly sinless. To satisfy it is the natural action of
a perfect Man. The hunger is a God-created sense. To
feed it, to satisfy it, is to fall in with the Divine purpose.

Now mark the subtlety of the enemy. God had created the need, but there was no provision there for its satisfaction. The temptation proceeded along this avenue, and virtually may be stated in this form. Thou art hungry, according to Divine arrangement, but in the Divine arrangement of this moment there is no provision for the satisfaction of Thy hunger. It is now competent for Thee to act upon Thine own initiative, " command that these stones become bread."

Long centuries before, the devil had asked a question in the Divine presence. A servant of God, a perfect and upright man was living in such conditions that all the necessities of his life seemed to be met, and the enemy coming before God, said, " Doth Job serve God for nought ? " [1] Around that question and insinuation of evil, the magnificent book of Job circles. The suggestion made was, that Job's loyalty to God was ensured by the satisfaction of all physical need. Job was full and wealthy through the beneficence of heaven. Let him be emptied and impoverished, and the strain put upon his loyalty would break down. To put it in the more vulgar language of the street, Job feared God for what he could get. Thus the devil's estimate of human life is, that the only reason for man's loyalty to God is that God meets every demand of his need as it arises ; and, moreover, that man's happiness consists in the satisfaction of his material nature, in a word, that he lives by bread alone.

That same thought underlay the temptation of the Master. It is as though he had said to Him, Thou art hungry. That sense of hunger is a part of the Divine arrangement. Therefore it must be right to satisfy it. If God has made no provision for the satisfaction of a need

[1] Job 1 : 9.

which He has created, then act independently, command
that the stones be made bread.

The subtlety of the temptation lies within the fact that
the devil suggested to Christ that He should satisfy a perfectly legitimate craving. The evil of the temptation lies
within the fact that he suggested that a legitimate craving
should be satisfied in an illegitimate way.

Thus Christ, impoverished and hungry, faced the old-
time lie, by meeting temptation, not when filled with the
plentitude of Divine gifts, but when needing that which
God provides for all His creatures. So much for the
avenue of approach.

Now notice the argument the enemy used, "If Thou be
the Son of God," marking carefully the meaning of the
"If," and the reason of its use at this particular crisis.
The temptation closely followed upon the baptism. But
forty days ago the silence of the long thirty years had been
broken, and the Divine voice had said, "This is My beloved Son in Whom I am well pleased."[1] Thus the seal
of God was set not merely in approbation upon the perfection of the life, but in identification of the personality of
Jesus. "*This is My beloved Son.*" Now hear the enemy's
"if." "*If* Thou art the Son of God."[2] If that experience of forty days ago was really anything more than a
phantasy, a vision; if what the voice declared be true, why
remain hungry? What is the use, said the enemy in
effect, of a position without its privileges? What value
is there in being the Son of God unless Thou shalt make
use of all that the name implies? Mark well that the
devil's idea of the privileges of sonship is that of selfish
gratification.

This temptation moved wholly in the physical realm.

[1] Matt. 3 : 17.   [2] Matt. 4 : 3.

The Man Jesus was hungry, and the enemy took advantage of this fact, and, moving along the avenue of His hunger, and using the argument of His Sonship, he suggested that He should exercise His Sonship for the satisfaction of His hunger, without reference to the fact that His hunger at the moment was a part of the will of His Father.

To sum up. The objective point was the loyalty of Jesus to the will of God. The avenue of approach was the perfectly natural and sinless hunger of His manhood. The argument used was that if He were the Son of God, He might use that privilege to minister to His necessity, without consulting the will of His Father.

There was nothing in that temptation which had the slightest suspicion of vulgarity. The devil did not suggest that He should minister to any craving of life that was not in itself right. Indeed such suggestion would have been utterly useless, for there was no such craving in Him. It was so, even then, as He said afterwards, that the devil "cometh: and he hath nothing in Me." [1] The enemy asked Him to do a right thing in a wrong way, to satisfy a lawful appetite in an illegal fashion, to make use of the privileges of Sonship for violating its responsibilities. The temptation was an attempt to pervert the will. This was done by a subtle suggestion of the unkindness of God, in order to quench love towards God. This suggestion was of the nature of an attempt to cloud the intelligence, by mixing the privileges and responsibilities of Sonship.

II. Turning to the repulse of the enemy, notic first, the weapon which the Master used. His first words reveal it. "It is written." These words He addressed to Satan in answer to the suggestion. He was not, however, by any

[1] John 14: 30.

means entering into an argument with the devil. There is nothing of the nature of argument through the whole process. It is rather that Jesus defined, in the hearing of the enemy, His own position. By the very first words He declared His submission to law. As against the enemy's suggestion that He should use the privileges of Sonship, He declared the binding nature of its responsibilities. " It is written," is a declaration of the fact that He stood within the circle of the will of God, and what that will permitted, He willed to do ; and what that will made no provision for, He willed to do without.

That which was written was part of the law of God as given to Moses, and recognizing the Divinity of this law, He at once revealed that He lived by words proceeding out of the mouth of God. Thus the opening words reveal the weapon of His defence, and define the position of His safety.

His citation of the Mosaic law serves to rebut the argument made use of by the enemy. That argument had been suggested by the words, " If Thou be the Son of God." Let it be particularly noted that in the first word of the quotation Christ made answer to the false suggestion of that argument. That first word was the word " man," " man shall not live by bread alone." The devil said, " If Thou be the Son of God." Jesus said, " man." Thus to put the emphasis on the first word is to discover the philosophy of Christ's answer to this particular temptation, a declaration of position rather than an argument, and yet in the declaration a great argument is involved. It is as though Jesus had said to the enemy, I am here as Man, and as Man I meet thy temptation. That temptation had been to over-emphasize the privileges of a Son, and to minimize the responsibilities of humanity. Christ's answer restored the true balance, and with magnificent courage inferentially declared that His presence in the wilderness was a challenge to the devil on the part of a representative Man. In all probability in the temptation of the devil there had also been a recognition of the larger thought of the Divine pronouncement, namely, a recognition of the Deity of Christ as indicated in the title "Son of God," and therefore the craft of the attack was even yet more marked, in that he may have suggested that the weakness of humanity should be strengthened by the exercise of Deity. If that was indeed so, then all the more forceful and remarkable was Christ's answer. He declined to use the prerogatives or powers of Deity in any other way than was possible to every other man. He did not face temptation nor overcome it in the realm of His Deity, but in the magnificence of His pure, strong Manhood, Manhood tested for thirty years in ordinary private life, and for forty days in the loneliness of the wilderness. "Man" is the first word and the forceful word. Jesus has been in the wilderness as man's representative, and that He declared when, repulsing the attack of the enemy, He did so by defining thus clearly His position.

And yet consider still more closely. "Man shall not live by bread alone, but by every word that proceedeth out of the mouth of God." [1] Weak from the hunger following upon forty days of fasting, the devil suggested that He should strengthen Himself with bread. His reply, "It is written," is a revelation of the true sources of strength. The strength of manhood does not lie in the assertion of rights, but in submission to the will of God. Mark well how that answer of the perfect One drags into light the false philosophy of evil, which the fallen race has uni-

[1] Matt. 4 : 4.

versally accepted. The most applauded position that man takes is that in which he declares, I prove my manhood by the assertion of my rights; but this perfect Man declares that the strength of manhood lies in the absolute abandonment of His will to the will of God, that being the only right He possesses.

In the last analysis the argument of the devil had been a presupposition that all man needed for his sustenance was food for his physical life. That unwarrantable assumption Christ answered by declaring that no man's whole life can be fed by bread that perishes. He needs more, that his spirit shall be fed, and its strength sustained by feeding upon the word proceeding from the mouth of God, and its safety ensured by abiding within the will of God.

This answer was given out of the midst of hunger, and consequently the force of the argument is increased by the attitude, that attitude plainly declaring not only that man cannot live by bread alone, but that the life sustained by bread is not of first importance. If there must be a choice between the sustenance of the spiritual and the feeding of the physical, the latter must make room for the former.

Thus the citadel is held against the first attack,—and how magnificently! Reverently declaring the thought of Jesus by paraphrasing His actual words, it is as though He had said: I am hungry, but as that lies within the will of God for Me, I choose the hunger in that will, rather than to find any satisfaction outside it. What a glorious vindication of the essential greatness of the spiritual man! Even though hunger should be so long continued that the physical, that which is sustained by bread alone, should cease to exist, even then man, fed to all fullness by the Word of God, would live. In every man in this probationary life there coexist the physical and the spiritual, and in all the ordinary dealings of God, both of these will be fed where the whole man is abandoned to His will. Where, however, for some purpose homed in His perfect love, the physical must suffer hunger, by the suffering of that hunger, because it is the will of God, the spiritual is strengthened and sustained. In that philosophy of life the perfect Man Jesus won His victory in the wilderness, continued through three years, and at last emphasized and vindicated it by passing with kingly majesty to the death of the Cross. If, on the other hand, man seeks to satisfy his physical need by disregarding the Word of God, which is the food of the spiritual, then the spiritual destroyed, the physical, also, at last shall perish, and the whole man be lost. Jesus, living ever and only according to the Divine plan, at last laid down His life and took it again, and lives forever as the deathless One, at the right hand of the Majesty on high.

Thus in the first temptation is a startling revelation of the purpose and the method of Satan, and of the true sources of man's strength. As to the purpose and method of Satan, his first purpose is to lure man into some position outside the will of God. His method is that of appealing to something perfectly lawful in itself, but suggesting that it should be satisfied by an unlawful method. As to the sources of man's strength, the Lord's answer and attitude reveal that man is not merely a fed animal. He is essentially spirit, and spirit depends for its sustenance upon its true correspondence to God. This correspondence can only be secured by the knowledge of God, and submission to the will of God, as revealed in the Word of God. He abode in the will of God, with which He was familiar in the Word of God, and choosing the hunger that resulted from dwelling in that will, rather than the passing satisfaction obtainable at the cost of disobedience, He repulsed the foe. As representative Man, He hurled back the attack which was directed towards the spoiling of the beauty and perfection of the life which had so often been tried in the thirty years and forty days preceding, and yet had always conquered.

Thus the first attack of the foe is seen as being directed against God's Man, and the first victory of Jesus is seen as been gained by Man, as He quietly remained within the sphere of Divine government. The Man of Nazareth, the second Man, the last Adam, stands erect at the close of the first attack, because He has resolutely refused to be enticed by any argument from His simple and unquestioning allegiance to His God. Man with God is equal to all strain, and superior to all temptation.

XII

THE SECOND TEMPTATION

THERE is no definite data for determining the length of time elasping between these several attacks. In all probability they followed each other in quick succession. This seems to be suggested by the word with which Matthew introduces the account of the second attack. " *Then* the devil taketh Him into the holy city." [1] This would suggest immediateness, that directly he was repulsed at the one point, he commenced the attack from some new vantage ground. He had attempted the overthrow of obedience through an attack upon the physical nature. In renewing the attack he no longer appeals to the element of weakness created by hunger, but to that which was the very strength of spiritual life, namely, the Master's trust in God.

Following the order of the previous consideration, first consider the attack; and secondly, the repulse.

I. In this renewal of temptation the enemy passes to that which lies behind the citadel already unsuccessfully assailed. Having endeavoured to seduce Jesus from His position of unswerving loyalty to the will of God, he now flings all the force of his subtle art against that which was the strength of His abiding in the will of God, namely, His perfect confidence in God. There can be no question that the element of strength in Christ's resolute steadfastness in the will of God was that of His absolute confidence in His Father, His quiet and perfect trust. It was this

[1] Matt. 4 : 5.

trust which made Him deliberately choose to suffer hunger which lay within the Divine will, rather than to satisfy that necessity of His life by deviation from the Divinely-marked pathway by a hair's breadth. The enemy, having failed to persuade Him to turn aside from that pathway, now directed his forces against the principle of strength which was the secret of the previous triumph of Jesus.

Too much emphasis can hardly be laid on this introductory thought. God's perfect Man was perfectly victorious, and that because His trust in His Father was so complete that His relation to the will of God was something infinitely beyond that of resignation or merely of determined submission. It was that of delighting in whatever was the will of One Whom He so absolutely trusted. He knew that He was safer, hungry, in the will of God, than He could have been, satisfied, outside that will.

This being the objective point, now carefully mark the terrible subtlety of the approach. " Then the devil taketh Him into the holy city ; and he set Him on the pinnacle of the temple, and saith unto Him, If Thou art the Son of God, cast Thyself down : for it is written,—

> " He shall give His angels charge concerning Thee : "

and,

> " On their hands they shall bear Thee up,
> Lest haply Thou dash Thy foot against a stone." [1]

The choosing of the place is first evidence of the subtlety of the foe. " The holy city," and in the holy city " the temple," and in the temple " the pinnacle." How largely the mind is often influenced by surroundings. Changes that are no less than marvellous are brought about in the attitude of the mind by the change of bodily situa-

[1] Matt. 4 : 5, 6.

tion. Location constantly stirs the pulses of patriotism.
All the nature is made tender in the neighbourhood of the
old homestead, and some of the deepest springs of religious
feeling well forth into new power in some place where
long ago the streams of living water refreshed the
thirsty spirit. It is always impossible to revisit any place
of tender, sacred, or holy associations without being profoundly influenced.

How much this place meant to Jesus we are hardly in a
position to understand. Every sentence in the account is
descriptive, and has its own peculiar value. " The holy
city." It is doubtful whether we are able to appreciate just
what that meant to a Hebrew. In order in any measure
to do so, we have to go back to Hebrew poetry, and read
some of the sentences which throb with such devotion as
we know little of, in these days of many cities and constant
travelling. " Beautiful in elevation, the joy of the whole
earth, the city of the great King," [1] " whither the tribes
go up," [2] " as the mountains are round about Jerusalem." [3]
These and all such sentences minister to our understanding. Jerusalem was the very centre of the deepest life
of the nation, and all the aspirations of the people
centred therein. The devout child of Abraham, in whatever part of the earth he found himself, turned his face towards the city, as his heart went out to the God of his
Fathers in prayer; and concerning it thousands would join
in the prayer of the Psalmist of old

> " If I forget Thee, O Jerusalem,
> Let my right hand forget her skill." [4]

Jesus of Nazareth was no exception to the rule. How
He loved the city. He came to it again and again, and

[1] Psa. 48 : 2.   [2] Psa. 122 : 4.   [3] Psa. 125 : 2.   [4] Psa. 137 : 5.

when at last it had finally rejected Him, as He knew, and it was necessary that He should pronounce its doom, He did so in a voice choked with emotion, so that the very curse pronounced was wet with the tears of His pity.

To this city the devil conducted Him. Into the midst of all that reminded Him of God's past dealings with His people, and of that city which was the centre of the promises, Satan brought the Master when he would attack His trust in God.

If the city was dear to the heart of the Jew, the temple was much more so. It was the centre of the city; indeed, the city was only great because it contained, and was gathered around, the temple. The Hebrew nation was a theocracy. They were under the immediate government of Jehovah, and His place of revelation was the temple That temple was therefore the peculiar glory of Jerusalem. Even when spiritual values were at a discount, there still remained in the heart of the people a veneration for the temple, and devout members of the nation ever associated with that temple all that was highest and best in their history, experience, and hope. It was indeed the very house of God.

How dear it was to the heart of Christ is proven in many ways, but most especially, perhaps, by the fact that at the beginning and close of His ministry He cleansed it from the traffickers. How often He stood in its courts, and walked in its porches, and addressed Himself to the multitudes, or held conversation with the smaller groups. To that centre of the national life, the point at which the religion of the Hebrew had its supreme manifestation and expression, the splendid symbol of that principle of faith in God, upon which the whole nation had been created, the enemy conveyed the Christ.

And yet once more note the particular place in the temple where the devil set Him. The word " pinnacle " conveys a false idea. As a matter of fact there were no pinnacles on that temple. The marginal reading suggests the word " wing," and in all probability the point referred to was that of the southern wing of the temple made magnificent by Herod's royaĺ portico. Josephus tells us that standing on the eastern extremity of that portico, " any one looking down would be giddy, while his sight could not reach to such an immense depth." This was the one point in the temple which might be described as of a great height. It was the most magnificent, the most strategic point, that point to which any one would be taken whom it was desired to impress with the solemnity and splendour of the city and its temple.

Thus to the heart of the nation, the city; to the heart of the city, the temple; to the most awe-inspiring situa tion of the temple, the devil brought Jesus. How well and subtly chosen, with what awful cunning and malice! Everything in the surroundings was calculated to appeal to the sense of trust in God. It would seem as though this were the last place in which to attack the principle of trust, and yet considering the enemy's suggestion, the malicious cunning of the foe will be seen in making such selection of situation.

Now hear the suggestion. Notice, first, the palpable and actual proposal of the enemy. " Cast Thyself down." [1] It is a direct attempt to force Jesus to act upon that principle of trust, which has been ministered to by the selection of this particular place. In the city of the great King, in the house devoted to His worship, at its most awe-inspiring point, exercise trust in Him by casting Thyself

[1] Matt. 4 : 6.

from this great height. Behind this palpable suggestion lay one inferred and indirect. It was the suggestion that trust most perfectly expresses itself in daring something unusual, out of the common, heroic. It was as if the enemy had said to Jesus, There is no necessity for Thee to cast Thyself down. It does not come in the ordinary line of duty, but so much the greater opportunity for a venture of faith,—trust in God most perfectly expresses itself in the doing of extraordinary things for God. The enemy suggested that the trust of Jesus should be put to the test and proven by being placed outside the realm of the commonplace. Jesus had repulsed the first attack of the enemy in the strength of His trust, and while the sense of that victory based on trust is fresh in His soul, the enemy suggests the unusual exercise thereof. " Cast Thyself down." Could anything be conceived more full of subtlety, more likely to entrap the unwary, and bring about the overthrow of what had seemed to be an impregnable life ?

The plausibility and force of the temptation is even more vividly seen in the argument which the devil makes use of, " If Thou art the Son of God." [1] This is the same argument used in the previous temptation, but almost certainly with a different emphasis. In the first in all probability it lay upon the word " art," " If Thou *art* the Son of God." [2] Here it seems as though it must have been upon the word " *God*," " If Thou art the Son of *God*." The emphasis would be upon the nature of God. In the first temptation He has proved the fact of His relationship. Now the appeal is to that relationship. He is prepared to enlarge upon the goodness of God, and the care He bestows upon such as put their trust in Him. Foiled and

[1] Matt. 4: 6.   [2] Matt. 4: 3.

wounded at the first by the Master's use of the weapon of the Word, he now makes use o. the self-same weapon. Behold the very sword of Christ in the hands of the devil. Its flash is seen as he says, " It is written."

In endeavouring to appeal to the principle of trust, he made use of Scripture. Jesus had declared that man lived not by bread alone, but by words proceeding from the mouth of God, and in an attempt to urge Him to a new exercise of trust, the devil quotes the Word of God. He now accepts Christ's definition of human life as something more than animal. He acknowledges that it is the spiritual life that needs to be strong for the exercise of trust; and moreover, that spiritual life is only strong as it feeds upon the Word; so he attempts to minister to Him in the realm of that very spiritual nature. It is a startling and an appalling picture. " It is written,"—

> " He shall give His angels charge concerning Thee: "

and,

> " On their hands they shall bear Thee up,
> Lest haply Thou dash Thy foot against a stone." [1]

That is the very acme of subtlety. The psalm from which the quotation is made, opens with the words,—

> " He that dwelleth in the secret place of the Most High
> Shall abide under the shadow of the Almighty." [2]

This is a description of the perfect safety of the trusting soul. Its rhythm, its music, and its sweetness have cheered the heart of such as put their trust in God through all the centuries; and as the enemy now attempts to press the Master towards some new exercise of trust, from that great psalm of confidence he quotes these words.

[1] Matt. 4 : 6.   [2] Psa. 91 : 1.

So far something has been seen of the subtlety and force of the attack, and yet the final revelation of that only comes when our Lord's answer lays bare its inner meaning.

II. Turn now to consider the victory of Jesus, and in doing so note first of all the weapon He used. Again the flash of the sword is seen as He says, " It is written." It is as though He first replies to the very subtlety of the enemy's attack by revealing the fact that He is still living upon the Word of God, and that as His physical being was content to be conditioned by the law of God, so also it is that law which defines His spiritual responsibility. He no more attempted to live outside the realm of His Father's will in spiritual life than in physical ; and was no more prepared to trespass upon the limits God set upon His spiritual liberty, than He was to trespass upon the limits set upon His physical being. And yet notice the slight variation in the form of His use of the weapon. In the first temptation He said, " It is written." In the second He said, " Again it is written." [1] In the use of the word " again " is a revelation of our Lord's perfect mastery of the weapon. In comparison with Christ the devil was a poor swordsman, when he attempted to use the sword of the Spirit. It would seem as though with quiet and yet mighty movement of His strong arm Jesus wrested the sword from Satan. The force of the " again " lies in the fact that it is an answer to Satan's, " it is written." He does not deny the correctness of the satanic quotation, but He replies to it by saying, " Again it is written." That is to say, there must be proper use made of the words of God. No one statement wrested from its context is a sufficient warrant for actions that plainly controvert other commands. " It

[1] Matt. 4: 7.

is written," but "Again it is written," and for the proper
definition of life, no one isolated text is sufficient. It is
necessary that there should be acquaintance with the whole
scheme of the Divine will, and the true balance and proportion of life is only discovered in this way.

What infinite value there is in that word "again."
How excellent a thing it would be if the whole Church of
Christ had learned that no law of life may be based upon
an isolated text. It is ever necessary to discover the varied
sides of truth, for these limit each other in operation, and
create the impregnable stronghold of safety for the soul of
man.

In a study of the heresies of the Church—not a very
profitable one, be it said—it will be seen that all these have
been based upon Scripture used as the devil uses it—
Scripture taken out of its context, and out of its relation to
the whole of the revelation. Every false teacher who has
divided the Church, has had an "it is written" on which
to hang his doctrine. If only against the isolated passage
there had been the recognition of the fact that "again it is
written," how much the Church would have been saved.

To pass, however, to the actual Scripture with which
Christ resisted the attack, "Thou shalt not make trial of
the Lord thy God."[1] It has been somewhat commonly
understood that here Christ was addressing Himself to the
devil as though He should say to him, Thou art not to
make trial of Me. That, however, is surely to miss the
supreme value of the words. In these words, as in those
with which He defeated the enemy in the first temptation,
He was defining His own position. The command,
"Thou shalt not make trial of the Lord thy God," was
addressed to man, and in this quotation the Lord gave His

[1] Matt. 4: 7.

reason for refusing to cast Himself from the wing of the temple.

Here, then, is the exposure of the deepest meaning of this subtle attack. What could be more excellent to all outward seeming than that this perfect Man should trust in God? What more fitting than that He should prove His trust by daring something, by taking some great risk? In a sentence the Master strips the whole hypocrisy of its speciousness, and reveals the murderous intent. To have cast Himself from the wing of the temple into the abyss that yawned below would have been to tempt God, and in the last and fine analysis would have demonstrated not trust, but lack of confidence. It is when we doubt a person that we make experiments to discover how far they are to be trusted. To make experiments of any kind with God, is to reveal the fact that one is not quite sure of Him. Trust never desires to tempt, to test, to trifle. It calmly, quietly abides in sure confidence. With what matchless skill this perfect Man has revealed at once the strength and weakness of the satanic onslaught. The true territory of trust is revealed by the Lord's answer. That territory is again the will of God. In effect the Master declared that He could trust God perfectly so long as He remained within the sphere of His revealed will, but that if He passed out of that sphere, then He had no right to trust, and could not trust.

What infinite value for all men is there in this unfolding of the true nature of faith in God. The devil is perpetually saying, Do something adventurous, do something magnificent, do something out of the ordinary, and thus demonstrate your confidence. The Master is always replying: Trust is not evidenced by such action. That would be to tempt God, and to tempt Him is to reveal the death of trust. Trust never makes experiments outside the Divinely marked pathway. Such experiments are evidences of timidity rather than of trust.

Thus again the citadel is held, and the foe is vanquished. Jesus refusing to tempt God, demonstrated His perfect confidence in Him, and thus revealed for all time the fact that man, so devoid of selfish interest as to be willing not to appear heroic, in confidence may dare all hell, and issue from the conflict more than conqueror.

In these first two temptations the twofold nature of the second Man has been subjected to severest testing, and the last Adam, Head of the new race, has been proved invulnerable to the assaults of evil. Weakness in the physical realm was tested. Strength in the spiritual realm was attacked. Physical weakness, abiding in the will of God, proved stronger than the mightiest force of evil; and spiritual strength, calmly content with what seemed to be the commonplace of life, was demonstrated mightier than all the subtlety of spiritual wickedness. The Man Jesus is victorious over evil in both departments of His nature. Behold Him, God's perfect Man, standing still erect, not merely in the perfection of created and untried humanity, but having passed through trial and testing still triumphant. He has chosen hunger, rather than bread which God does not provide. He has selected to appear to lack daring, rather than to demonstrate His fear by testing God. When the alternative of hunger in the will of God, or food outside, was presented to Him there was not one moment's hesitation; and yet again He elected the commonplace of patient waiting, rather than the brilliant magnificence of an act, which would have revealed fear rather than faith.

In what clear shining the deepest facts of human life are

revealed in these hours of the temptation of the Son of
Man. Perhaps nowhere is life seen to be more simple.
Man in his fall has rendered it complex by endeavouring to
act upon a thousand different principles, and with complexity
has come confusion. This Man had but one principle, and
that the will of God, and whether the enemy approached
along the line of physical necessity, or of spiritual activity,
it mattered not, he was foiled and driven backward. It
is for man to remember that by the mystery of His Cross
and passion, and the triumph of His resurrection, this victorious One now dwells in him. In proportion as man is
loyal to Him, as He was to God, his loyalty is also loyalty
towards God, and as He conquered the subtlest temptations
of the evil one, so also may all be " more than conquerors
through Him that loved us." [1]

[1] Rom. 8: 37.

XIII

THE THIRD TEMPTATION

Twice repelled, the enemy returned for the third and last time. His attack upon the physical side had resulted in the demonstration of the possibility of righteousness to a Man Whose conception of life was that bread sustenance is secondary, and the spiritual relation preeminent. Thus foiled, he had proceeded to attempt the ruin of Jesus on the spiritual side of His nature, by endeavouring to interfere with the simplicity of His trust in God. Here again he was utterly defeated, and the truth demonstrated, that trust which refuses to make any unordained experiments, is proof against all opposition.

Now against this human being, in Whom the relation between body and spirit is perfectly balanced, because the whole life is lived in right relation to God, the enemy comes with a new attack, in which he attempts to work the ruin of Jesus in the sphere of His specific mission.

This is in many ways the boldest and most daring adventure of the devil. For this last attempt he casts off all disguise, and presuming upon the awful victories he has won in the history of the human race, he definitely asks the homage of Christ. Never up to that moment, in the history of the race, had any individual soul proved strong enough to finally resist this terrible foe. Through thirty years of lonely conflict, and forty days of special testing, and two fierce and fearful attacks, the Man Jesus has remained the Victor. There remains but one chance. Having failed to ruin Him in His essential manhood, it may yet be possible to lure the perfect Servant from the pathway of perfect service. Through the previous conflicts, the Victor has stripped the vanquished of his disguise, and again and again revealed the true motive and awful malice of evil, though it had been skillfully hidden behind arguments the most plausible.

Now the enemy strips himself of all disguise, ceases to make use of secondary causes, and definitely asks the homage of Christ. It is his last and most daring bid for possession of the citadel hitherto successfully held against him.

I. Here again in examining the attack of the enemy, the objective point is the first thing to be discovered.

This is no longer the ruin of the Man Himself, but the prevention of His accomplishment of that work for which He had been preparing, and for which, but forty days ago, He was solemnly anointed. As has been seen, at the passing of Jesus into the waters of baptism, He signified His consent to be numbered with the transgressors, and therefore His willingness to tread the pathway that must issue in death, in order that a new highway of life out of death might be opened for the ruined race. It is against the carrying out of this programme, and the accomplishment of this purpose, that the present temptation is directed. Having failed utterly in his attempt to ruin the Servant, he now would interfere with His service. Here, as always, there is a blindness and a folly about evil, and Satan does not seem to understand that the strengthening of the perfect Servant, resulting from His victory under temptation, is yet increased guarantee of His perfect victory in the pathway of appointed service.

Examine now the avenue of his approach. Conveying Him to some high mountain peak, he showed Him "all the kingdoms of the world, and the glory of them." [1] What that meant, it is not easy to comprehend, and yet for a moment, think of the statement. By some strange power, at the command of the enemy, he made to pass before the vision of Christ a gorgeous and magnificent scene. He revealed to Him the kingdoms of the world, and the glory of them. Not merely the few and imperfect kingdoms of Palestine, but all the kingdoms of the world, the great Roman empire, Greece, Pergamos, Bithynia, the Bosphorus, Syria, Pontus, Judæa, and Egypt, all the known kingdoms of the world. And yet more than this, for the statement has no such limitation as that indicated by the word made use of: "known kingdoms." All the kingdoms of the world, the great unexplored lands with their thousand nations and tribes. Any literal interpretation contradicts the real story. Luke tells us that the devil gave Christ the vision of these "in a moment of time." [2] It is evident that having taken Him to some great mountain height, where instinctively the mind would be impressed with the sense of greatness and of splendour, he flashed upon Him in one swift and supernatural manifestation, a vision of the kingdoms, and their glory. The possibility is that Christ saw more than the devil knew. Satan is not omniscient, and though in the marvellous wisdom of his created intelligence he may be able to forecast the issues of certain lines of action, beyond such forecasting, which is ever presumptive rather than positive knowledge, he is not able to go. The God-man on the other hand, while standing only in the realm of His manhood for testing and temptation, may yet have been conscious of all the prospective grandeur of

[1] Matt. 4 : 8.   [2] Luke 4 : 5.

these self-same kingdoms. He saw that day the glory of them as they were, the wealth, the strength, the cities where the treasures of the nations were gathered, all the resources of the far-spreading lands, the teeming populations, the scientific victories, and artistic achievements, the glory of the kingdoms of the world. It was a truly magnificent and overwhelming spectacle. I make no attempt to explain how the devil flashed the vision upon the consciousness of the Christ. That remains a mystery, but the fact is plainly stated that he showed Him all the kingdoms of the world, and the glory of them.

With the dazzling spectacle upon the mind of the Master, the enemy uttered the actual words of the temptation, "All these things will I give Thee, if Thou wilt fall down and worship me."[1] Notice here particularly the claim the devil set up, and let it not be forgotten that the claim was made in the presence of Jesus. He claimed some right to the kingdoms of the world, and the claim was based upon certain unquestionable facts. These kingdoms had become what they were, largely under his control. They were at the moment submissive to his sway, obedient to his laws, being led captive by him at his will. For the larger part, the whole of them were blindly asleep in the arms of the wicked one. By the very temptation, Satan seems to lay claim to a title, which Jesus Himself gave him incidentally at a later period, "the prince of this world."[2] The fact of his sway is undisputed. He was then as he is to-day, exercising authority over all those who are in darkness, and he is perpetually paying his price to those who serve him. If Judas desires thirty pieces of silver, the devil will find them for him, on condition. If men will but serve him, he will give them what they ask.

[1] Matt. 4 : 9.   [2] John 12 : 31.

Wealth, fame, position, power are all in the gift of the devil. He holds them, and he actually dispenses them, in order to attain ends upon which his malice is set. What these gifts are worth, in the last analysis, is another question, which will be answered in the process of this consideration.

And so in effect he declared to Christ that whether the people knew it or not, they were under his sway, that he was the prince of the world, and he offered to give Jesus the whole of the kingdoms, and the glory of them, if there on the lone mountain peak He would but render homage to him, and receive them as his gift. All other men had submitted to his direction in order to gain some imagined advantage, and now he boldly suggested to Christ that He should do the same.

The real point and force of the temptation can only be understood as the sublime and magnificent Psalm of the King is remembered. In that Psalm it is declared that God's anointed King shall be His Son.

> "Yet have I set my King
> Upon My holy hill of Zion.
> I will tell of the decree:
> Jehovah said unto Me, Thou art My Son;
> This day have I begotten Thee." [1]

At the baptism Jesus was identified by the Divine pronouncement, "This is My beloved Son." [2] Reverting again to the Psalm, the promise of God to the anointed King is given.

> "Ask of Me, and I will give Thee the nations for Thine inheritance,
> And the uttermost parts of the earth for Thy possession.
> Thou shalt break them with a rod of iron;
> Thou shalt dash them in pieces like a potter's vessel." [3]

[1] Psalm 2 : 6, 7.   [2] Matt. 3 : 17.   [3] Psalm 2 : 8, 9.

Thus Jesus is God's chosen King, to Whom He has promised the nations for an inheritance, and the uttermost parts of the earth for a possession. But He promised these to the King, when He shall ask them of God. That asking is to be along the line of a Divinely appointed approach, which includes the pathway through death, symbolized by the baptism, which had preceded the identification of Jesus as the King.

Here on a mountain peak of the enemy's choosing, in contrast to the holy hill of Zion upon which God will establish His King, this anointed One was offered the self-same kingdoms of the world. All that God has promised Him was here seen in the dazzling splendour of that momentary vision. There were the nations, there were the uttermost parts of the earth, the things guaranteed to the King by the covenant with Jehovah. The devil having surely understood something of the suggestiveness of the Jordan baptism, and the consequent uttering of the voice of God, now suggested to Jesus that He might miss that deeper baptism and passion, and yet possess these kingdoms. He pointed out a short cut to a Divine destination. He was willing to hand over his right and claim, if all might but be received from him, instead of from God. One act of fealty, one recognition of the devil's ownership, one moment of bending the knee, and all the kingdoms were promised. Sometimes one wonders whether there did not lurk in the temptation a revelation of the devil's cowardice. The fact that he revealed the kingdoms in a moment of time, may have been due to his fear, lest if this Man should have lingered to examine them, He might discover their worthlessness. His suggestion, moreover, that Christ should take the kingdoms as his gift, may have been due to dark and gloomy fear of the conflict with

Him, through which Christ would yet win them.   Here
the very element of the primal fall of Satan flames out.
Not merely for the ruin of this Man, but for the saving of
himself from defeat, and the maintenance of the false
position he has occupied, would he shun the terrible conflict that lies ahead.

And yet the temptation meant more to Christ than even
Satan in the deepest reaches of his subtlety could possibly
comprehend.   The terrible nature of the suffering through
which Jesus had yet to pass, could not be perfectly understood of Satan, neither did he absolutely know the measure of defeat that waited for him.   Christ knew that these
kingdoms were assured to Him in the programme of His
Father's will, but He knew also that in that same programme lay the unutterable agony of the immeasurable
darkness, and the fierceness of the temptation lay in the
suggestion that all the splendours of these possessions might
yet be His, without the pathway of shame and suffering
and death.   Not that He entertained or meditated for a
single moment the possibility of yielding to the foe, but
He saw into the very heart of the meaning, and understood
even as the tempter could not, the infinite cost at which
He was yet to possess.

II.   Now notice the repulse of the enemy.   For the first
time the Master spoke to Satan in the language of His
own authority.   That authority had been created by the
victories He had won in the previous attacks.   He had in
His manhood proved stronger than the strong man armed,
mightier than the terrible foe of humanity, and in that
manifested strength He now addressed him, " Get thee
hence, Satan." [1]   This was no longer a challenge.   It was

[1] Matt. 4 : 10.

a command. All the effort and power of evil failed to encompass His capitulation, and now from that citadel of mighty strength He dictated terms to the enemy without the gates, and named him Satan, the slanderer, the calumniator, the liar.

In that authoritative word, spoken in answer to this particular temptation, there was first the refusal of the devil's suggestion, and then a flashing revelation of the method by which He will yet possess the kingdoms of the world. The enemy said, Pay homage to me, and I will give Thee the kingdoms. Christ virtually replied, I will obtain these kingdoms not by paying homage to thee, but by thine eviction. The devil, the liar from the beginning, was attempting to rob Christ of that which he was promising Him; was aiming, in this last desperate adventure of his malice, to cast God out of His own world. The Master's answer was a word of tremendous authority, based upon the perfections of His manhood as against temptation, and also upon the victories to be won in that death from which the enemy dared to attempt to lure Him. From that moment in the wilderness until now, Christ has been repeating that word, by every victory won in the soul of man. By all the triumphs of the Cross among the nations, and by those victories to come in the final movements of the Divine programme, He is repeating the irrevocable edict of the wilderness, " Get thee hence, Satan."

The order thus issued is rendered emphatic and forceful by His use of the same sword of the Spirit. Again the flash of the sword is seen as He said, " It is written, Thou shalt worship the Lord thy God, and Him only shalt thou serve." [1] Again He declared that He stood, in service as well as in the facts of His own being, within the will of

[1] Matt. 4: 10.

God.   He had homage for none save Jehovah, and to Him alone would He render service.   How perfectly this word of the Master rebutted the argument of Satan.   As in each of the previous cases so here, the command quoted had application, not to Satan, but to Himself.   It was not that the Lord ordered Satan to worship God, but that He declared, in the presence of the enemy, that there was one all-sufficient reason for His refusal to render homage to him, namely that the Word of God enjoined that He should worship only God.   Thus for the winning of victory in the pathway of specific service, He took His place as Man, and declared it impossible that He, abiding in the Divine will, should worship or serve any but God.

Notice here particularly the linking of worship and service, and see how this applies to the temptation.   In the mind of Jesus it is evident that worship and service are closely identified, indeed, are two aspects of the same attitude.   To worship is always to serve.   To pay homage is ever to recognize an obligation.   The enemy said nothing in his temptation about service.   He asked for worship only.   Christ's answer reveals the fact that to worship him would be to serve him.   This the enemy in his terrible subtlety did not declare.   He had asked for worship, promising that the kingdoms should then belong to Christ.   Christ's reply declared that promise to be a lie, in that the act of homage would issue in the fact of service, so that the supreme authority would remain that of Satan.   It was the devil's deliberate attempt to deceive the last Adam as he had deceived the first, and so to prevent the creation of the new race, as he had ensured the ruin of the first.

His answer, moreover, revealed the fact of His self-emptying, and yet His consciousness that self-emptying must issue in a perfect crowning.   Not for Himself did He come to win the kingdoms, but for His Father, and yet it pleased the Father that in Him should all the fullness dwell, and for a period unmeasured by human calculation, by the way of the Cross He would ascend the throne, and reign over all these kingdoms. And even when in the distant ages He finally will deliver up the kingdom to the Father, yet in His eternal association with Him, He will possess and reign over the whole territory of the kingdom of God.

Thus the anointed King utterly routs the enemy, and perfectly holds the citadel against this his last attack, and how great the victory is, and upon what infinite wisdom His choice of the Father's pathway was based! To have received the kingdoms from Satan (even granting for the sake of argument, that which cannot be granted, that He had ascended the throne by submission to the prince of the world) would have been to have taken a position utterly worthless. The kingdoms, notwithstanding all their apparent glory and splendour, were permeated with evil. They were the kingdoms of the world, that is, of the Cosmos. The very glory of them was purely material. All the splendour manifest was that of the enthronement of things material, at the cost of the death of the spiritual. To Him, therefore, it was patent that within the splendour there lurked the shadow. The elements of destruction were surely at work. Disintegration was evident in the fact that they were kingdoms. The plurality was a proof of weakness. There was conflict, and strife, and manifestation of break-up, rather than of unity. Until this hour that fact remains, for those who have eyes to see. The world is still full of kingdoms, and these are armed to the teeth. If one shall move, the rest watch with envious eyes, and all the finest skill of the world's statecraft is directed to selfish purposes, and the prevention of the enrichment of others.   The evidence of weakness lies in the very fact that the devil showed Him kingdoms.   God's Man of perfect vision saw this, and clearly understood.   He knew, too, that the glory was the glory of tinsel, rather than of gold.   It was passing, fading, tarnished, even as He looked upon it.   The splendour was undoubtedly great, but it was not lasting.   It was that of the Cosmos only, and that ever lacked the element of permanence.   He knew the truth of what John afterwards wrote, " The world passeth away, and the lust thereof: but he that doeth the will of God abideth forever." [1]

When Jesus therefore refused the offer of the devil, He refused the imperfect thing, the perishing thing; and He was able to do it because doing the will of God He Himself, in spite of the death before Him, must abide forever, and through that death, and that alone, He was communicating imperishable force to all He gathered around Himself.   By the victory of His Cross the kingdoms would be of infinite value, for being permeated with righteousness under the government of God, they would be unified, and no longer should be spoken of as kingdoms.   Pass for a moment to those after-years when, His victory won and He ascended, He gave to His servant in the lonely isle visions and words, declaring the last movements in the mighty programme.   " The kingdom of the world is become the kingdom of our Lord, and of His Christ: and He shall reign forever and ever."   Note carefully " the kingdom."   In the Authorized Version the reading was plural.   In the Revision there is a correction which is of infinite value.   " The kingdom of the world," no longer the many, but the one, " is become the kingdom," not many, but one, " of our Lord, and of His Christ."   And

[1] 1 John 2: 17.

now because He has dealt with, and cast out the element of evil, disintegration is impossible. " He shall reign forever and ever." [1]

Thus Jesus chose to move towards the establishment of one throne and one kingdom. The contrast should ever be kept in mind. The devil showed the Master the kingdoms, tribes, divisions, containing the elements of conflict and of break-up. Jesus refused them. He did not desire the kingdoms. He had come for the kingdom. He refused the tarnished glory of a wrecked ideal, and chose the radiant splendour of a fulfilled purpose, even though the pathway to the goal was the pathway of the Cross.

It must also be borne in mind that the great word in Revelation " the kingdom of the world," does not refer in the first place to the nations, but to the actual kingdom of the Cosmos. All the splendour of material things shall, under the perfect reign of God, be beautified and perfected. In the final victory, the whole creation which to-day groans and travails in pain, will be redeemed ; and being restored to their proper place in the Divine economy, material things, subservient to spiritual things, shall also abide. The vision Jesus had of the issues of the Cross were far more magnificent than that which the devil gave Him of the kingdoms of the world, and the glory of them. It was because He saw the higher that He refused the lower. Escape from the pathway of pain could at best only have resulted in the possession of the lower. Not for one single moment did God's perfect Man hesitate. He did not pause to compare the proposal of Satan, and the purpose of God. The glorious consciousness of coming victory was the joy that was set before Him, and that joy made hell's offer paltry, mean, blasphemous, and impertinent ;

[1] Rev. 11 : 15.

and with stern and magnificent authority He commanded
Satan to depart, and announced the fact of His abiding in
the will of God, to Whom alone He would render worship, and Whom alone He was prepared to serve.

Thus His victory was won, not only in the realm of His
personality, but also in the sphere of His official position;
and the devil was routed in his attack at every point.

The triumph of Jesus was perfect in the realm of His
physical life, in that of His spiritual nature, and in that of
His appointed work. Let it never be forgotten that in all
human nature the work is the final thing. Man was created for work. God made him that he might act in cooperation with Himself, for the fulfillment of Divine purposes. That is true in every individual. The being thus
created for work, consists of body and spirit. The mind is
the consciousness, which is the outcome of this dual personality. Where there is right relationship and perfect
harmony between the physical and spiritual, man is equal to
the work appointed. Where the instrument is injured, the
work is made impossible of achievement. The enemy
first attacked this second Man in an attempt to ruin Him
by appealing to a necessity of His physical nature. He
was utterly unsuccessful, for Jesus recognized that the essential fact of human nature is spirit, and wherever there
comes the necessity for conflict between the need of the
material and that of the spiritual, the former, being subservient, must minister to the latter, which is essential.

Defeated at this point the enemy then flung the force of
his terrible subtlety against the spiritual nature, attempting
the ruin of the entire Man, by suggesting that He should
make unwarranted venture upon the basis of His trust in
God. Here again he was driven back by the quiet and
splendid heroism, which refused that which had all the ap-

pearance of heroic action, but which would have been proof of fear, and lack of confidence.

Then the enemy, driven from his earthworks, stood in the open, and manifested himself in all the diabolic daring of his actual desire. He asked for the homage of perfection. Then in the open he received his final defeat, as the perfect and unharmed Man chose still only to worship and serve Jehovah, and in the might of that choosing, authoritatively commanded the enemy to depart. The second Man, perfectly balanced in body and spirit, and resolutely abiding in the attitude of unswerving loyalty to God, was invulnerable against all the forces of evil. At every point where man had failed He was victorious. In every weakness of man's life He was strong, and in the great Crisis of temptation He overcame with majestic might, and so completely broke the power of the enemy, that forevermore Satan is the conquered foe of the race.

XIV

FINAL

AFTER studying a picture in detail, it is always well to look at it from a distance. In this way effects are discovered which cannot be discerned in a more critical examination. There are certain interesting facts connected with this crisis in the mission of Christ which have not come under the observation in the former studies. These facts, while closely connected with the whole story, belong peculiarly to no section thereof, and therefore have so far eluded notice, but they are altogether too valuable to be omitted.

Before passing from the general subject then, look at the temptation as a whole, making certain observations, principally concerning the two central figures, Satan and Jesus, the tempter and the Tempted.

I. Consider the tempter first. And the first point of interest is that of a perpetual method, incidentally revealed in his attack upon Jesus. Carefully read the quotations from Scripture in which Jesus replied to his attacks, side by side with the passages in the Old Testament.

In answer to the first He said, "It is written, Man shall not live by bread alone, but by every word that proceedeth out of the mouth of God."[1] That is a quotation from Deuteronomy. "And He humbled thee, and suffered thee to hunger, and fed thee with manna, which thou

[1] Matt. 4: 4.

knewest not, neither did thy fathers know; that He might make thee know that man doth not live by bread only, but by everything that proceedeth out of the mouth of Jehovah doth man live." [1]

In answer to the second temptation He said, " Again it is written, Thou shalt not make trial of the Lord thy God." [2] That is a quotation from Deuteronomy. "Ye shall not tempt Jehovah your God, as ye tempted Him in Massah." [3]

In answer to the third He said, " It is written, Thou shalt worship the Lord thy God, and Him only shalt thou serve." [4] That is a quotation also from Deuteronomy. "Thou shalt fear Jehovah thy God; and Him shalt thou serve, and shalt swear by His name." [5]

These answers of Jesus reveal the order of the attacks. First bread, then trust, and then worship. If the references in Deuteronomy are now observed, it will be discovered that they are quoted in opposite order to the way in which they occur in the book. In answer to the temptation concerning bread Christ uttered words to be found in Deut. 8: 3. In replying to the temptation directed against trust, His quotation was from Deut. 6: 16. While in replying to that in the realm of worship, the quotation is from Deut. 6: 13. In the law of God, the order is worship, trust, bread. That order the devil inverted, and his temptations proceeded as to bread, trust, worship. This is a revelation of the perpetual method of Satan, and also of his estimate of humanity. All attempts to work the ruin of man by the enemy are based upon a low conception of human life, to which he attempts to gain the consent of the tempted. His unfailing plan is to act as

[1] Deut. 8 : 3.   [2] Matt. 4 : 7.   [3] Deut. 6: 16.
[4] Matt. 4 : 10.   [5] Deut. 6: 13.

though man were less than God has called him to be,
while he endeavours to degrade him to the level of his
own suggestion. He appeals first to man as being animal
only, calling him to satisfy his material appetite, as though
that were the sum total of life. God never so appeals to
man, even in his fall. Notwithstanding the ruin and the
wreckage of human life, the message of God is always one
that calls man first to worship, and a recognition of his
spiritual nature. The Divine plan is ever that of recognizing the Divinity in man, the magnificence of his
spiritual being, ruined magnificence to-day, and yet truly
magnificent in the ruin, because capable of communion
with God. The Word of God is ever, " Seek ye first His
kingdom; "[1] and then He appeals to the trust in man,
and promises him bread and all things necessary. Satan
called this Man to feed His physical life, and endeavoured
to break down His trust in God, and to divert His worship
from the true to the false, and so change His allegiance
and His service to bondage and slavery.

Then again notice how the enemy silently confessed his
defeat. That is impressively evident by the fact that
in each temptation the Master gave him but one reply.
No second argument was needed. Looking back on that
threefold process, in the wilderness, on the wing of the
temple, and on the high mountain, there is seen a Man, on
each occasion occupying an impregnable position, standing
in a fortress that hell is utterly unable to capture, replying
to each attack in one brief sentence. The silence of the
enemy after the reply of the Lord was a clear confession
of his defeat, and a remarkable proof that he is unable to
gain any advantage over those who are content to abide, at
whatever cost, in the will of God.

[1] Matt. 6: 33.

To those who know anything of the devices of Satan, and the persistency of his opposition, his silence with regard to each several temptation after the first reply of Jesus, is evidence at once of the perfection of that reply, and the utter discomfiture of the foe.

Yet once again. In this temptation there is an intimation of the devil's estimate of the worth of Jesus. After showing Him the kingdoms of the world, and the glory of them, he declared his conviction that to capture the soul of Christ would be a greater victory than all his conquests. He reckoned this perfect Man to be worth all over which he claimed to have gained authority. "All these," said the enemy, and the offer included the result of the dreadful persistency of diabolical endeavour through long centuries, the evolution of evil through tedious processes. The spotless Son of God was, in the estimate of the devil, of more value than all. In effect the enemy said, I will give to Thee all that has cost so much, if I may but gain for one moment Thy homage. It is a stupendous and startling revelation, the devil's estimate of the worth of Christ. There are persons who say that they cannot understand the expiatory work of Christ on the Cross, because of the difficulty of believing that the suffering and death of One could possibly be sufficient for the redemption of the world. Those who speak of this difficulty evidently hold Christ at lower valuation than did the devil. He, comparing the world with the Master, tacitly acknowledged the greater worth of Jesus. Satan evidently reckoned that unless he could bring Christ into subjection, nothing he had, would he be able to hold. He evidently recognized the infinite value of this second Man; and understood, moreover, the relation of that undepreciated value to the redemption of the world.

And yet, moreover, remarkable as is this estimate, from another standpoint the offer of Satan was a piece of insufferable and impertinent blasphemy. The kingdoms of the world for this pure soul? It seems at first assuredly a great conception of the Master's value, and yet one day, Jesus, holding the scales of infinite accuracy in His right hand, revealed that any life, even though bruised and broken by sin, was worth more than all the world. Said He, "What doth it profit a man, to gain the whole world, and forfeit his life?"[1] and yet Satan dared to suggest that the pure and spotless One, heaven's delight and earth's hope, might be purchased for the kingdoms of the world and the glory of them.

Thus in these scenes of the testing of the Son of Man, Satan is revealed that men may nevermore be ignorant of his devices. The last Adam has dragged him from his hiding-place, and held him to view in the clear shining of the light, so that he is known for a liar, the father of lies, for the traducer, the calumniator; and, moreover, for the foe who is defeated, whose power is broken, and who must at last lose his kingdom.

II. Turning attention now to the tempted One Who became the Victor, notice, first, His use of the Word of God under the process. His attitude towards the Word is clearly revealed in the fact that under stress of these terrible onslaughts of evil, His life was wholly conditioned by the law found in Scripture. As defining His own position He quoted directly from the law of Moses. By so doing, He placed Himself under it, and acknowledged its authority. This, moreover, was no mere unofficial sealing of that law. He declared plainly that it had proceeded

[1] Mark 8: 36.

from the mouth of God. Thus He set His imprimatur upon the Divine authority of the Mosaic economy. This should never be lost sight of. While this is not the only occasion upon which He did this, there is no other more remarkable. When Jesus was tried as Man by the powers of darkness, He revealed the fact that He stood within the limits of life, dominated by the sacred writings with which He was familiar; and in simple but explicit statement sealed those Scriptures as of Divine origin and authority.

In this connection notice also His marvellous familiarity with the Word of God. This is proven, not by the length of the quotations, for they were brief, but by their immediate applicability to the need of the moment. This could only be done by a Man Who was familiar with the sacred writings, and of Whom it might be said, even more fully than of Timothy, that from a child He had known the holy Scriptures.

This fact of His familiarity, and of its value in the hour of temptation, should ever be borne in mind by those who are still in the place of testing. Strength to overcome in the hour of such testing, is assured to those, and to those only, who are familiar with the Word of God, not merely as to its letter, but as to its spiritual value.

Without hesitation Jesus quoted the one verse in all the Library that perfectly defined His own position, and revealed the evil lying behind the plausibility of the foe. To do this was proof, not merely of familiarity with the letter, but of His clear understanding of the application thereof to human life.

In the second place notice the relation that the temptation bore to the public ministry of the Master. He passed into the wilderness full of the Spirit; "and Jesus, full of the Holy Spirit, returned from the Jordan, and was led in the Spirit in the wilderness during forty days." [1]   At the close of the temptation it is recorded, " And Jesus returned in the power of the Spirit into Galilee : and a fame went out concerning Him through all the region round about." [2] Mark well the two statements.   " Full of the Spirit," " in the power of the Spirit "; and between the fact of fullness and the fact of power He was led by the Spirit through these severe processes of temptation.   " Full of the Spirit " He went down to the wilderness.   " In the wilderness " He was " led in the Spirit."   From the wilderness to public ministry He passed " in the power of the Spirit."

Between the condition prior to temptation and that following it, there is a distinction and a difference.   It is that which exists between the plenitude of the Spirit and the power of the Spirit.   The plenitude of the Spirit is the result and evidence of holiness of character, and is in itself capacity and sufficiency for service.   The power of the Spirit is the consciousness which is born of victories won, and triumphs achieved.   He entered upon temptation full of the Spirit, that is to say, in possession of all power necessary for the fulfillment of His work.   But power bestowed, becomes truly powerful when it has been tested through the process of temptation.   What is seen in perfection in Christ, is a lesson that men do well to lay to heart.   Fullness of the Spirit, becomes the power of the Spirit, through processes of testing.   Herein is revealed the value of the trials and temptations that beset the pathway of the Christian worker.   In the experience of all those who know anything of what it is to follow in the footsteps of the Lord in God-appointed service, the power of the Spirit is never realized save through some wilderness of

[1] Luke 4: 1.   [2] Luke 4: 14.

personal conflict with the foe. From such experience entered upon in the fullness of the Spirit, men go out either broken and incapable of service, or with the tread and force of conscious power; in which way, depends upon the attitude in which the enemy is met. If in the spirit of self-complacency, then the devil is invariably the victor. If in the spirit of resolute abandonment to, and abiding in the will of God, the foe is routed, and consciousness of power is the inevitable sequence.

And once again. That whole temptation gives a very valuable insight into the relation of Jesus to the principalities and powers. First with regard to those which are fallen. Luke writes, "And when the devil had completed every temptation, he departed from Him for a season." [1] The wording is most expressive. "When the devil had completed every temptation" can only be interpreted into a statement of the fact that the devil had exhausted himself, and had no other line upon which he found it possible to approach the uncaptured citadel of the Son of God. "Then the devil leaveth Him," [2] says Matthew; and Luke declares, "the devil departed from Him for a season." Both are right. Matthew leaves the fact stated in all its magnificence, the King perfectly victorious over the foe. Never again did the enemy approach Christ in the same way. Never again is the perfect Man seen in defensive conflict with the foe. His presence in the wilderness was a challenge to the enemy, but it was a challenge in which He forced Satan into attack, rather than one in which He attacked the enemy. The victory is perfect. From that moment the records only reveal Him speaking to Satan, and to all demons under his sway, in words of quiet, absolute, Kingly authority. In the power of the Spirit He

[1] Luke 4: 13.   [2] Matt. 4: 11.

passed from the wilderness to cast out demons, and He drove before Him all the emissaries of the prince, having routed in this supreme conflict the arch-enemy of the race. It is interesting to notice how few words He addressed to demons afterwards, and that they were always words of command, and that the command He uttered was always obeyed. The story of the man possessed with a legion of devils as recorded in Matthew, chronicles the fact that they "besought Him, saying, If Thou cast us out, send us away into the herd of swine." Jesus answered them with one word only "Go,"[1] and immediately they obeyed. That is but one illustration out of very many. The same facts are patent through all the Gospel story subsequent to the victory of the wilderness. He at once assumed the position of authority over a conquered foe, and drove him and his forces, until at last in a final conflict in which He attacked the strongholds of evil,

> "He hell in hell laid low,
>   And Satan's throne o'erthrew;
>   Bowed to the grave, destroyed it so,
>   And death by dying slew."

And yet again is seen His relation to the unfallen principalities and powers in the words, "Angels came and ministered unto Him."[2] There is a beautiful touch of tenderness here. During the conflict He had received no help from these ministers of love. They had been restrained from coming to His aid during the temptation. Directly the fallen foe was driven forth, they gathered round in solicitous and tender service. This same restraint and readiness were manifest later in the garden of Gethsemane, when, the victory won and the conflict over, there

[1] Matt. 8: 31, 32.   [2] Matt. 4: 11.

also they ministered to Him; and when soon after the Master rebuked Peter for the rashness of his action in smiting Malchus, in one sentence He illumined the whole upper spaces, and showed how great hosts of them were ready to succour Him. "Thinkest thou that I cannot beseech My Father, and He shall even now send Me more than twelve legions of angels?"[1] They were ready at His bidding, to sweep to destruction the blasphemous rabble, approaching Him to do Him violence. And yet He did not ask for them, and even the hosts of light were held in restraint by the infinite love of God for man. Their rendering of assistance was rejected, when for man's redemption the pathway had to be trodden in loneliness. Yet with what haste they sped to minister to Him in the moment of triumph, and with what exultant gladness at last they were permitted to roll the stone away, and watch the sepulchre, and be the first messengers of the resurrection to men.

Our Lord and Master is seen to be King over fallen and unfallen angels. All the fearful host of demons obey His simplest word, and all the companies of the unfallen ones are eager to minister to Him, and go forth gladly as they are sent to minister to the heirs of salvation. The victory of Jesus over temptation is victory over all the forces of hell; and all men who, abandoned to His Lordship, abide in His will, must share in His triumph. He is, moreover, Master of the innumerable company of the angelic host, who have never fallen; and enthroned above them, He gives them also to the service of the saints, who through testing are passing to triumph.

Thus standing back and viewing the whole temptation, two figures stand out in clear light. The enemy of the

[1] Matt. 26 : 53.

race is seen in all his subtlety and terrible power, but yet spoiled, defeated, crushed. The Redeemer is seen in all the terribleness of conflict, upon the issue of which depends the carrying out of the purpose of God, and the deliverance and uplifting of man; but yet victorious, crowned, and exercising the functions of the Conqueror.

BOOK IV

THE TRANSFIGURATION

XV. Introductory
XVI. The Master Himself
XVII. The Celestial Visitors
XVIII. The Dazed Disciples
XIX. Final. The Things That Remained

' In the old days on Sinai
    Were tempests and dark cloud,
And God was there, in lightning,
    Thunder, and trumpet loud:
Upon a fairer mountain,
    Where pure snows lay congealed,
Stood Jesus in His glory,
    The very Christ revealed.

" His raiment white and glistering,
    White as the glistering snow;
His form a blaze of splendour,
    The like no sun can show;
His wondrous eyes resplendent
    In ecstasy of prayer;
His radiant face transfigured
    To heaven's own beauty there.

" Deep shadows are the edging
    Of that short transient peace,
For spirit-forms come warning
    Of the fore-doomed decease.
Words from the cloud give witness —
    ' This, My Beloved Son';
The three look round in terror,
    And Jesus is alone.

" Soon passed that scene of grandeur;
    But stedfast, changeless, sure,
Our blest transfiguration
    Is promised to endure;
The manifested glory
    Of our great Lord to see
Shall change us to His likeness;
    As He is, we shall be.

" O vision all surpassing,
    Filling the heavenly height!
The Lamb, once slain, transfigured
    In the throne-rainbow's light!
There for the endless ages
    All glorified is He,
And His eternal glory
    Shall ours forever be."
        —GEORGE RAWSON. " The Transfiguration."

And after six days Jesus taketh with Him Peter, and James, and John his brother, and bringeth them up into a high mountain apart: and He was transfigured before them; and His face did shine as the sun, and His garments became white as the light. And behold, there appeared unto them Moses and Elijah talking with Him. And Peter answered, and said unto Jesus, Lord, it is good for us to be here: if Thou wilt, I will make here three tabernacles; one for Thee, and one for Moses, and one for Elijah. While he was yet speaking, behold, a bright cloud overshadowed them: and behold, a voice out of the cloud, saying, This is My beloved Son, in Whom I am well pleased; hear ye Him. And when the disciples heard it, they fell on their face, and were sore afraid. And Jesus came and touched them and said, Arise, and be not afraid. And lifting up their eyes, they saw no one, save Jesus only.

And as they were coming down from the mountain, Jesus commanded them, saying, Tell the vision to no man, until the Son of man be risen from the dead.—*Matt. 17 : 1–9.*

*　　*　　*　　*　　*　　*　　*

And after six days Jesus taketh with Him Peter, and James, and John, and bringeth them up into a high mountain apart by themselves: and He was transfigured before them; and His garments became glistering, exceeding white, so as no fuller on earth can whiten them. And there appeared unto them Elijah with Moses: and they were talking with Jesus. And Peter answereth and saith to Jesus, Rabbi, it is good for us to be here: and let us make three tabernacles; one for Thee, and one for Moses, and one for Elijah. For he knew not what to answer; for they became sore afraid. And there came a cloud overshadowing them: and there came a voice out of the cloud, This is My beloved Son: hear ye Him. And suddenly looking round about, they saw no one any more, save Jesus only with themselves.

And as they were coming down from the mountain, He charged them that they should tell no man what things they had seen, save when the Son of man should have risen again from the dead. And they kept the saying, questioning among themselves what the rising again from the dead should mean.—*Mark 9 : 2–10.*

*　　*　　*　　*　　*　　*　　*

And it came to pass about eight days after these sayings, that He took with Him Peter and John and James, and went up into the mountain to pray. And as He was praying, the fashion of

His countenance was altered, and His raiment became white and dazzling. And behold, there talked with Him two men, who were Moses and Elijah; who appeared in glory, and spake of His decease which He was about to accomplish at Jerusalem. Now Peter and they that were with Him were heavy with sleep: but when they were fully awake, they saw His glory, and the two men that stood with Him. And it came to pass, as they were parting from Him, Peter said unto Jesus, Master, it is good for us to be here: and let us make three tabernacles; one for Thee, and one for Moses, and one for Elijah: not knowing what he said. And while he said these things, there came a cloud, and overshadowed them: and they feared as they entered into the cloud. And a voice came out of the cloud, saying, This is My Son, My chosen: hear ye Him. And when the voice came, Jesus was found alone. And they held their peace, and told no man in these days any of the things which they had seen.—*Luke 9 : 28–36.*

XV

INTRODUCTORY

In approaching the subject of the transfiguration it will be well first to take a general survey of the field, by considering,—first, its occasion; secondly, its witnesses; and thirdly, its purpose.

I. Each evangelist commences his account of the transfiguration with a suggestive word—"after." Matthew and Mark say "After six days." [1] Luke writes "Eight days after." [2] There is here no real discrepancy. The first two count the intervening days only, and the third reckons also the two days, on which the two events in mind occurred. This uniformity in the use of the word "after" arrests attention, and the question is naturally asked, after what? A study of the context will show that the reference is to the conversation between Peter and Jesus, the first part of which contained Peter's confession, and our Lord's commendation; and the second part Peter's shrinking from the cross, and the Master's stern denunciation.

Beyond these events, "after six days Jesus taketh with Him Peter, and James, and John his brother, and bringeth them up into a high mountain apart: and He was transfigured before them." [3] The first meaning, therefore, of the transfiguration to the men who witnessed it, was a confirmation of the truths uttered on that memorable occasion. In the splendours of the mount the two facts of the Messiahship and Saviourhood of the Christ were confirmed.

[1] Matt. 17 : 1; Mark 9: 2.   [2] Luke 9: 28.   [3] Matt. 17: 1, 2.

They saw the Messiah in the glory of His Person, they looked upon Him standing in the glory of God, and conversing with the spirits of just men made perfect. They beheld no longer the Man of sorrows, upon Whose face was the mark of a perpetual pain, but a Man shining in all the splendours of His own perfect character, as it transformed and transfigured the veil of His flesh.

The mount was also a confirmation of the necessity of the Cross of which the Lord had spoken, and from which His disciples had shrunk. They listened to the conversation between Jesus, and Moses and Elijah, and it was of His coming exodus. The Cross, concerning which Peter had rebuked his Lord, was the subject of conversation in the strange and marvellous light of the holy mount.

Thus the mount endorsed the confession of Peter, and the teaching of Christ.

There is, therefore, a distinct connection between the transfiguration and the events immediately preceding. "After six days," but what happened during those days? There is no detailed record of them. Follow the clue carefully, and it will be seen that during the period there had been a sense of estrangement between the disciples and the Master. They were amazed, afraid to ask Him questions, and do not seem to have walked in very close companionship with Him. He was going towards Jerusalem, moving with determination towards the very Cross of which they were afraid. They, being afraid, followed at a distance reluctantly, full of perplexed wonderings. Do not blame them. They had arrived at the moment when one of their number had confessed the Messiahship of Jesus, and He had not denied, but had rather crowned the confession with His blessing.

Then, suddenly, by His foretelling of the Cross, all that

Messiahship meant to these men seemed to have been rendered impossible of achievement. The Cross of shame loomed ahead, and they were bewildered, they fell back, fear possessing their hearts, and mystery enshrouding their pathway. Those six days must have been among the saddest in the life of the Master; six days of silence, six days in which His loneliness was the supreme fact in His progress. He had chosen these men, but there was not one of their number who fully followed Him now. They loved Him, and He loved them, and having loved them, He loved them to the end; but the way to the end lay through the desolate days in which He realized, and they proved, their present incapacity for fellowship with Him in suffering. He was moving in sublime loneliness to His Cross.

When the six days had passed, He called three of them, and leading them to the mount, was transfigured before them. In that sacred vision He spoke to their fear, and flung new light upon the overshadowing mystery, as He revealed the inward fact of the glory and strength of His Person and character, permitting, for a moment, that glory to shine through the veil of His flesh, that He might allay their fear, and clear away, as much as might be, the cloud of mystery that enshrouded them.

In this light Peter spoke again : " Lord, it is good for us to be here : if Thou wilt, I will make here three tabernacles; one for Thee, and one for Moses, and one for Elijah." [1] It was a sad blunder, and yet a revelation. " Be it far from Thee, Lord," [2] he had said in sight of the Cross. " It is good to be here," he said in the light of the glory. The Cross? No. The glory? Yes. It was as though he had said : Suffering and passion, and blood and death, I cannot look upon. This glory is what I crave for Thee,

[1] Matt. 17 : 4.   [2] Matt. 16 : 22.

my Lord and Master. It was still the speech of love, blind
and blundering, but yet love. It seemed as though the
Master said in effect: I spoke to you of the Cross, and
you were afraid. I spoke also of resurrection, and you did
not hear, but come with Me into a mountain apart, and in
its light and glory My converse shall be still of the
Cross.

He repeated the teaching of six days ago, but under different circumstances. For the strengthening of feeble
faith, and the quieting of the hearts of terror-stricken men,
He was transfigured before them.

II. There can be no doubt that these men, Peter, James
and John, were the most remarkable in the apostolate.
Peter loved Him, John He loved, and James was the first
to seal his testimony with his blood. Even their blunders
proved their strength. They were the men of enterprise,
men who wanted thrones, and places of power, complacent
and satisfied while the Lord spoke of keys, desiring to sit
on His right hand and on His left in His kingdom.
Mistaken ideas, all of them, and yet proving capacity for
holding the keys, and occupying the throne. What men
from among that first group of apostles reign to-day as
do these men? James, ever supreme among the apostles,
as having been first of their number to receive the crown
of martyrdom. John, in inspired writing, unveiled the
wonders of His commandments and His love, His light
and His life; and the whole Church, in its mystic relationship to Christ, is under the sway of the apostle of love.
Peter held the keys, and in Pentecostal preaching opened
the door of the kingdom to Jews and Gentiles, first at
Jerusalem and then in the house of Cornelius. These
were the men taken to the mount. There can be no doubt

that these among the apostles were the greatest three. To them He had shown His supreme miracles, and they subsequently came nearest to the sacred enactments of Gethsemane's garden. The transfiguration was after, and also before—"after six days," but before Gethsemane, flashing its light backward and forward to strengthen their faith after the mystery of the six days, and to be a light of hope even amid the gloom of the garden.

III. " He was transfigured *before them*." [1] The whole emphasis should be laid upon these last two words. It was wholly for their sakes that upon this occasion He was transfigured. There are no means of knowing, but perchance those silent mountain heights, and the starlit sky of night, had often witnessed such wondrous scenes. Luke declares that as He prayed He was transfigured; and he, moreover, tells that the ostensible purpose of this journey to the mount was that of prayer. [2] Who knows but that during those years of public ministry, when withdrawn from the crowd, and even having left His chosen disciples behind Him, He spent the hours of the silence with God, the angels saw Him transfigured? Be that as it may, the emphasis here is surely upon the words " before them." The outshining of this light, and all the radiant glory of the holy mount, was for their sakes.

This vision of their Master was a revelation to them of God's thought of Him. In the events preceding, He had asked, and they had given, man's opinion. Human voices had expressed different thoughts. These opinions are all suggestive and valuable, showing how the fulfillment in His Person and character of all that was great in the past, had impressed itself upon the minds of different men. Some

[1] Matt. 17: 2.   [2] Luke 9: 28, 29.

said He was John the Baptist, the stern prophet who had
dared to denounce the king. They had heard Him in some
sterner moment of His preaching, had been reproved by
Him for some willful sin, and they found John the Baptist
risen from the dead. Others said, This is Elijah, the man
who came to bring the people back to the law. Others,
who perchance, had seen such tears as He shed over Jerusalem, and heard such words as He spoke of her ruin,
were reminded of the weeping prophet of old, who in his
agony had cried, "Oh, that my head were waters, and mine
eyes a fountain of tears, that I might weep day and night
for the slain of the daughter of my people!"[1] and some
said He was Jeremiah. Others again had said, "one of
the prophets," being unable to decide which. All had discovered the prophetic genius and power of speech, and yet
all fell short of the supreme fact that He was Messiah.
This was the opinion of a man, not resulting from his own
observation, but created by distinct revelation, "Blessed art
thou, Simon Bar-Jonah: for flesh and blood hath not revealed it unto thee, but My Father Who is in heaven."[2]

And even now Peter and his comrades did not understand
the full significance of their own confession, and it is as
though the Master had said, having heard the expressed
human opinion at its best, "Come now to the mount, and
learn God's thought of the Christ." That thought is expressed in a threefold way, first, in the glory streaming from
His Person; second, in the visit of Moses and Elijah; and
third, in the actual speech of Deity. The mount revealed
the sublime fact that the Divine opinion included, and
glorified all human conceptions. Moses and Elijah conversed with Him, and withdrew. When they had departed,
and no one remained save Jesus only, then God said,

[1] Jer. 9: 1.		[2] Matt. 16: 17.

" Hear ye Him." [1]   He is sufficient, all that other prophets have spoken is fulfilled in Him, their messages have been but gleams of truth; He is the Truth.

Thus upon the mount, standing in the light and glory of the transfigured Christ, they learned the Divine thought of their Master, as they had given expression to the human thought six days before.

There are certain practical applications of this preliminary study, which will prove profitable. God's " afters " are worth the waiting for. However dark the " now " is, there will be light enough in God's " after " to explain the darkness. The very genius of Christianity consists in living in the dark " now," with the hope of the " after " upon it. Wait ever for

> " Light after darkness, gain after loss." [2]

Remember also, that beyond the mount lies the valley. It may be that the experience of the present moment finds expression in the language of the poet:

> " I stand upon the mount of God,
> With sunlight in my soul;
> I hear the storms in vales beneath,
> I hear the thunders roll.

> " But I am calm with Thee, my God,
> Beneath these glorious skies;
> And to the height on which I stand
> No storms nor clouds can rise." [3]

Do not forget, however, that it is not intended that the follower of Christ should abide on the mount. Just beyond lies the valley, and away further still, out of sight at present, but surely to be reached, is the sombre shade of the

[1] Matt. 17 : 5.   [2] F. R. Havergal.   [3] G. B. Bubier.

olives of Gethsemane. For that, this is preparation; this is a Divine process of training, and it is full of grace. The valley and Gethsemane lie beyond the holy mount. To them God never leads save by the way of the mount. The mount forever stands after the six days, before the deepest darkness and the severest trial.

It is also true that revelation is according to capacity. There are those to whom God cannot reveal some of the methods of His government. Peter, James, and John were taken to the mount, but eight others saw no trans-figuring glory. Do not ask for the vision of the mount. He takes there whomsoever He will. The light of trans-figuration creates new responsibility. The men who saw its glory were taken also to the vision of Gethsemane's sorrow. Let there be no asking for visions. When transfiguration, and garden, and Cross, and resurrection, and ascension hours are passed, the Master will not ap-portion His rewards according to the number of visions, but according to fidelity to the opportunities He creates. Is there no vision? Then let there be faithfulness with-out, and after all, this may be the more heroic life. The man to whom God grants a vision should find it easy there-after to be heroic. To the larger company of apostles and disciples, no vision comes. They patiently follow "until the day break, and the shadows flee away." [1] Ask for no vision, O, my soul, lest its coming bring also testing which God had not intended for thee. Take what He gives, and follow in His steps.

Lastly, communion with God issues ever in transfigured life. It was when He was praying that He was trans-figured. When the disciples pray as He prayed, they also will be transfigured as He was transfigured. This will not

1 Cant. 2: 17.

be until salvation is completed. While there lurk within possibilities of unbelief, fellowship is not perfected, and final transfiguration cannot be. And yet, the measure of fellowship is the measure of transfiguration, even here and now. How often, even amid the shadows of the little while, the faces of the saints are seen lit with the light of the inward glory. Those who, indeed, would shine amid the darkness of the world, must be transformed and transfigured by union with God. May the communion of the saints with the Son be such, that, in some measure, upon all of them may rest the light and glory of the holy mount

XVI

THE MASTER HIMSELF

HAVING thus taken a general survey of the occasion, the company, and the purpose of the transfiguration, it is possible to pass to a more detailed examination of its chief features. It is the Lord Himself upon Whom the attention is first fixed, and that in regard, first, to the fact of His transfiguration, and secondly, to the place it occupied in His life and mission. In each of these separate studies the subjects will overlap. It is impossible to consider the Master without having also to look both at the disciples and the celestial visitors, just as it will be impossible to consider either of these alone. All must be seen in connection with each, yet each demands special attention, and such attention is now directed to the principal Person in the glorious scene.

I. The books of Daniel and Revelation record visions of a glorious One which are remarkable for their similarity to the manifestation on the holy mount. Very little is said in Scripture concerning the glory and majesty of Christ. A stranger reading the Bible, especially the New Testament, would be impressed far more with the majesty of the Messiah's character, and the glory of His moral qualities, than in any other way. This, undoubtedly, was part of the Divine plan, for the search of men was rather for tokens of material glory, than for signs of moral excellence. His coming was principally for the display of the latter; and such signs, as might have appealed to the de-

224

sire of the men whose only conception of glory had come to be that of manifested splendour, were denied. The word of the prophet spoken in another connection had a supreme fulfillment in the Person of Jesus, "There was the hiding of His power."[1] Consequently, that which arrests a person in the study of the life of Christ, is not outward magnificence, not pageantry or pomp, but something more wonderful, and without which mere outward pageantry and pomp would be nothing worth, even His moral glory. No man can study the life of this remarkable One, Who passed through the ways of men devoid of attributes that attracted the attention of the mob, without finding that the beauty of His character lays hold upon the inmost spirit, and commands its admiration. To see the Christ in the glories of His character, is to be prostrate before Him in adoration.

Yet while the glory of His power is hidden, and the radiant splendours of His Person are veiled, occasionally during His sojourn upon the earth, they flashed into prominence. Here upon the mount, before the eyes of the disciples, there flamed forth the magnificence and the majesty of Him, Who, in order that the weakest and most trembling might hold intercourse with Him, had veiled these splendours behind the human.

What an outshining it was may be gathered from the accounts of the evangelists:

"He was transfigured before them; and His face did shine as the sun, and His garments became white as the light."[2]

"And He was transfigured before them: and His garments became glistering, exceeding white; so as no fuller on earth can whiten them."[3]

[1] Hab. 3:4.   [2] Matt 17:2.   [3] Mark 9: 2, 3

"And as He was praying, the fashion of His countenance was altered, and His raiment became white and dazzling." [1]

The accounts vary somewhat, and this is doubtless due to the different impression made upon the minds of the men who beheld the vision, and told the story to the evangelists. Yet in the differences there is unity.

Matthew describes the change that passed over Him as one of light: "His face did shine as the sun, and His garments became white as the light."

Mark gives the impression of snow: "His garments became glistering, exceeding white." The word "glistering" suggests the sparkling of the snow as light falls upon it.

Luke writes, "His raiment became white and dazzling," the word "dazzling" suggesting the blinding light of the lightning's flash.

That which is common to all the descriptions is the thought of whiteness and of light. "White as light" says Matthew's story. "White as snow glistering in the light" is Mark's utterance. Not as light merely, not even as snow glistering upon the mountain heights, but as lightning flashing forth in glory, dazzling in its brilliancy, is Luke's account.

The one fact of white light is here declared in threefold statement—the beneficence of light, the purity of snow, the majesty of lightning.

With what overwhelming awe must these men have looked upon their Master! They had become familiar with Him as with a Man sharing their nature—His face lined with the furrows of care, His visage sorrowfully marred, beautiful, yea, passing beautiful, and yet always

[1] Luke 9 : 29.

overshadowed with the signs of sorrow.   As they looked
up from their bewildered sleep in the darkness of the
night, they beheld Him white as the light, His raiment
glistering as with the radiance of the snow-capped peaks
behind Him, His whole Person standing out in clear relief
against the dark background, like lightning flashing upon
the bosom of the night.   Long years after, Peter, writing
of the vision, said, "We were eye-witnesses of His
majesty." [1]   The word "majesty" occurs three times only
in Scripture.   Once it is translated "mighty power," once
"magnificence," and once "majesty."   The thought it
suggests is that of splendour, of overwhelming beauty and
glory, and that which arrests and subdues the mind to the
point of adoration and worship ; and Peter, looking back
to the splendours of that night scene, wrote, "We were
eye-witnesses of His majesty."

This glory was not the light of heaven falling upon
Him from above.   Nor was it a merely reflected radiance
which resulted from communion.   When Moses descended
from the mount, his face shone so that men could not look
upon it.   That glory was the reflection of the light in
which he had sojourned in the solemn days of his absence,
and even that was so brilliant that men could not look upon
it, and he had to veil his face.   Later on, when the first
martyr was about to pass from earth to heaven, upon his
face there rested a glory so that when men looked upon
him "they saw his face as it had been the face of an
angel." [2]   But these are very different matters from the
radiant splendour of the Master on the mount.   That was
the glory of His own face, of His own Person, shining
through the veil that had hidden it, until the very raiment
of His humanity sparkled and glistened and flashed with

[1] 2 Peter 1 : 16.   [2] Acts 6 : 15.

the splendour of light and snow and lightning. The transfiguration was effected, not by glory falling on Him, but by inherent glory flashing forth. To depict that splendour is impossible with brush, or pencil, or pen. To-day it may only be seen partially, when in some place of silent solitude, the spirit of man communes with the Christ, under the immediate illumination of the Spirit of God.

II. The transfiguration had a close connection with the human life and the Divine mission of Jesus of Nazareth. Indeed, it may be said to have been the connecting link between the two. It carried the one over into the other. It was the consummation of ideal human life, and the beginning of the pathway that ended in the accomplishment of the purposes of God in the redemption of fallen human nature.

It is astonishing to find how many there are who look upon the transfiguration as an experience granted to Christ for the confirmation of His own consecration, and how large a number of writers on the subject say that He was led to the mountain, in order that His own faith might be confirmed, and His devotion made more complete in view of the death that lay before Him. Without doubt the experience was of value in His human life, in the way of a satisfaction and strength. But to imagine that He needed such an experience to confirm His consecration, is to misunderstand the whole of His life prior to this period. The consecration of the Christ to His Father's will and work, was settled before He was born a Man. In that Voice which comes out of the past, and Whose words are written in the volume of the Book, "Lo, I am come. . . . To do Thy will, O God,"[1] is the declaration of a perfect

[1] Heb. 10: 7.

and complete consecration, from which there was never the swerving of a hair's breadth, or the drawing back of a single moment. He needed no vision of glory such as this to confirm Him in His consecration to His Father's will. The vision of the Father's face was never clouded for a moment to Him until the dark hour on Calvary's Cross, which as yet was not reached. So perpetual was His sense of the Divine presence that in conversation with Nicodemus, He spoke of Himself as "the Son of Man, Who is in heaven."[1] No, this was not something given as an encouragement to devotion. It was part of the perfect whole.

The transfiguration of Jesus was the consummation of His human life, the natural issue of all that had preceded it. Born into the world by the Holy Spirit, He had lived a life linked to, and yet separate from, humanity : linked to it in all the essential facts of its nature, separate from it in its sin, both as a principle and activity. He had taken His way, from His first outlook upon life as a human being —a babe in His mother's arms—through the years of childhood and growth, through all temptation and testing of manhood, and through the severer temptation of public ministry ; and here, at last, that humanity, perfect in creation, perfect through probation, was perfected in glory. The life of Jesus was bound to reach this point of transfiguration. It could do no other.

In Jesus of Nazareth there was the perfect unfolding before heaven and before men, of the Divine intention as to the process of human life. Beginning in weakness and limitation, passing through difficulties and temptation, gaining perpetual victory over temptation by abiding only, at all times, and under all circumstances, in the will of God,

[1] John 3: 13.

at last, all the testing being ended, the life passed into the presence of God Himself, and into the light of heaven, not through the gate of death, but through the painless and glorious process of transfiguration. The transfiguration of Jesus was the outcome of His unceasing victory in every hour of temptation. The garrison of His life had been kept against every attack of the foe; no room had been found in any avenue of His being, nor in all the circle of His manhood, for anything contrary to the will of God. His life was a perfect harmony, and the unceasing burden of its music was the goodness, and perfectness, and acceptableness of the will of God. He had ever done the things that pleased God; He had thought the thoughts of God, and spoken words, and done deeds under the inspiration and impulse of communion with God; and at last, having triumphed over every form of temptation, He passed, not into the darkness of death, but into a larger life; and as He was transfigured, He was filled with the answer of God to the perfection of His life—an answer that came, not as a glory from without, but as the perfect blossoming of that which He had always enfolded in His human nature.

Reverently take a flower as an illustration of the process, watching it in its progress from seedling to perfect blossoming. The blossom rested in the seed in potentiality and possibility. Take a seed and hold it in the hand, strange little seed, without beauty, the very embodiment of weakness. But within that husk in which the human eye detects no line of beauty or grace, no gleam or flash of glory, there lie the gorgeous colours and magnificent flower itself. From that seed, through processes of law, plant and bud proceed, until at last the perfect blossom is formed.

God's humanity has blossomed once in the course of the

ages, and that transfigured Man upon the holy mount, flashing in the splendour of a light like the sun, glistering with the glory of a whiteness like that of the snow, and flaming with the magnificent beauty of the lightning which flashes its radiance upon the darkness, that was God's perfect Man. That was the realization of the thought that was in the mind of God when He said, "Let Us make man in Our image."

The mount of transfiguration was the consummation of the life of Jesus, and if He had not been in the world for other purposes, if He had not been here because He loved man, if He had not been here in order to win life out of the deep dense darkness of human sin and death, He might have passed back with Moses and Elijah to the heights of the glory of God—God's Man, having won His way to heaven by the perfection of His life. Such then is the place of the transfiguration in the life of Jesus.

With regard to His mission, the transfiguration was the prelude to His death. It was the crowning of the first part of His mission, that of realizing perfect life. Because of this crowning, He was now able to pass to the second part of His mission, that of atoning death. It will at once be seen how closely united these things are. The death of Christ would have been of no avail for the redemption of the world, had it not been preceded by His perfect life. To say this is not for one single moment to undervalue the death of Christ. Had the life not been perfect, the death would have been nothing more than the tragic end of an ordinary life, ordinary because conformed to the tendency and habit of the centuries, that of sin. But blessed be God, there had been no such conformity in the years that had preceded the Cross. Amid the self-idolatry of all the race, He alone had stood erect, and therefore His death became the very door of life for a lost race, because of the infinite value of the life that had preceded it. No other man could be found as ransom for his brother, for every other man in coming to death had nothing in life that made death of value. When God had found none that could by any means ransom his brother, it was not that He had not been able to find one man willing to die for another. Men have always been found ready to die for others. The old story of how a soldier found a comrade ready to don his uniform, and take his place in the ranks, and answer " Here " when his name was called, is well-known. But on the higher plane, no man can answer " Here " for his brother, for each must answer for himself, and every man's life is in itself imperfect, and the life of one cannot avail for that of another, for that " all have sinned and fall short of the glory of God." [1] Men have in all ages been willing to die for others. Savonarola died for Florence, but he could not redeem Florence by his death. George Whitfield died for England, but he could not redeem the country by his dying. But this Man on the mount finished His life, wrought it out to absolute perfection, crowning it with the glory of heaven in the sight of men and God. Having done this He took that life—perfect, spotless, entire—and poured it out in death. His death thereby became more than the end of life. It became the mystery of Atonement, the darkness through which the eternal morning broke, the death through which life as a river passed through the ages, for every man, who forsaking sin, commits himself to the Perfect One Who died and lives.

The transfiguration divided the ways. Amid the glory of that resplendent hour, the first part of His mission was

[1] Rom. 3 : 23.

ended. There was ushered in the second part, as He descended from the mountain, turning His back for the second time upon the light of heaven, and taking His way to the Cross, passed into the darkness of death. Follow carefully the life of Jesus from that mount to the green hill without the city wall. The one thought in His mind was that of His death, and of His Cross. May it not be said that after the mount He was eager for death? There was no drawing back, there was no flinching. He set His face towards Jerusalem, and it almost seems as though He were impatient of delay. With straight undeviating course, He passed from the mount of transfiguration to the Cross. Death was the goal, the Cross the throne, the passion-baptism the loosening of prison bonds, the darkness of Calvary the prelude of the dawn of the age for which He longed. So the transfiguration came into the life of Jesus as the crowning of His humanity, and therefore His preparation for the death by which man is redeemed.

In conclusion, it may be well to glance at the companions and the converse of the mount as they affected Him. His disciples were dazed, half asleep, not with the sleep of carelessness, but with that overpowering that follows the vision of glory. As He stood in the glory of that crowning moment, these men spoke to His heart, by their very blindness and blundering, of the incompleteness of His work. The words of Peter and the needs of these men were two different things. Said the words of Peter, " Let us stay here." Said the need of the men, even expressed in the blunder of Peter's prayer, Stay not here, but pass to the Cross. In the light of the mount Jesus looked upon these men, and heard the cry they themselves did not understand, their cry for the Atonement of His death, and the light that should follow the darkness of His passion.

Then, again, Moses and Elijah, the spirits of just men made perfect. They talked with Him of His Cross. In this there is deep significance. What they said to Him, or He to them, concerning that Cross is not chronicled, but may it not have been that as He looked at them He saw again the necessity for His Cross? Did He not know that the perfecting of the just had been through the faith they had reposed in the purpose of God? And did He not know that the purpose, in which He had had fellowship, was that of redemption by blood? Did not these men say to Him by their very presence, Heaven as well as earth waits Thy Cross, and unless Thou dost pass from the mount of crowning to the mount of crucifixion, heaven must be unpeopled, for we are of the company of those who have died in faith looking for Shiloh, our Desire and our Redeemer. We wait amid the splendours of the upper world, and all is lost to us if Thy work of redemption be unfinished?

With reverent daring follow the thought to its issue. Had He, the crowned and perfected Man, passed upward into light, heaven would have been unpeopled, and in its splendour there would have been one only Man. The plea of heaven and earth in the ears of Christ was a great cry for the deeper work, that lay as yet beyond Him. Earth with no language but a cry, which itself did not understand, was asking for the Cross. Heaven in its glory of perfected vision was looking for the same; and because He willed one will with God, He left the glory of the mount, and with resolute step trod the way to Calvary; and from the darkness that overwhelmed Him has broken a light, that falls in radiance of hope and certainty upon the ruined race.

XVII

THE CELESTIAL VISITORS

Next to the actual transfiguration of the Master, perhaps the most interesting fact of these hours of glory on the holy mount was the presence there of Moses and Elijah, two of the most remarkable and prominent figures in the Old Testament economy. They were among the number of those of whom the writer of the letter to the Hebrews said, " These all died in faith." [1] Their presence in the heavens was due to their faith in the promises of God, promises which were to find their fulfillment in Jesus. On the transfiguring mount He had reached a crisis in the process of the work, and they came to greet Him in the moment of triumph, and to speak with Him of the work yet remaining to be done.

By their conversation with Him they revealed the interest of the dwellers in heaven in His approaching work, for they talked with Him of the exodus which He was about to accomplish. To look at them, listen to their conversation, and consider the thoughts suggested by their presence, is the purpose of the present study.

First, look at the men, Moses and Elijah; secondly, notice the significance of their presence and passing, the fact that they came, and the fact that they disappeared; and thirdly, notice the message they inferentially brought concerning the condition of those who have departed this life in the faith and fear of God.

[1] Heb. 11 : 13.

235

I. Moses and Elijah—Moses, the heroic law-giver of the people ; Elijah, the lion-hearted prophet of God. Moses, the founder of the economy in the midst of which Christ carried on His earthly mission up to the point of His rejection ; Elijah, the reformer, the messenger of heaven to a decadent age, to a people who were heirs of the oracles, and yet were disobedient to them, to a people of whom it could be said, " They feared Jehovah, and served their own gods," [1] to a people who very largely were given over to the worship of Baal, while still professing to have covenant relations with Jehovah.

Moses had received the law, and given it to the people. Elijah had called the people back to the law. They were the two most remarkable figures in the whole of the Mosaic economy, the founder and the reformer, the law-giver and the vindicator of its authority, who called the nation to return to its allegiance ; men who both had led the people in some great Divine movement, the one initiating a new order of things in the world, the other repeating the principles upon which that order was based, in the days when the chosen nation had become disobedient.

Yet from what different experiences had they come to the holy mount ? This was Moses' first visit to Palestine. Never before had he stood in the land of promise. He had seen it from afar at the close of his work, and now he had come to stand —

> " With glory wrapped around
>   On the hills he never trod,
> And speak of the strife which won our life,
>   With th' Incarnate Son of God." [2]

If it is possible in any measure to ap eciate the feelings

[1] 2 Kings 17 : 33   [2] Mr. Alexander.

of those who dwell in the light of heaven, by those of the dwellers on earth, one can imagine with what keen interest Moses stood upon that holy mount. He had seen it from afar, had led the people almost to the verge of possession, and then had died in the land of Moab, and received the high and holy honour of burial by God. Centuries had passed, and at last he stood within the land, not having won his way thereinto by the law as given to him on Sinai, but by the infinite grace of God as manifested in the Person of His Son, with Whom he now held converse.

Elijah's experience was very different. In all probability he was familiar with every part of the holy land. He had moved across it, founding the schools of the prophets, and endeavouring therein to prepare men to carry on his ministry when he had departed. He must have loved the land with a great love, wherein once he had stood —as he wrongfully thought—the only man loyal to God.

Now he was back in the land again, but under such different circumstances. He who did not die—for the chariots and horses of fire had separated him from Elisha, and the whirlwind had caught him to the saints' abode— had returned to the earth to talk of the one and only death with the Son of God.

II. The significance of their presence and passing, suggested by these facts of their personality, is of deep interest. The religion in which they were so deeply interested was about to be changed, not destroyed. The transfiguration of Jesus was symbolic of that which was taking place, through His presence and mission, in that old economy of which one of these men was the founder, and the other the restorer.

It is somewhat difficult to speak of the old form of religion, for if one speaks of it as Judaism, the mind of the believer associates it with the thought of bondage. There are many words which have a double meaning, and care must be taken to distinguish which meaning is intended, whenever the word is used. The word Judaism, used in reference to a system of bondage to form and ceremony, ever refers to the yoke with which the saints are not again to be entangled. Yet the very heart and soul of Judaism is the heart and soul of Christianity. It was the religion of the one God, the religion that insisted upon the Divine right to govern human life, and perpetually taught the truth of the nearness of God to the affairs of men. All that abides until this hour. The old forms and symbols and signs were perishing; and the old economy which Moses had founded, and to which Elijah had recalled the people, so far as it was outward, material, and temporal, was passing away. But the heart and soul of it remained, and was rediscovered in the mission of Christ. These men in the past had been great and powerful, because they had understood the spirit underlying the letter, and in converse with Jesus upon the mount they knew that nothing was passing away which was of value.

Moses stood upon that mount of glory the representative of the law. Elijah there represented prophecy. Moses for the law, with its requirements, its provisions, and its shadow of sacrifice. Elijah for prophecy,—not *foretelling* merely, but *forthtelling*,—that wonderful gift bestowed upon various men among the ancient people, and continued at intervals in unbroken succession, until it ceased with Malachi.

Moses' presence signified that in Jesus the shadows

of the law were all fulfilled and now withdrawn. In Jerusalem men were still fighting, not merely for the law of Moses, but for the traditions of the elders, and priests and leaders were still arguing about the tithe of mint and cummin, while here upon the mount was the great law-giver himself, by his presence acknowledging that this glorified One, Who should presently be crucified in the name of the law, did in Himself gather up all that was hinted at, suggested, included in the economy of the past.

The law, with its commands, its forbiddings, was fulfilled in the Person of Jesus; and the law-giver Moses, by the will of God had left the heavenly places to greet upon the mount of transfiguration the One, Who in His own Person, had magnified the law, and made it honourable.

So also with Elijah. He had spoken the word of God. From place to place he had journeyed, speaking to kings in their corruption, to courts in their degradation, and to individuals in their need, that one unceasing word, "Thus saith Jehovah."[1] He had certainly been one of the most remarkable men in the history of the nation from the prophetic standpoint. God had spoken in times past by divers portions in the prophets, but by no man had He said more to the nation than by Elijah.

And now he stood upon the mount in converse with One Who had said to His disciples, "I am the truth,"[2] and concerning Whom Peter, on a subsequent occasion, speaking under the inspiration of the Spirit, said, "To Him bear all the prophets witness."[3] Every word that had passed the lips of Elijah in the olden days had been but the spelling out in simple syllable and speech, of that

[1] I Kings 21: 19.   [2] John 14: 6.   [3] Acts 10: 43.

which was embodied in the Person of Christ; and he stood now upon the mount to acknowledge, that in this transfigured One, all the speech of heaven begins and ends that in Him every prophecy of the past is fulfilled, and that the prophet of the days to come, will gather from this Man and His teaching, his inspiration and his power.

They "spake of His exodus," [1] of His going out. The word here unfortunately translated "decease" signifies infinitely more than our Lord's death. It includes everything that was necessarily bound up in the thought of departure—His death, His resurrection, His ascension. His death was the first fact, but because "it was not possible that He should be holden of it," [2] resurrection was the necessary sequence, and if resurrection, having triumphed over death, then ascension to the heavenly places.

How much the word meant to these men! How familiar "exodus" must have been to Moses, carrying his memory back to that wonderful movement from Egypt. He would recall the moment of peril and of victory, when from imminent death God made a way of life through the cleft waters of the sea. Elijah, too, would comprehend the true significance of the word. What had his mission been but a leading out of the people, an "exodus" from a new slavery to a new freedom, in the government of Jehovah. Both these men had led in an exodus, and now they have come to speak of that of which those of the past were but a shadow. They talked with Him Who is "the Author and Perfecter of faith." [3] That word "Author" literally means a file-leader, the Man in front, Who makes a track through the forest in which all that come after Him shall walk in safety. His exodus was to be a passing through death into life, through the baptism of passion into the

[1] Luke 9: 31.   [2] Acts 2: 24.   [3] Heb. 12: 2.

infinite spaces of His Father's kingdom. The surging of
the waves upon the shore of old, would speak to Moses of
the waves and billows, that soon should break over the head
of Him with Whom he held speech upon the holy mount
as He should lead the way through death to life. Alone
He breasted the waves, alone He broke the pathway
through the forests. And until this moment those who
have believed in Him are following in the way He led
and because of His exodus, they also have theirs, and
are led out to the infinite reaches of the kingdom of the
heavens.

The presence of Elijah upon the mount, and his conversation with Jesus, was almost a more wonderful story.
His message to men had been that they should live the life
of righteousness, but this Man is about to give His life to
be the new dynamic of righteousness. Elijah had only
been able to tell men of the things of God, but this Man
will not only teach, but will energize, will Himself pass
into the lives of men, and give them power to do the things
that He shall tell them they ought to do. Moses and
Elijah talked to Him of His exodus, and found that in His
outgoing through death there should be the fulfilling of their
own dreams, the realization of their own ambitions.

If their presence meant much, their passing was also full
of significance. A cloud of glory overshadowed and
removed them, and in their removal taught the completion
of their work in Him. There was now no need for Moses,
nor yet for Elijah. All that the Mosaic economy foreshadowed found its substance in Him, and Moses may pass
back to the rest of the Father's house. All that Elijah had
heroically said in the midst of much opposition, with faltering and even failure, Christ is now to say with absolute
certainty, and never failing, and Elijah may pass back to

the celestial spaces, to wait the consummation of the work of Jesus.

A significant statement by Luke is worth passing notice in this connection. "When they were fully awake, they saw His glory, and the two men that stood with Him." [1] The significance of the statement is that the glory in which Moses and Elijah stood upon the mount was *His* glory. They stood, these saints of the old covenant, in the light in which they shall abide forever. There upon the mount stood these representatives of the service of the past. Moses had died with sadness in his heart. The people whom he had led for forty years, were still outside the promised land, and yet he had to lay down his work ere it was completed. Elijah was translated very quickly after the terrible experience under the juniper tree, and while the people were still living in idolatry, he had been called away. These men did their work, and laid it down unfinished, but God had gathered them into the glory of His final kingdom, and now upon the mount had given them the promise that all they had left undone would yet be perfectly accomplished.

So through all the ages He will gather His workers, and at the last, in the light of the final victory, they will understand the meaning of their work. Presently every one will have to lay down unfinished life's work. Nothing can be completed here. And yet, at last, no piece of work faithfully done will be lost. He will gather Moses and Elijah and all the company of His faithful servants, and show how their work merges into the work of Jesus, and there finds its crown and reward.

III.   The presence of these men suggests a message

[1] Luke 9: 32.

from heaven. The teaching of this last section is inferential rather than direct, but may not on that account be the less valuable. Looking upon them something is learned about the condition of the departed, something about their knowledge, and something about the central interest of their existence.

" There talked with Him two men, who were Moses and Elijah." [1] Only Luke states the matter exactly in this form, and the statement is of value. Note the absence of wings. " Two men," that is to say, they still were what they had been in the essential fact of their being. Their presence in heaven was not due to a change in essential nature.

Then, notice that they were in a conscious state. Their minds still followed the same line as when upon the earth, though now they saw and understood clearly. Matters at which Moses had looked in his own economy through a glass darkly, he now saw face to face. Gleams of truth that had fallen upon the soul of Elijah and compelled obedience, even while he knew there were infinite possibilities beyond which he could not fathom, now fell in full radiance upon his mind. The presence of these men suggested not merely existence after life, but conscious existence, and not conscious existence only, but the continuity of the same existence with enlarged powers.

It is evident that Peter, James, and John knew Moses and Elijah. How they knew them, of course, cannot be told. But the fact that they knew them suggests that the identity of personality is maintained in the world that lies beyond, and in some wonderful manner, men know those whom here they never saw. Men will certainly then know their own loved ones when they meet them in the Father's

[1] Luke 9: 30.

home. The holy mount lights for a moment the land where our loved ones wait for us. They are still human, they are still conscious, and they are what they were. We shall know them.

There is yet another suggestion here in the interest these men took in the earth and what was passing on it. They came and talked to Him of His exodus, spoke of the mystery of His passion, of the joy of His resurrection, of His loving lingering amid the ways of men, and His triumphant ascension to the Father's right hand. These are only suggestions. Sometimes the question is asked, if the loved ones in the heavens know what is going on upon the earth. The answer seems to be that upon occasion, under the express command of God, they are able to find their way back and watch the process of the spirits that yet move amid probationary things. It is sometimes declared that if this be so, then there must be sorrow in heaven. And why should men shrink from this conclusion? Faber was surely right when he said :—

> " There is no place where earth's sorrows
> Are more felt than up in heaven."

Let it be remembered, however, that it is always sorrow in the light of joy, the sorrow of a present sympathy with pain, in the knowledge that the pain moves towards a purpose which in its blessedness far outweighs the present endurance. Moses and Elijah could talk of His coming sorrow, because with Him they looked on to the joy that was yet to be revealed.

If to-day men pass through sorrow, and the loved ones beyond the vale, visiting them, feel the sorrow in comradeship, they also joy, knowing that presently the song of triumph shall end the sigh of trial.

" ' Hath it ever been granted those who have passed
  The river, to appear and show themselves,
Unchanged in form, in heart unchangeable,
  To loved ones they have left behind ? ' ' It is true
It hath been so.
      But only by His sovereign will and word
    Who holds the keys of Hades and of death,
    And opens, as He wills, the mortal eye
    To see the mysteries of things unseen.' "

[1] Bishop Bickersteth.

XVIII

THE DAZED DISCIPLES

HAVING considered the transfiguration of Jesus, and the presence and passing of Moses and Elijah, it now remains to turn the attention to the disciples, and this subject is of supreme interest. The principal purpose of the transfiguration is declared in the statement, " He was transfigured *before them*." [1]

The experience of the holy mount had its place in the process of the work of the Master, in that it was the fitting consummation of a life innocent in Childhood, and holy through all the testing of growth into Manhood. Born without sin, triumphing over every attack made upon Him by the powers of evil, He at last passed not by the way of death, but by that of transfiguration into communion with the spirits of just men made perfect, into the very presence of God.

Moreover the presence and passing of Moses and Elijah, representing as they did the great movements of the past, have been seen to be full of suggestiveness.

The aspect of the transfiguration, however, which is of supreme value, is that the disciples were taken to the mount, were permitted to behold His glory, to listen to His converse with Moses and Elijah, themselves to speak in the light of the glory, and to hear the answer of God to that speech.

The consideration proceeds along three lines. First, a

[1] Matt. 17 : 2.

246

contemplation of the men; secondly, a consideration of their speech; and thirdly, attention to the answer of heaven to the suggestion of Peter.

I. The names of Peter, James and John are associated on more than one occasion, and the fact certainly must have significance. Very many reasons have been suggested for the fact that the Master took these men to certain places to which the other disciples were not taken. Without discussing those theories, one reason may be considered. To discover this it will be helpful to call to mind the occasions upon which it happened. They are three in number. These men were taken to the house of Jairus, to the mount of transfiguration, to the garden of Gethsemane.

In each case they were brought into the presence of death, and in that fact lies a partial solution of the problem. Peter's attitude towards death was revealed in the memorable conversation with his Lord chronicled in Matthew.[1] While Jesus had spoken of a kingdom and keys, Peter had listened with calm complacency, but when He proceeded to speak of death upon a cross, Peter had been strangely moved, and had exclaimed, " Be it far from Thee, Lord." [2] Thus it will be seen that he had followed Jesus to the point of death, and then had halted. This distinctly proves that Peter had no true conception of his Master's attitude towards death.

Mark gives the account of the coming of James and John to Jesus, and their asking that when He should come into His kingdom they might sit one on His right hand and one on His left. In great pity and love the Master had looked at them and said: " Ye know not what ye ask. Are ye able to drink the cup that I drink? or to be baptized

[1] Matt. 16: 14–19. [2] Matt. 16: 21–23.

with the baptism that I am baptized with?" They answered,
"We are able,"[1] feeling that there was no cup that He should
drink that they were not able to share with Him, and no
baptism through which He should pass in which they were
unable to have fellowship with Him. They were "sons
of thunder" and what could make them afraid? If He
could pass through baptism, so also could they. If He
were able to drink some strange cup, so also were they.
James and John had followed Jesus to the point of death,
and dared all results. Peter was afraid. James and John
were blindly courageous. Both attitudes were wrong.
None of these men understood the death towards which
the Master moved, nor the triumph that awaited Him
through death. They must be taught, and the teaching
began before their speech revealed their attitude, and was
continued after the experience of the holy mount. The
sequence of the teaching is most clearly revealed in the
Gospel of Mark.

First there is recorded the story of the visit to the house
of Jairus. "He suffered no man to follow with Him, save
Peter, and James, and John. . . . He, having put
them all forth, taketh the father of the child and her mother
and them that were with Him, and goeth in where the child
was. And taking the child by the hand, He saith unto
her, Talitha cumi; which is, being interpreted, Damsel, I
say unto thee, Arise."[2] She obeyed, and He handed her
to her parents. That scene, proving Christ's Lordship
over death, was witnessed by Peter, James and John.

Then follows the account of the transfiguration, and the
fact that these same three men listened to the converse
with Moses and Elijah concerning His own death.[3]

And finally the experience in Gethsemane, concerning

[1] Mark 10: 35-40.   [2] Mark 5: 37-41.   [3] Mark 9: 2.

which Mark says, " And He taketh with Him Peter and James and John, and began to be greatly amazed, and sore troubled. And He saith unto them, My soul is exceeding sorrowful even unto death : abide ye here, and watch." [1]

Thus it is at once seen that each time He took these men aside, He conducted them into the presence of death, and He revealed His threefold attitude towards death. In the house of Jairus He was Master of death. On the mount of transfiguration He stood superior to death, transfigured, and yet conversing of death to be accomplished. In Gethsemane He bowed and yielded Himself to death— a strange progression. These men, of whom one was afraid, and the other two imagined there was nothing to fear, were led through this private and special ministry of infinite patience, that they might see the Master's connection with death. In the house of Jairus He addressed the dead child, using the familiar speech of a living love, " Little lamb, I say unto thee, arise." [2] There was no thunder about His voice, no magnificence of majesty, suggesting the assertion of authority, but the sweet whisper of an infinite Love, in response to which the spirit of the little one came back from the spirit land to its clay tabernacle. He stood in the home evidently Master of death, with a strength and dignity that needed no outward pageantry.

Then upon the mount He was seen to be in His own Person absolutely superior to death, passing without its touch into the breadth and beauty of life in the places where death never comes, and yet there talking of it as an experience through which He would soon pass.

Then, strange and marvellous thing, in Gethsemane He came towards the hour of His dying, and as He approached

[1] Mark 14 : 33, 34.   [2] Mark 5 : 41.

that hour, said to those same men, " My soul is exceeding sorrowful even unto death." [1]   To Peter and James and John were these visions granted.

Thus the presence of these men on the mount was part of a perfect scheme.   These were experiences which the Master was storing for them, which should have their explanation in days that were yet to come.   Presently, when the work of the Cross was accomplished, and the Paraclete had been poured upon them, these men would begin to understand what happened in the house of Jairus, upon the holy mount, and most wonderful of all, how that when His soul was sorrowful unto death, they had beheld the Master of death bowing to death, in order that He might slay death.   After that, Peter writing a letter, and speaking of his own death, did not so name it, but borrowing the word he heard upon the mount, wrote, " after my exodus." [2] Thus death was transfigured for these men through the patient process of a special training which the Master gave them.

II.   In turning from this consideration of the men, to give attention to Peter's words uttered in the glory of the mount, it is important to notice their condition at the time. Of Peter, Mark says, " He knew not what to answer; for they became sore afraid," [3] and Luke affirms " not knowing what he said." [4]   These statements confirm the opinion that the whole speech was a blunder.

Luke's account alone makes reference to the fact that the disciples had slept.   It is probable that here, as in the garden, they fell asleep while the Master was at prayer. Awakening, and while yet in a half-dazed condition, they looked upon the marvellous scene before them ; remember-

[1] Mark 14: 34.   [2] 2 Pet. 1: 15.   [3] Mark 9: 6.   [4] Luke 9: 33.

ing, as people waking suddenly so often first remember matters but recently impressed upon the mind, the six days of estrangement which had followed upon their shunning of the Cross. How changed the scene and the Master. Jesus, Whose face had borne the marks of an infinite sorrow during those days of silence, now stood in the midst of splendour such as they had never beheld. His face shone with the brightness of the sun, and the seamless robe, which, perchance, love had woven for Him, was white and glistering, beyond the glories of the snows of Hermon. How everything would rush back upon the minds of the men. Peter would remember the rebuke that had fallen from his Master's lips, " Get thee behind me, Satan," [1] and then the cause of that rebuke, the fact that he had desired for his Master not a Cross, but a kingdom. And now behold that loved One, just as Peter would fain see Him, and desired to keep Him. In the mind of the waking man there would be the contrast between this and that ; between the splendour of the glory, and the fact of converse with heaven's own inhabitants ; and that strange announcement of a week ago, concerning Jerusalem, and the chief priests' hatred, and the culminating death. The outcome of this contrast was the speech of the man : " Lord, it is good for us to be here "—not there, but here. Talk no more of the Cross, but stay here upon the mount in glory. " If Thou wilt, I will make here three tabernacles, one for Thee, and one for Moses, and one for Elijah." [2]

How strangely confused the mind of the man was, is evident by this suggestion. Imagine making tabernacles for Moses and Elijah, to say nothing of the Master. Had he said, Let us stay here and make three tabernacles, one for Thee, and one for me. and one for James and John,

[1] Matt. 16: 23.   [2] Matt. 17: 4.

it would have had more of reason in it. What did Moses and Elijah want with tabernacles? The word tabernacle simply means a booth, or boughs made into a shelter for present use. Peter's suggestion was that he should go to the trees and bear back boughs with which to construct three temporary resting-places. Think of Moses sojourning in a tabernacle, or Elijah settling down to rest in a booth. The whole suggestion is grotesque. " He knew not what to answer," and for him, as for all men in like circumstances, it were infinitely better to say nothing. He had lost the sense of the spiritual, and his mind, moving wholly within the realm of material things, imagined that the spirits of the just made perfect could find shelter in tabernacles constructed of boughs.

There was, however, a darker side to the mistake of Peter. When he suggested building three tabernacles, one for the Master, one for Moses and one for Elijah, he seems to have been forgetful of his own confession made but eight days before. Jesus had asked, "Who do men say that the Son of Man is?" and had received the reply, "Some say John the Baptist; some, Elijah; and others, Jeremiah, or one of the prophets." Then, in answer to His second question, "Who say ye that I am?" Peter had placed his Lord in a position far higher than that of Elijah, " Thou art the Christ, the Son of the living God." [1] Yet now he suggests making a tabernacle for Jesus, and one for Moses, and one for Elijah, thus putting his Master upon the same level with these men of the past.

The mistake is by no means an obsolete one. Men are still attempting to make tabernacles, one for Christ, one for Confucius, one for Buddha. Beware of such blasphemy.

[1] Matt. 16: 12–16.

More harm was done in 1893 in the world's parliament of religions at Chicago than has yet been undone. Men from the East, who then heard arguments to show the comparison between the religion of Jesus and that of others, while perhaps to-day thinking no less of Christ than before, yet cling more tenaciously than ever to the system in which they have been brought up. It is ever dangerous to allow that it is possible for a moment to put the best of religious teachers in comparison with the Christ. One for Jesus, one for Moses, and one for Elijah is utterly and hopelessly wrong. The man who suggests it has lost the sense of the absolute and sovereign supremacy of Jesus Christ over all teachers.

III. Matthew describes the cloud which overshadowed the mount as a bright cloud. Darkness glorified, shadow illuminated! Wherever there is a bright cloud, the brightness is proof of the light behind. Who has not seen the clouds piled mountain high on the horizon, lit with gorgeous splendour? Only the clouds are seen, but the lights upon them speak of the sun shining in power behind them. A bright cloud overshadowed them, a symbolic cloud. The transfiguration is passing, the outshining of the splendour of His presence is to cease, and the clouds are gathering over the green hill far away, but they are smitten through and through with light. It is impossible to hide the glory again from these men. They will never again wholly forget the radiant vision. James will pass to his martyr baptism with that glory still upon his mind, and that holy mount will abide with Peter until, his work ended, he, too, shall enter the cloud, and beyond it, find the never-fading light.

It was indeed a bright cloud, but it overshadowed them

while yet Peter was speaking. It interrupted and silenced the speech of earth, that the speech of heaven might be heard. What Peter would have said had he been allowed to proceed, none can tell. While he was yet speaking the cloud came. This blundering speech of men must be interrupted, this gross misunderstanding of the Divine must be corrected, this incoherent prayer of a disciple but half awake, must be hushed.

Out of the bright cloud came the heavenly voice, and there are three matters of importance to notice in the words spoken. First, the identification of this Man Who has been seen in resplendent glory—" This is My beloved Son "; secondly, the announcement of the Divine satisfaction—" In Whom I am well pleased "; and thirdly, the injunction laid upon these men, and upon the Church and all the ages through them—" Hear ye Him." [1]

First, identification—" This is My beloved Son." Moses and Elijah were servants, this is the Son. The messages of the economies of the past were for the unfolding of the law, He and His message constitute the epiphany of grace.

Then the statement of Divine satisfaction—" In Whom I am well pleased." God had said this before at the baptism in Jordan, when the private life of Christ drew to a close, and His public life was beginning. And now that the second stage had come to an end, when the public life was closing, and the sacrificial and atoning work beginning, as He was about to pass from the culminating glory to take His way into the shadows and into death, again God said " I am well pleased." Satisfied with the private life in Nazareth, with the honest toil of the carpenter's shop, with the years of public ministry, with the deeds of love

[1] Matt. 17 : 5.

that had been scattered over all the pathway, the whole life of Jesus from beginning to end had given satisfaction to the heart of God.

Then the injunction—" Hear ye Him." Moses and Elijah have passed. Let there be no tabernacle built for Moses; his mission is ended. " This is My Son." Let there be no attempt to retain the fiery reformer; Elijah's work is over. " This is My Son." " God, having of old time spoken unto the fathers in the prophets by divers portions and in divers manners, hath at the end of these days spoken unto us in His Son," [1] " Hear Him." No other voice is needed. Let them be hushed in silence. Let Moses and Elijah pass back to the upper spaces. The dwellers upon earth have the speech of the Son, and nothing else is needed—" Hear Him."

It was a word of rebuke silencing the blunder of Peter. It was a word of comfort by which God attested the value and virtue of Christ. It was a word of encouragement, for if the speech of Moses and Elijah were over, and their presence had passed within the veil, the Son is to abide, and through all the exigencies and intricacies of the coming days His voice, sweet as the music of heaven, clear as the voice of a brother man, shall lead through the mists to the dawn of the eternal light.

What wonderful effect was produced upon these men by this scene. James died sealing his testimony with his blood, a martyr. Nothing more is recorded of him. John takes his way to long life, and in his writing, says, " The Word became flesh, and dwelt among us . . . full of grace and truth." [2] The parenthesis follows as a flash of glory from his pen, as he remembered the mount, he wrote, " We beheld His glory, glory as of the only begotten from the

[1] Heb. 1 : 1, 2.   [2] John 1 : 14.

Father." John can never forget. Peter in his last epistle wrote, " We did not follow cunningly devised fables, when we made known unto you the power and coming of our Lord Jesus Christ, but we were eye-witnesses of His majesty. For He received from God the Father honour and glory, when there was borne such a voice to Him by the Majestic Glory, This is My beloved Son, in Whom I am well pleased: and this voice we ourselves heard borne out of heaven, when we were with Him in the holy mount." [1]

Thus Peter and John to the end of their ministry were influenced by the vision of that wonderful night, and influenced supremely by the speech of heaven and the bright cloud that overshadowed them.

To many there comes no mount of transfiguration, but there is for all the speech of the Son. If the majority are not called to some mount of vision where they may behold the glory as these three men beheld it, yet to every soul amid the multitudes of the redeemed He speaks in every passing day. God forbid that the babel of earth's voices should drown the accents of His still small voice. To His children He speaks softly and sweetly in the innermost recesses of the heart day by day, saying ever, " This is the way, walk ye in it," [2] and out of God's heaven God's message ever speaks, " This is My Son, hear ye Him." [3]

[1] 2 Peter 1 : 16–18.   [2] Isa. 30 : 21.   [3] Matt. 17 : 5.

XIX

THE THINGS THAT REMAINED

AFTER some heavenly vision it is well that a pause should be made, and the question asked, What is left when the actual vision has passed, and what is the result of the vision? After the bright cloud that interrupted the ignorant speech of the disciples, and after the heavenly voice had ceased, what happened? When the cloud overshadowed them, and they heard the voice of God, they fell on their faces in fear. When they opened their eyes and looked around, what was left? The answer to that question is to be found in a few minutes' pause on the mountainside, whence the glory had passed away, and then in a descent from the mountain in the company of Jesus.

I. The transfiguration had been a night scene, and the whiteness of the light radiating from the Person of Christ had been more brilliant and glorious than the dazzling splendour of the snows on Hermon; but the light had passed, and morning was breaking in the eastern sky, with its suggestion of the coming day. But a few moments ago Jesus seemed to be no longer Jesus of Nazareth, but the veritable Son of God—God the Son. But a few moments ago Moses and Elijah were there. But a few moments ago was heard the incoherent suggestion of Peter—"Let us make here three tabernacles." All this has now passed, and waiting in the quiet hush of the solemn morning hour, upon the mount, see what follows the transfiguration.

Moses and Elijah have gone, gone also is the flashing

splendour that lit the night, silenced is the speech that fell upon the astonished ears of Peter, James, and John.

Imagine the disciples for a moment as they looked around them,—the silence after the speech, the loneliness after comradeship with celestial visitors, and the usualness of everything. "Lifting up their eyes, they saw no one, save Jesus only." [1]

It was a solemn moment. Moses and Elijah had passed, the glory had vanished, the heavenly voice was silent, and they saw "Jesus only." He was the same Jesus that they had known. Oh, the exquisite beauty of the statement. "Jesus came and touched them and said, Arise, and be not afraid." [2] It was the old familiar touch, the same touch that they had felt so often before. Who shall say that when talking with them, His hand had not rested upon them; or walking with them, His hand had not arrested them, and stayed them for a moment while He spoke to them? The old touch, the human touch of the Son of Man, a Man among them once again, just as they had known Him. It was the old familiar voice, the same Jesus, "Jesus only."

The same, but yet so utterly different! "Jesus only," containing in His own Person as now they knew, a glory that was hidden, a veiled splendour that at any moment might flash out, yet hidden for some inscrutable reason. How strangely these men were perplexed will be gathered from all the history of the days that followed the transfiguration until Calvary was reached. They never could think of Him again as they had thought of Him before. For once they had been permitted to look at Him changed, altered, transfigured, shining with all the splendour of that indwelling glory; and even though He had come back to the old form, and the voice of their Friend and Teacher, and the

[1] Matt. 17 : 8.   [2] Matt. 17 : 7.

touch of the Man Jesus, they knew that underneath the veil of that humanity there was hidden a radiant splendour.

In those last days how they would watch Him, and wonder whether at some moment the glory would not flame again in the sight of men. He was never the same again because they had seen more of Him. He was to them "Jesus only," forevermore the Centre of all things. He remained, the One Who fulfilled the promises of the past, and realized all the hopes created by the messages of God. And not merely was He the One in Whom all past history culminated, but the One from Whom all future history should take its form. From that moment until to-day every upward movement, every movement that has had for its issue the bettering of human condition, the ennobling of the race, all have found their inspiration in the thought, teaching, character, and Person of Christ. He was the essential Light of men, the Light of the world, and all the men who have flung light across the pathway of human life from that moment until now, have not been *the Light*, but light-bearers, and they have lit their torches from the Light, the Son of God.

"Jesus only"—finality, God's perfect speech. All the new in the future will be but the more perfect comprehension of Him, and the great ones of all the coming days will learn what He meant, when in simple speech He spoke great eternal verities, which the listening ears of men did not at the time perfectly understand.

If the first impression produced upon the minds of the apostles as they looked around them was that of silence, now that the voice had ceased; and loneliness, now that Moses and Elijah had gone; and the usualness of everything, now that the unusual had passed away; the answer to that first impression was found in the presence of "Jesus only," for if no heavenly voice sounded, His speech was heard. If Moses and Elijah had passed, He remained, the perpetual Comrade of saintly souls for all the future. If the unusualness had ceased, they began to find that they were now in the company of One Who could transmute the usual into the unusual, Who could pass with them into the valley, into the home life, into the service of all the coming years until the end; and touching the common-places of life, make them flash with splendour, as His body of humiliation shone with glory upon that mount of trans-figuration. This was the first thing that these men realized as they rose from their overcoming fear. The vision had passed, Moses and Elijah had gone, the voice was silent, "Jesus only" remained.

II. It is most interesting to trace what happened as these men left the mount. First, notice that as they were com-ing down with Him, their same Lord and Saviour, the One they had known so well during the three years of ministry, He charged them that they should tell the vision to no man, and there is deepest significance in the command. He enjoined silence upon them because it would be im-possible for them to tell aright the story of the things they had seen, for such visions always transcend explanation. There was a limit put upon their silence; " Tell the vision to no man, until the Son of Man be risen from the dead." [1] The real reason, undoubtedly, was that these men were to wait until the Holy Spirit Himself should equip them for the telling of that story.

But other things lay within that injunction of silence. The theme for the coming days was not to be the theme

[1] Matt. 17 : 9.

of glory, but of the Cross; and Matthew inserts here the fact that He told them again the story of the Cross that had so alarmed Peter six days before the transfiguration. The vision of the glory had its place and purpose, but it must pass away. The multitudes were waiting, the lunatic was in the valley, the Cross and the exodus were before Him. The mountain was the place of vision, but yonder lay the pathway of accomplishment, and in order that His heart might be set upon His exodus, and that they might come as much as possible into comradeship with Him in His great work, nothing was to be said of this vision. It was to be one of the sealed stories during the days of suffering. After the triumph of His resurrection and ascension, then it might be remembered, understood, and told in all its meaning.

Probably there was another reason why silence was enjoined on these men. Visions are of no value save to those who see them. No help comes from a recital of some vision granted to another child of God. There is a Divine intention and purpose in that fact. The fact of the vision is not denied. What is affirmed is this, that the vision given to one is not for another, and the repetition of it cannot help another man. The vision of God granted immediately to the soul of man is for the man to whom it is granted. No man can tell his own vision and help another as that vision helped him, so it is infinitely better to be silent about the deepest things that God says to the heart. Each must for himself have the vision, if it is to be of use and of blessing. Peter and James and John were taken to the mount of transfiguration for a set purpose, in order that their conception of death might be changed and altered, that these men who boasted or feared might come to see— as they had seen in the house of Jairus and as they were to

see in the garden of Gethsemane,—His outlook upon death.
The telling of that story of transfiguration to others would
not be a help to them, until the Holy Spirit should take the
story up and make it part of the unveiling of the glory of
the Christ, then out of it should come help for all the
Church to the end of the age.

Now they have reached the valley, and there are two
things to be noticed. First, the group around the lunatic;
and second, the fellowship of the shekel.

There is a touch of great beauty in Luke's account of
the man who brought his son to Jesus, not to be found in
Matthew or Mark, which flings a wonderful light upon the
whole picture. Luke records that the man said to Jesus,
not only " This is my son," but " mine only child," [1] and
the Greek word is " my only begotten son," the very word
that is used of Christ's relation to God; and here it is used
of this devil-possessed child.

It seems to have been a symbolic moment, proving the
necessity for the descent from the mount and the approach
to Calvary. There in the valley, foremost in the scene,
was the father with his boy, his only begotten child; round
about were the disciples, defeated, absolutely unable to do
anything with such a case as this; and around the disciples
was a circle of sceptical scribes ready to taunt these men
with their failure. It was a picture of the human race, the
only begotten child of man, mastered by evil, and no one
to deliver. A father's love was unable to break the slavery;
the loyalty of disciples, as disciples merely, was quite help-
less; the cheap cynical sneer of the unbeliever did nothing
to relieve the suffering of the devil-possessed boy. Such
was the scene in the valley.

Looking upon it one seems to see approaching, the Only

[1] Luke 9 : 38.

begotten of the Father in Whom He is well pleased, Who speaks with the voice of the authority of heaven, Who will act with all the power of the Godhead behind Him; and the only begotten child of man, beaten, bleeding, and bruised upon the highway and none to deliver.

Hear the words of Christ, which come as a rebuke to the faithless generation,—" Bring him hither to Me." [1] For that moment He left the mountain, for that work He turned His back for the second time upon the glory, for that need He declined to have tabernacles made which would detain Him on the mount, while here in the valley humanity was suffering.

" Bring him hither to Me." Now mark His mastery over all things. " Bring him hither to Me "—Master of men. He rebuked the devil, " and the demon went out from him: and the boy was cured from that hour " [2]— Master of demons. The only begotten son of a man was cured by the only begotten Son of God; and Peter, James, and John and the rest stood round and saw the wondrous work that never could have been performed had Jesus stayed upon the mount of vision.

Then note what follows. They went down to Capernaum, and the men who were gathering the shekel for the Temple came to Peter. It is quite a mistake to imagine that the men who asked for this money were collecting a tax for the Roman power. What they were collecting was the half-shekel for the support of the Temple, which according to the old Mosaic economy, was paid at the taking of the census. But gradually it had become an annual payment, and it was for this purely voluntary tax that the Temple authorities came to Peter and said, " Doth not your Teacher pay the half-shekel?" and he answered,

[1] Matt. 17 : 17.   [2] Matt. 17 : 18.

" Yea." [1] It has been suggested that he made a mistake, but no doubt he simply stated a fact. Most probably that half-shekel had been paid during the three years that had passed whenever it had been demanded. Yet Christ had a lesson to teach, and speaking to Peter said, " The kings of the earth, from whom do they receive toll or tribute? from their sons or from strangers?" And when Peter said, " From strangers," Jesus said unto him, " Therefore the sons are free." [2] He meant to teach Peter by this that He was what Peter, but a few days ago, had said He was, the Son of God. He was the King's Son, the Prince of the Temple. There was no need for Him to pay the half-shekel. By His nature and position He was exempt from this contribution to the Temple, nevertheless—and whatever else is forgotten in this study, catch this thought,—" Lest we cause them to stumble," [3] I will pay it. The word is " lest we become a scandal to them." These men would not understand His claim of freedom from the payment of the half-shekel, and rather than cause them to stumble He forfeited His personal right.

Then mark what He said, " Go thou to the sea, and cast a hook, and take up the fish that first cometh up; and when thou hast opened his mouth, thou shalt find a shekel." A shekel? But they wanted a half-shekel. " That take, and give unto them for Me and thee." There are no sweeter words in the gospel than these, " for Me and thee,"—comradeship, companionship, fellowship with Peter, even to the contribution to the Temple.

Oh, how wondrously was Peter discovering his Master, and how when the Spirit came, and lit up these events, did he love Him and worship Him! King of glory on the

[1] Matt. 17 : 24.   [2] Matt. 17 : 25, 26.   [3] Matt. 17 : 27.

mount, Master of human life and of devils in the valley, Comrade of every child of His love, sharing responsibility even to the payment of taxes. He need not have paid the shekel, but He did so with Peter for two reasons: first, not to be misunderstood of the men who collected the tax; and secondly, that He might enter into companionship to the last detail of the commonplaces of daily life with His own disciples. These are the things that follow the mount.

In closing this series there yet remain one or two inferences worth gathering. Although only three disciples saw the transfiguration, while eight others who were loyal in their love and service were shut out, yet not one of these eight was excluded from that which remained when the transfiguration glory had passed. "Jesus only" was not only for Peter, James and John, but for all the rest, and by this time they have seen Him in His glory, so the vision was only postponed.

And concerning these men, the words of the Master in another connection have application: "Blessed are they that have not seen, and yet have believed."[1] There are still those to whom no visions come, no moments upon the mount suffused with a glory that never was on land or sea. Let such not envy the men of vision. It may be that the vision is given to strengthen a faith that else were weak. It is to the people who can live along the line of what others call the commonplace, and yet trust, that the Master says, "Blessed are they that have not seen, and yet have believed." The morning will reveal the reason why visions are given to some and not to others, but if tempted to wish for such an experience as these men had, let it never be forgotten that the majority of the

[1] John 20: 29.

apostles had no share in it, and yet they fulfilled His will and reached His home, and their names also flash with splendour from the foundations of the city that God is building. Let those who have had no vision trust Him still. Let such as have seen a vision walk in its light, but remember that more precious than the vision is that which remains when the vision passes, the common heritage of all the disciples,—" Jesus only."

Lastly, it is all-important to remember that all mounts of vision, save the last, must be left, for the valleys. In the valleys to-day are men possessed of devils; and the scepticism of cheap literature, of which there is much abroad, never took a devil out of a man. It is all in succession to the sneer of the scribe and Pharisees. Jesus Christ standing in the valley to-day can say as He said then, " Bring him hither to Me."

It is the challenge of His might and the voice of His love, and the business of the disciples is to bring such to Him. He will still cast out the demon as He ever did. Men must leave the mountain for the valley, but they can carry the mountain with them into the valley. They who visit the mount may pass back into the commonplaces of life in new power, taking with them the truth, that behind the commonplace lies the light that flashed upon the mount of transfiguration. Happy are the men who can say with Peter on the mount, " Lord, it is good to be here "—and then, with not a word about the tabernacles, pass to the valley with Him; there they will see Him casting out a demon, and repeat, " Lord, it is good to be *here* also." Then, returning to the commonplace, to the payment of taxes, they will hear Him say, " For Me and thee "; and will reply, " Lord, it is good to be *here* also." Whether on the mountain, in the valley, or in the home, wherever

He is, it is good to be.   No house is common where He dwells, no valley is dark and hopeless through which He passes, and no solitary mountain height on which He stands is without possibility of vision.   Man's one safety lies in being with, and listening to " Jesus only."

From the resplendent glory of this Crisis in which, in the fulfillment of His human life, He has faced anew the fact of His dying, the Christ passes on towards the Cross, with the tread of One Who having conquered goes forth to yet sterner battles, and more glorious triumphs.

BOOK V

THE CRUCIFIXION

XX. The Approach
XXI. The Sufferings of Christ
XXII. Sin Unveiled, Grace Outshining
XXIII. The Kingly Exodus
XXIV. The Representative Crowds

.   .   .   .   *As the load*
Immense, intolerable, of the world's sin,
Casting its dreadful shadow high as heaven,
Deep as Gehenna, nearer and more near
Grounded at last upon that Sinless Soul
With all its crushing weight and killing curse,
Then first, from all eternity then first,
From His beloved Son the Father's face
Was slowly averted, and its light eclipsed;
And through the midnight broke the Sufferer's groan,
Eli, Eli, lama sabachthani?
The echo was the mockeries of hell,
Reverberate in human lips. We heard,
And shudder'd. Gabriel lean'd on me a space,
And hid his face within my vesture's folds,
As if the sight were all too terrible
Even for archangelic faith. But now
Once more the agonizing Victim moan'd,
Uttering His anguish in one dreadful plaint,
I thirst; His last: for, when the cooling sponge
Had touch'd His lips, a loud and different cry,
As if of triumph, It is finish'd, rang
Upon our startled ears; and with a child's
Confiding tender trustfulness, that breathed
Father, to Thy hands I commend My Spirit,
He bow'd His head, and yielded up the ghost."
                —E. H. Bickersteth.
                " Yesterday, To-day, and Forever."

And as they came out, they found a man of Cyrene, Simon by name: him they compelled to go with them, that he might bear His Cross.

And when they were come unto a place called Golgotha, that is to say, The place of a skull, they gave Him wine to drink mingled with gall: and when He had tasted it, He would not drink. And when they had crucified Him, they parted His garments among them, casting lots; and they sat and watched Him there. And they set up over His head His accusation written, THIS IS JESUS THE KING OF THE JEWS. Then are there crucified with Him two robbers, one on the right hand and one on the left. And they that passed by railed on Him, wagging their heads, and saying, Thou that destroyest the temple, and buildest it in three days, save Thyself: if Thou art the Son of God, come down from the Cross. In like manner also the chief priests mocking Him, with the scribes and elders, said, He saved others; Himself He cannot save. He is the King of Israel; let Him now come down from the Cross, and we will believe on Him. He trusteth on God; let Him deliver Him now, if He desireth Him: for He said, I am the Son of God. And the robbers also that were crucified with Him cast upon Him the same reproach.

Now from the sixth hour there was darkness over all the land until the ninth hour. And about the ninth hour Jesus cried with a loud voice, saying Eli, Eli, lama sabachthani? that is, My God, My God, why hast Thou forsaken Me? And some of them that stood there, when they heard it, said, This Man calleth Elijah. And straightway one of them ran, and took a sponge, and filled it with vinegar, and put it on a reed, and gave Him to drink. And the rest said, Let be; let us see whether Elijah cometh to save Him. And Jesus cried again with a loud voice, and yielded up His Spirit. And behold, the veil of the temple was rent in two from the top to the bottom; and the earth did quake; and the rocks were rent; and the tombs were opened; and many bodies of the saints that had fallen asleep were raised; and coming forth out of the tombs after His resurrection they entered into the holy city and appeared unto many. Now the centurion, and they that were with him watching Jesus, when they saw the earthquake, and the things that were done, feared exceedingly, saying, Truly this was the Son of God. And many women were there beholding from afar, who had followed Jesus from Galilee, ministering unto Him: among whom was Mary Magdalene, and Mary the mother of James and Joses, and the mother of the sons of Zebedee.—*Matt. 27 : 32–56.*

*　　*　　*　　*　　*　　*　　*

And they bring Him unto the place Golgotha, which is, being interpreted, The place of a skull. And they offered Him wine mingled with myrrh : but He received it not. And they crucify Him, and part His garments among them, casting lots upon them, what each should take. And it was the third hour, and they crucified Him. And the superscription of His accusation was written over, THE KING OF THE JEWS. And with Him they crucify two robbers ; one on His right hand, and one on His left. And they that passed by railed on Him, wagging their heads, and saying, Ha ! Thou that destroyest the temple, and buildest it in three days, save Thyself, and come down from the Cross. In like manner also the chief priests mocking Him among themselves with the scribes said, He saved others ; Himself He cannot save. Let the Christ, the King of Israel, now come down from the Cross, that we may see and believe. And they that were crucified with Him reproached Him.

And when the sixth hour was come, there was darkness over the whole land until the ninth hour. And at the ninth hour Jesus cried with a loud voice, Eloi, Eloi, lama sabachthani ? which is, being interpreted, My God, My God, why hast Thou forsaken Me ? And some of them that stood by, when they heard it, said, Behold, He calleth Elijah. And one ran, and filling a sponge full of vinegar, put it on a reed, and gave Him to drink, saying, Let be ; let us see whether Elijah cometh to take Him down. And Jesus uttered a loud voice, and gave up the ghost. And the veil of the temple was rent in two from the top to the bottom. And when the centurion, who stood by over against Him, saw that He so gave up the ghost, he said, Truly this man was the Son of God. And there were also women beholding from afar : among whom were both Mary Magdalene, and Mary the mother of James the less and of Joses, and Salome ; who, when He was in Galilee, followed Him, and ministered unto Him ; and many other women that came up with Him unto Jerusalem.—*Mark 15 : 22–41.*

*　　*　　*　　*　　*　　*　　*

And there followed Him a great multitude of the people, and of women who bewailed and lamented Him. But Jesus turning unto them said, Daughters of Jerusalem, weep not for Me, but weep for yourselves, and for your children. For behold, the days are coming, in which they shall say, Blessed are the barren, and the wombs that never bare, and the breasts that never gave suck. Then shall they begin to say to the mountains, Fall on us ; and to the hills, Cover us. For if they do these things in the green tree, what shall be done in the dry ?

And there were also two others, malefactors, led with Him to be put to death.

And when they came unto the place which is called, The skull, there they crucified Him, and the malefactors, one on the right hand and the other on the left. And Jesus said, Father, forgive them ; for they know not what they do. And parting His garments among them, they cast lots. And the people stood beholding. And the rulers also scoffed at Him, saying, He saved others ; let Him save Himself, if this is the Christ of God, His chosen. And the soldiers also mocked Him, coming to Him, offering Him vinegar, and saying, If Thou art the King of the Jews, save Thyself. And there was also a superscription over Him, THIS IS THE KING OF THE JEWS.

And one of the malefactors that were hanged railed on Him, saying, Art not Thou the Christ ? save Thyself and us. But the other answered, and rebuking him said, Dost thou not even fear God, seeing thou art in the same condemnation ? And we indeed justly ; for we receive the due reward of our deeds : but this Man hath done nothing amiss. And he said, Jesus, remember me when Thou comest in Thy kingdom. And He said unto him, Verily I say unto thee, To-day shalt thou be with Me in Paradise.

And it was now about the sixth hour, and a darkness came over the whole land until the ninth hour, the sun's light failing : and the veil of the temple was rent in the midst. And Jesus, crying with a loud voice said, Father, into Thy hands I commend My spirit : and having said this, He gave up the ghost. And when the centurion saw what was done, he glorified God, saying, Certainly this was a righteous man. And all the multitudes that came together to this sight, when they beheld the things that were done, returned smiting their breasts. And all His acquaintance, and the women that followed with Him from Galilee, stood afar off, seeing these things.—*Luke 23 : 27–49.*

*   *   *   *   *   *

They took Jesus therefore : and He went out, bearing the Cross for Himself, unto the place called The place of a skull, which is called in Hebrew Golgotha : where they crucified Him, and with Him two others, on either side one, and Jesus in the midst. And Pilate wrote

a title also, and put it on the Cross.   And there was written, JESUS
OF NAZARETH, THE KING OF THE JEWS.   This title therefore read
many of the Jews, for the place where Jesus was crucified was nigh
to the city ; and it was written in Hebrew, and in Latin, and in
Greek.   The chief priests of the Jews therefore said to Pilate,
Write not, The King of the Jews ; but, that He said, I am King of
the Jews.   Pilate answered, What I have written I have written.

The soldiers therefore, when they had crucified Jesus, took His
garments, and made four parts, to every soldier a part ; and also the
coat : now the coat was without seam, woven from the top throughout.   They said therefore one to another, Let us not rend it, but
cast lots for it, whose it shall be : that the scripture might be fulfilled, which saith,

> They parted My garments among them,
> And upon My vesture did they cast lots.

These things therefore the soldiers did.   But there were standing
by the Cross of Jesus His mother, and His mother's sister, Mary
the wife of Clopas, and Mary Magdalene.   When Jesus therefore saw His mother, and the disciple standing by whom He loved,
He saith unto His mother, Woman, behold thy son !   Then saith
He to the disciple, Behold, thy mother !   And from that hour the
disciple took her unto his own home.

After this Jesus, knowing that all things are now finished, that
the scripture might be accomplished, saith, I thirst.   There was set
there a vessel full of vinegar : so they put a sponge full of the vinegar
upon hyssop, and brought it to His mouth.   When Jesus therefore
had received the vinegar, He said, It is finished : and He bowed
His head, and gave up His spirit.

The Jews therefore, because it was the Preparation, that the
bodies should not remain upon the cross upon the sabbath (for the
day of that sabbath was a high day), asked of Pilate that their legs
might be broken, and that they might be taken away.   The soldiers
therefore came, and brake the legs of the first, and of the other
that was crucified with Him : but when they came to Jesus, and
saw that He was dead already, they brake not His legs : howbeit
one of the soldiers with a spear pierced His side, and straightway
there came out blood and water.   And he that hath seen hath
borne witness, and his witness is true : and he knoweth that he
saith true, that ye also may believe.   For these things came to
pass, that the scripture might be fulfilled, A bone of Him shall not
be broken.   And again another scripture saith, They shall look on
Him Whom they pierced.—*John 19 : 17–37.*

XX

THE APPROACH

THERE is considerable divergence of opinion as to whether Jesus was conscious of the full meaning of His mission during the days of His boyhood and young manhood. A full discussion of this subject is not here attempted. Neither recorded word of His, nor clear statement of scripture, give any decisive declaration on the point. Believing in the perfection of His unfallen human nature, it would seem as though all the probability were in favour of the opinion that He saw the Cross, and knew through all the quiet processes of preparation, that therein lay the final fact of His wondrous work.

His communion with His Father was perfect, and in unclouded intelligence He would understand the meaning of the sacred writings of His people. It is unthinkable that He shared their blindness as to that portion of the prophetic writings, which had reference to the suffering of the Messiah. His first utterance declares His consciousness of relation to His Father, and understanding of the fact. This in itself would seem to warrant belief that He realized the fact of His Messiahship. If this be so, then there can be no doubt that He also knew that the pathway of the Messiah to the throne was the pathway of suffering and the Cross.

This position is strengthened by His accurate apprehension of the meaning of the symbolism of the Hebrew worship. All the types and shadows of the ceremonial law were luminous to Him. The very calendar of the feasts must have spoken to His heart its true message.

From this study of the approach of Jesus to His Cross, eliminating any further reference to the early years, and confining attention to those of the public ministry, there is no longer room for doubt or uncertainty. It is perfectly certain that from the commencement of His public ministry He was perfectly conscious of the Cross. Through the three years of preaching, of working of miracles, of conflict, and of training of His own, He moved with quiet dignity, and set determination, towards the Cross of His passion.

The present study is an attempt to demonstrate this consciousness by an examination of many of the things He said, which while not revealing the fact of the Cross to the men of His age, clearly prove His consciousness of it, in the light of subsequent events. Behind all the teaching and activity of the Master there is evidently a sub-consciousness of the Cross, and on at least five occasions this flames out, declaring itself in unmistakable ways. These may safely be spoken of as the lowlands of sub-consciousness, and the mountain peaks of immediate consciousness. A consideration of each will now be attempted.

I.   In the first place then an examination of words of His, which while not immediately revealing the fact of the Cross, do yet conclusively prove that it was present to His mind, in the midst of all the ceaseless activity of three years of public ministry.

There is a notable silence concerning it as to open declaration until the moment when His Messiahship was confessed by Peter. He then began to speak plainly of the Cross, but yet during all that period of preaching and teaching, it was present to His mind, and is the only explanation of certain things He did, and words He uttered.

In such a study as this, the principal factor is that of careful attention to the Master's own words. Comments upon them are of minor importance, and will only be made in an attempt to indicate their true meaning.

" Verily, verily, I say unto you, Ye shall see the heaven opened, and the angels of God ascending and descending upon the Son of Man." [1]

The Lord had spoken of Nathanael as " an Israelite indeed." [2] In response to his evident wonder He makes a statement closely connected with His declaration that this man was a true child of Israel. It calls to mind the revelation made to the patriarch concerning the communication existing between heaven and earth by the ladder, and the ascending and descending angels, and of the fact that in the King of Israel there shall be the fulfillment of all that was suggested by that dream. How were these words of Jesus fulfilled? Only by the way of His Cross, and resurrection, and ascension.

" Jesus saith unto her, Woman, what have I to do with thee? Mine hour is not yet come." [3]

This is the first of a series of references in the Gospel of John to an hour yet to come. A comparison of them will show that they all refer to the Cross. His mother evidently thought that now at the commencement of public ministry, He would demonstrate His Divine calling, and accomplish His work, and in the first fact she was correct, but her understanding was limited. He wrought the miracle she suggested, and it was His first sign, but His words prove His understanding of the fact that His mightiest work could only be accomplished by the way of the Cross.

[1] John 1 : 51.   [2] John 1 : 47.   [3] John 2 : 4.

"Destroy this temple, and in three days I will raise it up." [1]

The Pharisees demanded His authority for cleansing the temple, and His answer, which was utterly misunderstood at the time, declared His Cross and resurrection to be the authority.

"And as Moses lifted up the serpent in the wilderness, even so must the Son of Man be lifted up; that whosoever believeth may in Him have eternal life." [2]

Utterly perplexed by the strange words that have fallen upon his ear, Nicodemus at last said, "How can these things be?" that is to say, granting the truth of the assertion made, by what process can there be accomplishment? The reply of the Lord, almost certainly not then understood by Nicodemus, yet reveals His clear understanding, that life could only be communicated through His uplifting in the sorrows of death.

"My meat is to do the will of Him that sent Me, and to accomplish His work." [3]

In the absence of the disciples He had been dealing with a lost woman, and winning her back with inimitable strength and tenderness to the pathway of virtue. When they, returning, offered Him food, He declared that the very sustenance of His highest life consisted in the doing of the will, and the accomplishment of His work. How evidently here His mind was dwelling upon that mighty work by which He would seek and save the lost.

"The Son of Man hath authority on earth to forgive sins." [4]

Here by a miracle of healing, He demonstrated to His critics His power to forgive sins, while His very claim to

[1] John 2 : 19.   [2] John 3 : 14, 15.   [3] John 4 : 34.
[4] Matt. 9 : 6. (See also Mark 2 : 10; Luke 5 : 24.)

be able to do this, proves His consciousness of the fact that "His own self bare our sins in His body upon the tree,"[1] for by this bearing of sin alone has He power to forgive.

"Can the sons of the bride-chamber mourn, as long as the bridegroom is with them? but the days will come, when the bridegroom shall be taken away from them, and then will they fast."[2]

In astonishment at the absence of fasting in the lives of His disciples, men contrasted this fact with the fasting of the disciples of the Baptist, and asked His explanation. In answer He declared that while He was with them, there was no room for mourning, and then there is evident His consciousness of the coming Cross, as He declared that when the bridegroom should be taken away, the sons of the bride-chamber would mourn.

"Even so the Son also giveth life to whom He will."[3]

In controversy with His foes He made this sublime assertion of His power to give life to those who are dead, an assertion He could only make in view of His victory over death through the Cross and resurrection.

"And he that doth not take his cross and follow after Me, is not worthy of Me. He that findeth his life shall lose it; and he that loseth his life for My sake shall find it."[4]

In these words, uttered when first He commissioned the twelve, there is a meaning far deeper than they then understood, or were intended to understand. They were to take up the Cross and follow after Him, and as He uttered the words, most surely there was present to His

---

[1] 1 Pet. 2 : 24.
[2] Matt. 9 : 15. (See also Mark 2 : 19, 20; Luke 5 : 34, 35.)
[3] John 5 : 21.   [4] Matt. 10 : 38, 39.

mind His own Cross. And yet He declared that " he that findeth his life shall lose it; and he that loseth his life for My sake shall find it." He knew how afterwards such declaration would find its full explanation and vindication by the way of that Cross, in which He found His life by losing it, and lost His life to find it.

"As Jonah was three days and three nights in the belly of the whale; so shall the Son of Man be three days and three nights in the heart of the earth." [1]

In answer to the scribes and Pharisees, who sought a sign, He declared that He would give them none save that of Jonah, but He linked that with a coming fact, namely, that of His Cross, and burial, and resurrection. He understood perfectly that no sign He wrought would be final, save that mightiest of all, of a man cast out in death, yet winning his victories by return to life.

"The kingdom of heaven is like unto a treasure hidden in the field; which a man found, and hid; and in his joy he goeth and selleth all that he hath, and buyeth that field. Again, the kingdom of heaven is like unto a man that is a merchant seeking goodly pearls; and having found one pearl of great price, he went and sold all that he had, and bought it." [2]

In the midst of the parables of the kingdom, these have evident reference to His coming passion. The popular interpretation of them fails to discover this, in supposing that lost man sells all to buy the field, and possess the pearl. That is an utter failure to appreciate the essential value of the parable. What has man to sell to buy the pearl of price? He is a bankrupt beggar on life's highway, and nothing that he has to sell will purchase for him the field of the world, or the pearl of price. It is

[1] Matt. 12 : 40. (See also Luke 11 : 30.)   [2] Matt. 13 : 44–46.

Christ Who sold all to possess the pearl, and in that double declaration of the cost at which He purchased the field of the world, and the pearl which is the Church, there was evidently present to His mind His Cross. We " were redeemed, not with corruptible things, with silver or gold, . . . but with precious blood, as of a lamb without blemish and without spot, even the blood of Christ." [1]

" I am the living Bread which came down out of heaven : if any man eat of this bread, he shall live forever : yea, and the bread which I will give is My flesh, for the life of the world. The Jews therefore strove one with another, saying, How can this Man give us His flesh to eat ? Jesus therefore said unto them, Verily, verily, I say unto you, Except ye eat the flesh of the Son of Man and drink His blood, ye have not life in yourselves. He that eateth My flesh and drinketh My blood hath eternal life ; and I will raise him up at the last day. For My flesh is meat indeed, and My blood is drink indeed. He that eateth My flesh and drinketh My blood abideth in Me, and I in him." [2]

In this memorable discourse on the true sustenance of man's spiritual life, while not declaring in detail, no argument is needed to prove that He was speaking out of the consciousness of that Cross by which He would give His flesh for the meat, and His blood for the drink of the world.

So far the references have been indirect, proving the consciousness of the Cross in His own mind. Those which follow are clearer, because they come after Peter's confession, and are subsequent therefore to His clear announcement of the Cross as the issue of His work, to His own disciples.

" If any man have a hundred sheep, and one of them be

[1] I Pet. I : 18, 19.   [2] John 6 : 51-56.

gone astray, doth he not leave the ninety and nine, and go unto the mountains, and seek that which goeth astray ? " [1]

In this most wonderful chapter which deals with the child and the Church, these words clearly reveal His consciousness of the long journey into the uttermost darkness that He must take for the finding and restoration of that which had gone astray.

" Jesus therefore saith unto them, My time is not yet come ; but your time is always ready.   The world cannot hate you ; but Me it hateth, because I testify of it, that its works are evil.   Go ye up unto the feast : I go not up unto this feast ; because My time is not yet fulfilled." [2]

Here is another reference to the hour that had not yet come, this time spoken to His brethren, as at the first it was addressed to His mother.   They were urging Him to manifest Himself, and accomplish something.   He declared that the supreme moment had not arrived, knowing perfectly that between Him and any manifestation of real power, there lay the Cross.

" Jesus therefore said, Yet a little while am I with you, and I go unto Him that sent Me.   Ye shall seek Me, and shall not find Me : and where I am, ye cannot come." [3]

To the officers sent to arrest Him, He uttered these words, and in common with all those of a like nature, spoken to those outside the immediate circle of His disciples, they prove His consciousness of the Cross, while not openly declaring it.

" Jesus therefore said, When ye have lifted up the Son of Man, then shall ye know that I am He, and that I do nothing of Myself, but as the Father taught Me, I speak these things." [4]

[1] Matt. 18 : 12.
[2] John 7 : 6–8.
[3] John 7 : 33, 34.
[4] John 8 : 28.

Here again is the consciousness of limitation until the lifting up of the Cross, after which men shall know.

" I beheld Satan fallen as lightning from heaven." [1]

At the return of the seventy, as they recounted the story of their journeying and their work, He uttered these most wonderful words, which, while variously interpreted, certainly indicate the discomfiture and defeat of the enemy which was only wrought in the Cross. The words therefore prove the Lord's consciousness of that Cross.

" We must work the works of Him that sent Me, while it is day : the night cometh, when no man can work." [2]

This declaration of Christ has very often been taken out of its setttng and its relation, and has been made to teach that which is undoubtedly true, but what is not here declared. Through John, as has been seen, there is a reference to an hour which was coming. It was to be an hour of darkness, of night ; and here He said to His disciples in connection with the healing of the man born blind, " *We* must work," and then declared that presently the night was coming in which no man could work. His mind was almost certainly fixed upon that deep, dense, dark night, in which man should be excluded, and God alone should accomplish the redemption of the lost race.

" I am the good Shepherd : the good Shepherd layeth down His life for the sheep. . . . I lay down My life, that I may take it again. No one taketh it away from Me, but I lay it down of Myself. I have power to lay it down, and I have power to take it again." [3]

No comment is necessary here to prove the Lord's consciousness of His Cross.

---

[1] Luke 10 : 18. [2] John 9 : 4. [3] John 10 : 11, 17, 18.

" But I have a baptism to be baptized with; and how am I straitened till it be accomplished!"[1]

Here is an almost startling declaration of His sense of limitation of the work of preaching, and miracle working. He seems to have gazed on towards the dark and awful passion-baptism with eagerness for it, that He might be no longer straitened, but able to accomplish all that could only be accomplished through its mysterious experiences.

" Behold, I cast out demons and perform cures to-day and to-morrow, and the third day I am perfected."[2]

How closely this follows upon, and adds emphasis to, the last quotation. The Pharisees were warning Him of Herod's hatred and opposition, and in calm and dignified language He declared His present work, and that presently He would be perfected. He looked towards the perfecting by the way of His Cross and resurrection.

" Whosoever doth not bear his own cross, and come after Me, cannot be My disciple."[3]

Here is another instance similiar to that recorded in Matthew[4] in which the value of His word, as subsequent events would prove, was created by the fact of His own Cross.

" What man of you, having a hundred sheep, and having lost one of them, doth not leave the ninety and nine in the wilderness, and go after that which is lost, until he find it? And when he hath found it, he layeth it on his shoulders, rejoicing."[5]

In this wonderful parable of the lost sheep, the lost piece of silver, the lost man, a parable thus indicating the order of the Divine plan of salvation, is the whole gospel of redemption; the saving of the sheep, illustrative of the work

[1] Luke 12: 50.   [2] Luke 13: 32.   [3] Luke 14: 27.
[4] Matt. 10: 38.   [5] Luke 15: 4, 5.

of Jesus; seeking for the silver, illustrative of the work of
the Church indwelt by the Spirit, and the welcome of the
prodigal, illustrative of the attitude of God to man. At
the first in His declaration concerning the Shepherd seeking the wanderer, one finds His Cross and passion.

"Jesus answered, Are there not twelve hours in the
day? If a man walk in the day, he stumbleth not, because
he seeth the light of this world." [1]

The Master proposed to go to Jerusalem that He might
wake Lazarus from sleep, and His disciples protested because of the opposition that had been stirred up against
Him, and the certainty they felt that men would lay hands
upon Him to kill Him. To their objection He replied in
words that are in harmony with some already considered in
this Gospel of John, which show His consciousness of a
working day, merging into a terrible night; and while His
attitude is a revelation of His sense of security until the
day's work be over, it also clearly indicates His consciousness of the Cross.

"But first must He suffer many things, and be rejected
of this generation." [2]

"Behold, we go up to Jerusalem; and the Son of Man
shall be delivered unto the chief priests and scribes; and
they shall condemn Him to death, and shall deliver Him
unto the Gentiles to mock, and to scourge, and to crucify:
and the third day He shall be raised up." [3]

"But Jesus answered and said, Ye know not what ye
ask. Are ye able to drink the cup that I am about to
drink?" [4]

"Even as the Son of Man came not to be ministered

[1] John 11: 9.   [2] Luke 17: 25.
[3] Matt. 20: 18, 19. (See also Mark 10: 33, 34; Luke 18: 31-33.)
[4] Matt. 20: 22. (See also Mark 10: 38.)

unto, but to minister, and to give His life a ransom for many." [1]

Upon these no comment is necessary. Here He was teaching His disciples that second lesson, which they utterly failed to learn, until the accomplishment of the facts.

" For in that she poured this ointment upon My body, she did it to prepare Me for burial." [2]

Mary, conscious of some dark sorrow settling over His life, with the keen intuition of a great love, perceiving the very shadow of death upon Him, anointed His feet; and in His recognition of the gracious action there is a revelation of the overwhelming consciousness of the Cross, which was yet unappreciated by the many, and discovered only by Mary.

" But afterwards he sent unto them his son, saying, They will reverence my son. But the husbandmen, when they saw the son, said among themselves, This is the heir; come, let us kill him, and take his inheritance. And they took him, and cast him forth out of the vineyard, and killed him. . . . Jesus saith unto them, Did ye never read in the scriptures,

> The stone which the builders rejected,
> The same was made the Head of the corner:
> This was from the Lord,
> And it is marvellous in our eyes ?

Therefore say I unto you, The kingdom of God shall be taken away from you, and shall be given to a nation bringing forth the fruits thereof. And he that falleth on

[1] Matt. 20 : 28.   (See also Mark 10 : 45.)
[2] Matt. 26 : 12.   (See also Mark 14 : 8; John 12 : 7.)

this stone shall be broken to pieces : but on whomsoever it shall fall, it will scatter him as dust." [1]

Thus, in what was probably Christ's last appearance in the temple, in a parable and an application of Scripture, He openly declared the issue of His ministry to be the Cross.

" Ye know that after two days the passover cometh, and the Son of Man is delivered up to be crucified. . . . My time is at hand; I keep the passover at thy house with My disciples. . . . Verily I say unto you, that one of you shall betray Me." [2]

These Scriptures are the records of His last messages to His disciples, all of them delivered under the very shadow of His Cross, the fact of which is evident to-day ; and yet though openly declared to them, it seems as though they had no clear understanding of its nearness.

Thus we have, in hurried fashion passed over a wide field, and consequently nothing is perfect save the actual Scriptures as recorded. Enough though has surely been done, to show that from the moment when His public ministry began, there was present to His mind its consummation in the Cross. In great love and tenderness He hid it from His disciples until they had learned the first lesson, that, namely, of His Messiahship. And even then, appreciating their weakness and inability to perfectly understand, He seems to have spoken to them seldom concerning it. The pathway of the three years was a pathway ever resolutely trodden towards the Cross, and while the consciousness of its pain was ever upon Him, so was also the sense of its value, for upon the triumph there to be won, He based His authority for all the wonders which He

[1] Matt. 21: 37-44. (See also Mark 12: 6-10 ; Luke 20: 13-18.)
[2] Matt. 26: 2, 18, 21. (See also John 14-17.)

wrought, and the blessings which He scattered were in His view made possible thereby.

II.   There is no necessity to do more than tabulate these occasions which have been referred to at the beginning, as the mountain peaks of full consciousness. For the most part they have been considered in connection with their proper setting, and it is not necessary therefore to do more now than indicate them as the occasions upon which Jesus seems to have come through some special circumstance face to face with the fact of His Cross.

The first of these occasions is the baptism. Then, as has been seen, His very consent, nay, His request for baptism, and His insistence upon it, was the outward symbol of His identification with sinners, and therefore, moreover, of His identification with all that sin meant. For Him the whelming in the water foreshadowed the passion-baptism.[1]

The second occasion was that of Peter's confession, when, having consummated the teaching required to reveal to His disciples His Messiahship, in a few words, startling and comprehensive, He declared the whole pathway to and through the Cross. "From that time began Jesus to shew unto His disciples, that He must go unto Jerusalem, and suffer many things of the elders and chief priests and scribes, and be killed, and the third day be raised up."[2]

The third instance of this clear consciousness of, and consent to, the Cross is to be found in His transfiguration. While the light of His human victory illumined the darkness of the night, and He held familiar converse with the lawgiver and the prophet, it was of His Cross and resurrection that they spoke.[3]

[1] Matt. 3: 15.   [2] Matt. 16: 21.   [3] Luke 9: 31.

Again for the fourth time at the coming of the Greeks with their request to see Him, it is evident that the sense of the Cross, as one of great sorrow, was upon Him, for He declared that His soul was troubled. Here again, however, He deliberately chose and asked that His Father's name should be glorified, whatever the cost might be to Himself, and then declared His conception of what the Cross would mean.[1]

And lastly in the Garden of Gethsemane, having passed outside the last limit of human comradeship, in awful loneliness He looked into the heart of the great passion, and trembling at the prospect, yet with a strength of purpose that astonishes, and fills man with deep reverence, He chose the will of God, including, as it did, the emptying of this cup of all its bitterness, that He might fill it with the wine of life for the sons of men.[2]

Thus in deepest sense He is seen to have been " a Man of sorrows, and acquainted with grief." [3] Yet though His whole life was based upon conformity to the Divine purpose, even though He knew its issue was this mystery of deep pain, He nevertheless exercised a ministry of beneficence which was ever a magnificent prophecy of final victory by the way of the Cross.

[1] John 12: 28.　　[2] Luke 22: 39-44.　　[3] Isa. 53: 3.

XXI

THE SUFFERINGS OF CHRIST

THAN this there is no subject more mysterious and yet more sacred in the whole realm of revealed truth. This is the heart of that mystery of the love and wisdom of God, which wrought towards, and made possible the salvation of man. At the commencement of this study I would place on record not idly, and not for the mere sake of doing so, but under the urgency of a great conviction, that I am deeply conscious of approaching things too high, and too profound for any finality of statement. Personally I increasingly shrink from any attempt to speak in detail of the great fact of the Cross. This is not because I am growing away from it, but rather on account of the fact that I am more deeply conscious every day of my need of all it stands for, and as I have pressed closer to its heart, I have become almost overwhelmed with its unfathomable deeps, and its infinite majesty.

It is impossible, however, that any consideration of the mission of Jesus should be complete, if this subject were omitted. Let all therefore who approach the subject do so with abandonment to that Spirit of God Who "searcheth all things, yea, the deep things of God,"[1] praying earnestly to be led, so far as it is possible, to see and understand the mystery of His pain.

In the light of the earlier studies, it may here and now be stated that the Cross solves two problems that have

[1] I Cor. 2: 10.

found solution nowhere else. These problems may thus be stated.

First, How can God be just and justify the sinner?

Second, How can righteousness of conduct be made possible to those who are poisoned and paralyzed by sin?

As to the first it must be remembered that the word "justify" means the clearance of the soul from guilt. Justification must be infinitely more than forgiveness. Sin must be put away, and made to be as though it had not been. For justification the soul must be put into a place of purity, so restored that there shall be no spot, or blemish, or stain, not merely upon the record, but what is of infinitely deeper significance, upon the character. To be justified before God is to be put into such condition, that no trace remains of the guilt of sin. That is the problem which is solved in the Cross. How can God be just, that is, true to Himself in nature, and yet justify the sinner, that is, receive him upon the basis of freedom from sin?

The second problem touches practical life, and deals with an actual condition, rather than a relative one. How can righteousness of conduct be made possible to those who are poisoned and paralyzed by sin? The difficulty of the problem is at once discovered if the impossibility of producing right conduct in man is thought of, apart from the subject immediately under consideration, that, namely, of the Cross. It is a problem that has never been solved in the past, neither can it be at the present hour. Right conduct can only issue from right character, and therefore is not possible to man whose whole nature is poisoned and paralyzed by sin.

These are the problems with which the Cross is approached. Can a man be justified before God, and sanctified in his own actual experience? Can a sinner be so cleared from guilt that he may have a conscience void of offence ? Can a man, whose powers have become paralyzed by the virus of sin, be so changed as to enable him to do the things he cannot do ? Can a man be made able to translate the vision of an ideal into the actuality of daily life ? These problems baffle all the wisdom of man apart from the Cross, and still defy all attempts at solution. These are the problems solved by the mystery of Christ's sufferings.

The present study is not directed to an examination of the results of the Cross, but to a reverent contemplation of the way by which they were made possible.

It is impossible to follow the Lord into the place of His mightiest work. Alone He entered and wrought. No man followed Him, nor could follow Him at all, in help, or in sympathy, or in understanding. Fallen man was degraded in will, emotion, and intelligence, and therefore was not able to help, or sympathize, or understand. From that inner mystery, therefore, man was excluded.

Tracing the Lord through the three years in which He was constantly conscious of the Cross, it will be noticed how gradually and yet surely, He moved out into the loneliness of the final fact of His work. While living in Nazareth He was a favourite. He " advanced in wisdom and stature, and in favour with God and men." [1] At the commencement of His public ministry both the rulers and the multitudes gathered round Him. The men of light and leading were at least interested in Him, and ready to listen to Him, and more than inclined to patronize Him. They were among the first to fall back from Him. As He, in the great progress of His teaching, uttered deeper and yet deeper truths, men who were merely curious be-

[1] Luke 2 : 52

came excluded, and only His own disciples remained in
anything approaching close association with Him. Yet
further on, the ranks of the disciples were thinned. After
the discourse recorded in the sixth chapter of John, in
which He declared He would give His flesh for the meat,
and His blood for the drink, of the world, many went
back and walked no more with Him. Without closely following the details, it will be seen that His approach to His
Cross is marked by constant withdrawals, until at last the
nearest flee, the story of their going being recorded in one
tragic sentence, "Then all the disciples left Him, and
fled."[1]

He passed into the actual place of His passion, the
region of that mystery of pain through which He was
about to solve these problems, in utter loneliness. No
man could help, no man could sympathize, no man could
understand. Let this always be borne in mind when His
suffering is followed and contemplated.

Men may gather reverently to the place of the passion,
but can only know of it from what is revealed in the words
that fell from His own lips. That should be accepted as a
canon and principle of interpretation concerning the sufferings of Christ. What others may think or say, can
only be of value as it harmonizes with, and expresses the
meaning of the words He Himself uttered. Nothing can
be known of that mystery of pain save from Himself.
Any attempt to go beyond this limit is a mistaken attempt,
and borders upon the realm of unholy intrusion. The subject had infinitely better be left where He left it, considering
reverently, and only, His own words.

Of these there have been recorded seven several utterances. The first three manifest His keen and marvellous

[1] Matt. 26: 56.

insight, even on that Cross of shame, into the deepest things and simplest necessities of human life. The last four are expressions of His own Spirit's experience in utter loneliness, and come out of that awful isolation.

The first three : " Father, forgive them ; for they know not what they do " ; [1] " To-day shalt thou be with Me in Paradise " ; [2] " Woman, behold, thy son ! Behold, thy mother ! " [3]   In these is evident His pity for men in the issue of their sin, His power towards those believing in Him, and His provision for those upon whom His love is set.

Then the last four : " Eloi, Eloi, lama sabachthani ? " [4] " I thirst " ; [5] " It is finished " ; [6] " Father, into Thy hands I commend My Spirit." [7]   Here man stands in the presence of the process of His mightiest work, through strife and suffering to the consciousness and calm of victory.

I repeat emphatically that beyond what these words reveal of the Cross, man has neither ability nor authority to go.

From the present study the first three sayings are eliminated, and save for a final moment, the last two also. Thus two words are left which express all that man can ever hope to know of the sufferings of Christ.   First, the spiritual anguish, expressed in the cry, " My God, My God, why hast Thou forsaken Me ? " [8] and second, the physical agony revealed in the brief but awful exclamation, " I thirst." [9]

While believing that this was the true order of the saying, that the physical pain was not mentioned until after the cry of the spiritual anguish had been uttered, I propose

[1] Luke 23 : 34.   [2] Luke 23 : 43.   [3] John 19 : 26, 27.
[4] Mark 15 : 34.   [5] John 19 : 28.   [6] John 19 : 30.
[7] Luke 23 : 46.   [8] Mark 15 : 34.   [9] John 19 : 28.

to notice, first, the words " I thirst," [1] considering them in few words, remembering ever, that silence is often the most perfect exhibition of true understanding and deep sympathy ; and then to attempt a somewhat closer examination of that awful cry of the spiritual anguish, which revealed all that man may ever know of the mystery of that pain by which He redeemed the lost.

I.   The word of the physical agony, " I thirst." [2]   What can any say concerning that ?   Is it not rather subject for lonely contemplation and meditation ?   It is hardly possible to approach it without fearing lest the approach may be that of sacrilegious curiosity.   From such we would utterly be delivered, and therefore I do not propose to dwell for a single moment upon the actual physical pain of Jesus.   The whole of it surges out in that cry, " I thirst."   To know all that was behind those words, rather recall briefly, quietly, and slowly, almost without comment, the facts that had immediately preceded the Cross :—

The night watches in Gethsemane.

The flash of the light of the torches upon the darkness of the night.

The kiss of the traitor.

The arrest.

Still in the darkness of night, the arraignment before the high priests.

The hours of waiting, and of tension.

The appearance in the morning before the high priests and the council.

The palace of the Roman governor with that strange interview between Jesus and Pilate, withdrawn from the rabble into some quiet apartmer*

[1] John 19 : 28.   [2] John 19 : 28.

The journey from the house of Pilate to the palace of Herod.

The first and final meeting with Herod, the corrupt, the depraved, Herod who had so often sought an interview with Him, and had never obtained it until that last hour, Herod who never heard the voice of Jesus, for to his curiosity Christ vouchsafed no single word.

The rough handling of Herod's brutal soldiery.

The journey back to Pilate.

The awful scenes through which Pilate strove to save Him, while priests and people clamoured for His blood.

The scourging.

The pathway to the Cross.

The crucifixion.

Hours into which eternities were compressed! Through all in silence He endured the Cross, despising the shame; in silence, with no word of complaint and no word expressive of pain, " as a lamb that is led to the slaughter, and as a sheep that before its shearers is dumb, so He opened not His mouth."[1] In the hours of darkness, three words breathing tender interest and infinite love, one outcry of the spirit, and then, not so much a wail as a smothered sob of pent-up human agony, " I thirst "; the very expression of human agony, dignified, neither complaint nor appeal, but simply the statement, a terrible revelation of such suffering as is beyond explanation.

And now let it be remembered that all this is outward and physical, and human, and is but the symbol of the inward, and spiritual, and Divine. If in loneliness we pass over this pathway, and consider these scenes in contrition and tears, we have not then reached the heart of the mystery. Beyond all these stretch the infinitudes of suffering

[1] Isa. 53 : 7.

II.   With sorrowful silence and fearfulness of utterance we approach the deepest darkness.   " My God, My God, why hast Thou forsaken Me ? " [1]   These words reveal a mystery, and represent in mystery a revelation.   To them we turn for a theory of the Atonement, only to discover that theorizing is impossible.   Alone in the supreme hour in the history of the race, Christ uttered these words, and in them light breaks out, and yet merges, not into darkness, but into light so blinding that no eye can bear to gaze. The words are recorded, not to finally reveal, but to reveal so much as it is possible for men to know, and to set a limit at the point where men may never know.   The words were uttered that men may know, and that men may know how much there is that may not be known.   In that strange cry that broke from the lips of the Master there are at least three things perfectly clear.   Let them be named and considered.   It is the cry of One Who has reached the final issue of sin.   It is the cry of One Who has fathomed the deepest depth of sorrow.   It is the cry of One Himself o'erwhelmed in the mystery of silence.   Sin, sorrow, silence.   Sin at its final issue, sorrow at its deepest depth, silence the unexplainable mystery of agony, and agony of mystery.   These are the facts suggested by the actual words.   In that order let them be pondered reverently.

" My God, My God, why hast Thou forsaken Me ? " [2] The logical, irresistible, irrevocable issue of sin is to be God-forsaken.   Sin in its genesis was rebellion against God.   Sin in its harvest is to be God-abandoned.   Man sinned when he dethroned God and enthroned himself. He reaps the utter harvest of his sin when he has lost God altogether.   That is the issue of all sin.   It is the final penalty of sin, penalty not in the sense of a blow inflicted

[1] Mark 15 : 34.   [2] Mark 15 : 34.

on the sinner by God, but in the sense of a result following upon sin, from which God Himself cannot save the
sinner. Sin is alienation from God by choice. Hell is the
utter realization of that chosen alienation. Sin therefore
at last is the consciousness of the lack of God, and that
God-forsaken condition is the penalty of the sin which for-
sakes God. Now listen solemnly, and from that Cross
hear the cry, " My God, My God, why hast Thou forsaken
Me ? " [1]   That is hell. No other human being has ever
been God-forsaken in this life. Man by his own act alienated himself from God, but God never left him. He
brooded over him with infinite patience and pity, and took
man back to His heart at the moment of the fall, in virtue
of that mystery of Calvary which lay within the determinate counsel and foreknowledge of God, long before its
outworking in the history of the race. What explanation
can there be of this cry from the lips of Jesus ? None
other is needed than that declared by His herald three years
before, and considered in previous studies. " Behold, the
Lamb of God, that taketh away the sin of the world ! " [2]
He has taken hold upon sin. He has made it His own.
He has accepted the responsibility of it. He has passed to
the ultimate issue. There is a statement in the writings
of Paul, to my own mind the most overwhelming, the most
profound of the New Testament : " Him Who knew no
sin He made to be sin on our behalf; that we might become the righteousness of God in Him." [3]   Reverently
hear the strange and sublime words, " Him Who knew no
sin He made sin." A man says, I do not understand that.
Neither do I. But there is a declaration, and in the hour
of the Cross is the fact. On that Cross He was made sin,
and therein He passed to the uttermost limit of sin's out-

[1] Mark 15 : 34.   [2] John 1 : 29.   [3] 2 Cor. 5 : 21.

working. He was God-forsaken. He knew no sin. He was made sin. He was forsaken of God. Because He knew no sin there is a value in the penalty which He bore, that He does not need for Himself. Whose sin is this that He is made, and for which He is forsaken of God? My sin. I can say no other in the presence of that sublime miracle. Each must for himself stand there alone,—*my sin.* He was made my sin. If in passing to the final issue of my sin, and bearing its penalty, He created a value that He did not need for Himself, for whom is the value? It also is for me. " He bore my sin in His body upon the tree."[1]

And yet the broader fact must be stated. He bore the sin of the world. Himself knowing no sin, by such bearing He created a value which He did not require. For whom then is the value of that awful hour? For the whole world, whose sin He bore. Behold Him, on the Cross, bending His sacred head, and gathering into His heart in the awful isolation of separation from God, the issue of the sin of the world, and see how out of that acceptance of the issue of sin He creates that which He does not require for Himself, that He may distribute to those whose place He has taken.

Turn for one brief moment only to the next fact, closely allied to that already considered, never to be separated in the final thought, and only now taken separately for the sake of examination and contemplation. This cry is not merely that of One Who has reached the final issue of sin, but it is therefore, and also, the cry of One Who has fathomed the deepest abyss of sorrow. Sorrow is the consciousness of lack. What is the sorrow of sickness but the consciousness of lack of health? What is the sorrow of bereavement but the consciousness of the lack of the loved

[1] 1 Pet. 2 : 24,

one? What is the sorrow of poverty but the consciousness of the lack ot the necessities of life? What is
the sorrow of loneliness but the consciousness of the
lack of companionship? All sorrow is lack. Then it
fol.⁓⁓ by a natural sequence of that, that the uttermost
depth of sorrow is lack of God. There is no sorrow like
it. There is no pain comparable to it. The human
heart through the infinite mercy of God has never in
this life really known this uttermost reach of sorrow.
There are moments in life when it would seem as though
God had hidden. His face as men pass through dark experiences, but if He had actually withdrawn Himself, the
sorrow of the hiding of His face would have been as nothing, to the sorrow of the actual absence from Him. In
this hour when Jesus was made sin, and was therefore God-
forsaken, He knew as none had ever known, the profundities of pain. The vision that had been His light through all
the dark days in the three and thirty years, was lost. The
strength of that fellowship with the Father which had been
His on every rough and rugged pathway, was withdrawn.
In perfect harmony with the purpose of God He passed
into the place of separation from God, and in the awful
cry which expresses His loneliness, there is revealed the
most stupendous sorrow that has ever been witnessed through
the ages.

And yet once again. If man imagines that he has now
fathomed or understood the Cross, he is reminded by the
very fact, that this cry is a question that something, perchance the mightiest and most marvellous of all the facts,
eludes him, and defies his every attempt at final analysis.
He is in the place of sin as to its final issue, and in the
place of sorrow in its abyssmal depth, and yet now note
that while He states the fact that He is God-forsaken, He

in the midst of the experience asks the question, " Why ? "
It is never recorded that He asked such a question before.
Never again is there record of so strange a fact. In that
withdrawal of the Divine presence, which is the issue of sin,
and the depth of sorrow, there is the enshrouding of the
Spirit of the Christ in a great and awful mystery of silence.
If these infinitudes may be measured by the small standards of human individuality, it may be at once declared that
there is no experience of life through which men pass, so
terrible as that of silence and of mystery, the hours of isolation and of sorrow, in which there is no voice, no vision,
no sympathy, no promise, no hope, no explanation, the hours
in which the soul asks why. The river, the darkly flowing
river, how men dread it, and yet there is something more
fearsome than the darkly flowing river. It is the mist that,
rising from the river, wraps men round in its chill embrace,
until they do not know where they stand, or where the
river is. There is no agony for the human soul like that
of silence. The perfect One, made sin, and suffering all
sorrow, had reached that place of silence and of mystery.
Who shall explain it ? I cannot. When I am asked for
a theory of the Atonement I ever reply that in the midst of
the mighty movement, the Lord Himself said " Why ? "
and if He asked that question, I dare not imagine that I
can ever explain the deep central verities of His mystery
of pain. Men stand outside the circle of that incompre-
hensible agony, they behold Him forsaken of God, at the
uttermost issue of sin, in the deepest profundities of sorrow, in the mystery of an awful silence, and all this as they
hear Him say, " My God, My God, why hast Thou forsaken Me ? "[1] Let there be no attempt to penetrate further
into that hallowed and awful realm.

[1] Mark 15 : 34.

And yet the subject of the sufferings of Christ cannot be so left. Standing overwhelmed in the presence of these sufferings, feeling increasingly man's utter inability to understand or explain, with a great sense of might and majesty overwhelming us, we hear the next words that pass His lips. "It is finished." [1] Immediately the heart sings a new song,—

> "O Jesus, Lord! 'tis joy to know
> Thy path is o'er of shame and woe,
> For us so meekly trod."

How in the depth of the darkness the mighty work was accomplished, men will never perfectly understand. Eternity cannot suffice for the unfolding of the dread mystery of the passion, but this is known, "He bare my sins in His body upon the tree," [2] He stood where man should have stood. The pains of hell that were man's portion, gat hold on Him, and man passes into the light of the heaven which was His by right, and which He brings to him.

Such were the sufferings of Christ, so far as we have been allowed to come near them in the inspired narrative. What have we seen? So little and yet so much. Unable to appreciate all the meaning of the words, yet great facts now shine in radiant revelation, and from the study we may make statements which constitute the evangel of hope and of power. These deductions may be expressed in old words, the theological words of our fathers. I pray God that we may restore them. I would not plead for the restoration of mistaken interpretation of the words, but that we may lay hold upon them in their true and infinite value.

Gazing then in astonishment at the sufferings of Christ

---

[1] John 19 : 30.　　　　　[2] 1 Peter 2 : 24.

I declare them to have been vicarious sufferings, expiatory sufferings, atoning sufferings.

They were vicarious sufferings, for He stood in man's place when He suffered. The penalty He bore had no relation to the life as lived. He stood connected with all human sin and failure, and seeing that He bore it, man is delivered from it.

They were expiatory sufferings. Through what He bore, He exhausted human sin, He put it away, He made it not to be.

They were atoning sufferings in that through them He has dealt with all that separated between man and God. He has now made possible the restoration of the lost fellowship, and man may henceforth live in communion with Him.

Thus has He solved the problems first suggested. By the way of that Cross, and by that way alone, God may be just, that is, true to Himself in nature; and justify the sinner, that is, place man into the position of one for whom sin is made not to be, and who is therefore clear from guilt.

The second problem is assuredly solved by the mystery of the Cross, as will be more fully seen when contemplating His resurrection. As He passes out of death, He comes into a new life which He may now communicate, and which is to be for paralyzed men a new dynamic and a new purity, in the power of which all life may be transformed, and all victories won.

Thus we have foregathered on the outer margin of that deep sea of sorrow through which the God-man wrought with God, though for a while in separation from the consciousness of His presence, a redemption which meets all difficulties, and solves all problems, and opens the kingdom of heaven to all believers.

XXII

SIN UNVEILED; GRACE OUTSHINING

WOULD we know the true nature of sin, and the deepest facts concerning the grace of God, we must come to the Cross. In Peter's first message after Pentecost, referring to the Cross he said : " Jesus of Nazareth, a Man approved of God unto you by mighty works and wonders and signs which God did by Him in the midst of you, even as ye yourselves know ; Him, being delivered up by the determinate counsel and foreknowledge of God, ye by the hand of lawless men did crucify and slay." [1]   Herein is a most remarkable statement, declaring two facts concerning the Cross, which seem to contradict each other, but yet which reveal the actual causes of the Cross.   " Delivered by the determinate counsel and foreknowledge of God."   Therein is declared the purpose and action of that grace which lies at the back of the whole plan of redemption.   " Ye by the hand of lawless men did crucify and slay."   Therein is contained a statement of how God's plan was carried out in history by the very principle of lawlessness, which His grace operating through the Cross contradicted and overcame.   The first declaration is that of the cause of the Cross from the Godward side, and in the light of it the Cross is seen as the epiphany of grace.   The second statement is the cause of the Cross so far as man was concerned, and in the light of it the Cross is seen as the reve-

[1] Acts 2 : 22, 23.

lation of human degradation.   These facts of the unmasking of sin, and the unveiling of the Divine heart are now to receive attention.

In the fact of the Saviour's sufferings, sin deepened into densest darkness, and grace broke forth in brightest brilliance.   In the strange mystery upon which we have already reverently looked, sin and love met in fiercest conflict.   All other forces were withdrawn, and alone in a death grapple in the darkness, sin took hold on love, and love took hold on sin.   The issue of the conflict is not now the subject of consideration, but only the contemplation of the opposing forces, as seen in this supreme hour. Love incarnate has taken hold upon sin, and the issue must be a decisive victory for one or the other.   In this hour sin or grace will triumph forever.   If sin and grace are seen as here revealed, there will be no possibility of mistake as to the nature of both.   Whoever may be inclined to judge sin by the superficial measurements of much so-called new thought, should be brought back to the Cross for a revelation of its true nature; and all those, moreover, who would confine the river of grace within small human channels, should stand again in the presence of the Cross for an understanding of the irresistible sweep and might of this river of life, flowing from the throne of God.

Let us then examine sin and grace as here revealed, in each case considering the essence, the expression, and the end.

I.   These studies are unified in certain directions by the analysis of human personality, which was accepted at the beginning.   In speaking of the essence of sin as revealed in the Cross, therefore, it will be considered in the realm of the intelligence, the emotion, and the will of man, takin

these in the reverse order.   As at the first, man's sin
proceeded through the avenue of the darkening of the
intelligence, the deadening of the emotion, and the
degradation of the will, so here is the ultimate expression of degraded will, deadened emotion, and darkened
intelligence.

The casting out of Jesus on the Cross was the protest of
license against law.   It was the most daring act of man in
his revolt against the government of God.   The Cross was
man's response to the fact intimated in the superscription
which Pilate in mockery of those Jews had written and
placed over His head.   There can be no doubt that the
Roman governor was far more angry with the priests than
with Jesus, and yet driven by the false principle of ex-
pediency, He handed Christ to crucifixion, and in doing so
mocked the men that had clamoured for the blood of the
Nazarene, by placing over His head in letters of Hebrew,
and Latin, and Greek the words, " THIS IS JESUS THE
KING OF THE JEWS." [1]   Thus from whatever cause, man
wrote above the Cross the supreme fact, and in the Cross
expressed his attitude towards it.

At the time of Christ's life and death, the three great
world forces were all represented in that little land of
Palestine, and it is not without deep significance that over
His Cross these words were written in letters of Hebrew,
and Latin, and Greek, the national language, the official
language, the common language; the language of religion,
the language of government, and the language of culture.
The attitude of all the forces represented by these things
was antagonistic to Christ.   Out of the religion of the
time, the Hebrew, arose the inspiration of the crucifixion,
while the power of the time, the Roman, was the agent for

[1] Matt. 27 : 37.

its execution, and the culture of the time, the Greek, was scornfully indifferent to Him and His claims. Sinful religion rejected Him, s nful power murdered Him, sinful culture neglected Him. He was cast out. The reason is to be found in the burden of His ministry as revealed in the first word of His preaching, the word " repent." In the uttering of this word, He called all men to a course of life exactly opposite to that being pursued. This first note of His message was a criticism and condemnation of all things as He found them. He practically declared that man had lost the true centre of his life, and that all the lines of human activity were proceeding in wrong directions. In the statement which immediately followed the first word, He revealed the nature of the wrong and of the right, " the kingdom of heaven is at hand." [1] This word is a declaration of the departure of man from the Divine government. It was an announcement, moreover, of the setting up of that government, and the whole burden of His preaching was that of a call to men to submit to God. It was a stern, severe, revolutionary cry that He sent ringing forth over all the manners and methods of men. The sternness was that of a great love, the severity was that of a great tenderness, the revolution was that of restoration. Men did not understand this. They recognized the meaning of the word, and the nature of the call. They knew that if they listened and obeyed, the whole current of life would be changed as to course, because changed at the centre. There was no apology in the preaching of Jesus. He did not submit to men a proposal which they might discuss and vote upon. He spoke with authority, and not as the scribes, and the great burden of His message as men heard it, is perfectly expressed in that one word, " Repent."

[1] Matt. 4: 17.

Through the years of His public ministry, they criticised Him, they entered into conflict with Him, they endeavoured to entrap Him in His talk, and at last they gave their final answer to His message, and the answer was the Cross. If Calvary's Cross means anything, it means that men have said, We decline to repent, we will not have this Man to reign over us, we will not submit ourselves to the Divine government.

Jesus had come into the world for the restoration of the lost order. In the midst of the chaos that He found, He uttered the first word, " repent," and then enunciated the principles of life within the Kingdom of God, proceeding to illustrate the breadth and beauty and beneficence of that kingdom, by all the deeds of tenderness and of love with which He filled the days. Men appreciated the benefits, but declined to submit to the authority. There is one startling instance of the attitude of man towards Christ. He passed over into the country of the Gadarenes, and at once came into contact with a man who must have been the very plague of the whole life of the district. He freed him from the possession of the evil spirits, and in the account of how the men who watched the working of His mighty power told the story in the city, there is this somewhat strange and yet revealing statement, " They . . . told everything, and—— " Is it then possible to tell " everything, and—— " ? What can there be to tell, when everything is told ? Now hear the whole statement, " They . . . told everything, and what had befallen " to the man " possessed with devils." [1] Now mark this inversion of values. What was the " everything " in the sight of these men ? The destruction of their pigs. What was the " and " ? A man was delivered from demon posses-

[1] Matt. 8 : 33.

sion, and set upright in the dignity of his manhood.   Is it
to be thought for a single moment that these men did not
desire the benefit offered in the casting out of devils?
There is no doubt that they would gladly have accepted
all such benefits, and yet it is written, "they besought Him
that He would depart from their borders." [1]   What can
the explanation of such strange conduct be?   This simply.
They were not prepared to pay the price.   This is not the
occasion upon which to enter into any discussion of the
vexed question as to our Lord's permitted destruction of
the swine.   It is enough that He permitted it to vindicate
the action.   And yet it may be declared in a sentence that
at this period Jesus was exercising His Jewish Messiahship,
and when He permitted the devils to destroy the swine, He
but rebuked an unholy traffic, forbidden among these people
whose Messiah He was.   They fain would have the benefits of the kingdom, but this revolutionary interference with
their profits they were not prepared to tolerate.   This is
but illustration of the fact evident through all His ministry,
which had its final expression in the Cross.   Men were
determined to silence His voice, because they would not
submit to that actual Kingdom of God which He proclaimed among them.   The Cross is the incontrovertible
proof that sin has degraded man's will.

Few words need be uttered to prove that the Cross is
the supreme evidence of the prostitution of emotion.   If
it be indeed true that the same capacity operates along the
lines of love and hate, then of all fearful revelations of
prostituted emotion, there is none equal to the Cross of
Jesus.   There, in all the details, is an expression of the
brutal and barbarous in human life, such as the world has
never seen at any other point.

[1] Matt. 8 : 34.

But was not this also the revelation of the darkening of human intelligence ? There is nothing more patent in the Cross than the blindness of the sin which erected it, both as to immediate interests, and as to far-reaching issues. What utter folly was this murder of the Emancipator, the giving over to death of the Life-giver, the whelming in darkness of the one and only Light of life. Thus the essence of sin is revealed in the Cross, as madness, and hatred, and rebellion.

This statement will cover also the fact, as the considera- tion leading to it has already covered the subject, of the expression of sin.

Sin as the rebellion of the will expressed itself finally in the murder of God's anointed King. Sin as degraded emo- tion expressed itself most fully in the refined cruelty and malicious brutality of the whole process by which Christ was apprehended and cast out. Sin as darkened intelli- gence expressed itself most surely when it found no room in its counsels for the Voice which alone was that of per- fect wisdom.

What then was the end of sin as expressed in the Cross ? The rejection of the King, the destruction of the Priest, the silencing of the Prophet. The exercising of authority must not be permitted, so sin murdered the King. Man's return to God must be prevented, so the great High Priest was refused. The shining of light upon the darkness sin loved, must not be allowed, so the voice of the Prophet was silenced. Thus sin has finally expressed itself in anarchy, for the King is dethroned ; in irreligion, for the Priest is destroyed ; in ignorance, for the Prophet is silenced.

II.   There is, however, another side to the Cross, and to it

we turn with great gladness of heart, for therein is revealed
the grace of God answering and triumphing over everything that sin is.   Grace in the Cross is the assertion of
the unquestioning authority of God.   It is the revelation
and working of His unquenchable love.   It is the outshining of His unclouded wisdom.

First, grace asserted itself in unquestioning authority.
It asked no permission.   It took no counsel with man.   It
moved along the line of a great right and authority, in
spite of man's willful rebellion against the throne.   Man
had not dethroned God when he erected the Cross, neither
did man destroy God's King therein.   God is love, and
He did not abandon man, even when man abandoned Him.
That is the great lesson of the Cross.   Men said, We will
not be governed by God, and yet there in the Cross expressing that attitude, love is seen still retaining the throne,
still holding the reins of government, still declaring to men
that without Him they can do nothing.   Apart from His
authority, they are hopelessly and forever ruined.   Even
in the blood-baptism of that awful passion, in which man's
sin has declared its refusal of God, God enthrones Himself, and asserts the will of essential love as superior to the
will of rebellion.   Never for one moment did He vacate
the throne.   Men cast His appointed King out into darkness, but in the darkness He was still the King, and prose-
cuted His reign in love.   It was not merely the enforce-
ment of authority.   It was not merely an insistence upon
government.   It was not merely the defence of a right, for
it seems as though if these had been all, God might have
established all these things by ridding Himself of man.
These are not the principles vindicated and revealed in the
Cross.   The Cross is the insistence of love.   It is the
persistence of love.   It is love that holds the throne in the

darkness. But for love there would have been no Cross. Every violated fact within the Divine purpose might have been reestablished by the destruction of that which had so signally and awfully failed. Love by determinate counsel and foreknowledge permits man to express his sin in the Cross; and in that very act of full and final expression, grace occupies the throne, sways the sceptre, and reveals, as in no other way, the authority of God, and its reason of love.

For one moment, to slightly change the angle of observation, let it be borne in mind that in that Cross of Jesus God expressed His unqualified hatred of sin. The very fires that burn the sacrifice were the fires of His wrath against all evil. The fierceness of the flame was created by the intensity of love. God will not be dethroned, though His enthronement cost Him the Son of His love; and therein is most awfully visible the severity and the judgment of God. Yet that severity and judgment can never be understood save as it is clearly recognized that the force of them is His compassion. Of this there is no perfect illustration other than the Cross itself. Let me attempt one faint and far-away, and yet perhaps appealing to us in the realm in which we most perfectly find an expression of human love. Once it was my lot to see a mother snatch up her child from a railway track, just as the rushing train was almost upon it. I do not know that I ever saw anything much more roughly done. The mother was transformed for the moment into a veritable fury, as she caught up the child with hands that must have bruised it and carried it out of danger. Yet never did I see love more radiant than in the wild fury of that mother. How imperfect the illustration none can be more conscious than am I. I lift my eyes again to the Cross, and this I see, that in the mystery of its unfathomable anguish I discover that God will not be dethroned, though all hell be against Him, and this because of His mighty love. Let me utter it slowly and carefully, and yet out of my profoundest heart, if there be nothing to vindicate but His authority, then there is no necessity for the Cross; for the vindication of justice, or judgment, or righteousness, or holiness in the last analysis may be realized by the destruction of man. In such destruction, however, love would have been defeated, and for the vindication of that love, and what is infinitely more than its vindication, for its own satisfaction, He will not permit man to dethrone Him. Amid the depth of the darkness of Calvary it is grace that triumphs in a great authority. He will not consult with man in his folly, but He will retain the throne for very love of the foolish one. God found even in the midst of the ruin the possibility of redemption, and while God in Christ—for They cannot be separated—became the butt of brutal malice, He responded with tenderness; and when man's sin has done its worst in nailing Christ to the Cross with lawless hands, in that very Cross God plants the kiss of forgiveness upon the face of the murderers. It is the magnificent and majestic authority of love. He will love. We cannot prevent Him loving, and let me add reverently to that statement, He cannot help loving because He is Love. Love is stronger than death, mightier than the grave. Many waters cannot quench love. That is the anthem of the Cross. God retains the throne of authority because of His infinite love. He will never cease to love a single soul He has created.

In that Cross, moreover, there is revealed the unclouded wisdom of God. Seeing all that man in his blindness failed to see, and knowing perfectly the whole fact of the depravity wrought by man, He yet originated and carried out a plan of redemption so wonderful that the very unfallen intelligences of the upper world have ever desired to look into this great mystery of wisdom, and no man has been able perfectly to fathom its depths. To the Jews a stumbling-block, something in the way over which they fall; to the Greeks utter foolishness; and yet blessed be God, both to Jew and Greek, not only power, but wisdom. What wondrous words were those that passed the lips of Jesus. "It is finished."[1] What is finished? Sin was finished as to its power to work the final ruin of any man. In the mystery of the passion of Jesus, sin which had mastered men, and held them in slavery, was in turn mastered and robbed of its force. Whatever bruised, broken, beaten slave of sin will but hide in the cleft of that rock, and trust in the Crucified, for such an one sin is no more master. To the truth of this statement, testimony can be borne by the great multitudes of men and women who, standing at the Cross, have said, and still can say, The impossible has become possible, for all the forces of sin have been broken by the way of this victory of grace. Sin as a force that ruins, is ended in the Cross. It is not ended anywhere else. If men will not come into relation with that Cross, then sin is still an element of force, so great that no man is equal to its overcoming. In the cleft rock there is perfect security and perfect victory. "It is finished," said the Master, and because He meant that sin was finished, He meant that the work was finished through which grace might flow out like a river.

Not very long ago in London on a cold raw winter day, in the midst of the squalour and the degradation of the East End, I saw a little group of Salvationists, and I

[1] John 19: 30.

heard them sing, and never anthem sounded half so sweet.
These were the words :—

> " Grace is flowing like a river,
>   Millions there have been supplied,
>   Still it flows as fresh as ever
>   From the Saviour's wounded side."

Did I hear some one say something about doggerel? It is
the poetry of heaven. Did some one ask as to the balance
of the music? It had in it all the harmonies of the heart
of God. Grace is flowing like a river. How is it that
grace is thus flowing for the healing and the uplifting of
men? Because Jesus has said, " It is finished." He accomplished the work that made possible the outflowing of
this river of God.

Let us pause for a moment. Is some soul conscious of
sin that masters, of pollution that blights? The river is
flowing even here and now, and you may be cleansed, purified, saved. Oh, the matchless splendour of this outshining grace! In that Cross in very deed we see the deepest
meaning of sin, and the fullest force of grace. There sin
refuses God's King. There grace announces —

> " Jesus shall reign where'er the sun
>   Doth his successive journeys run." [1]

There sin manifested its prostitution of emotion in the
brutality of an awful tragedy. There grace through the
untold abyss of suffering smiled back with love ineffable,
until the very murderers of Christ found the highway open
to the heart of God. There sin in its ignorant madness
put out the light of life. There grace in infinite wisdom
shone through the gloom and there fell upon the pathway
of the race the light that leads to God.

[1] Watts.

Oh, wondrous Cross! Therein sin rejected the King, and grace crowned Him. Therein sin destroyed the Priest, and grace through the Priest made atonement. Therein sin silenced the voice of the Prophet, and grace caught up the message and repeated it to all the race, for a new law of life and love. In the Cross I see my sin. In the Cross I see God's grace. And, hear me, His grace is mightier than my sin, for " where sin abounded grace did abound more exceedingly." [1] Yet let me try to show that I cannot put all into it that is suggested by it. Did you ever watch the children playing on the seashore? How have I watched them, the golden-haired, laughing-eyed, dimple-fisted darlings! I ask this little group what they are doing, and they tell me that they are digging a big hole. What for, I say to them, and they reply, We want to see if the sea can fill it. The hole is dug, and the bairns stand on the mounds of sand, and I wait with them. We wait and watch and wonder as the waves come nearer in, those white horses of the mighty deep, and at last one, the seventh, perchance, stronger and bigger than his brothers, breaks up, and over the hole with the sweet swish of summer music, and I look and they look. What has happened? Is the hole filled? More exceedingly, more exceedingly! And the sea is yet behind! " Where sin abounded grace did abound more exceedingly." [2]

[1] Rom. 5 : 20.   [2] Rom. 5 : 20.

XXIII

THE KINGLY EXODUS

HAVING traced the very evident revelation of our Lord's consciousness of the coming Cross during the three years of His public ministry, and having endeavoured, moreover, reverently to come as near to that Cross as it is right that we should in contemplation of His suffering, and having stood before the Cross and considered its revelation of sin and grace, we are now to approach it from a new standpoint.

This study is devoted to a consideration of the Cross in relation to the Kingly position of Christ, and in the course of it we shall endeavour to observe Him as He wins the victory which issued in the redemption of His people from the slavery of a false authority, and opened the way into a new land of freedom under government.

The slavery of sin is a part of its penalty. When man yielded himself to sin, he became the servant of sin. By the way of the Cross the King made provision by which man could be redeemed from that slavery. In the mystery of His passion, the King led the exodus of all such as following Him, leave forever behind them the tasks and taskmasters of evil, and pass into the glorious liberty of the children of God.

In Luke's account of the transfiguration we read, " And behold, there talked with Him two men, who were Moses and Elijah; who appeared in glory, and spake of His decease which He was about to accomplish at Jerusalem."[1]

[1] Luke 9: 30, 31.

317

The writer of the letter to the Hebrews says, "By faith Joseph, when his end was nigh, made mention of the decease of the children of Israel." [1]   The word used by our translators is not the word "decease," but "departure," and such translation is undoubtedly correct.   The word translated "departure" in Hebrews is the identical word translated "decease" in Luke, and a more literal translation of the Greek word in each case would convey the correct meaning on both occasions, that word being ἔξοδον. The simplest translation would be in the use of our word exodus.   Use the word exodus in both connections, and it will be seen how it perfectly fits each : "Behold, there talked with Him two men, who were Moses and Elijah ; who appeared in glory, and spake of His exodus which He was about to accomplish at Jerusalem."   "By faith Joseph, when his end was nigh, made mention of the exodus of the children of Israel."   Peter, in referring to his own approaching end wrote, "Yea, I will give diligence that at every time ye may be able after my *departure* to call these things to remembrance." [2]   Here again we have altered the word, for it is translated "decease."   In the alteration on this occasion no incongruity was discovered. Here again adopt the suggested word, "Yea, I will give diligence that at every time ye may be able after my exodus."   This word ἔξοδον only occurs in the New Testament on these three occasions.   It is a word which means very literally, a highway out of, and so in use, a going out.   This is the word which describes the subject of conversation between Jesus, and Moses and Elijah. The word "decease" is not wrong, always providing that it is understood correctly.   It is derived from the Latin word "decessus," which means a going from, so that the true meaning of the word decease is not death, as cessation of being, but a going out, or liberation of life. This decease is really a word marking the Christian thought of death, although so seldom understood in that way. Upon the mount of transfiguration the heavenly visitors conversed with Jesus of His exodus. Joseph, when his end was nigh, spoke of the exodus of the children of Israel; and Peter, referring to his approaching end, used the word concerning it which our Lord had used of His, on the holy mount, " after My exodus."

We have occupied so much space with this word in order that we may be brought face to face with this particular aspect of the Cross of Jesus. We have considered our Lord as He passed into the place which was the necessary outcome of His assuming the responsibility of sin. We are now to consider Him as leading the way out from that very place, and so are to consider His death as in the pathway of His exodus. In this exodus He broke down all barriers, and left behind Him open doors through which those submitted to His Kingship, surrendered to His government, might have their exodus also from the bondage and slavery of sin into the glorious liberty of the children of God. In order to our contemplation of this aspect of the Cross, we shall first make a statement of the case, and then take the supreme illustration of this truth given in the case of the malefactor, who by faith in Jesus, passed with Him along the pathway of His exodus.

I.   In stating the case there must first be a remembrance of certain foundation facts. Of this the supreme one is that of the Divine Kingship. God is King. His claim is based upon the fact that He is the Creator, and Sustainer, of all life; and therefore His Proprietorship is based upon this original relationship, and His governmental right is the necessary and logical sequence. From this fact there can be no final escape. The history of human sin is the history of man's attempt to deny the Divine Kingship, and to resist its claims. In spite of all this terrible history of rebellion and failure, God has not resigned His throne, He has not abandoned His sceptre, He has not yielded the reins of government. He is absolute King in the very nature of the case. His right to rule does not depend upon the vote of a crowd. He has created, He has sustained, and in these facts lies the right of His Kingship. In the fullness of time God revealed and represented the fact of His Kingship in the Person of His Son.

Let us again revert to the second Psalm, and read it as it bears on our study.

First we have the question of the Psalmist in which we discover the touch of irony :—

> " Why do the nations rage,
> And the peoples meditate a vain thing ? "[1]

Then follows his description of the attitude of the kings and the rulers of the earth towards God and His anointed, with a declaration of their resolve :—

> " The kings of the earth set themselves,
> And the rulers take counsel together,
> Against Jehovah, and against His Anointed, saying,
> Let us break their bonds asunder,
> And cast away their cords from us."[2]

The next stage in the Psalm reveals the attitude of God towards the kings and the rulers, and declares the words

[1] Psa. 2: 1.   [2] Psa. 2: 2, 3.

of Jehovah, in answer to the resolve of these kings and rulers :—

> " He that sitteth in the heavens will laugh :
> The Lord will have them in derision.
> Then will He speak unto them in His wrath,
> And vex them in His sore displeasure :
> Yet have I set My King
> Upon My holy hill of Zion." [1]

At this point there is a change, and the Psalmist records the words of the anointed King, in view of the fiat of Jehovah :—

> " I will tell of the decree :
> Jehovah said unto Me, Thou art My Son ;
> This day have I begotten Thee.
> Ask of Me, and I will give Thee the nations for Thine inheritance,
> And the uttermost parts of the earth for Thy possession.
> Thou shalt break them with a rod of iron ;
> Thou shalt dash them in pieces like a potter's vessel." [2]

And yet once more there is a change. With the ceasing of the voice of the Anointed, the Psalmist addresses the kings, and the rulers of the earth :—

> " Now therefore be wise, O ye kings :
> Be instructed, ye judges of the earth.
> Serve Jehovah with fear,
> And rejoice with trembling.
> Kiss the Son, lest He be angry, and ye perish in the way,
> For His wrath will soon be kindled.
> Blessed are all they that take refuge in Him." [3]

Notice specially the announcement of Jehovah, " I have set My King upon My holy hill of Zion." Jesus Christ, the Son of God, was the visible representation and revela-

[1] Psa. 2: 4–6. [2] Psa. 2: 7–9. [3] Psa. 2: 10–12.

tion in time, of the perpetual inward fact of the Divine Sovereignty. He is God's anointed King for the accomplishment of certain purposes, for the carrying out of specific work. The eternal and unalterable fact is that of the sovereignty of Jehovah, and looking on over the far and immeasurable distances, I see the point described in the words of the apostle, "Then cometh the end, when He (the Son) shall deliver up the kingdom to God, even the Father." [1] In the Divine economy therefore there will finally be restored the actual and immediate Kingship of God. In order to that issue for the carrying out of the wonderful processes which will result therein, the Son is the King anointed, set upon the holy hill of Zion. These facts must be clearly before the mind in the contemplation of the Cross as the exodus of the King.

In certain respects, this fact of the Divine Kingship has become inoperative in human lives. In no human life has it absolutely become inoperative. Every man, woman, and child is under the government of God, and can by no means escape from it. The supreme illustration and proof of this lies in the fact that no man has been able to fix the day of his death. Or if by an act of unreasoning folly man has taken his life, it has been but to discover that he has not escaped from, but has hurried himself into, the consciousness of the supremacy of the Eternal God. Yet in the realm of will, and therefore of certain lines of conduct, the Divine Kingship is not acknowledged, and in that sense has become inoperative. Insomuch as this is true, man has passed under the false authority, and has become its slave. In an earlier study we noticed how the will necessarily demands a governing centre, a reason, a because. Will can only be exercised upon the basis of reason, and the reason

[1] 1 Cor. 15 : 24.

behind the exercise, is the governing authority of the life.
The true reason for the exercise of the will of man is the
will of God. Man dethroned God, declined to consider His
will as the abiding law, and abandoned by that act the true
principle of life. He did not, however, escape from the
necessity of a central authority, and a governing principle.
In place, however, of the good and perfect and acceptable
will of God, he enthroned the foolish, varying, imperfect
desires of the flesh and the mind. Instead of continuing
to say, I will because God wills, he came to say, I will because I wish. That is the essence of sin, and the issue
is obvious. Man yielded to sin, becomes the servant of
sin, is oppressed by sin, and is unable to do any other than
respond to the mastery of sin. He may catch fair glimpses
of that freer life, actuated by the will of God, but being
under the dominion of sin, he is not free to obey the
Divine Kingship. In the words of the apostle, he has to
say, " to me who would do good, evil is present." [1] That
is the supreme and overwhelming degradation of human
life. It is, moreover, the whole story of man. Yielded
to sin he is the slave of sin, bound hand and foot, bruised
and ruined in the whole fact of his life.

This principle of sin expressed itself towards God's
anointed King in His rejection and casting out. The will
of man, governed by a wrong reason, acting from a wrong
motive, rejected, crucified the One Who revealed the true
centre of authority in human life.

The great problems, therefore, facing the King in His
work of redeeming man, were those of how he should be
freed from the penalty of sin, and delivered from its paralysis. The inevitable issue of sin is death. Sin committed
cannot be undone by sorrow, or by promise of amendment.

[1] Rom. 7 : 21.

Sowing demands the harvest. It cannot possibly be avoided. Before man can be delivered from the slavery of sin, the penalty of sin must be borne.

The deeper and more terrible problem is that of the paralysis resulting from sin. Sin working death makes obedience impossible. Man is the slave of sin, is paralyzed in all the highest powers of his being, in the whole of which the poison operates with ever increasing and terrific power. These problems are solved in the mystery of the King's passion. Having reverently come to the margin of that passion, and observed Him as He passed into a realm where we could by no means follow, we see Him in the Cross emerging from the slavery.

As our previous study has shown, the King in His sinlessness has carried the sin of His people, and having done so has created a value which He did not require for Himself, and which is therefore at the disposal of those in whose place He has suffered. Thus by identification with man in the penalty and paralysis of sin, He brings man into identification with Himself in the pardon and power of His life. Yet when I hear Him saying: "It is finished,"[1] "Father, into Thy hands I commend My spirit,"[2] I know that He is on the highway of His exodus, Egypt is behind, the power of the oppressor is broken, the mystery of sin is at an end, and as He emerges from the slavery, He sets the door wide open, that those who follow Him by the way of the Cross, may have their exodus also from all that sin means as to penalty. It was, moreover, the pathway of freedom from the paralysis of sin, in virtue of the fact that the life laid down was taken again, that it might be communicated to the sin-enslaved. This will only be fully dealt with as we pass to the subjects of resur-

[1] John 19: 30.   [2] Luke 23: 46.

rection and ascension, which are also within the highway of His exodus.

Thus we reverently contemplate the anointed King as He leads His people from the Egypt of their bondage, through a divided sea, towards the place of liberty under the Kingship of Jehovah. The King Himself has taken hold upon that which has enslaved man, He has borne its penalty, and broken its power, and thus provided the value of forgiveness for the race, and a dynamic of life for all such as put their trust in Him. We see Him passing by the way of the Cross with the step of a Conqueror, the Leader of the great hosts, who by His victory shall be delivered from the bondage of sin and the bondage of death, into all the spacious freedom of the Kingdom of God.

II. A singularly beautiful illustration of the truth is supplied in the story of the malefactor. Carefully note the setting of that story in the Gospel of Luke. Immediately preceding it is the account of the superscription over His cross, " THIS IS THE KING OF THE JEWS." [1] Immediately following it is the declaration: " It was now about the sixth hour, and a darkness came over the land until the ninth hour, the sun's light failing, and the veil of the temple was rent in the midst." [2]

The superscription expressed the fact that the Hebrew nation did not believe. So far as Pilate was concerned it was undoubtedly an expression of his contempt for the men who had encompassed the death of Jesus. These are the human elements. The Divine fact is that the superscription was written with the finger of God even though Pilate all unconsciously was His penman. As of old He girded Cyrus, though he did not know Him, so He

[1] Luke 23: 38. [2] Luke 23: 44, 45.

inspired Pilate who was all unconscious. The Jewish nation in the purpose of God was a revelation of His government, a theocracy through which He would express the
benefits of His rule to the nations of the world, that they
might all share in them by submission. In the economy
of God, therefore, the King of the Jews was the Holy
One set upon the hill of Zion, King of the whole earth.
The Hebrew people had their exodus from bondage long
centuries before, but it had never been completed. The
letter to the Hebrews makes this perfectly clear. They
passed over the sea, and yet died in the wilderness. The
God-appointed King, talking with Moses who had led that
old-time exodus, and yet who himself had failed as the people had failed, spoke of an exodus which He would accomplish. The other exodus was never accomplished. It
was begun, but not finished. He had come to accomplish,
to finish the exodus, and the superscription marks Him as
the King Who is leading His people, and all people who
bow to His sceptre in that exodus which is perfect freedom
from the bondage of false authority.

At last the hours of darkness are ended, and then it is
written, "the veil of the temple was rent in the midst." [1]
The rent veil was the sign that the exodus so far as the
King was concerned, was accomplished. This exodus
which has been considered as a going out of, a liberation
from the bondage, is now seen as an introduction to relationship with God.

Between this declaration concerning the superscription,
and the account of the rent veil, there is the story of the
malefactor, and his coming into association with the King,
in the process of the exodus. That dying man is a super-
lative illustration of the slavery of sin. He is suffering

[1] Luke 23 : 45.

the penalty of death, which is the issue of the paralysis of ruined character. In that hopeless condition he becomes conscious of his nearness to the King. There is, as it seems to me, no record of faith in the New Testament so wonderful as that of the dying malefactor. In the very moment of the defeat of Jesus to all human seeming, in the presence of the sign and symbol of His casting out, this man recognizes the King moving towards a Kingdom, and he appeals to Him before the exodus is accomplished, before the crowning is reached. His cry is the cry of conscious need as it casts itself in all its helplessness at the feet of supreme authority. " Jesus, remember me when Thou comest in Thy kingdom." [1] What did the King say to such an appeal ? He was on His way from Egypt to the land of liberty. He was at the moment grappling with the bonds that bound the race. He, whelmed in the billows of the sea, was yet in infinite power dividing a pathway through its waters, and without hesitation, in a great consciousness of the coming victory, He said, " To-day shalt thou be with Me in Paradise." [2] We care nothing for the moment as to discussions concerning the Paradise. " With Me." That is the word of value. Explain the Paradise as you will. Let it mean for the moment, if you so please, simply the abiding place of disembodied spirits. What matters it ? The fact remains that the sin-slaved and ruined man is in that abode to be with the King. Abandonment to Him will issue in identification with Him. If that issue is His defeat, then also will abide the defeat of the man. Yet this is a suggestion ventured only by way of contrast to the glorious fact. The King really said to him, I am going on My exodus, you come with Me. I am passing to the depth of this slavery. I am

[1] Luke 23 : 42.   [2] Luke 23 : 43.

breaking these bonds. I am liberating the prisoners. Come with Me. From that moment until this He has been leading souls who have trusted Him through the pathway of His passion with all its values, into the place of His victory with all its virtues.

Thus the presence and the plea of the dying malefactor reveals the Cross as the condemnation and death of rebellion and unbelief, and the commendation and life power of loyalty and faith.

So comes the kingdom of God! The King has accomplished the exodus! Are we living in the bondage, or in freedom? The answer to this question will be found in the answer to another. Have we yet come into the place of trusting identification with Him in His Cross? If so, then for us

> " Bars are riven,
> Foes are driven "

and our bondage is at an end.

The King accomplished the exodus for all such as put their trust in Him, and these have already passed with Him from darkness to light, from slavery to freedom, from death to life.

XXIV

THE REPRESENTATIVE CROWDS

THE Cross was the outworking in history of the redemptive purposes of God. In it the Lamb slain from the foundation of the world, was slain in view of those for whom His passion and death provided redemption and life. It would seem as though all the facts and forces of human life appeared in the presence of the passion of the Son of God. What the Cross was to those composing this assembly, depended upon the attitude of mind and heart in which they gathered around it. To some it was the evangel of hope. To others it was a sentence of doom. In the present study we shall attempt to look at those gathered to the Cross, and to enquire what the Cross meant to them.

In an examination of the records of the crucifixion preserved for us by the four evangelists, we shall be able to fill in for ourselves a picture of that Cross with the persons surrounding it. As we have been intent upon the vision of the suffering Saviour, we now turn to look at those who are round about Him, and at once are arrested by the strange mixture, and representative character of the multitude gathered to the mount called Calvary.

Let us first state without reference to classification, the persons mentioned in the Gospels, and then proceed to separate them into groups, and consider the suggestiveness in each case.

I. All the writers in some way refer to the presence of

the women.   Matthew speaks of the women from Galilee, and of these he names " Mary Magdalene, Mary the mother of James and Joses, and the mother of the sons of Zebedee." [1]   Mark mentions these same three women, " Mary Magdalene, Mary the mother of James the less and of Joses, and Salome," [2] the wife of Zebedee, and therefore the mother of James and of John, the sons of Zebedee.   Luke gives no names, but he declares the fact of the presence of the women in the words, " there followed Him a great multitude of the people, and of women who bewailed and lamented Him." [3]   John names the three referred to by Matthew and Mark, but adds another.   It is he who declares the presence of the mother of the Lord. There has been some difference of opinion concerning John's account of the women present, which reads, " But there were standing by the Cross of Jesus His mother, and His mother's sister, Mary the wife of Clopas, and Mary Magdalene." [4]   Some interpret that verse as referring to three women.   In that case it is understood that His mother's sister was Mary the wife of Clopas.   My own conviction is that John mentions four women, that Mary of Clopas was not the sister of Mary the mother of Jesus. To tabulate the statement of John, you would write :—

" His mother."
" His mother's sister."
" Mary the wife of Clopas."
" Mary Magdalene."

The only difference between this account, and those of Matthew and Mark, is the addition of the mention of Mary the mother of the Lord.   In that case her sister was Salome, the wife of Zebedee, and mother of James

[1] Matt. 27 : 56.   [2] Mark 15 : 40.   [3] Luke 23 : 27.   [4] John 19 : 25.

and John. It is interesting to note in passing, the effect that this understanding of the passage has upon certain facts in the Gospel history. The woman who came to the Lord, and asked that her sons might sit, one on His right hand and one on His left hand, was according to the flesh, related to Him, being His mother's sister, and these men for whom the boon was asked were His own cousins. This gives some clue to what otherwise appears as a very strange request. If it be granted that Salome was His mother's sister, we have at any rate some explanation of her request in the fact that she suggested to Him that when He came into the place of power He should find preferment for His family relations.

We take it then for granted that four women are mentioned as being present at the crucifixion of the Lord. In John we see two pairs, the unnamed women, the mother of the Lord and her sister; and the two women who are named, Mary of Clopas, and Mary Magdalene. As Luke records, there were many other women, but these stand prominently out, as having been most closely associated with Him.

All the evangelists speak of the presence of the soldiers, and of the two malefactors crucified one on either side of Jesus. Matthew, Mark, and Luke draw special attention to the centurion in charge of the carrying out of the crucifixion, and they give some account of how he was impressed in the presence of the Crucified. According to Matthew he said, " Truly this was a Son of God "; [1] according to Mark, " Truly this Man was a Son of God "; [2] according to Luke, " Certainly this was a righteous Man." [3] Let me at once say that there is no con-

---

[1] Matt. 27 : 54 (margin).   [2] Mark 15 : 39 (margin).
[3] Luke 23 : 47.

tradition between Matthew and Mark on the one hand, and Luke on the other. It is almost certain that the centurion said both of these things. It is certainly conceivable that as this man watched Jesus on the Cross, he gave utterance to more than one sentence, and we believe therefore that while Matthew and Mark chronicle the statement which impressed them, Luke chronicled what appealed to him, and was in perfect harmony with his whole scheme of teaching. The accounts are rather complementary than contradictory.

The presence of the chief priests is recorded by Matthew, Mark, and John, Luke making no reference to them. Matthew, Mark, and Luke refer to the scribes, elders, or rulers, comprising the Sanhedrim, while John ignores their presence.

Luke, the burden of whose Gospel is that of the universality of the work and relation of Jesus, declares the presence of great multitudes of the people.

John alone tells us that the disciples were also there, and he only, moreover, refers to the fact of his own presence, and this in order that he may record Christ's committal of His mother to his care. Standing back and gazing out upon that mixed multitude, we notice the women, the soldiers, the malefactors, the centurion, the chief priests, the members of the Sanhedrim, the group of His own disciples, and in addition to these, the vast multitudes of people from the whole surrounding country. All sorts and conditions of men are gathered to the Cross, representative crowds, the whole scene being a picture and a prophecy of how, through all the centuries, every sort and condition would be gathered to the uplifted Cross of the Son of man.

II. Let us now look at these crowds in another way.

We will attempt an analysis of the multitude, not so much with reference to the persons as to the conditions represented at the Cross, illustrating the fact by an examination of the people.

Sorrow was supremely represented by the presence of the women. Worldly government by the centurion, the soldiers, and the malefactors. Religious failure by the chief priests and the Sanhedrim. The great shepherdless crowd over which Christ had so often mourned, and in the presence of which His heart had ever been moved with compassion, was largely represented in the great multitude of which Luke speaks. Familiarity with Jesus had its representation in the presence before the Cross of His kinsfolk and acquaintance. Discipleship was there, in the person of His own, and particularly of John.

See, first, human sorrow as represented in the women, noticing the groups as we have them in John, taking first the women who are named, and then the women known but unnamed.

Of the former, the principal figure attracting attention is that of Mary Magdalene, for we know very little concerning Mary of Clopas, save that she was the mother of James the less and of Joses. The sorrow of Mary Magdalene must have been very profound. I would that it were in my power to redeem this woman from a popular and terrible misconception concerning her. For some reason almost without explanation the term Magdalene has become a synonym for impurity. There is absolutely no warrant in Scripture for the idea. Mary Magdalene simply means Mary of Magdala. That was her city, and the title is used undoubtedly by the evangelists, simply to distinguish her from other women who bore the name of Mary. She had been delivered from seven demons. This phrase was certainly sometimes used by Jewish writers as descriptive of some terrible form of sin, such as drunkenness or impurity, but it was as often used to describe different forms of disease, such as epilepsy. Attempts have been made to link her with the woman that was a sinner, but the case has never been proven, and in the absence of positive proof we have no right forever to link her memory with the sin of unchastity. We prefer to believe that the demons possessing her had afflicted her as they did the son of the man who met Jesus at the foot of the mount of transfiguration, seeing that we have no positive proof of impurity. This woman was present at His Cross, watching the cruel crucifixion and fearful death of the One Who had forever endeared Himself to her, and proved His power, by that marvellous deliverance He had wrought. By the way of that Cross she had lost her Deliverer. How her heart must have been wrung with anguish.

Yet in the clearer understanding of the Cross which has come to us, we see how in it she recovered her Leader, and by it He gained possession of her forever, as the One Who in the mystery of its darkness, conquered and dispossessed the devil and all demons of their power over human lives. So that while hers was the sorrow of a lost Leader, a dead Deliverer, it was in process of time transformed into the joy of a Leader that cannot be lost nor will suffer those He loves to be lost, of a Deliverer Who has conquered death and will deliver those who trust Him, even from death itself. Thus for Mary of Magdala the Cross was the process by which her greatest sorrow was transmuted into her highest joy.

Notice next the second pair of women, Salome the mother of James and John, and the Lord's own mother Mary.

Concerning Salome may it not be said that she stood before the Cross disappointed in the emotions of motherhood? Her sons had left their fishing, and had gone to follow Jesus. With the true instinct of motherhood she had been anxious that they should succeed. One can imagine that she did not feel perfectly in harmony with their action. If I may use an expression of the present day in application to her attitude, I should say that she had questioned the wisdom of their giving up a certainty for an uncertainty. When, however, they had left their nets and followed Him, she endeavoured to use her influence with Him on their behalf. Expecting the possibility of His at last coming into power, she had asked that in that event her sons, His cousins, James and John, might sit one on His right hand, and one on His left. And now the folly of their action is revealed in His evident failure. I see in this woman the sorrow of disappointed motherhood. It may be objected that this is placing her sorrow on a low level. Is it not true that most human sorrow is sorrow on a level that is certainly not high? I do not question for a moment that this woman sorrowed in sympathy with Him in His defeat and awful pain, but her previous action makes it more than probable that she thought of her own sons in the presence of the crucified Jesus. And yet what did that Cross do for this woman? It was by it that James and John found their thrones of power. They passed out into the ages crowned men, seeing that He permitted them to drink of His cup, and to be baptized with His baptism, as He said that He would. And so by the way of that Cross her motherhood was crowned with gladness, and she found her joy just where she had seemed to lose it.

Who shall speak of the sorrow of His own mother? Let us describe it by the words in which it was foretold in those early days in which her neart was glad at the birth of Jesus. The sword had pierced through her own soul. What anguish of spirit, what heart-break Mary passed through, perhaps only motherhood can ever perfectly comprehend. And yet she also found her salvation there, and is known to-day as most highly favoured among women, because she was the mother of Him Who was crucified for the redemption of man. Blessed virgin in very deed. It is absolutely certain that we of the Protestant faith have in our rebound from the worship of this woman gone to another extreme, utterly unwarranted by Scripture. We have relegated Mary into the improper position of obscurity. We need to remember that an angel addressed her, saying, " Hail, thou that art highly favoured," [1] and this we should all be prepared to say of her, as a recognition of her exalted position, having in it not the slightest suspicion of worship rendered. In Mary all womanhood was crowned and elevated, and yet she found her way into heaven, not because of the honour bestowed upon her, but by the way of that Cross and passion, which for the moment was a sword piercing her soul also.

Thus sorrow is seen at the Cross where sorrow is always seen at its deepest, in the wounded, stricken, smitten heart of womanhood; and yet in each case by the Cross the sorrow was turned into joy. Upon the dark cloud there flashed the great light, until the very cloud became a sea of glory. Oh, rough and rugged Cross of Calvary! We gather round thy stern sublimity of suffering with our own hearts' agony, and find heart's-ease. We come to thee with faces stained with tears, and in the strength of His victory our tears are wiped away, our sorrow is turned into joy.

[1] Luke 1 : 28.

But now turn abruptly to another group, the representatives of worldly government, the centurion, the soldiers, and the crucified malefactors. Look at each of them for a moment, for the Cross is to the fact of worldly government, just what the fact of worldly government is to the Cross.

The centurion was a representative of discipline and duty. It is worthy of passing notice that every centurion mentioned in the New Testament was a good man. It was a centurion who said to Jesus: "I also am a man set under authority, having under myself soldiers: and I say to this one, Go, and he goeth; and to another, Come, and he cometh."[1] In that statement there is contained a remarkable philosophy of authority and discipline. I am under authority, I obey; therefore I have authority, I command others to obey. The true philosophy of human government lies within that statement. The man who has a right to rule is the man who knows how to be ruled. The only man fit to issue orders is the man accustomed to obey orders. "I am under authority, I have authority." This centurion in the presence of the Cross was a man of authority, and he had soldiers under him. He was a man of law, of order, of discipline, of duty, and from that standpoint of life he had watched the dying man until at last he said, "Truly this was a Son of God."[2] To properly appreciate this statement we must understand the Roman thought rather than the Hebrew in the phrase "a Son of God." I believe the centurion meant that He was one of the sons of the gods. The Roman idea of God was that of heroic, courageous manhood, magnified in all its powers, and looking upon this man in His suffering, the heroism, the courage and the dis-

Luke 7 : 8.   [2] Matt. 27 : 54.

cipline manifested in submission, appealed to him as being Godlike.

And yet he said another thing, "Certainly this was a righteous Man."[1] This was the conviction of one who was himself a man of duty. To this Roman soldier the one governing principle of life was that of duty. He lived in the midst of a system. He marched in rhythm and time. He obeyed and insisted upon obedience with inflexible regularity. Rightness was the one word of value to him, at least in the sphere of his soldierhood. He saw in the Man upon the Cross One evidently acting in the realm of order, submissive to authority, and therefore authoritative, keeping time with eternal principles in the quiet majesty of His submission, "a righteous Man." The centurion as a man of duty discovered order in the Cross, and as a man who worshipped high ideals, saw the Son of God crucified.

What did the Cross for the centurion? We have no record of his after life, but this much at least is certain, that it commanded the respect and the confession of that which was highest in human government. And if we may follow the story along imaginative lines, it is more than probable that the King upon Whose brow the centurion placed the diadem of his loyalty, crowned him with the realization of his own highest ideals of life.

We look at the soldiers with pity rather than anger. They were brutalized men, and yet brutalized by the system in the midst of which they found themselves. We watch them as gathered around the Cross upon which they have nailed the Son of God, they gambled for His garments and presently one of their number pierced His side with a spear. As we have seen in the former considera-

[1] Luke 23 : 47.

tion, that spear thrust was the ultimate expression of man's rebellion against God. So far as the man was concerned who thrust it in His side, I am never quite sure that the action was not prompted by pity. How brutalized and vulgarized these men were, is evident from the fact that they cast lots for His garments under the shadow of the Cross, and their only idea of help, granting that to have been the motive, was that of the thrust of the spear.

One wonders if these soldiers ever saw the true vision. Did they ever understand that the seamless robe of which they sought to gain possession by gambling, was the prophecy of the new robing being provided for men in the mystery of that Cross? Did they ever discover that the flowing blood which answered their spear thrust was for the putting away of sin? I do not know. Personally I expect to meet some of those men in heaven. It is certain that the Master prayed for them, and I cannot forget that on the Day of Pentecost thousands were swept into the kingdom of God, and in all probability among the number some of the Roman soldiery, and, perchance, the men also who nailed Him to the Cross.

Look for one moment at the malefactors, and there we have sin on the one side persisted in, and on the other, turned from. The crucified malefactors both express the uttermost that human government has ever been able to do with sin. It can but punish. Both these men are in the presence of the Cross. One in that presence persisted in his sin, and added to it. For him the Cross was the penalty which deepened into the darker death that lay beyond it. One turning from his sin, flung himself upon the tender notice of the King, Who was passing over the pathway of His exodus, and for Him the Cross was the gate of Paradise, and just beyond this darkness flamed the splendour of the light of the presence and companionship of the Lord, which makes unnecessary the light of sun, or moon, or stars, or candle. To these things no words need be added. Sin in the presence of the Cross, on the one hand, persisting in rebellion, goes down into the unutterable and awful and inexpressible darkness. Sin on the other hand, turning to Him, confessing, believing, passes triumphantly with Him through the darkness of the Cross to the light of Paradise.

Notice yet again earth's religious failure as represented by the high priests and the Sanhedrim. What a terrible picture this is of priestism. These men were rejoicing in the Cross because it had secured power to them by destroying Jesus. Is this sufficiently realized? Do we always remember why the priest encompassed the death of Christ? Watch carefully the history, and notice that their trouble was that they were losing power, and their constant question was, What shall we do? The people were slipping away from their grip, but at last they have put an end to His influence, they have Him now nailed to a Cross, and by His destruction they secure their own power. O blind men, infatuated men! While they gloat over their fancied victory, God rends the veil of the temple in twain, and for-ever more does away with the priest. Just as they thought they had ensured their dominance of humanity by crucifying Him, He by His dying spoiled their power, rent the veil, and by abolishing the priest, created the priesthood of all believers.

Turn for one moment and look at the Sanhedrim as represented by the scribes, the elders, the rulers. How are they occupied in the presence of the Cross? They are indulging in diabolical pleasantry. They are laughing at the dying Man. They say, " He saved others, Himself He cannot save." [1]   They are making merriment over the fact that the Cross is the evidence of His folly.   He Who had been saving men, and calling men to the pathway of salvation, is unable to save Himself.   How can any really save others who are not able to save themselves ?   Such is the wisdom of the world, and the world's wisdom laughs at the folly of the Cross.   It has never ceased laughing at the Cross !   It is doing so still !   In this new century the trouble is that not the world only makes mock of the Cross.   The laughter has invaded the so-called Church of Jesus.   I have heard a man, claiming to be in the ministry of Jesus, who objected to sing —

" There is a fountain filled with blood."

What gain it would be for the Church and the world if these men would be honest and go outside the Church. The man who has lost his sense of the need of blood-cleansing from sin has no right to stand and call himself a messenger of Christ.   The Sanhedrim laughed at the Cross.   And yet in that Cross there is being shown forth before the gaze of heaven and in the presence of men, so sadly blinded that they cannot understand, the wisdom of God.   In the foolishness of Christ's Cross there flames out the glory of the Eternal Wisdom, for what man has never been able to do will be done through that Cross. And the very people who have become brutalized, and degraded, and wrapped in the grave clothes of ritualism, by the Sanhedrim and the priests; will cast aside their grave clothes, and pass into nobler life by the way of that Cross of shame.

Oh, how foolish and pitiable is the mockery of the Cross by the wisdom of the world !

[1] Matt. 27 : 42.

Look for one moment upon the multitudes around, the great shepherdless crowd. That was Christ's picture of them, sheep having no shepherd. How perplexed, how disappointed many of them must have been that day. For three years they had followed a Leader, a Deliverer, followed Him foolishly, it is true, not from high motive, and never able thoroughly to appreciate Him. Moved by the signs of His power, and drawn by the tenderness of His compassion, they have followed still, though imperfectly, and now the end of it is His crucifixion. They had hoped that " it was He Who should redeem Israel," [1] and now He is nailed to the Roman, and the cursed, tree. Jesus had spoken of them as being without a shepherd, and many of them had come to hope that perhaps He was their Shepherd. Oh, could they but see, He was indeed the good Shepherd, and in the mystery of that awful Cross, He was laying down His life for them! Presently they will come back, by tens, by hundreds, and by thousands. Never tell me that Christ's ministry was a failure. It has sometimes been said that He only gathered about one hundred and twenty disciples. But let it never be forgotten that the results of the preaching of Jesus were gathered upon the day of Pentecost, and gathered wherever those men afterwards proclaimed His death and resurrection. In the days of His public ministry He had done what He is now doing in the present day. He gathered a few in association with Himself, as He is now calling out the Church to Himself; but He prepared thousands of others to be gathered in, in the fullness of time, as He is now preparing the whole world for the preaching of the Gospel that shall succeed the present dispensation and economy. And of those multitudes around the Cross there can be no doubt that

[1] Luke 24: 21.

presently many came to know Him as the good Shepherd Who had laid down His life for the sheep.

Luke alone refers to the fact of the presence of His acquaintance at the Cross. The reference is undoubtedly to His kinsfolk and His neighbours from Nazareth, and their presence may be suggestive of a deepened interest. In all probability His own brothers, the sons of Mary, were among the number. It would seem as though James, the author of the epistle, who was undoubtedly the Lord's own brother, did not come into true sympathy with Him during the life of Jesus. May it not be that in the presence of that Cross and through the events following, he was led to a knowledge of the truth concerning the Master? In the attitude of these kinsfolk and acquaintance of Jesus, and if the foregoing supposition concerning His own brothers be correct, what a revelation there is for all time that familiarity may be most distant.

Discipleship was represented at the Cross especially by John. He seems to have been the only one who came very near the place of his Master's suffering, and his nearness issued in the sacred charge of Mary, which was committed to him by his dying Lord.

Looking back at that whole scene, how truly remarkable it is. The first impression is that of a Roman gibbet surrounded by a promiscuous mob, while one frail, weak Man finds relief from overwhelming agony in the act of death. But look again, and it is seen to be the place of a throne. The throne is occupied by One Who is at once King and Judge, finding verdicts and pronouncing sentences, and all in the neighbourhood of the Cross are judged by the Cross. His dying is the condemnation of evil in every form. His dying is the pathway of deliverance for those who at the Cross turn from the things the Cross condemns, to put their trust in Him. Such He leads by the way of the Cross to the broad life that stretches away on the other side.

> " I take, O Cross, thy shadow,
>   For my abiding place ;
> I ask no other sunshine
>   Than the sunshine of thy face.
> Content to let the world go by,
>   To know no shame nor loss.
> My sinful self my only shame,
>   My glory all the Cross." [1]

[1] E. C. Clephane.

BOOK VI

THE RESURRECTION

XXV. Perfect Victory
XXVI. The Divine Seal
XXVII. Faith's Anchorage

"The foe behind, the deep before,
 Our hosts have dared and pass'd the sea;
And Pharaoh's warriors strew the shore,
 And Israel's ransom'd tribes are free.
Lift up, lift up your voices now!
The whole wide world rejoices now!
Happy morning, Turning sorrow
  Into peace and mirth!
Bondage ending, Love descending
 O'er the earth!
Seals assuring, Guards securing,
  Watch His earthly prison.
Seals are shattered, Guards are scattered,
 Christ hath risen!

No longer must the mourners weep,
 Nor call departed Christians dead;
For death is hallowed into sleep,
 And ev'ry grave becomes a bed.
Now once more
  Eden's door
   Open stands to mortal eyes;
For Christ hath risen, and man shall rise!
Now at last,
  Old things past,
   Hope, and joy, and peace begin;
For Christ hath won, and man shall win!
It is not exile, rest on high:
 It is not sadness, peace from strife;
To fall asleep is not to die:
 To dwell with Christ is better life.
Where our banner leads us,
 We may safely go:
Where our Chief precedes us,
 We may face the foe.
His right arm is o'er us,
 He our Guide will be:
Christ hath gone before us,
 Christians, follow ye!"
                    —DR. NEALE.

Now late on the sabbath day, as it began to dawn toward the first day of the week, came Mary Magdalene and the other Mary to see the sepulchre. And behold, there was a great earthquake; for an angel of the Lord descended from heaven, and came and rolled away the stone, and sat upon it. His appearance was as lightning, and his raiment white as snow: and for fear of him the watchers did quake, and became as dead men. And the angel answered and said unto the women, Fear not ye; for I know that ye seek Jesus, Who hath been crucified. He is not here; for He is risen, even as He said. Come, see the place where the Lord lay. And go quickly, and tell His disciples, He is risen from the dead; and lo, He goeth before you into Galilee; there shall ye see Him: lo, I have told you. And they departed quickly from the tomb with fear and great joy, and ran to bring His disciples word.—*Matt. 28 : 1–8.*

*   *   *   *   *   *   *

And when the Sabbath was past, Mary Magdalene, and Mary the mother of James, and Salome, bought spices, that they might come and anoint Him. And very early on the first day of the week, they come to the tomb when the sun was risen. And they were saying among themselves, Who shall roll us away the stone from the door of the tomb? and looking up, they see that the stone is rolled back: for it was exceeding great. And entering into the tomb, they saw a young man sitting on the right side, arrayed in a white robe; and they were amazed. And he saith unto them, Be not amazed: ye seek Jesus, the Nazarene, Who hath been crucified: He is risen; He is not here: behold, the place where they laid Him! But go, tell His disciples and Peter, He goeth before you into Galilee: there shall ye see Him, as He said unto you. And they went out, and fled from the tomb; for trembling and astonishment had come upon them: and they said nothing to any one; for they were afraid.

Now when He was risen early on the first day of the week, He appeared first to Mary Magdalene, from whom He had cast out seven demons. She went and told them that had been with Him, as they mourned and wept. And they when they heard that He was alive, and had been seen of her, disbelieved.—*Mark 16 : 1–11.*

*   *   *   *   *   *   *

But on the first day of the week, at early dawn, they came unto the tomb, bringing the spices which they had prepared. And they found the stone rolled away from the tomb. And they entered in, and found not the body of the Lord Jesus. And it came to pass, while they were perplexed thereabout, behold, two men stood by them in dazzling apparel: and as they were affrighted and bowed down their faces to the earth, they said unto them, Why seek ye the living among the dead? He is not here, but is risen: remember how He spake unto you when He was yet in Galilee, saying that the Son of Man must be delivered up into the hands of sinful men, and be crucified, and the third day rise again. And they remembered His words, and returned from the tomb, and told all these things to the eleven, and to all the rest. Now they were Mary Magdalene, and Joanna, and Mary the mother of James: and the other women with them told these things unto the apostles. And these words appeared in their sight as idle talk; and they disbelieved them. But Peter arose, and ran unto the tomb; and stooping and looking in, he seeth the linen cloths by themselves; and he departed to his home, wondering at that which was come to pass.—*Luke 24: 1–12.*

*   *   *   *   *   *   *

Now on the first day of the week cometh Mary Magdalene early, while it was yet dark, unto the tomb, and seeth the stone taken away from the tomb. She runneth therefore, and cometh to Simon Peter, and to the other disciple whom Jesus loved, and saith unto them, They have taken away the Lord out of the tomb, and we know not where they have laid Him. Peter therefore went forth, and the other disciple, and they went toward the tomb. And they ran both together: and the other disciple outran Peter, and came first to the tomb; and stooping and looking in, he seeth the linen cloths lying; yet entered he not in. Simon Peter therefore also cometh, following him, and entered into the tomb; and he beholdeth the linen cloths lying, and the napkin, that was upon His head, not lying with the linen cloths, but rolled up in a place by itself. Then entered in therefore the other disciple also, who came first to the tomb, and he saw, and believed. For as yet they knew not the Scripture, that He must rise again from the dead. So the disciples went away again unto their own home.

But Mary was standing without at the tomb weeping: so, as she wept, she stooped and looked into the tomb; and she beholdeth two angels in white sitting, one at the head, and one at the feet, where the body of Jesus had lain. And they say unto her, Woman, why weepest thou? She saith unto them, Because they have ʳaken away my Lord, and I know not where they have laid Him.

When she had thus said, she turned herself back, and beholdeth Jesus standing, and knew not that it was Jesus. Jesus saith unto her, Woman why weepest thou? whom seekest thou? She, supposing Him to be the gardener, saith unto Him, Sir, if Thou hast borne Him hence, tell me where Thou hast laid Him, and I will take Him away. Jesus saith unto her, Mary. She turneth herself, and saith unto Him in Hebrew, Rabboni; which is to say, Teacher. Jesus saith to her, Touch Me not; for I am not yet ascended unto the Father: but go unto My brethren, and say to them, I ascend unto My Father and your Father, and My God and your God. Mary Magdalene cometh and telleth the disciples, I have seen the Lord; and that He had said these things unto her.—*John 20: 1–18.*

XXV

PERFECT VICTORY

In considering the crisis of the resurrection, arguments for the actual historical fact will be taken in the last section. First assuming the fact, its value as a demonstration of Christ's perfect victory will be considered.

Referring again to Peter's discourse on the day of Pentecost, a most remarkable epitome of Christian doctrine, there will be found an argument concerning the resurrection which is briefly stated in the words " It was not possible that He should be holden of it," and is defended by quotation from ancient Scripture, full of value and of suggestiveness. It will be well to read in full, Peter's statement, and the Psalm from which it is quoted. Having set the Cross in relation to the sin of man, and the grace of God, the apostle continued,

" Whom God raised up, having loosed the pangs of death : because it was not possible that He should be holden of it. For David saith concerning Him,

" I beheld the Lord always before My face ;
For He is on My right hand, that I should not be moved ;
Therefore My heart was glad, and My tongue rejoiced :
Moreover My flesh also shall dwell in hope :
Because Thou wilt not leave My soul unto Hades,
Neither wilt Thou give Thy Holy One to see corruption.
Thou madest known unto Me the ways of life ;
Thou shalt make Me full of gladness with Thy countenance." [1]

[1] Acts 2 : 24-28.

The actual words of the Psalm quoted, as they appear in the Old Testament are as follows,

> " I have set Jehovah always before Me :
> Because He is at My right hand, I shall not be moved.
> Therefore My heart is glad, and My glory rejoiceth :
> My flesh also shall dwell in safety.
> For Thou wilt not leave My soul to Sheol ;
> Neither wilt Thou suffer Thy holy One to see corruption.
> Thou wilt show Me the path of life :
> In Thy presence is fullness of joy ;
> In Thy right hand there are pleasures forevermore." [1]

Perhaps the true values of the simple statement of the apostle may be gathered, by laying emphasis upon the pronoun having reference to Jesus, and the final one referring to death. " It was not possible that He should be holden of it." In this way the statement is seen to be a sublime and magnificent one, in which the apostle, conscious of the victory Jesus had won in life and death, treats almost with contempt the last enemy.

" He " that is " Jesus of Nazareth, a Man approved of God unto you by mighty works and wonders and signs," the One Who " being delivered up by the determinate counsel and foreknowledge of God, ye by the hand of lawless men did crucify and slay." This same Person, God " raised up, having loosed the pangs of death : because it was not possible that He should be holden of it." [2] The unifying fact in the whole discourse is the Person of Jesus of Nazareth, and having set in order the movements of that wonderful life, the apostle now declares that God raised Him because He was bound to raise Him. Not to have done so, if this may be reverently supposed, would have been to have violated every principle of law. The necessities of the Divine nature demanded it. The eternal order required it. If death had held Him, the issue must have been disorder, and the defeat of all the purposes of God.

So far this is a bare statement. It remains now to consider why " it was not possible that He should be holden of it." This is revealed in the apostle's use of the language of the Psalmist. Peter distinctly declared that what David wrote, he wrote concerning Christ, and was careful by subsequent statements to show that the language of the Psalmist could not have been fulfilled by the experience of the one who wrote it ; but its perfect fulfillment was in the Person and victory of Jesus of Nazareth.

Turning to the Psalm, let it be carefully noted that its gladness is caused by the fact of resurrection, and that resurrection is the necessary outcome of a threefold fact in the character and conduct of the One so rejoicing. These facts may thus be tabulated. First, " I beheld the Lord always before My face." Second, " For He is on My right hand, that I should not be moved." Third, " Therefore My heart was glad, and My tongue rejoiced ; Moreover My flesh also shall dwell in hope : Because Thou wilt not leave My soul unto Hades, Neither wilt Thou give Thy Holy One to see corruption." The issue of this threefold assertion is " Thou madest known unto Me the ways of life ; Thou shalt make Me full of gladness with Thy countenance." [1]

The distinction between the three facts, issuing in resurrection may not be clear, and yet on close examination it will be found that they indicate the threefold victory of Christ, which captured the whole ground of death's domain, and made necessary the resurrection. This threefold victory may be stated, and then considered as, first, victory

[1] Acts 2 : 25–28.

over the possibility of originating evil; second, victory over evil as suggested from without; and third, victory over evil as responsibility assumed.

I.   Victory over the possibility of originating evil, is suggested by the first statement, " I beheld the Lord always before My face." Jesus was, in some respects, an entirely new creation. He indeed stood in the same relation to God as that occupied by the angels, who were created prior to man. In emptying Himself of the form of God, it is first stated that He took upon Him the form of a Servant. That is a fact even deeper than that He was made in the likeness of men. In this stoop of the Eternal Son, He passed, as has been seen in a previous chapter, from the place of Sovereignty to the place of submission. In that very fact, there is the possibility of a new beginning of sin. The fall of Satan can only be comprehended by recognizing that as to his original creation he was made a servant of God. All the powers of his being were to act under the direction of the Eternal. There was to be no choice of the will save under the guiding principle of the will of God. He was created with his face towards God, and the secret of his fulfillment of the highest possibilities of his marvellous being lay in his setting the Lord always before his face. His fall consisted in the fact, to continue the figure, that he set before his face another purpose, another reason, and thus turned his back upon Jehovah. The new Servant of God in all the facts of His being was able to say, " I have set Jehovah always before My face." When divesting Himself of the form of Deity, He took the form of a Servant, and entered upon the life of subjectivity. He stood in a place where it was within the possibility of His nature to act apart from the governmental direction of

Jehovah. This He never did. Jude the apostle declares in what lay the sin of the angels. " Angels that kept not their own principality, but left their proper habitation." [1] Let it be carefully noted that their leaving their proper habitation was not the punishment of their sin, but the sin itself. They refused to remain in the habitation marked out for them by the law of God. The punishment of their sin lies in its sequence, that they are cast forth from their habitation by their own act, they are reserved in the bonds or limitations of their false position " under darkness unto the judgment of the great day." Their own principality, that is, the realm over which God had intended them to rule, they did not keep, because they left their habitation. They turned their back upon Jehovah. Here, so far as has been revealed, is the primal origin of sin in the universe of God. Instead of exercising the magnificent endowment of will under the governing principle of the will of God, they exercised it under another domination, that namely of their own desire, and then turning their backs upon God they left their proper habitation, their first habitation.

Herein by contrast is manifested the first fact in the marvellous victory of Jesus. He, the new Servant of God kept His principality by abiding in His true habitation. He never exercised will under the constraint of desire, but always setting Jehovah before His face, He lived in unceasing and glad response to all the volition of that will of infinite wisdom, of perfect holiness, and unfathomable love. The first phase of the victory of Jesus was therefore that of victory over the possibility of sinning, by the prostitution of will power, without suggestion made from without.

[1] Jude 6.

II.   The next phase of the victory is marked by the words, " For He is on My right hand, that I should not be moved." [1]   Here is something distinct from that already considered.   The first fact may be stated by the declaration, I have not moved.   But here it is, I should not be moved. That is to say, not merely that there has been no movement from the place of submission to the Divine will, simply on the basis of personal choice ; but also that there has been no movement from that position in response to suggestion or temptation from without.   It is here that man fell.   The fall of the angels was that of ceasing to set the Lord before their face, acting upon their own initiative.   The fall of man consisted in his allowing himself to be moved from his loyalty to God, in response to a suggestion coming to him from without himself.   Man did not originate sin.   He fell under the power of it by yielding to an attack made upon him from without.   In this realm also Jesus was victorious. Having held the citadel of His will against the possibilities of His subservient position, He held it moreover, against all attacks of the enemy from without.   Recognizing the presence of God Who was at His right hand as a wall of defence, He ever acted by remaining in such position, so that God was between Him and every attack of the enemy ; and thus the second phase of His victory over sin is that of remaining unmoved, in spite of every attack of the foe to change His relationship to God, by moving Him from the sphere of perfect trust.

III.   But now follows a victory, if possible more remarkable.   At least it may be said to be of even profounder interest to man, for in it lies the great pathway of his own escape from the guilt and power of sin.   Let the

[1] Acts 2 : 25.

examination be careful. "Therefore My heart was glad,
and My tongue rejoiced." [1] Why? Because having beheld the Lord always before His face, there had been perfect victory over the possibility of the origination of sin,
and because having recognized always the presence of
Jehovah at His right hand, He had not been moved.
Therefore His heart was glad, glad in the victories won,
and in the strength of righteousness resulting. Again the
question comes, Why was He glad of the victory? Was
it simply because of the triumph? Surely that, and surely
more. That double triumph creates the strength for another triumph. His heart, His tongue, His flesh rejoice
because "Thou wilt not leave My soul unto Hades,
Neither wilt Thou give Thy Holy One to see corruption."
It is evident that this victorious Person intends passing into
Hades. He is going to death, and through death into
Sheol. But because of the first victories, it is now certain
that death and Hades cannot hold Him. God must raise
Him, and bring Him back into life. Herein lies the explanation of the triumphant notes. I rejoice. My heart
is glad, My tongue rejoiceth, My flesh rests in hope. The
great Person, Who in experience fulfilled this song of the
past, declares that because He has set the Lord before His
face, because, having the Lord at His right hand He has
not been moved, when He descends into Hades, God cannot abandon Him. He must bring Him forth again, and
the final note of triumph issuing upon this double victory
achieved, and third victory assured, is expressed in the
words "Thou madest known unto Me the ways of life;
Thou shalt make Me full of gladness with Thy countenance." [2]

Here again the question forces itself upon the mind

[1] Acts 2 : 26.   [2] Acts 2 : 2o.

Why did this Holy One pass into Hades? The answer is already in our possession from the study of the former crisis in the life and mission of the Christ. As the Lamb of God He had made Himself responsible for the sin of the world, and the issue of that responsibility was death, essential death, the separation of the spirit from God, and death expressed in the separation of the spirit from the body. To that issue the perfect One Who had assumed the responsibility of all human guilt, passed by the way of the Cross. In the deep and unfathomable mystery of the Cross, His Spirit was separated from God, and that Spirit separated also from the body, passed down into Hades. Think reverently, and in solemn stillness of this fact in God's universe. One Who has obtained a double victory over sin, as a possibility within the very nature of the subservient life, and over sin as a suggestion made by a foe without, has taken upon Himself the responsibility of the sin of a race, and in those solemn hours between the passing of the Spirit of Christ on the Cross, and the resurrection morning, the holy body of the Man lies in the tomb. His Spirit has passed into hell, the place of lost spirits. Now hear His words. "Thou wilt not leave My soul unto Hades." In the mystery of the Cross, all the penalty of sin has been borne. In the place of fire there is no pain for the Holy One, Who has exhausted all its fierceness in the terrible experience of His Passion. In His body has He borne man's sin, and that work having been as He said finished, the corruption which means the disintegration of the body, cannot touch Him. "Thou wilt not give Thy Holy One to see corruption."

In that great expression of triumph which Peter quoted, there is evident the twofold nature of the perfect Man, and in both realms there is the cry of victory. His soul cannot be left in Hades. The body cannot see corruption. Here then is the third fact of the victory. The penalty of death, in its first and deep meaning, was due to sin. He took sin, and because there was no place for death in His life, by dying He exhausted the penalty due to some one else. Thus in the moral realm His death has created a new value, a value that He does not require for Himself, but that He holds for others. Here then is evident the reason of Peter's confident affirmation. " It was impossible that He should be holden of it." " It " was the issue of sin. " He " is Victor over sin as to the possibility of origination, as a suggestion coming from without, as a terrible fact for which He has made Himself responsible. Having thus gained a victory over every conceivable form of sin, covering the whole territory of its domain, death cannot hold Him.

The resurrection therefore is the unanswerable argument for the accomplishment by Jesus Christ, of God's purpose of destroying the works of the devil. There are infinite possibilities of application. Let it only be said that it is from the empty grave that the true song of hope has sounded. Every worker with God is conscious of the presence of evil in the world. Let that consciousness always be held in connection with the glorious fact that over all, Christ is absolute Master. The Church is not fighting a conflict, the issue of which is uncertain. The victory has been won, and therefore it must be won. The battle often thickens, and presses upon the weary soldiers of the King, but these are but conflicts of administration. There is no question left as to the final issue. Sometimes the process may seem tedious, and the waiting long, and yet this is but false seeming. The movements of God must never be measured by the slowness of a human life, or by the inadequacy of an earthly almanac. Standing by that risen Man of Nazareth, each one putting trust in Him may say with reverence and holy fear, and yet with certainty and absolute boldness, My heart is glad, my tongue rejoices, my flesh also shall dwell in hope. He has won His victories, and evil is doomed. Therefore, at last the victory of souls trusting in Him must also be won. The glories of the resurrection demonstrate forever the absolute and final victory of the Man of Nazareth over every form and force of evil.

XXVI

THE DIVINE SEAL

THE supreme value of the resurrection lies in the fact that it was a Divine act, by which God gave attestation to His perfect satisfaction with the work of Christ. It is well to remember that the deepest question of all for the heart of man is not whether he is satisfied, but whether God is satisfied.

In the contemplation of the matchless beauty of the life of Jesus, the heart of man may have found perfect satisfaction. Standing on the margin of the mystery of His Passion, the deepest consciousness of the life may have been that of the sufficiency of the work wrought for personal redemption. And yet so perpetually has the mind of man been at fault, that not in its own satisfaction can it find its deepest rest. Therefore it is that the question of greatest moment is as to whether God has found in the life and death of His Son, that which has accomplished His purpose, and will issue in blessing to men, and the glory of His name.

The answer to all this questioning is found in the resurrection. In the passage which perhaps is the most remarkable of all the utterances of Christ concerning His Passion, He declares " Therefore doth the Father love Me, because I lay down My life, that I may take it again. No one taketh it away from Me, but I lay it down of Myself. I have power to lay it down, and I have power to take it again. This commandment received I from My Father." [1]

[1] John 10 : 17, 18.

This is so strange a statement as to baffle all attempts at explanation. Its correctness, however, is demonstrated by the fact that He did lay down His life, and that He did take it again. Carefully note, He claims His right to do this was received from His Father. Thus the whole work committed to Jesus by the Father was that of laying down through death His perfect life for the making of Atonement, and right to lay hold again upon that life for its communication to others, as the context shows.

The proof then that the work of the Cross was perfect lies in the fact that He not only laid down His life, but that He took it again, thus carrying out the Divine authority to its utmost limit.

In writing to the Ephesians the apostle in praying for them that they " may know . . . the exceeding greatness of His power " describes it as the power " which He wrought in Christ, when He raised Him from the dead, and made Him to sit at His right hand in the heavenly places." [1]

Thus it is evident that He, Jesus, laid hold upon His own life, taking it again, but He did this by the authority of His Father, and so it is remarkably true, as Paul declares, that His resurrection was by the act of God. There is no contradiction in these two statements, but rather the revelation of that perfect harmony of action between the Father and the Son, which characterized the whole work of Christ.

The resurrection then is the Divine seal upon the work of Jesus, as perfectly meeting the purpose of God. In examining this, notice first how the resurrection was the culminating act, marking the perfect approbation of God; secondly, how the resurrection was the final act, marking God's rejection of man; and thirdly how the resurrection

[1] Eph. 1: 18-20.

was therefore the Divine ratificat on of the new and living way, by which rejected man could be accepted.

I. It has been seen through the whole progress of this study how that again and again in different ways, God bore testimony to the sacred nature of the mission of Christ, and to the satisfaction of the Eternal heart with the outworking of the Divine purpose in history, in the Person and work of Jesus of Nazareth. At His advent when earth gave Him no welcome, and there were no evidences of preparation, remarkable signs were granted to the sons of men, the shining of the star, the singing of the angels, the voices of prophecy, the moving of the under world of evil, the coming of the wise men from afar. During the days of His public ministry there was the thrice repeated breaking of the silence of the heavens in the speech of approval, at the baptism, at the transfiguration, and at the coming of the Greeks. Moreover through all those days there were the miracles by which God approved Him among men. The awful and supernatural manifestations at the crucifixion were of the same nature; the earthquake, the opening of graves, the darkening of the sun, the rending of the temple veil.

The resurrection is the central and supreme declaration of this fact. It is well to notice that associated with it was the resurrection of some of the saints. He was the First-fruit, for coming forth He led others with Him. The account of the rending of rocks, and opening of graves, which were among the supernatural signs attending the crucifixion, very clearly declares that though the graves were opened, the saints did not arise until the day of resurrection. That opening of the tombs was in itself a wonderful thing, but none could move from them until He had risen.

He must lead the way forth.   Yet the very graves seem
'o feel upon them the touch of the hand of the Master of
life, and the earth yawned to yield to Him the conquest He
was winning.   The Divine seal did not end with the
resurrection.   His ascension was by the act of God, Who
exalted Him.   The coming of the Spirit at Pentecost was
God's great outpouring of the new force of redemption,
and was consequent upon His satisfaction with the work
of His Son.

And yet again in the glory of that advent which is to be,
the Divine approval will be manifested before all creation.

The value of the resurrection as a Divine act, is threefold.   First it is God's attestation of the perfection of the
life of the Man Jesus.   Secondly it is God's attestation of
the perfection of the mediation of the Saviour Jesus.
Thirdly it is God's attestation of the perfection of the
victory of the King Jesus.   Upon all the virtue of His
life, and the value of His death, and the victory of His
conflict, God set the seal in the sight of heaven and earth
and hell, when raising Him from the dead, He fulfilled the
confident assertion of the old time Psalmist concerning
Him, that He did not leave His soul unto Hades nor suffer
His Holy One to see corruption.

II.   All this is a startling and terrible fact in its first application to fallen and degraded humanity.   By that solemn act
of God in the midst of the history of the race, an act in
which He accepted perfect humanity, He rejected all imperfection, and forever made impossible the hope that any
man should find acceptance with Him upon any other
ground than that of a perfect realization of His purpose
and His will.   The real value of the resurrection will
never be appreciated save as this fact is recognized.   The

risen perfect Man was the condemnation of the imperfect.
In the midst of the age, in the sight of all the universe, the
Eternal God declares that He cannot and will not be satisfied with anything short of the fullest realization of His
perfect purpose. The resurrection of Jesus is the establishment in the midst of the human race of a Divine testimony
concerning righteousness. In that magnificent moment of
the emergence of Jesus from death into life, the Eternal
God took hold upon perfection, and setting Him in the
front of all the race, declared that Jesus was His standard
of human life. He raised Him from the dead, because of
His perfect realization of all the purposes of His will. By
that act the doom of imperfection is sounded. If that be
the standard of the acceptance of God, then all such as
have failed are rejected.

The resurrection is more than God's acceptance of the
perfect Man. It is His acceptance of Him as the Victor
over evil, and the recognition of His right to claim the
spoils of victory, that is to say, by resurrection God
accepts the redemptive method of the Son. The Father
declares that by the life laid down, a work has been done
which is sufficient for the salvation of men. Yet carefully
mark the sequence of this truth. By the resurrection of
Jesus, God rejects and refuses all other methods of salvation. He declared in that stupendous act, not only His
rejection of imperfect man, but His rejection of every
attempt imperfect man may make, to save or reinstate
himself.

And yet when by resurrection God declared the victory
of Jesus, He announced the defeat of all others in their
conflict with sin. Standing in the search-light of the resurrection, man becomes more conscious of his helplessness
than when standing in the shadow of the Cross. The

risen One is Victor, and Victor in virtue of the perfection of life, of the perfection of mediation. Man in his imperfection of life, and his inability to work out a salvation of his own is declared to be vanquished, and unable himself to become master of the forces which have wrought his ruin.

It is because the resurrection has not been properly appreciated as the message of God, which is the severest condemnation of sinning man, that men have still imagined that apart from the Passion and passing of Jesus of Nazareth, it may be possible for them to be accepted of God.

Gazing into the darkness of the grave which Jesus has left, man should recognize the utter hopelessness of his condition, and the utter folly of attempting to please God. When the Eternal raised Jesus from the grave, and took Him to Himself, He by that act hurled the whole race to destruction. Think of the resurrection for a single moment, not merely with reference to the truths now considered, but as an illustration of them in the fact of history. No man saw Him rise. The very disciples were denied the vision. It may be urged that the weakness of their faith was the reason of their failure in this respect. And yet in that very fact is evident the act of God. As in the Cross there was manifest the element of lawlessness, crucifying the Son, and the element of Divine counsel and foreknowledge; so also in the resurrection there is manifest man's failure in his absence, and God's rejection of man, in that he was not permitted to see the stupendous glory of the acceptance of the perfect One.

The act of God in the resurrection of Jesus, was one characterized by marvellous majesty, and overwhelming power. In describing this, Paul speaks in language which almost seems to be redundant, and yet is surely necessary to give some indication of the stupendous fact. He writes:

"That working of the strength of His might."[1] The might of God, the strength of the might of God, the working of the strength of the might of God. Simply to read this is to feel the irresistible throb of omnipotence. In the quietness of that first day of the week, when the first shafts of light were gleaming on the eastern sky, the disciples being absent, and the enemies, as represented by the soldiers, being rendered blind by the glory of the angelic splendour, God raised Him.

Notice what this meant with regard to the powers that had been against Him. The priests had laboured to encompass His death, and had been successful. They had done their worst, and God lifted Him out of the death to which they had condemned Him, and by this act forever rejected them. The world powers had united in religious hatred, and cultured indifference, and material power to cast Him out; and God placed Him over the whole of them, crowning Him at the centre of all authority, and by that act rejected false religion, imperfect culture, and merely material power. This is no mere dream, though for twenty centuries the priest has fought for his position in the world. He has been defeated again and again, and must ultimately be defeated, and always in the power of the Priesthood of the risen Christ.

So also have false religions, the religions of externalities striven for the mastery, only to be superseded by the religion of the Christ.

False culture has repeatedly attempted, with self-satisfied cynicism, to treat with indifference the Christ of God, only to find that He takes hold upon all the domain of true culture, and rules supremely over it.

And moreover, the kingdoms of the earth in their pride

[1] Eph. 1 : 19.

have set themselves against the Lord and His Anointed, only to find that the King of kings, and the Lord of lords defeats their purpose, spoils their programme, and paralyzes their power. All the forces of the world were placed below Him in resurrection. In the act of the crucifixion of the Christ, man turned his back upon God. In the fact of His resurrection God turned His back upon man. The risen Christ was the One with Whom God entered into covenant, to the exclusion of all others.

The resurrection has no message to men who are attempting in the energy of their own will to please God, save that of declaring that by the fact of His pleasure in the perfect One, He cannot be pleased with imperfection in any degree. The resurrection attests to every successive age that in God's acceptance of the way of salvation provided by Christ, He forever refuses to lend a listening ear to any who shall attempt that which is impossible, the working out of a salvation in the energy of a depraved and degraded nature.

III. And yet this is but the dark background to a picture radiant with the colours of hope. God's rejection of imperfection is the act of Love. His refusal of all human attempts at renewal and reconstruction, is the refusal of a great compassion. If the acceptance of Christ was the rejection of man, it was also the acceptance of a new and living way, through which rejected man might find his way back to God. If in the resurrection God accepted the perfect Man, He also accepted Him in that representative capacity, indicated by the fact of His wounding and His death. He raised in Him, all those who commit to Him their whole life, in a deep sense of its direst need, and full confidence in His power to save. Not in loneliness did

He rise, but in the possession of a life to be placed at the disposal of others. On the resurrection side of the grave Jesus stood as the Head of the new race, the second Man, the last Adam. How often is this wording confused in quotation. Men speak of the last Man, and the second Adam. It may be objected that this is a matter of small significance, and yet it is not so. In His perfection He was the second Man. The first man failed, the second Man succeeded. That is the statement of a lonely fact. The first Adam was the head of a race, and in his failure the race was involved. The last Adam created the force of renewal even for the fallen, and became the Head of the new race, to whom that new force should be communicated. Not merely was He the second Adam, as though there might be a third. He was the last. Beyond Him, and all included in the communication of His life, there is to be no new race.

Thus the resurrection is seen to be the Divine announcement of the evangel. According to the words of Jesus, on the Cross He laid down His life for the sheep, that is, that they might receive it as their own. When God raised Him from the dead, He ratified that intention, and declared it to be an established fact. The life laid down all received in resurrection, and all who receive that life are accepted, received by God. They are accepted in the Beloved. From the resurrection morning until now, God has been, and still is, receiving Christ; and the groundwork of the acceptance of any man with God is that there has been communicated to him the life of Christ. There is no verdict upon fallen man so final in its declaration of his rejection, as is the risen Christ. There is no door of hope so radiant with light for the fallen people as this way into acceptance through the reception of the Christ.

Oh wondrous Shepherd of the sheep. The hireling careth not for the sheep, and fleeth because he is an hireling. The Shepherd came into conflict with the wolf, and by His dying overcame. The scattered frightened sheep, receiving the life liberated through the death of the Shepherd, receive all the values and the virtues which God accepts, and thus in Christ are accepted of God.

XXVII

FAITH'S ANCHORAGE

THE importance of the resurrection may be gathered from the position its proclamation occupied in the preaching of the apostles. It was the first article in the creed they professed and proclaimed. When the apostles were surrounded with the high priests, and the whole senate, and the council of the children of Israel, Peter as the spokesman of the rest, in declaring the facts for which they stood, and of which they claimed to be witnesses, put the resurrection in the forefront,[1] and this notwithstanding the fact that he knew it must run counter to the prejudices of that assembly, seeing that the high priest was himself a Sadducee, and therefore one who denied the resurrection of the body.

The words of Paul in writing his first letter to the Corinthians, " I determined not to know anything among you, save Jesus Christ, and Him crucified,"[2] have almost perpetually been used as serving to define the whole subject of his preaching. A reasonable and careful examination of the context will prove that this is a misinterpretation. " Jesus Christ and Him crucified " is not the whole burden of preaching, neither is it the final nor central fact thereof. It would be far more correct to say that the keynote of apostolic teaching was expressed by the same apostle when he wrote, " It is Christ Jesus that died, yea, rather, that was raised from the dead."[3] This is not to minimize the

---

[1] Acts 5.   [2] I Cor. 2 : 2.   [3] Rom. 8 : 34.

value of the preaching of Christ crucified, but if Christ crucified be all, then there is no value in preaching Christ
crucified. It was His resurrection from among the dead
that demonstrated the infinite value of the mystery of His
death. When the apostle declared to the Christians in
Corinth that he was determined not to know anything
among them, save Jesus Christ and Him crucified, the reason lay in the fact of their carnality. All kinds of disorders
had crept into the church, and the tone of the life of the
members was carnal and not spiritual. It was necessary to
hold their thinking in the realm of the Cross, for they had
not learned this first lesson, and could not therefore be led
into the deeper and fuller truth.

In his letter to the Romans Paul distinctly places the
resurrection before the mind as the anchorage for faith unto
salvation. " If thou shalt confess with thy mouth Jesus as
Lord, and shalt believe in thy heart that God raised Him
from the dead, thou shalt be saved."[1] And writing in the
epistle to the Corinthians he makes a simple statement that
at once reveals the true place of the resurrection in preaching and in faith. " If Christ hath not been raised, then is
our preaching vain, your faith also is vain. Yea, and we
are found false witnesses of God; because we witnessed of
God that He raised up Christ: Whom He raised not up,
if so be that the dead are not raised. For if the dead are
not raised, neither hath Christ been raised: and if Christ
hath not been raised, your faith is vain; ye are yet in
your sins."[2]

While the preaching and teaching of the apostles were
constantly occupied with the fact of the Cross, as to its
place and value in the economy of redemption, they never
failed to direct attention to the resurrection as the central

[1] Rom. 10: 9.   [2] 1 Cor. 15: 14–17.

verity, demonstrating to man's intelligence, and communicating to his life, the value of the Cross.

The resurrection gave meaning to all that had preceded it. By it the Cross was proved to be more than a tragic death, and the life of Jesus infinitely more than an example. Upon the fact of the historic resurrection stands or falls the whole fabric of Christianity. Unless Jesus of Nazareth actually came back from the grave, then indeed have we followed " cunningly devised fables "[1] and have been hopelessly deceived. This has been recognized by the very enemies of Christianity. It was Strauss who said that " the resurrection is the centre of the centre."

In contemplating the resurrection as the anchorage of faith, first let the historic fact be taken for granted and considered as an anchorage; and secondly, let an enquiry be instituted as to whether faith has actually the anchorage of the resurrection.

I. Let the facts as recorded in the Gospels be accepted as true. An appreciation of the value thereof will be discovered, by suggesting the questions arising in the mind of man, seeking redemption, as he stands outside the grave in which Christ has been laid to rest; and secondly, by noticing how such questions are perfectly answered as the grave is opened, and the Man of Nazareth comes forth.

Having reverently attempted to trace in order the work of Jesus in fulfillment of the mission of redemption, the mind is now fixed upon His grave. Against the entrance of that tomb a stone is laid. Upon that stone is the seal of the Roman governor. Within the tomb there lies the dead body of the Man of Nazareth. The questions arising, are questions of reverence, and yet are questions hon-

[1] 2 Pet. 1 : 16.

estly forced upon the mind. These are two, which may thus be simply stated. His life in its perfection was ever lived with the culminating fact of death upon His consciousness. This has been seen in the study of the approach to the Cross. In the process of the death, the declared intention has been that of dealing with sin, and creating a new moral value to be placed at the disposal of such as are enslaved by sin. Has the Man of Nazareth succeeded in this great work?

Closely allied is the second question. In looking forward to His death this Man has spoken of it as the pathway to something infinitely more. Having declared that He had come that men might have life, He moreover claimed that though He laid down His life, He would take it again, in order that it might be communicated to those who needed life. Is He equal to this declared purpose? With great reverence the mind has contemplated the passing of the King into the darkened way where lay the enemies of the race, with the avowed purpose of gaining victory over them, and accomplishing an exodus. In the death grapple in the darkness has He won, or have they? Is He merged beneath the swelling waters of the unfathomable sea, or are they? Standing before the sealed tomb of the Man of Nazareth, man asks in the deep consciousness of his heart's need and anguish, whether there has been accomplished in the mystery of the Passion, that which will issue in the loosing of man from his sin? He asks moreover, whether the infinite promises of individual life, which will enable him to overcome the things that have overcome him, can be fulfilled? A question concerning pardon, and a question concerning power surge upon the mind in the presence of the entombed Jesus.

The contemplation of His life and death have kindled

within the heart a sense of love towards Him, and even though He have failed, He must ever hold His place for what He was, in the love of those who have beheld the vision. He meant well, He strove towards redemption, yea, so mightily, that none other can ever repeat the process. Has He failed, or has He succeeded? He is in the grave, and there is no answer so long as He abide there.

It would seem as though the very statement of these questions is all that is necessary to an unfolding of the infinite value of the glorious fact of His resurrection. How precious it is to stand in imagination in the tender light of the first day of the week, in the company of the women who are first at the tomb, and to listen to the first uttering of the evangel of hope, as sounding from the empty grave, its music breaks upon the heart, " He is not here; for He is risen, even as He said. Come, see the place where the Lord lay." [1] What tenderness is in the message, what glad exultant joy, and yet what a touch of quiet irony. And yet again, what gentle rebuke. " He is risen, even as He said." These women and these apostles He had told again and yet again that He would rise, and yet they had come bringing spices to anoint Him dead. The angel revealed heaven's rebuke in the phrase " even as He said." And then what quiet majestic irony. All sin and all malice had united to put Him within the silent tomb. And now the angel quietly says " Behold the place where the Lord lay." The grave is there, but it is empty. He is not here, for He has risen superior to all the forces that united to silence and entomb Him. That resurrection is indeed the centre of the centre, and all the questions of the seeking heart are answered, in the radiant splendour of the light that streams from the vanquished grave.

[1] Matt. 28: 6.

The exodus is complete, the foes met in the darkness are mastered. The waters have not o'erwhelmed the King. In their unfathomable deeps, only the enemies have perished.

Almost with trembling, and yet reverently let this fact be stated from the other side. If the mighty work attempted had failed of accomplishment, the grave would have held Him. Unless He had vanquished sin, there could have been no resurrection. Unless He had still retained in the mystery of laying down His life the authority to take it again, there could have been no impartation of these values of His death, and the virtues of His life. His own perfect confidence in victory was declared when out of the darkness of the experience of the Cross He cried, " It is finished." [1]   The absolute vindication of that cry is to be found in the resurrection, in which God answered declaring also " It is finished."

Here then indeed is faith's firm foundation, its assured anchorage. By that empty grave man knows that sin is put away, and the infinite value of the Atonement is at his disposal. By that grave man is assured of the fulfillment of the promises made, and he knows indeed that the life taken again is at his disposal. Glad unutterable peace possesses all the soul, as faith takes reasonable action upon the testimony of the resurrection, and trusts without question or controversy, the accomplished work of the Redeemer.

II.   The remaining section of this chapter is that of a restatement of the arguments for the historic fact of resurrection. Having considered how that fact, if granted, is indeed the anchorage for faith, it now remains to repeat in briefest form, the lines of proof. And yet nothing can be

[1] John 19: 30.

of more importance. It is utterly false to declare that it is unimportant, whether the Man of Nazareth did actually rise from the dead. It is unfair, and illogical, and outside the final possibility of reason's acceptance, to affirm that the value of the resurrection remains if its fact be denied. The idea that the matter of supreme importance is value, apart from fact is absurd, because it is presupposing an impossibility. The value has been created by the fact. Had there been no fact, there could have been no value. Permanent values can only exist upon the bases of established facts. A value of perpetual force has never been created upon the basis of a so-called working hypothesis. Sooner or later the hypothesis will almost invariably cease to work, and when that happens, the value passes like the mirage of the desert. If the hypothesis is to continue, it will be because it is finally demonstrated as being based upon fact.

The permanent value therefore is the outcome of established fact. All the working values of the Gospel of grace are founded upon the fact of the resurrection of Jesus.

To follow this statement further. It is declared that the value is here, and we need take no time in arguing concerning the fact. That may be abandoned seeing that the value is now at the use of men. This again is evidence of short-sightedness. Abandon the fact, and the value will be lost. This may not be seen immediately, but in the process of years it will be seen. When the great rock foundations of our faith are reckoned of no account, the values that have accrued may seem to abide, but they will inevitably even if slowly, lose their transforming power.

The fact of the resurrection has created the value of high life. Once deny the fact, and its value will cease to grip, and regulate the consciences of men, and they will revert, sooner or later, to the bestial materialistic ideal of life, which issues in such rottenness as that of Rome, and of Greece. To trifle with the foundations of God is to render the building insecure. The actuality of the resurrection of the Man Jesus, is necessary to the permanent value of the Christian Gospel.

It is therefore absolutely necessary that the question be asked, did He rise? Take the apostolic formula of supposition. "If Christ be not risen," there are certain inevitable deductions will follow.

First, His teaching was false for He distinctly declared that He would rise again, and so faith's central claim was never realized, and all other claims are valueless. His one final sign was that of His own resurrection. "What sign showest Thou unto us, seeing that Thou doest these things." "Destroy this temple, and in three days I will raise it up."[1] "We would see a sign from Thee." "As Jonah was three days and three nights in the belly of the whale; so shall the Son of Man be three days and three nights in the heart of the earth."[2] When He said these things, men did not understand them. But looking back at them, it is perfectly patent that to the mind of the Master, the resurrection was the one indisputable seal of the Divinity of His mission. Yet again earnestly and solemnly it must be declared that if He did not rise, either He was Himself deceived, or He was intentionally a deceiver.

"If Christ be not risen," then to adopt the first supposition, He was mistaken, for He thought He would; or else, to adopt the second, if He never expected to rise, He deliberately attempted to deceive men, by promising them that He would.

And yet again, if He did not rise, His work was the

[1] John 2: 18, 19.   [2] Matt. 12: 38, 40.

direst failure.   At the erection of the Cross, there was indeed to all human seeming, a final failure for Him.   His
own were against Him, His disciples abandoned Him, and
they are seen scattering as fast as they knew how to fishing
nets.   They had had a dream of exquisite beauty in the
days of their discipleship, but the whole thing had melted
like the mirage of the desert.   To affirm this in the face of
the stupendous victories of Christ during nineteen centuries
is an absolute absurdity.   If He did not rise, then the
victories were not gained by Him, but by the men who
were His followers, who reconstructed an idea out of a
dismal failure, and made it the dominating and all-victorious
force that it has been in human history.

And yet this cannot be, for they abandoned hope of the
Christ, and scattered.   There must have been something
which regathered them, and reunited them.   Not the
Cross, but something other, for the Cross broke up the
unity, and scattered the units.   Not one of them waited to
watch.   They are seen drifting away, with the sadness
of a great love for a lost Leader in their hearts, feeling that
while He was true indeed to them, He was utterly mistaken, and that the only logical sequence of the Cross is
that they shall go back to their fishing.

But to take the larger outlook.   " If Christ be not
risen," then the atoning value of His death cannot be maintained, and it is worthy of careful notice that the doctrine
of Atonement always goes, where men call in question the
fact of the resurrection.

And yet again.   " If Christ be not risen," then the
world has no authoritative message concerning the life
hereafter.   If indeed He did not return, then has man no
well-established hope of seeing again those faces loved long
since and lost awhile.   A man often says—thoughtlessly in

all probability—that no one has ever come back to tell us anything concerning the life beyond. That statement is absolutely correct if Christ be not risen. No one, however, whose faith is fastened upon the resurrection can make that assertion. One has come back, and in His coming has brought life and immortality to light.

If Christ be not risen then there is no type of humanity, for all the perfections, which seem to be resident in Him, are spoiled by the revelation of His ignorance, or His attempt to impose upon the credulity of man.

"If Christ be not risen" there is no new power at the disposal of man, and he is left alone to struggle, and altogether unavailingly, with the forces of evil.

If Christ did not rise, what then did happen? What was it that recalled that scattered group of frightened souls, and turned them into men and women of such marvellous force, that within one brief generation they had filled Jerusalem with their doctrine, spoken to the known world, and undermined the corrupt Roman empire? How are these facts to be accounted for? It may at once be declared that every attempt to account for the victories of the Church apart from the resurrection is philosophically absurd, and historically without proof.

It has been affirmed that the early disciples were guilty of fraud, that they invented a story. Will this stand the test of one moment's consideration of the fact that for this particular story they endured almost untold suffering, being excommunicated, ostracized, and in thousands of cases put to death? It may be that in the history of the race, individual men have been found, who, swept by some fanaticism, have been willing to die for fraud. Cases have not been wanting in which men have suffered and perished, in order that evil may reach the goal, and something dastardly be accomplished. But this is not a case of isolated individuals, but a whole company and society of men and women and children, ever increasing in number, all of them more or less having to suffer in those early centuries; and the central fact, for the declaration of which they endured all things, was this story of the resurrection, which, forsooth, it is announced they invented. Let the apostles be the first and most conspicuous illustration. All of them save one died violent deaths, and he was exiled to a lonely island.

The breaking out of persecution as chronicled in the Acts of the Apostles was based upon the fact that these men declared that the Man Who had been crucified to put an end to His teaching and influence, had been raised, and was alive. It is not within the compass of rational consideration to believe that men who so suffered, suffered for a story themselves had invented.

Again it has been said that Jesus never really died, but that He swooned upon the Cross, and that being placed in a grave He recovered. How then it may be asked, did He escape from the tomb so carefully guarded by Roman soldiers, and from grave-clothes so marvellously wrapped, as those of Eastern burials were? Of course such a statement is to take away not only resurrection, but the death of the Cross, and all the value connected with it.

And yet His death is proven by the fact that it was carried out by Roman authority, and Roman soldiers, and is a matter of the world's history, as apart from the story of the Gospels. In the crucifixion of malefactors the Romans were ever careful to be certain of death, and for this purpose broke the bones after a lapse of certain time. His bones were not broken for the simple reason that He was dead already. Before His body was granted to Joseph ot Arimathea, the Roman governor made careful enquiry concerning the actuality of death.

And yet one other argument may be referred to. It is asserted that the disciples saw certain visionary appearances after the crucifixion, and that they thought they saw Him. Under stress and strain of terrible excitement they imagined they had a vision of their lost Leader again alive. The statement has been made in this connection that they saw what they wanted to see, as people overwrought often seem to do. The answer to such a statement is of the simplest. There need be no argument. They had no expectation of seeing Him again. No thought was further from their minds than that of His resurrection. As to the hypothesis of visionary appearances, it might have been considered if but one or two had testified. No less than ten distinct appearances are recorded, and these not only to individuals, but to companies and crowds. First to the women. Then to Peter. Then to two men walking to Emmaus. Then to ten apostles, and subsequently to eleven. Yet later to seven men approaching the seashore. Yet again to the whole number of the apostles, and afterwards to five hundred brethren at once. Then to James, and finally to the little group gathered round Him when He ascended.

Is it conceivable that all these were deceived by visionary appearances, and were so deceived that whatever else their faults and failure in the coming years, there is absolutely no record of any one of them questioning the historic fact of the resurrection ? Of course it may now be said that this is all upon the authority of the New Testament. That is at once admitted. The authenticity of the Gospel narratives is not now under discussion, but is taken for granted. And therefore there may be added to the

proofs already cited, the wonderful history of Saul of
Tarsus, who declared through over thirty years of con-
sistent Christian life and testimony, that the miraculous
change wrought in his attitude towards Christ, and in the
whole fibre of his character, was brought about by an actual
vision of Jesus of Nazareth, risen and glorified. It has
been said that the true account of what happened to Saul
of Tarsus was that he had an epileptic seizure in a
thunder-storm. So puerile is such a statement, that the
only answer possible to it, is a suggestion that if it be indeed true, then men ought always to pray for a multiplica-
tion of thunder-storms, and an epidemic of epilepsy.

And yet finally these outside proofs are not the supreme
one. The supreme proof is the Church of Jesus Christ.
As has incidentally been seen, at the Cross the disciples were
frightened, and scattered. By the way of resurrection
these were gathered, and held in patient waiting, until the
outpouring of the Holy Spirit, Whose coming created the
new society, which consisted not merely in the gathering
together of individuals, but their fusing into one mystic
unity. Then followed the growth and influence of that
Church in every successive century. Within its border
to-day there is the deposit of the only regenerative Gospel
that man has ever heard. The resurrection of Christ is
proven to-day by the Church on earth, with its ordinances,
its living ministry, its Gospel of grace, and the marvellous
victories won in every age, and in every land by its
toil, in spite of its weakness and its worldliness. The
Church of Christ is the supreme credential of Christ.

Turning from this subject of resurrection with the great
glad exultant cry, Christ is risen, there is in the cry the
affirmation of His perfect victory, the declaration of the
Divine seal set upon that victory, and the proclamation of

a sure anchorage for the faith of men. The living risen Christ is the Centre of the Church's creed, the Creator of her character, and the Inspiration of her conduct. His resurrection is the clearest note in her battle-song. It is the sweetest, strongest music amid all her sorrows. It speaks of personal salvation. It promises the life that has no ending, it declares to all bereaved souls that "them also that are fallen asleep in Jesus will God bring with Him," [1] and therefore the light of His resurrection falls in radiant beauty upon the graves where rest the dust of the holy dead.

[1] 1 Thess. 4 : 14.

BOOK VII

THE ASCENSION

XXVIII. God's Perfect Man

XXIX. Man's Wounded God

XXX. The New Union

" *Over against His Dead*
God sat in silence : for the Earth was dead,
And dimly lay upon her awful bier,
Wrapped round in darkness ; yea, her shroud was **wrought**
Of clouds and thunders : for the Earth had died
Not gently and at peace, as tired men die
Toward the evening ; but as one who dies
Full of great strength, by sudden smiting down.
The Earth was dead, and laid upon her bier,
And God, Sole Mourner, watched her day and night —
The living God a Watcher by the dead,
Sole Mourner in the Universe for her
Who had been once so fair.

      *   *   *   *   *   *

Sole Mourner, for in the dark outer Room
The devils danced and sang for dreary joy,
Because God's so beloved Earth was dead,
And must be shortly buried out of sight
To perish.
        Still,—over against His Dead
God sat in silence.
           But, behold, there came
One, treading softly to the House of Death,
Down from among the Angels, through the room.
He came, as comes a King, unto the place
Where lay the Dead ; and He laid His right hand
Of strength on her, and called her tenderly
Saying, ' Arise, beloved, from thy sleep,
For I will ransom thee by Death to Life ;
Arise and live.'   And He did raise her up
By His right hand, presenting her to God,
All glorious, as one who hath been dead
But hath found life and immortality.
And God, the Mighty God, did there rejoice,
And rest in His great love ; for this His Earth,
Which had been dead, was living in His sight.
Therefore He crowned with many crowns His head
Who had prevailed to ransom her from Death ;
And also, laying joy upon her head
For everlasting, He hath made her Bride
Of Christ, the King."—B. M.
               " *From Death to Life.*"

So then the Lord Jesus, after He had spoken unto them, was received up into heaven, and sat down at the right hand of God. —*Mark 16 : 19.*

* * * * * * *

And He led them out until they were over against Bethany: and He lifted up His hands, and blessed them. And it came to pass, while He blessed them, He parted from them, and was carried up into heaven.—*Luke 24 : 50, 51.*

* * * * * * *

And when He had said these things, as they were looking, He was taken up ; and a cloud received Him out of their sight. And while they were looking steadfastly into heaven as He went, behold two men stood by them in white apparel ; who also said, Ye men of Galilee, why stand ye looking into heaven ? This Jesus, Who was received up from you into heaven, shall so come in like manner as ye beheld Him going into heaven.—*Acts 1 : 9–11.*

* * * * * * *

And I saw in the right hand of Him that sat on the throne a book written within and on the back, close sealed with seven seals. And I saw a strong angel proclaiming with a great voice, Who is worthy to open the book, and to loose the seals thereof? And no one in the heaven, or on the earth, or under the earth, was able to open the book, or to look thereon. And I wept much, because no one was found worthy to open the book, or to look thereon : and one of the elders saith unto me, Weep not ; behold, the Lion that is of the tribe of Judah, the Root of David, hath overcome to open the book and the seven seals thereof. And I saw in the midst of the throne and of the four living creatures, and in the midst of the elders, a Lamb standing, as though it had been slain, having seven horns, and seven eyes, which are the seven Spirits of God, sent forth into all the earth. And He came, and He taketh it out of the right hand of Him that sat on the throne. And when He had taken the book, the four living creatures and the four and twenty elders fell down before the Lamb, having each one a harp, and golden bowls full of incense, which are the prayers of the saints. And they sing a new song, saying,

> Worthy art Thou to take the book, and to open the seals thereof: for Thou wast slain, and didst purchase unto God with Thy blood men of every tribe, and tongue, and people, and nation, and madest them to be unto our God a kingdom and priests ; and they reign upon the earth.

—Rev. 5 : 1–10

XXVIII

GOD'S PERFECT MAN

THE ascension of Jesus of Nazareth was the final crisis in His great work. To omit it would be to omit that which is a necessary link between His resurrection from among the dead, and reappearance amid His disciples; and the coming of God the Holy Spirit on the day of Pentecost. It is not easy to follow Him as He passes out of human sight. This difficulty is recognized inferentially in the very brevity of the Gospel narrative. Very little is said because little can be said which could be understood by those dwelling still within the limitations of the material, and having consciousness of the spiritual world only by faith. Still the positive fact is definitely stated, and following closely the lines laid down, we may reverently attempt their projection beyond the veil of time and sense.

It is almost pathetic that it is necessary to pause one moment to insist upon the actual historic fact of the ascension into the heavenly places of the Man of Nazareth. If the resurrection be denied, then of course there is no room for ascension. If on the other hand it be established, that Jesus of Nazareth did indeed rise from the dead, then it is equally certain that He ascended into heaven. No time need be taken in argument with such as believe in the authenticity of the New Testament story, and with those who question this, argument is useless. That there is an unconscious questioning of this fact of ascension is evident from the way in which reference is sometimes made to the

Lord Jesus. It is by no means uncommon to hear persons speak of what He did or said "in the days of His Incarnation." Such a phrase, even when not used with such intention, does infer that the days of His Incarnation are over. This however is not so, any more than it is true that Abraham, Moses, and Elijah have ceased to be men. Indeed the presence of Jesus of Nazareth in heaven as a Man, is more complete than that of any other save Enoch, Moses, and Elijah. All others wait the resurrection for the reception of their body. He in bodily form has passed into heaven. So also Enoch passed, as a sign in the dim and distant century of the triumph over death that God would win in the Person of His Incarnate Son. Thus also Elijah passed, for a testimony in the midst of corruption, which was issuing in unbelief in immortality. Moses' body was brought out of the grave by Michael the archangel, for reunion with his spirit for the purpose of communion with the Man Jesus. This again was an act of God's faith in Christ, and though the devil disputed with the archangel his right to appropriate the benefits of redemption, until redemption were accomplished, by this very act God declared the absolute accomplishment of redemption in the Divine economy, long before it had been wrought out into human history. Jesus therefore through Whom, and through Whom alone eventually, men as such will be found in the heavens, ascended in bodily form to those heavens, being Himself as to actual victory First-born from the dead.

The stoop of God to human form was not for a period merely. That humiliation was a process in the pathway, by which God would lift into eternal union with Himself all such as should be redeemed by the victory won through suffering. Forevermore in the Person of the Man of

Nazareth, God is one with men. At this moment the Man of Nazareth, the Son of God, is at the right hand of the Father. Difficulties arising concerning these clear declarations as to the ascension of the Man of Nazareth must not be allowed to create disbelief in them. Any such process of discrediting what is hard to understand, issues finally in the abandonment of the whole Christian position and history. It may be objected for instance that if He be indeed localized as a Man, in heaven, how can He be present with His people on earth. In answer to that, it must be stated, that working in the inverse way, the same difficulty obtains in understanding His presence on the earth as a Man. In the very mystery of the Being of the God-man, as has been shown, there is the limitless and the limited, the omnipresent and the localized. Just as He was here upon the earth in order that the grace of God might have its outshining in a Person, and yet while here, spoke of Himself as the " Son, Who is in the bosom of the Father " ; [1] so to-day the Man Christ Jesus is in heaven, and through Him the glory of God is having its outshining in a Person, while He is yet in the deep and unfathomable reaches of His Being, the infinite and eternal I AM.

In considering the ascension first as the coming into heaven of God's perfect Man, there are three things to be noted,—first, His perfection in the realization of the Divine purpose for man; second, His perfection in the accomplishment of the Divine purpose of the redemption of ruined man; third, His investiture with a name.

I. The coming of Jesus of Nazareth into heaven was the arrival of such an One as had never before been there. The coming to heaven of Abel was the coming of the first

[1] John 1 : 18.

human being, and so far as it is competent to measure the interest of heaven by earthly interest in the things of God, it may be reverently declared that it was a great occasion when this first soul representing a new race, and, more marvellous still, representing a fallen race, appeared in the unsullied light of the home of the unfallen. He came by faith, ransomed by love, at the cost of sacrifice. As the Scripture declares that "the angels desire to look into"[1] these things, this must indeed have been a mystery of life and love demanding their close attention, and not per- chance, even fathomed by them, until the explanation of the mystery of sacrifice enfolded in the sublimer mystery of love, was wrought out upon the Cross of Calvary. It is more than probable that Abel, and all who succeeded him, had to wait the fullness of the earthly time for the ex- planation of the method of their acceptance with God. They passed into the dwelling-place of Infinite Love, upon the basis of their faith in God, so far as they were con- cerned. In the Divine economy they were received upon the basis of God's faith in His Son. The Father trusted the Son to accomplish His purpose in the fullness of time, and upon the foundation of that confidence of God in Himself, the sinner was admitted to heaven.

On ascension day something still more marvellous oc- curred. The Man of Nazareth, the First of the new race, the last Adam, passed into the Divine presence in the right of His own perfect humanity. In His coming, He asked for no mercy. No mediator opened the door of heaven for Him. He proceeded along the line of the outworking of the infinite order to consummation, basing His claim to reception upon the even and inexorable justice of God. He passed from earth to heaven, and stood unafraid in the

[1] I Pet. I : 12.

white light of the Eternal Purity. In all the record of the race there has been no other like unto this Jesus of Nazareth.

The greatest of Old Testament characters are seen overshadowed by their own sin and failure, and the men of the New have no claim or merit, save that which is imputed to them, and outwrought through them, by the Spirit as He reveals to their understanding, and realizes in their character, the perfections of the Christ. Jesus stands in heaven, having perfectly realized the original thought of God which found expression in the first covenant of creation, " Let Us make man in our Image, after Our likeness." [1] Both in character and in conduct do men learn the meaning of that Divine thought as they know the Man of Nazareth.

Perhaps the sublimest description of perfect character is that which Paul uses in writing to Timothy, when he says " God gave us . . . a spirit . . . of power and love and discipline." [2] This exactly describes the character of Christ ;—the spirit of power, the spirit of love, the spirit of discipline. It should be noted here that discipline does not signify self-control, so much as power of ruling others. It is the spirit of order, of authority. This indeed is perfection of character. Out of this sprung His perfection of conduct. The whole conduct of His life was the outward expression of this perfect character whether at the feast, or the funeral ; whether with the scholars, or the simple ; whether with the adults, or the children ; whether in loneliness on the mountain height, or amid the crowds that surged around Him, He was ever acting in response to the impulse of the spirit of power, the spirit of love, and the spirit of discipline. At last this Man Whose creed was truth, Whose character was true, and Whose conduct was

[1] Gen. I : 26.   [2] 2 Tim. I : 7.

triumphant, was received into heaven upon the basis of His own absolute perfection.

II.　Yet that is not the greatest wonder of ascension day.　It would seem as though one could hear the antiphonal singing of the heavenly choirs, as this perfect One passes into heaven,

> " Lift up your heads, O ye gates ;
> And be ye lifted up, ye everlasting doors :
> And the King of glory will come in," [1]

is the exulting challenge of the angels escorting Him.　To this comes back the question, inspired by the passion to hear declared again the story of the victory,

> " Who is the King of glory ? "

And yet gathering new music and new meaning the surging anthem rolls,

> " Jehovah strong and mighty,
> Jehovah mighty in battle.　.　.　.
> He is the King of glory." [2]

Thus the song is also of One who was mighty in battle. Looking upon Him the glorified One, and listening to His words, the wonder grows.　In that form all filled with exquisite beauty are yet the signs of suffering and of pain. The marks of wounding are in hands, and feet, and side, and His presence declares in His own words, " I am .　.　.　the Living One ; and I was dead, and behold, I am alive forevermore." [3]

This is indeed a mystery demanding explanation.　In the life of the Perfect, there is no reason for death.　Death

[1] Psa. 24 : 7.　　[2] Psa. 24 : 8, 10.　　[3] Rev. 1 : 17, 18.

is the wage of sin, and apart from sin there is no place for death. Sometimes men declare that death is a necessity, a part of a process. This may be declared, but cannot be demonstrated. The mystery of life has eluded all scientific examination, and therefore so also has the mystery of death. The reason for death in ordinary human life has never yet been declared. The human frame, according to scientific testimony, reconstructs itself once in every seven years. Why may not this process go on indefinitely? Why is there any necessity for death? The scientists are unable to answer the question. They can do no more than declare what seems to be a necessity from the perpetual recurrence of the experience in the human race.

What science has failed to do, revelation has clearly done. It simply and sublimely states that death is penalty for sin. Such is the meaning of the story of Genesis, and such the meaning of the explicit declaration of the apostle. "Through one man sin entered into the world, and death through sin; and so death passed unto all men, for that all sinned." [1] If then pain be the issue of sin, and death its penalty, why has the Perfect suffered and died? As was seen in the consideration of the transfiguration of Jesus on the Holy mount, His human nature, having passed through all temptation victoriously, was metamorphosed, and might so far as it was concerned, have been received into heaven. Between that crisis and ascension, He has been to the deepest depth of suffering, and through death itself. There can be but one answer to all these questionings. He has wrought a victory for others. The One in Whom death had no place, has died in the place of those who ought to die. Gazing upon the perfections of the ascended Man, the heart is filled with astonishment, and humbled with a

[1] Rom. 5 : 12.

great shame, as the light of His glory falls upon the failure of all others.   Gazing upon that Perfect One, the " Lamb as it had been slain," realizing that the wounds tell of penalty borne, and the words of death vanquished, the heart is filled with unutterable sense of the infinite Love, the lips break out in song,

> " Rock of Ages, cleft for me,
>   Let me hide myself in Thee.
>   Let the water and the blood
>   From Thy riven side which flowed,
>   Be of sin the double cure,
>   Cleanse me from its guilt and power." [1]

III.   Thus ascending, He led captivity captive, He passed into the presence of God with the defeated foes of the race dragged at His chariot wheels, the Master of sin, the Vanquisher of Satan, the Overcomer of death, the insignia of Whose victory were the wounds that He bore, and the fact that He lived the life taken up after having been laid down in death.   For Himself He stood in the perfection of His manhood.   For man He stood in the perfection of His Saviourhood.

It is now that He is invested with the Name.   In that sublimest of all passages dealing with His descent and ascent, the apostle declares that God gave unto Him " the Name which is above every name," [2] and the occasion of the giving of the Name was His exaltation to heaven, after the perfect carrying out of that Divine work of Love which included humiliation and suffering and death.

In the ascension light what Name is this now bestowed upon the all conquering Man ?   It is the old Name, full of ineffable music, the Name of Jesus.   It is the Name by which His mother first called Him in the innocence of

[1] Toplady.   [2] Phil. 2 : 9.

infancy. It is the Name by which men knew Him in the purity of His boyhood. It is the Name by which men called Him in the victory of His Manhood. It is the Name by which disciples knew Him in the days of His teaching. It is the Name which men wrote over His Cross in the hour of His dying. It is the old Name, and yet He had never received it in all fullness until now. At His Incarnation the Name was a prophecy. " Thou shalt call His Name JESUS; for it is He that shall save His people from their sins." [1] That prophetic Name He carried through all life's mystery and ministry, the Name that told to those that understood, that God's faith was centred in this innocent child, and holy Man. And now having accomplished all, perfected to finality the infinite plan of the Eternal Love, He is invested with the Name which at His birth was prophetic. The issue is reached, and in the centre of the universe of God, the Man of Nazareth is enthroned, and named by the sweet Name that ever speaks of perfect humanity, and ever declares the fulfillment of the purpose of salvation. At His birth the Name of Jesus was the proclamation of a Divine purpose. On ascension day it was the ratification of a victory won. He gave Him the Name—JESUS.

[1] Matt. I : 21.

XXIX

MAN'S WOUNDED GOD

THE title of the chapter is startling, and needs some explanation. In the previous chapter has been considered the coming into heaven of God's perfect Man, bearing in His body the marks of His wounding, the evidences of His dying.

Attention still being fixed upon Him, it must be remembered that in that glory as ever, two things are true concerning Him. First He is God's Man ; and secondly, He is man's God.

Apart from Him, man has no perfect understanding of God. In Him man finds the full and final revelation of the Father. It is impossible for men to come, either in understanding or in actual communion, to the Father save through the risen glorified Son.

To state this positively therefore is to declare that man approaching God, does so forevermore, as He has revealed Himself in and through Jesus of Nazareth. Thus the ascended One is man's God.

It is impossible to omit from that ascended and reigning One the wounds He bears. They are part of His Personality, and speak of the fulfillment of a purpose which was the purpose of God, and which was carried out by God in and through Jesus. If the perfect Manhood of Jesus be the perfect unveiling before the eyes of men of the essential glories of God, so the wounded Personality of Jesus is the unveiling before the eyes of men of that wounding of the heart of God, through which His grace was manifested, and wrought its mightiest victory.

In Apocalyptic vision John saw " in the midst of tne throne . . . a Lamb as though it had been slain." [1] The reference is without question to Christ. Two things are manifest, first that He occupies the position of proper Deity. He is in the midst of the throne. Secondly that He retains the evidences of suffering. It is " a Lamb as though it had been slain." This double fact speaks forevermore of the deepest fact that lies behind man's redemption. This fact is that of the pain of God.

In the book of Proverbs, the preacher asks,

> " The spirit of a man will sustain his infirmity;
> But a broken spirit who can bear ? " [2]

Therein is a recognition of the fact that while the spirit of a man gives him strength for bearing physical infirmity, the deepest fact of sorrow possible to man is sorrow of the spirit.

Bearing in mind that illustration taken from the lower realm of human experience, turn now to a passage in the prophecy of Isaiah. " I gave My back to the smiters, and My cheeks to them that plucked off the hair; I hid not My face from shame and spitting." [3] Whatever the local and incidental application of these words, there is a general consensus of opinion that they are Messianic in their final application, finding their perfect fulfillment only in the experience of Jesus.

Turning to another passage in the same prophecy, " Surely He hath borne our griefs, and carried our sorrows; yet we did esteem Him stricken, smitten of God, and

[1] Rev. 5 : 6.　　　[2] Prov. 18 : 14.　　　[3] Isa. 50 : 6.

afflicted.   But He was wounded for our transgressions, He
was bruised for our iniquities; the chastisement of our
peace was upon Him; and with His stripes we are healed." [1]
The idea that He was smitten of God and stricken of God
is not accurate.   It is rather the portrayal of One Who in
perfect cooperation with God is bearing the smiting and
the bruising that comes upon human guilt through the
operation of the inexorable law of God.   The suffering
Servant is seen here as receiving those stripes which will
make possible the healing of such as ought to have borne
their own penalty.   The word to be specially noticed now
is the word "smitten."   That is the word translated
"broken" in the quotation from the Proverbs.   While the
wounding of the body of Jesus was the outward and visible
sign, it was in the wounding of the Spirit that the deepest
mystery of His atoning suffering lay.   Thus in Jesus, God
is revealed, not only in His love, in His holiness, and in
His justice; but in His sorrow, and in His pain.

At this point there are strong divergences of opinion.
It has been maintained that God is incapable of sorrow, and
that it was only in the fact of His Manhood that Jesus
suffered in the place of man.   Such a conception of God
would seem to be utterly unwarranted by the whole revelation made of Him in Scripture, and finally in the Person of
His Son.   If the Man was a revelation of God, surely the
Man of sorrows was a revelation of the God of sorrow.
This capacity for sorrow is most evidently pre-supposed in
the injunction of the apostle, " Grieve not the Holy Spirit
of God." [2]   The word "grieve" here is purely a word indicating sorrow.   There is no suspicion of anger in it.
The injunction does not mean, Do not make the Spirit
angry.   It most certainly means, Do not cause Him sor-

[1] Isa. 53 : 4, 5.   [2] Eph. 4 : 30.

row. The fact to be established is that of the possibility
of sorrow in the consciousness of God. If once this is established, then a new light shines through all the book.
The final proof of the proposition is most evidently to be
found in the simplest statement concerning God, namely,
" God is love." [1] Love is the capacity for joy. It is
therefore, moreover, the capacity for sorrow. Joy and
sorrow are twin sisters. They are so closely related that
it is impossible to have capacity for one, without having
also capacity for the other. That Jesus was the revelation
of God in His marvellous wisdom, in His splendid strength,
no one denies. When against tyranny, and oppression, and
wrong, His anger flamed, it is at once conceded that the
indignation of God was being revealed. Can it then be
denied that the tears He shed in presence of the grief of
the bereaved sisters, were revelations of the exquisite tenderness of the heart of the Divine, or have we any right to
affirm that when the Man of Nazareth gazed upon beautiful Jerusalem the curse alone was the revelation of the
Divine will? Were not the tears, and the tones of emotion in the voice, equally means of manifesting to men the
love and the sorrow of the heart of God. It must of
course be at once granted that God can never have any
sorrow which is merely that of limitation, or that caused
by the sense of mystery. His sorrow must ever be that of
sympathy, with that which is the result of His entering
into the actual experiences of another, and making His own
what that other feels. To understand this is to read with
new intonation the startling questions that occur in the first
book of the Bible. When God cried to Adam " Where
art thou," [2] it was not so much the voice of outraged holiness,
speaking in anger, as a violated love, wailing in compassion.

[1] I John 4 . 8.   [2] Gen. 3 : 9.

Jesus the wounded is therefore in expression to man, and in the fact of His own Personality, man's wounded God. As the God-man on the earth was the Revelation of the Father in all the wondrous facts of His Personality, so the Lamb slain in the midst of the throne is still the Revelation of the Father in the unsullied light of the heavenly places. The harmony between Father and Son is unbroken. In the High Priest, Who can be touched with the feeling of our infirmities, there exists One Who expresses thus the fact of God's consciousness of all human infirmity and all human sorrow.

The risen and ascended God-man, having received His Name, now assumes His place in the economy of God, and the Divine purpose is declared that every knee shall bow, in submission; and every tongue shall confess in acclamation that He is Lord to the glory of God the Father. Thus we may see in Him the order of a new economy as to its central Personality, and as to the nature of its administration.

I. The central Personality being that of the ascended Man, is described as a " Lamb as though It had been slain," and the throne is the symbol of order. That order had been violated through the terrible catastrophe of human sin. There was no possible way for its restoration but the way of the Cross. Jesus of Nazareth having wrought righteousness in life, and atonement in death, and having received the seal of perfect victory, in the miracle of resurrection, now passes to the very throne of power.

While it is thus seen that the only way to the throne was the way of the Cross, it is at once demonstrated that there could be no issue to the Cross of Christ other than His crowning and the ultimate restoration of the lost order. The ascended Man of Nazareth in the midst of the throne is none other than God the Son, invested in the counsel of the ever-blessed Trinity with all authority, upon the basis of redemption work accomplished, and victory won over all the enemies of the human race.

II. The issue of this is self-evident. The Man of Nazareth in the midst of the throne, occupies the seat of final authority, and therefore constitutes the last court of appeal. There can be no appeal beyond that throne. His word is the universal law, His verdict the irrevocable sentence. As in resurrection, God rejected man apart from Christ, so in Christ's enthronement, He receives man in Him. Thus those who are united to Him are already seated in Him in the heavenlies. Forevermore therefore the word of the Church is that which so often occurred in apostolic preaching, " Jesus is Lord." [1] It is the word of salvation to the individual, the word of reconstruction to society, the word of ultimate deliverance to all the nations. Herein therefore lies the true centre of sin, as He Himself said, " of sin, because they believe not on Me." [2] It is still true of the world at large that

> " Our Lord is now rejected,
> And by the world disowned.
> By the many still neglected,
> And by the few enthroned." [3]

Yet He is God-enthroned, and the future of an individual, of society, of a nation is being determined by the relation of each to Him. The Man of Nazareth, ascending on high, led captivity captive, and passed beyond all principalities and powers, yea, beyond every name that is named to the very throne of God, and there to-day He sits, still re-

---

[1] 1 Cor. 12: 3.   [2] John 16: 9.   [3] Major Whittle.

jected by men, and yet being crowned by thousands who listening to His voice, obey it.

It is impossible to pass from this contemplation of the ascension of Jesus to the centre of all government, and to see in Him man's wounded God, without becoming conscious of a great comfort and of a great strength. The comfort ever comes as we behold on the throne of the Eternal, One Who bears amid the dazzling splendour, marks that tell of His having suffered and died for us men, that He might bring us into union with His unending joy and eternal Love.

Moreover when the work presses, and the battle thickens, and the day seems long in coming, it is good for the heart to remember that the present conflict is with defeated foes, and that there is no room for question as to the final issue, for the Man of Nazareth is not only seated in the place of authority, He carries forward the work of active administration. This is a fact too often forgotten amid the turmoil and the strife. High over all the thrones of earth, stands that throne of the Eternal, and seated on it is the ascended Man, watching, ordering, preventing, and through all the apparent chaos, moving surely towards the ultimate triumph of the Infinite Love. He initiates the true policies, selects the proper agents, and even when man least understands, moves ever onward.

In the Person of the crowned Man of Nazareth justice acts forevermore in mercy, and mercy moves in unerring justice. Justice acts in mercy by pardoning, purifying, perfecting upon the basis of that Passion, the signs of which are in the evidences of the slaying. Mercy operates in justice by the justification, sanctification, glorification of those who submitting to the King, receive the blessing of the Saviour

XXX

THE NEW UNION

HAVING attempted to follow the Lord as He ascended to the right hand of the Father, and having seen Him in the height of the heavenly glory, a perfect Man, fulfilling the Divine ideal, the perfect Saviour having provided a ransom for the lost; and having moreover, recognized anew the fact that this exalted Man is our God, there remains to be considered somewhat more closely, the new union between God and man, consummated when the Man of Nazareth received the promise of the Father.

In his first sermon after Pentecost, Peter, referring to the ascended Christ, declared that He " having received of the Father the promise of the Holy Spirit," [1] had poured forth the gift upon the waiting disciples. The present study is an attempt to understand what the apostle meant, when he said that Jesus had received the promise of the Spirit.

Most certainly this is a declaration that upon the basis of His finished work of life, and on the occasion of His arrival in heaven, Jesus of Nazareth did receive, by a solemn and official act from the Father, the Holy Spirit according to promise. The first question that suggests itself to the mind is, Why was the Spirit now given to this ascended Man, and in what sense was the Spirit given to Him? It cannot possibly be that the bestowment of the Spirit was for Himself. His whole human life had been conditioned by the abiding presence in Him of the Holy

[1] Acts 2 : 33.

Spirit of God, and that in fulfillment of the primal Divine intention concerning man. It is important that there should be perfect clearness of understanding of this fact. His reception of the Spirit in heaven was not the crowning by God of His Manhood. It was rather the answer of God to the claim this Man made upon Him, by the work He had accomplished for others.

To state this even more fully. The whole Being of Christ, and the whole mission of Christ were so closely associated with the presence and power of the Holy Spirit that there could be no necessity for any new bestowment of the Spirit merely for Himself. His very human life was due to the mystery of the overshadowing Spirit and through all the years of privacy, there can be no doubt that He lived under the immediate guidance of the Spirit of truth. He did not, at the baptism, receive the Spirit. At that crisis, the presence of the Spirit was manifest, and in a new symbolism that suggested the truth that His work would be carried out in the power of the Spirit. The dove-like form in which the Spirit then appeared,—a form in which He is never manifested in connection with any other person, save the Christ : a form suggestive of tender gentle patience—revealed the truth concerning the character of Jesus ; and announced that in keeping with that essential of His nature, all His work would be carried forward. Filled with the Spirit, He passed to the wilderness to be tempted of the devil, and in the power of the Spirit He went forth to His ministry, when all the temptation was accomplished. And at the last it was " through the eternal Spirit " He " offered Himself without blemish unto God."[1] And yet we have a declaration that having passed through death, and having ascended to the presence of the Father,

[1] Heb. 9: 14.

He received there from the Father the promise of the Holy Spirit.

An explanation of the declaration will be found in a correct apprehension of what is meant by the promise of the Spirit. Where, and to whom was the promise made? The whole subject may be considered under the following heads, first, the promise of the Spirit fulfilled in His bestowment upon the ascended Man; second, the Spirit received by the ascended Man for those whom He represented as Saviour; third, the union of God and man resulting.

I. In the final charges delivered to the apostles, Christ distinctly commanded them not to depart from Jerusalem, but "to wait for the promise of the Father."[1] Here is the same thought, uttered by the Lord Himself, and here also He distinctly tells them when the promise was made, "which, said He, ye heard from Me." Thus it is evident that we are approaching an explanation of this statement. Christ had promised the Spirit, and He had done that in the name of the Father, for Whom He ever spake to men. Is there no definite account of His having made such a promise? Most assuredly there is an account, which is not only definite, but also detailed, and it is to be found in the Paschal discourses, which are chronicled by John alone. "I will pray the Father, and He shall give you another Comforter, that He may be with you forever, even the Spirit of truth: Whom the world cannot receive."[2] "But the Comforter even the Holy Spirit, Whom the Father will send in My name."[3] "When the Comforter is come, Whom I will send unto you from the Father."[4] Thus in view of His approaching Cross, and in preparation of His

[1] Acts 1: 4.   [2] John 14: 16, 17.   [3] John 14: 26.   [4] John 15: 26.

disciples for the days when He in bodily form should be no more with them, He declared that in answer to His prayer, and in His Name, the Father would send them another Comforter, the Holy Spirit. Nothing is more evident in reading these discourses than the quiet majestic confidence of Christ. "I will enquire of the Father." "He will send you." "The Father will send in My name." "I will send you from the Father." That is the promise of the Father, and when the One Who made the promise to the band of disciples, ascended into heaven, the Father recognized the prevailing plea of His presence there, and gave Him the Spirit that He might fulfill the promise to the waiting men upon the earth.

It is evident therefore that His reception of the Spirit was, as has been shown, not for Himself but for others. This however will be dealt with more fully subsequently. It would be sufficient to leave the statement at this point, and yet that phrase "the promise of the Father" has more in it than is indicated by this answer. As the whole of the Old Testament economy had culminated in Christ, and as in His teaching He had fulfilled all that was symbolized and suggested in that economy, so His uttering of the promise of the Father concerning the Spirit was the explanation of a constant message, sounding through the previous centuries, concerning a new dispensation of power. The seers and the prophets of the past all saw and spoke of a day full of light, full of force, a day of restoration that was yet to come. Through these prophets the Father had promised the Holy Spirit to men in larger, fuller measure than had ever been experienced. In the midst of the darkness that characterized the age in which these men of old had spoken, they had looked on towards the suffering Servant, Who was yet to be the all-conquering Deliverer, anᴄ stretching away beyond His day of suffering, they caught the light and glory of the dispensation of the Spirit. One or two illustrations will suffice.

Isaiah, in lofty and terrible language is announcing the coming of judgment. He tells of woe and of desolation, and ends with a paragraph pulsating with hope, which begins with the words " until the Spirit be poured upon us from on high, and the wilderness become a fruitful field, and the fruitful field be esteemed as a forest." [1] Here the prophet, telling the message of Jehovah, promises the Spirit.

And yet again the same prophet, " I will pour water upon him that is thirsty, and streams upon the dry ground; I will pour My Spirit upon thy seed, and My blessing upon thine offspring: and they shall spring up among the grass, as willows by the watercourses. One shall say, I am Jehovah's; and another shall call himself by the name of Jacob; and another shall subscribe with his hand unto Jehovah, and surname himself by the name of Israel," [2] again an inspired promise of the Spirit.

There remains the most radiant and remarkable foretelling of the Spirit's dispensation, which Peter quoted on the day of Pentecost itself. " I will pour out My Spirit upon all flesh; and your sons and your daughters shall prophesy, your old men shall dream dreams, your young men shall see visions: and also upon the servants and upon the handmaids in those days will I pour out My Spirit. And I will show wonders in the heavens and in the earth: blood, and fire, and pillars of smoke. The sun shall be turned into darkness, and the moon into blood, before the great and terrible day of Jehovah cometh. And it shall come to pass, that whosoever shall call on the name of

[1] Isa. 32: 15.   [2] Isa. 44: 3–5.

Jehovah shall be delivered." [1] Thus it is seen that the men who kept alive in the heart of the nation this spiritual hope, were men who served, and spoke in the hope of the coming of a new day, which should be a day of the poured out Spirit of God.   Thus the promise which Jesus made in the Paschal discourses was the repetition of the promise made to the fathers by the prophets, by the One Who now not only promised, but was working towards the mighty consummation, which should consist in fulfillment.

In order to catch a true perspective, let this argument now be summarized.   God, through the prophets in the past had promised the Holy Spirit to men.   These heroic souls hearing and seeing, declared to their age the gracious announcement, and yet passed away without seeing the day of which they spoke.   In fullness of time the Messiah came.   He accomplished the will of God, and at last, passing into the presence of God, claimed as the inevitable issue of His victory, the fulfillment of the Divine promise, made to, and through the prophets, and finally uttered by His own lips.   In answer to that claim, God acting at once in love and justice, gave Him the Spirit.   Through Him the dreams of the prophets moved into the realm of deeds.

II.   Having clearly seen that this bestowment of the Spirit was not for Himself, it becomes perfectly evident that it was a bestowment for such as were represented by that infinite work accomplished through His death and resurrection.   The fact of His death makes righteous demands upon God, which, God answering, Jesus receives for bestowment, that which He Himself already had possessed for personal life and victory.   His death having been accomplished for sinners, the Spirit is now bestowed

[1] Joel 2 : 28–32.

for them also. What symbols or figures of speech are equal to helping men to understand this solemn and wondrous transaction? Reverently conscious of the inadequacy of all figures of speech, it may be said that God placed the Spirit at the disposal of Christ, that He might bestow Him upon all such as trusting in Jesus have counted to them the value of His death upon the Cross. Having accomplished that Mediatorial work through which man may in the value of His death be brought back to God, He now commences that Mediatorial work through which God the Holy Spirit may come back into relation with man, for the administration of the virtue of His life.

III. Confining the attention exclusively for the moment to the new union as seen in the Man Jesus, it is evident that now God has moved into a new relationship with fallen man, and man is lifted in spite of his fall, into new relation with God in the Person of Jesus. Jesus the unfallen is yet Jesus, Who has borne the final issues, resulting from the fall. His reception of the Spirit is therefore a representative fact, declaring forevermore that in spite of sin, a way has been made back to fellowship with God. Such relation had never been nor could be, apart from this great fact. The Holy Spirit Who knows the mind of God, Who "searches all things, yea the deep things of God,"[1] Who is the Spirit of life forever proceeding from the Father, is now vested in the Man of Nazareth, and through Him is at the disposal of all such as submit to His Lordship. The Spirit of God Who had been grieved from humanity, and prevented operating in the human heart, as to the knowledge of God, and the life of God, and the power of God, is now through this perfect

[1] 1 Cor. 2: 10.

Man, in Whom was no sin, yet in Whom is resident the moral value of cancelled sin, at the disposal of the rebellious also. The ascended Christ has now become the new Centre of a new race. Henceforth the Spirit will plead with man the cause of Christ, demonstrating the fact that sin consists in rejection of Him, declaring the evangel that righteousness is possible because He has ascended to the Father, and denouncing forever the ultimate doom of evil, because the "prince of this world hath been judged." [1]

Having received this promise of the Father, the ascended Lord poured out upon the waiting disciples the gift of the Holy Spirit, and so the promise fulfilled to Christ, is fulfilled to those who have put their trust in Him, and herein is revealed the explanation of all the careful statements of His own discourses on the Paraclete. The Father has sent the Spirit, because He has bestowed Him on the Man that represents the fallen race. The Son has sent the Spirit, having received Him from the Father.

One brief glance at the fact on earth will serve to complete the present study, and prepare for those that remain. In the upper room at Jerusalem, a company of waiting souls received the gift of the Holy Spirit, not in answer to their prayer, but in answer to the prevailing prayer in high heaven of the ascended Man of Nazareth. The Holy Spirit falling upon them, took up His abode in them, coming to them from the crucified, risen, and ascended Lord. In the Person of Jesus the point of union between man and God has been found. Jesus is glorified by God in exaltation to the throne of power. Jesus is glorified by man in his submission to Him as enthroned.

The Spirit indwelling man, administers all the values o the finished work of Jesus.

[1] John 16: 11.

This means that the men so indwelt, are by that Spirit Who administers the values, made one with the risen Christ. His life is their life as to its nature, for it is life won out of death, risen, ascended and yet to be manifested; as to its expression, for it is life interested in the things of God, and devoted in its powers to the accomplishment of Divine purposes; as to its whole, for henceforth for them also the one and only rule of life will be the good and perfect and acceptable will of God.

And yet again, the Spirit's indwelling initiates a process of growth into perfect likeness to Christ by the subjugation of the whole man, spirit, soul, and body to the new life imparted in this miracle of regeneration. Thus the outpouring of the Spirit on the day of Pentecost is the demonstration of the fact that the stupendous work to which God set Himself according to His wisdom and His might in the Person and mission of Christ has been fully accomplished. It now remains to consider how Christ answers the call of man in all its deepest meaning.

RESULTANT

THE ANSWER OF CHRIST—MAN REDEEMED

XXXI. Man Restored to God by Christ
XXXII. Man Knowing God Through Christ
XXXIII. Man Made Like God in Christ

" *He found me the lost and the wandering,*
   The sinful, the sad, and the lone ;
He said ; ' I have bought thee, beloved,
   Forever thou art Mine own.

" ' *O soul, I will show thee the wonder,*
   The worth of My priceless Blood ;
Thou art whiter than snow on the mountains,
   Thou art fair in the eyes of God.

" ' *O vessel of living water,*
   From the depths of the love divine,
The glorious life within thee
   Flows from My heart to thine.

" ' *O soul altogether lovely,*
   O pearl for which Christ was given,
Wouldst thou know the joy and the glory
   That welcome thee into Heaven ?

" ' *Wouldst thou know how near to the Father*
   The place that is granted thee ?
Behold Me, O soul, in His bosom,
   And measure His love to Me.

" ' *Are the love, and the joy, and the glory*
   More than My Blood could win ?
In the Name of the Son Beloved,
   Beloved one, enter in.' "

—V. M. C.

" *Hymns of Ter Steegen, Suso and others.*"

Concerning the faith in Christ Jesus.—*Acts 24 : 24.*

God was in Christ reconciling the world unto Himself.—*2 Cor. 5 : 19.*

A man in Christ.—*2 Cor. 12 : 2.*

Approved in Christ.—*Rom. 16 : 10.*

Blessed . . . with every spiritual blessing in the heavenlies in Christ.—*Eph. 1 : 3.*

God Who always leadeth us in triumph in Christ.—*2 Cor 2 : 14.*

The dead in Christ shall rise first.—*1 Thess. 4 : 16.*

RESULTANT

THF ANSWER OF CHRIST—MAN REDEEMED

As at the first, in order to a correct understanding of the meaning of Christ's mission, it was necessary to consider the nature and extent of the calamity which constituted the call for Christ, so now at the close of the study it will be profitable to contemplate how perfectly He has responded, in the plenteous redemption He has provided.

The statement of the case concerning that provision may be made in three propositions, which correspond to the threefold statement concerning man's need,

First, Man restored to God by Christ.

Second, Man knowing God through Christ.

Third, Man made like God in Christ.

The actual experience of the threefold redemption in human life always results from the direct work of the Holy Spirit, Whom the Father had promised, and Who was given through the Son on the day of Pentecost dispensationally, and to each individual for indwelling life, when in response to His work of conviction from without, Jesus is glorified. As this book is to be devoted rather to an examination of the resulting facts than to the initial act, it is fitting that that act should first be dealt with briefly, as to its condition and its actuality.

The first work of the Spirit with fallen man is that of producing conviction concerning sin, righteousness, and judgment. All these subjects are dealt with, however, from the centre of Christ and His work. Sin is shown to consist in the rejection of the Saviour; righteousness is declared to be possible through the fact of His ascension; and judgment is pronounced against all rebellion, " because the prince of this world hath been judged." [1] The initial work of grace therefore is that of bringing the sinner to a consciousness of the truth concerning these vital matters. At this point human responsibility commences. If man refuses to yield to the truth understood, he remains outside the sphere of salvation. If on the other hand, he responds to conviction by submission to Christ, and trust in Him, then the spirit performs the stupendous miracle of regeneration. By communicating to the man " dead through trespasses and sins," [2] the life of Christ, He quickens his spirit. This act of God restores man to his own true balance and proportion, lifting to the throne of his personality the spirit so long neglected, and dethroning the flesh so long having occupied the place of power. More than this, the Spirit of God enters now into a perpetual partnership with the spirit of man, and thus initiates the life of power and of victory.

This of course is simply a condensed statement concerning most important truths dealt with more fully in another volume. [3] Upon the basis of this statement it is now possible to pass to an examination of the redemption provided, under the propositions stated.

---

[1] John 16: 8–11   [2] Eph. 2: 1.   [3] " The Spirit of God."

XXXI

MAN RESTORED TO GOD BY CHRIST

In previous studies two subjects have been dealt with, which must now be recalled and carefully remembered. First that man by his sin, distanced himself from God, passed out of the region of communion, and was " alienated from the life of God." [1] Second, in the raising of Jesus of Nazareth from among the dead, God accepted Him as the One Who perfectly realized His original design in the creation of man, and by that raising finally rejected man in his failure and in his sin. He nevertheless, in that same reception by resurrection, received in Christ all those for whom He stood in the sacred and awful mystery of His death on the Cross. It becomes evident therefore that when, by the regenerative work of the Holy Spirit, man is joined to Christ, he is restored to God. This restoration is marvellous in its completeness and overwhelming as a manifestation of the wisdom of God. Some understanding of it may be gained by an examination under three aspects, as judicial, vital, and governmental.

I. Man's judicial restoration to God is indicated by the great word justification. The term is forensic. Behind it lies the fact of law, and also the profounder fact of justice. The greatest problem in man's redemption was that of how it was possible for God to be just, and yet to justify the sinner. The answer is to be found in the res-

---

[1] Eph. 4 : 18.

toration of man in Christ Jesus. In the mystery of the Master's passion, He endured what was not His due. Considering this for a moment without reference to the need of the sinner, it is at once seen how that in the realm of law, and in the presence of the eternal principle of justice, these sufferings created a value which was not required by the One Who suffered, and apart from the fact of man's sin, is an overplus in the working of the Infinite Order. This value has been created for those who have violated law, and is placed at the disposal of all such. Those receiving the benefit by submission to, and trust in, the Saviour, are thus so far as the guilt of sin is concerned, justified before God and made nigh to Him.

Yet again, by thus cancelling sin, the perfection of the life of Jesus is made to count for others also, and God imputes it to those for whom the value of His death has cancelled the guilt of sin. This union with Christ is wrought by the Holy Spirit in the communication of life. This is done when man, under the conviction of the Spirit, believes in Christ, so that God may be " just, and the Justifier of him that hath faith in Jesus." [1] Man exercising faith in Christ, has imputed to him by the grace of God the value created by Christ's death, for pardon; and all the perfection of Christ's life for righteousness. Therefore the sinner standing in Jesus, is a sinner no longer, but a saint, separated in Christ to God, and so restored. He has no guilt; that is cancelled. He has righteousness; that is bestowed. Such an one is restored to God, because the reasons of his exclusion are all removed. The sword guarding the way to the tree of life becomes the light of truth, illuminating all the pathway. The veil, enclosing the Holy of Holies, and excluding man, being rent, becomes

[1] Rom. 3:26.

the glorious portal to the inner places of fullest communion. Henceforward neither hell, nor earth, nor heaven can condemn the trusting soul, for in Christ Jesus every claim has been fully met, and every provision perfectly made.

II. The fact of vital restoration has necessarily been already stated incidentally, but it now remains to be more fully considered. In order to a right appreciation of this, there must be a clear understanding of the nature of the life communicated by the Holy Spirit. In speaking of regeneration it is not sufficient to say that there is an impartation of new human vitality. Neither is it absolutely correct to speak only of the communication of a new measure of Divine life. It is neither, merely because it is both. Herein is the great mystery and wonder of Christianity. The Spirit imparts in regeneration the Christ life, and that is at once human and Divine. Thus, all essential human life is surcharged with new life of its own most perfect order, but it is also energized with the force of life Divine, in inseparable union therewith. Thus in Christ, man is restored to the possibilities of his own nature, but also he is introduced to a new vital union with God more marvellous as to its potentiality and possibility than that of original man.

> " Where He displays His healing power,
>   Death and the curse are known no more :
>   In Him the tribes of Adam boast
>   More blessings than their fathers lost." [1]

All man's inability is overcome in God's ability. The sinner is lifted from the impotence of his fallen nature, into

[1] Watts.

the potency of the perfect Man Jesus in cooperation with the might of the Eternal God. What wonder that Paul exclaimed, " I can do all things in Him that strengtheneth me." [1]

The great theme of the Colossian epistle is that of the perfection of the Church in the perfection of the Christ. All its sublime doctrine gathers around two main statements, first, " It was the good pleasure of the Father that in Him should all the fullness dwell; " [2] and second, " In Him ye are made full." [3] The fullness dwelling in Christ is fullness of Deity, which is fullness of life, fullness of light, fullness of love. It is in Him and in His fullness that man is made full. Can anything be added to such statements as these? Some idea of their value, and yet of the difficulty of expressing that value, and even of appreciating it, may be gathered from examining one paragraph in that letter. [4] Here the word " mystery " occurs thrice. First the apostle refers to the Church as the mystery " which hath been hid for ages and generations : but now hath it been manifested to His saints." He then declares the mystery lying behind the mystery of the Church to be that of " Christ in you, the hope of glory." And yet further on he speaks of " the mystery of God, even Christ." Evidently here the apostle is moving backward through great mysteries of effect to the primal mystery of cause. Let this threefold mystery be stated thus :

1. Christ.
2. Christ in the saints.
3. Christ in the Church.

The central mystery is that of Christ Himself, the mystery of His Person, in its unity of the human and the Divine, and the mystery of His passion in the preparation of the

[1] Phil. 4 : 13.   [2] Col. 1 : 19.   [3] Col. 2 : 10.   [4] Col. 1 : 24–2 : 5.

life, and the propitiation of the death; a veritable mystery, most evidently revealed, and most absolutely defying analysis or explanation.

Then follows the mystery of personal realization, "Christ in you, the hope of glory." Christ the human and the Divine, in one indissoluble unity in the believer, administering the virtue of His life through the value of His death.

Then finally the Christ in all believers, finding at last His own completion, His body, that through which in conjunction with Himself all the infinite fullness of the Infinite God, is to find through unending ages, a medium of manifestation, is to be in fact the new form of God through which His wisdom and His love may be known by other creations through the never ending ages.

This stupendous vision of the issue of the Christ and His work in its individual application with regard to trusting souls, reveals how in Christ, man is restored to God by actual sharing of the life Divine. God in Christ in a new sense, shares human life. Man in Christ in a new sense, shares Divine life. This is the final realization of the Atonement, and consists in man's restoration to God on a basis infinitely beyond that from which he fell by his sin.

III. The sequence of this vital restoration in the life of man is that of a governmental restoration. As at the first, man ruined himself by rebellion, so now his redemption being accomplished by the operation of God in Christ, within the realm of law and of justice he must abide in the will of God. This is not an arbitrary and capricious requirement. It is rather, as the whole history of man in his ruin demonstrates, a necessity upon the fulfillment of which love must insist, or cease to be love. Outside the realm of the Divine will, man is in the place of ruin and of death.   Within that will, he is in the sphere of permanence and of perfection.

Now however it is possible to refer to abiding in the will of God in new terms, which are the terms of a plenteous redemption.   To abide in that will is to abide in Christ. The restoration of man to God in Christ being, as has been shown, vital as well as judicial, it is therefore governmental also, in a way which reveals the infinite love and wisdom of God, as perhaps it is nowhere else revealed, because it appeals to man at the point of his supreme consciousness of weakness.   The God-man is the meeting place between God and man.   Rejecting man, God enthroned Jesus.   Rejecting himself, man enthrones Jesus. Thus the Divine and the human will move into union of decision and purpose.   God and man meet in Christ. Upon this basis, the Spirit communicates the life which creates vital relationship, and that life henceforth becomes the directing, controlling, suggesting principle in the life of the saint.   Moving along the line of the perfect will of God, as it ever has and ever must, it regulates all the life of the saint, within the government of God, " casting down reasonings, and every high thing that is exalted against the knowledge of God, and bringing every thought into captivity to the obedience of Christ." [1]   It is because of this that the Christian is no longer under the law, which consists in commandments outside the personality.   He in Christ, answers the law of the Spirit of life, which is at once a perpetual illumination, and a constant power.   God in Christ by the Spirit works in " to will and to work, for His good pleasure." [2]

It was in view of this great truth the apostle declared

[1] 2 Cor. 10 : 5 (margin).   [2] Phil. 2 : 13.

" for if, while we were enemies, we were reconciled to God through the death of His Son, much more, being reconciled, shall we be kept safe in His life." [1] Thus plenteously indeed, even in superabounding fullness, does Christ answer the call of man distanced by sin, in restoring him to God. In Christ, man is restored judicially, and there is no condemnation; vitally, and there is no separation; governmentally, and there is no alienation.

[1] Rom. 5 : 10. Bishop Handley Moule's translation.

XXXII

MAN KNOWING GOD THROUGH CHRIST

THE restoration of man to God necessarily issues in the restoration to man of the knowledge of God. The original purpose of man's creation was that he should be a being capable of the consciousness of, and in communion, and cooperation with, God Himself. To all this he is restored in Christ. As the vital union between God and man is created and maintained by the Spirit, so also is the work of revealing God to man that of the Spirit. He "the Spirit searcheth all things, yea, the deep things of God;" and these

> "Things which eye saw not, and ear heard not,
> And which entered not into the heart of man,
> Whatsoever things God prepared for them that love Him;"

that is, the things of the love of God in Christ, which man in clouded intelligence was ignorant of, "unto us God revealed them through the Spirit."[1] Thus while in Christ God has provided Himself with a Medium of Self-revelation, Christ is revealed to man by the Spirit. This scheme of revelation must be understood, if there is to be a true appreciation of the revelation itself. The whole perfect system is revealed in the last discourses of Jesus with His disciples, prior to His Passion. When Philip, speaking in larger degree as the mouthpiece of fallen humanity than he knew, said to Jesus "Show us the Father, and it sufficeth us,"[2] there was neither doubt nor uncertainty in the Lord's

[1] I Cor. 2: 9, 10.　　　　　　　　　　[2] John 14: 8.

428

reply. He distinctly declared, " He that hath seen Me, hath seen the Father." [1]

This declaration is in perfect harmony with the inspired statement of John that " no man hath seen God at any time; the only begotten Son, Who is in the bosom of the Father, He hath declared Him." [2] There is no way by which man can know God save through Christ. All attempts on the part of man, to formulate a conception of God, or declare a doctrine concerning Him, are futile, save as conception and doctrine are based upon, and perpetually true to, the Revelation He has made of Himself in Christ.

Recognizing man's inability to know God apart from Himself, the Lord also recognizes that men were unable to understand the revelation of God in Himself, save as it should be explained by that Spirit Who " searcheth all things, yea, the deep things of God." [3] He therefore immediately followed Philip's question with the promise of the Spirit, and such teaching concerning Him, as should fit the disciples for His coming and work. From the body of that final teaching, three main statements will be sufficient, as giving the teaching of Christ under this head.

1. " The Holy Spirit—He shall teach you all things, and bring to your remembrance all that I said unto you." [4]
2. " The Spirit of truth—He shall bear witness of Me." [5]
3. " The Spirit of truth—He shall glorify Me: for He shall take of Mine, and shall declare it unto you." [6]

These words clearly demonstrate two things. First, that the work of the Spirit is essentially that of revealing Christ to those in whom He has taken up His abode; and secondly, that man can only know Christ through the Spirit's illumination, as man can only know God through Christ's

[1] John 14 : 9. [2] John 1 : 18. [3] 1 Cor. 2 : 10.
[4] John 14 : 26. [5] John 15 : 26. [6] John 16 : 13, 14.

revelation. Any Christology which is not the direct issue of the Spirit's teaching, is false; for the mystery of His Person, and the meaning of His work, are alike inscrutable to the mind of man in its darkened condition, and can only be apprehended as the light of God falls upon them. Through Christ, the Spirit of truth indwells the believer, and through the Spirit of truth therefore Christ becomes the indwelling One; and as He by the Spirit is made known to man, man is restored to the knowledge of God, which he had lost through sin.

Man's knowledge of God through Christ by the Spirit may be contemplated therefore by considering; first, the unveiling of Christ by the Spirit; second, the apprehension of Christ through the Spirit; third, the consequent knowl. edge of God.

I. The Spirit's revelation of the Christ has been individual and historic. He commenced His work with individuals, and then for the sake of the generations to come, proceeded, in cooperation with such individuals, to prepare for the future. By personal revelation of Christ to individuals, He prepared men for the creation of a written record concerning Christ. He then through men thus prepared became the Author of the new record. That record being completed, He has given an exposition of it through the centuries, in constant cooperation with men. The Spirit commenced His work when upon the day of Pentecost He baptized the company of waiting souls into new union with God in Christ. In tracing His work therefore, it is necessary to begin with the Acts of the Apostles, while of course in a study of His revelation, the structure of the New Testament is the true order. In the Acts of the Apostles, the Spirit is seen communicating life to individual men, and then directing them definitely and immediately in all the affairs of their life. One of the special notes of the narrative of the early Church is that of how men were specifically led by the Spirit, and yet, it is always to be observed that their action under His guidance, is that of loyalty to Christ. The Spirit hinders, or impulses, but they are restrained when He hinders, or go forward when He impulses, as loyal to Christ. Thus it is evident that while these men were conscious of the immediate interference of the Spirit, they recognized that that interference was an interpretation to them of the will of their crowned Lord.

Eventually, for the consolidation of the Church in its relation to Christ, and for the continuity of its consciousness of Christ, it was necessary that such record of Him as a Person in history, as should form a perpetual basis for the Spirit's interpretation, should be written. Out of this necessity came what are known now as the New Testament Scriptures. In these writings the Spirit's one subject is Christ. In the Gospels there are recorded such facts concerning His Person and teaching, as are necessary. In them He is seen very largely in splendid loneliness, separated from, while yet in the midst of men; glorious in true Kingliness, as Matthew's story shows; patient in unceasing service, as Mark's record reveals; supreme in the realization of the Divine ideal of humanity, as Luke's evangel demonstrates; and mysterious in the essential majesty of Deity, as John's writings declare.

Then follows that treatise in which Christ is manifest in new union with men, continuing the work commenced in loneliness, in cooperation with such as are united to Him by the Holy Spirit. This record has to do almost exclusively with Christ as He calls outsiders to Himself for the remission of sins, for the renewal of life, for the restoration of the lost order.   Passing from this the Spirit in the great didactic writings reveals Christ as realized in the believer, and as expressing Himself through the Church.   While in the Acts He is almost exclusively seen calling the outsider, in the epistles He is seen again almost exclusively in His relation to those who have come in obedience to His call. Then in the Apocalypse, to a man who is "in the Spirit,"[1] there is granted Christ's own vision of His coming victory, and the consummation of all the purposes of God concerning men, realized in Christ.

At this point the writings being complete, the Spirit did not cease His work, but rather commenced it, in all its fullness and beauty.   Through the centuries of the Christian era, there may be traced an ever-broadening and deepening apprehension of Christ, due invariably to the Spirit's revelation to the Church of Christ, a revelation constantly proceeding in harmony with the inspired Writings, so that nothing has been revealed in addition to the facts recorded therein, while yet in an ever-enlarging understanding of their meaning, there has come this ever-increasing appreciation of the Christ.

It may safely be affirmed that the Person and work of Jesus are more perfectly understood than they have ever been, and that He, by the Spirit, is demanding and receiving a larger and profounder loyalty, than has ever been the case before.   This statement is made with a very keen recognition of the fact that the conflict which has been going forward in the outworks of the Christian revelation, is gathering around the central citadel of the Person of Christ. In view and in presence of that conflict, there is no fear in the heart of such as are conscious of the continued presence and work of the Spirit.   The issue must be a new

[1] Rev. I : 10.

vindication of the Personality of the God-man, and a new
appreciation of that concerning Him which will ever be
beyond the possibility of formulated statement on the part
of man.

Thus it is seen that the Holy Spirit of truth, through
processes of infinite patience, whether it be to the individual, or in the history of the race, continues His sacred
work of revealing Christ, interpreting His Word, and administering His work.

II. Leaving the subject now in its historic setting, it
will be well to consider somewhat more carefully the apprehension of Christ through the Spirit by the individual.
The first work of the Spirit of God towards this end, is that
of the preparation of the spirit of man. That spirit originally created as a medium for the knowledge of God, was
polluted, and disorganized by sin, and therefore became
useless for the fulfillment of its original intention. By the
impartation of Christ to the spirit of man, the Holy Spirit of
God cleanses from pollution. By uniting the spirit of man
with Christ He readjusts the instrument, and by lifting man
into the place where he looks out upon all things in fellowship with Christ, He focusses the lens, that so the pictures
may no longer be distorted, blurred, and inaccurate, but definite, clear, and precise. This preliminary work of the
Spirit is most immediate and most gracious. And yet its
value is only known in the results which follow.

Man's experience of this work is not in a new self-con-
sciousness, even though it be that of purity and illumination. It is rather an experience of the issue, that namely
of a new apprehension of Christ, and consequently a new
knowledge of God.

Then follows necessarily the work of the Spirit in pre-

senting the Object to this restored instrument. That
Object is Christ. The method of the Spirit here is always
governed by the individual necessity of the believer, and by
capacity. It may be safely affirmed that the Spirit of God
has no stereotyped system of theology to teach men. The
great facts concerning Christ are never taught by the Spirit
to companies of men, but to individual lives, and the
lesson now being learned by any single person, is the one
necessary for the growth of that particular individual. To
some to-day He will reveal the Master's sympathy, to
others His severity; and so, according to the necessity of
each, will He minister the revelation of the living Lord.

It is equally true that He does not measure His teaching
by the standards of time, but by the capacity of the disciple, revealing only that which each is able to bear. His
method is moreover perpetually characterized by the fact
that every individual revelation of Christ to the spirit of the
disciple has within it some new claim, demanding immediate obedience, and the measure of the obedience is the
measure of an increased capacity for yet new revelations.

Thus man, indwelt by the Spirit, is the subject of a
perpetually growing consciousness of the sublimities of
Christ, through a perpetually growing understanding of His
simplicities. Thus it is that while the youngest believer
may seem to be in possession of all the facts concerning
Christ; as the years pass, through the varied disciplines of
life, and the operation of an abiding communion, it is seen
that the things known were hardly known, that the facts
recognized were imperfectly realized; and gradually and
yet surely with the passing of the years, through every
window, new light is streaming, and new meanings are
dawning on the soul. In the earliest years of discipleship
there must be recognition of the simplicity of Christ, as the

story of His life is read; of His perpetual serenity as He passed through scenes that might have been expected to disturb the stoutest heart; of the sweetness of His disposition, in spite of all the occasions which so often end in the embittering of the human heart; of the severity of His Spirit against all forms of wrong and of tyranny; and of His ever active sympathy with all sorts and conditions of men.   All these things, however, are only learned as to their fullness of value, and of meaning, as the Spirit reveals them according to the demand of occasion, and the capacity of the learner.   Through this great process it is discovered that the simplicity of Christ is due to His subiimity of the consciousness of the straightness of the line of truth; and His serenity is due to the abiding sense of the permanence of righteousness; and His sweetness manifest because of His understanding of the ultimate victory of love; while His severity is the necessary out-flaming anger of that love against all that for the time may seem to violate it; and His sympathy is the natural, spontaneous relation of essential love to all the consciousness of those upon whom such love is set.

Thus the issue of the indwelling Spirit is not merely the unveiling before the spirit of man of the fact of Christ; but also the preparation of the spirit of man, which issues in a true and ever growing apprehension of the unveiled One.

III.   Thus God is known to man, and that after the method of the original Divine intention through a Man Who is His express Image.   Redeemed man acts upon the same principle as fallen man in his search after God, with a distinction and a difference both in method and in result. Man's darkened understanding still conscious of his need of a god, projected into immensity himself, with the result that his conception of God was that of a monster, because not only were the essentials of his nature, intelligence, emotion, and will, magnified in the process, but their degradation. Restored to God, man still projects Man into infinity, but not himself. It is now by the magnifying of the Man Christ Jesus, Who by the Spirit indwells the believer, that God is found. The intelligence of Jesus, characterized by clearness, freedom from questioning, and unanswerable statement of truth, surprises and startles the soul anew in every fresh understanding of it through the Spirit's interpretation. And as these lines are projected from the wisdom of Christ into infinity, the mind catches some conception of what the wisdom of the infinite God is in its perfectly clear understanding of all things, so that "in Him is no darkness at all." [1] His freedom from perplexity carried out into the immeasurable, aids man in his apprehension of that great reason for the quiet calm of Deity, in the midst of the things which, coming of their imperfect understanding, so trouble and vex the heart of the finite. Every century of consideration of the Word of Jesus proving as it has, that His teaching was not a deduction from appearances, but the uttering forth of eternal principles in the speech of man, has given to men a new conception of the authority of God, as based upon the necessity of the things that are.

Perhaps the supreme consciousness of God, however, has come by the projection into immensity of what may still be spoken of as the emotional fact in the Person of Jesus. In Him love proceeded out of the necessity of its own might, and expressed itself in self-forgetfulness to the point of absolute sacrifice, and that without regard to any worth

[1] 1 John 1 : 5.

in the object upon which it was set. In Him moreover, love was patient, optimistic, powerful. No lack of response was sufficient to quench its ardour, no degradation sufficient to extinguish its hopefulness, no opposition equal to overcome its might. It was this revelation of His love that made it possible for there ever to have been written the statement, so simple and sublime, so sweet in its constraint, so manifold in its beauty, that heaven's music will be needed to express its harmonies, while earth's discords are by it being changed towards the heavenly symphony, "God so loved the world, that He gave His only begotten Son, that whosoever believeth on Him should not perish, but have eternal life." [1] It was surely with his eye resting upon the Man of Nazareth, and his heart speaking of his consciousness of the marvel of the love of the Perfect One, that Paul wrote his classic passage descriptive of love.[2]

And yet again, the action of the will of Jesus as responsive ever to the supreme will of His Father, and moving always under the impulse of love, has revealed forevermore the truth of unutterable value, that the will of God operates not arbitrarily, but under constraint, the constraint of the essential fact of His own nature, that of an infinite and immeasurable love.

Thus Jesus the perfect Man, standing before the soul in all His perfection, is the gateway through which the mind passes out to a conception of God which arrests, subdues, and commands the loyalty of the life. It is in His presence that man exclaims "Lo, this is our God; we have waited for Him, and He will save us: this is Jehovah; we have waited for Him, we will be glad and rejoice in His salvation." [3]

[1] John 3: 16.   [2] 1 Cor. 13.   [3] Isa. 25: 9.

To say this is to declare also the difference in result. Man of old, projecting himself until he found an enormity, learned only to hate and to fear his conception of God. To-day, man, projecting the perfect One finds infinite satisfaction in the revealed Father, and his heart goes out in adoring love, and his life is spent in glad service. Thus in Christ, man is restored to the knowledge of God by the enlightening of his intelligence, and the presentation thereto of all the gracious facts, in such way, and in such measure as he is able to bear, and capable of receiving.

XXXIII

MAN LIKE GOD IN CHRIST

THE final fact in redemption is that of the restoration of man to the image and likeness of God. Underlying every creation of God is a most definite purpose. This it may not always be easy to trace, but the general principle is most certainly revealed in the vast majority of cases, and therefore it is reasonable to believe it to be universal, and the fact that it is beyond the power of human intelligence always to discover the reason, is to be accounted for by the limitation of that intelligence, rather than by the absence of the purpose. The purpose of angelic life is certainly that of service. In the great Psalm of thanksgiving, angels are referred to in such a way as to declare the very meaning of their existence :—

> " Bless Jehovah, ye His angels,
> That are mighty in strength, that fulfill His word,
> Hearkening unto the voice of His word," [1]

and the writer of the letter to the Hebrews asks, " Are they not all ministering spirits, sent forth to do service for the sake of them that shall inherit salvation ? " [2] while all the sacred history reveals them as occupied ever in serving in gladness the will of the King.

The purpose underlying the creation of man was far sublimer. He was made in the Divine image, in a sense that angels never were, and in the very nature of that creation there is revealed its purpose. Man was intended as a

[1] Psa. 103 : 20.   [2] Heb. 1: 14.

medium for the Divine manifestation, one through whom, because of his likeness to God, it would be possible for God to express Himself to other creations more perfectly. Redemption therefore is only complete when man is restored to the perfection of his own being, and thus to fitness for the fulfillment of the Divine purpose. This then is the ultimate issue of the work of Christ in man. For the accomplishment of this, vital restoration is the power, and restoration to knowledge is the process. The life of Christ imparted to man by the Holy Spirit is the constraining, transforming power, and the new vision of God in Christ is at once the pattern, towards the carrying out of which the power works, and therefore the governing principle to which the will of the saint being submitted, the Christ life is the product. The first fact in redemption, that of restoration to God, was perfected in justification; the second, that of restoration to the knowledge of God, is being perfected through sanctification; the third, that of restoration to the likeness of God, will be perfected in glorification. Redemption is thus seen to be the restoration of man to fellowship with the Father. John, who writes most minutely of the great subject under this aspect, affirms that as to standing, that fellowship is accomplished. " Now are we children of God," that as to finality it will be accomplished, " we know that, if He shall be manifested, we shall be like Him; " that as to process the work goes ever forward, " every one that hath this hope set on Him purifieth himself, even as He is pure." [1] The foundation fact is created by the reception of the Christ life in germ, the experimental advancement is being caused by the mastery of the whole being by that ever-conquering life; the final fact will be consummated by the complete

[1] 1 John 3: 2, 3.

comformity of the whole life to the Christ. Therefore as Christ is the express Image of the Father, in perfect likeness to Him, man will fulfill the primal Divine purpose, by becoming restored to the image and the likeness of God. Thus it is evident at once that the present life is, by comparison with the life to come, as utterly insignificant, as the days of school are, when compared with the sternness and importance of the days for which they are but preparatory. And yet this view of the finality, in another sense, lends new meaning and urgency to the life that now is; for school-days very largely determine the place to be occupied in the maturer opportunities of life.

In considering this last phase of the plenteous redemption, difficulties confront the mind, which it is better at once to recognize, as John did when he wrote, "It is not yet made manifest what we shall be." [1] It will be perfectly safe, however, to accept the certainty as declared by John, "We know . . . we shall be like Him," and within that assurance, consider first, man becoming like God in his realization of the character and conduct of Christ; second, man becoming like God in his realization of himself; third, man becoming like God, becomes a revelation of God.

I. There is no necessity to deal with the close relation existing between character and conduct, save to declare the fact as necessary to an understanding of the line of the present study. It must, however, be borne in mind that they are necessarily and indissolubly connected. Conduct is always an expression of character, and character therefore is the cause of conduct. Character is the condition of being, while conduct is the expression thereof in doing. In

[1] 1 John 3: 2.

both these, Christ was the Revelation of God, and in proportion as man is Christlike, he is therefore like God. Zacharias, filled with the Holy Spirit, referring to the coming of Messiah, declared that the purpose of His coming was that man should serve God "in holiness and righteousness."[1] These words cover the whole fact of life as to its general trend, holiness referring to character, and righteousness to conduct. It is at once seen that these words belong primarily to God, the first declaring the supreme truth concerning His character, and the latter that concerning His conduct. He is holy, and therefore acts righteously. Both these facts are however the result of another and profounder one, that namely, of the love which is of the very essence of His Being. Holiness of character is the result of the nature of love, and so also is righteousness of conduct. In Christ these facts concerning God have been revealed, and always in this setting and proportion. The holiness of the character of Christ was the inevitable necessity of His Love. His righteousness of conduct was the immediate outworking of His holiness of character, which resulted from Love. By the impartation of His life to man, and its realization progressively, man is subdued by Love, and obedience to this new nature issues in holiness of character, and righteousness of conduct.

The finality of all this is that man's essential nature being transformed into perfect conformity to that of God, his holiness of character will be forever established, and he will then be perfectly prepared for all that exercise of life, which expresses itself in righteousness of conduct, which is always that of cooperation with God. Here the point of difficulty is reached, because it is impossible to know to-day along what line the activities of God will be continued, in

[1] Luke 1 : 75.

the ages lying ahead. There are certain principles however which may contribute at least to a lofty conception of
what the activity of redeemed man will be. The question
of character need not therefore be discussed because conduct is its outward expression. It may therefore be
affirmed that as the activity of God is constructive, and
never destructive, man in union with Him will cooperate in
the expression of the Infinite Energy, along the pathway of
perpetually perennial manifestations of that essential Love,
which is fullness of joy, and pleasure forevermore.

For to-day man's likeness to God, in likeness to Christ,
is manifest in his approximation to the character of holiness,
and his cooperation in the work of redemption. Said
Jesus, "My Father worketh even until now, and I work." [1]
The work of God and the work of Christ are identical,
and the proportion in which man is already like God, is
manifest by his cooperation with Him in the sublime and
serious enterprises of seeking and saving the lost. Man is
only equal to this cooperation upon the basis of likeness to
God in character, and he is only holy in proportion as he
is indwelt and impulsed by love.

II. This consideration demonstrates without need of
argument that man being restored to the likeness of God
in Christ, is therefore restored to the essential possibility
and purpose of his own being. Referring once again to
that analysis of human personality, which was considered
in the earlier chapters of this book, intelligence, emotion,
and will, it will be seen how in becoming like God, man
becomes himself in all the spaciousness of that primal intention. The intelligence having passed from underneath
the eclipse which was the result of sin, is able to set all

[1] John 5 : 17.

things in their true perspective, and to value them in their right proportion. Not in measure or degree, but in method and direction, the human intelligence now apprehends with the Infinite Intelligence. In this realm, as in every other, all things have become new. The new understanding of God has issued in a new appreciation of man and of all that creation which is apparent to the mind, but which is now known to be a window through which the Infinite is seen; and which, consequently is of less value than that which it reveals. The feverish restlessness resulting from limitation ceases, as the mind recognizes that beyond all natural phenomena there exists the one Eternal Verity, of which all phenomena are but the transitory expressions.

The emotional nature having been freed from its degradation, now operates in conformity with the Divine Love. Affections are set upon the things above, the upper things, the dominant, the eternal. Every movement of love is henceforth conditioned by the relation of the object to God, and all its operation seeks the highest good of the loved one.

The will is restored to its relation to the true governing principle. It does not cease to be, and therefore its activity is not discontinued. Now however instead of choosing and deciding upon the false basis of rebellion against government, it perpetually elects to act under the compulsion of that Eternal One, Whose essence is Love. Thus by redemption man becomes a being, whose will decides in answer to the impulse of pure affection, in the light of unclouded intelligence. The centre and throne of personality being thus restored to the true Divine order, all the powers and capacities conditioned can be directed and employed at their highest and their fullest. The sense of beauty, expressing itself in music, or in art, becomes dominated by that unswerving holiness, which is the character of love. Wherever this is so, all discords cease, and harmonies are perfected; all that is grotesque and untrue is corrected by the lines of undeviating loveliness, and the colours of un-dimmed beauty. The capacity for investigation is now enlarged, and science emerging from the mists of mere hypotheses, affirms with actual accuracy of statement, for which she has so long sought, and yet been unable to dis-cover. At this point again the understanding of all that lies in the future for man is necessarily limited, but it may surely be affirmed that " whatsoever things are true, what-soever things are honourable, whatsoever things are just, whatsoever things are pure, whatsoever things are lovely, whatsoever things are of good report," [1] in human nature as we know it, will not be lost in the hereafter, but rather found and fulfilled in all power and perfection.

The present application of this consideration is that even to-day the measure of man's appropriation of the redemp-tion in Christ Jesus, is the measure in which, what he is in the essential of his Divinely created being, is realized and ennobled, and through such realization and ennoblement man is seen to be Godlike. The expression of this like-ness here, as in the former case, will be found in the conse-cration of man's own redeemed personality to such co-operation with God as shall move towards the future perfect unfolding of the Divine in the human.

III. Thus the redemption that is in Christ Jesus will finally make every individual a revelation of God, in the measure that is possible to each individual capacity. Here, however, again there breaks upon the consciousness that larger vision of the Divine purpose which consists in a race

[1] Phil. 4 : 8.

made up of individuals, each one contributing something to the final perfection, through which race, all the glorious fullness of the Deity is to have its perfect outshining. This also is according to primal intention. The creation of the first man was the creation of a race, and while he was in the image of God, it was in the larger creation of the whole family that the supreme manifestation of the glory of God was to be made. This is the true doctrine of the solidarity of humanity, and the inter-relationship of individuals. Towards this, man is ever attempting to grope his way, and ever signally failing. Perfect human society has never been realized outside the economy of grace, because perfect human individuality does not exist. In the redemption of the individual, Christ prepares for, and makes possible, the final realization of the race, through which the Divine glory will be manifested. The sublimest arguments concerning this are to be found in the writings of the apostle Paul, whose vision of the Church in its consummation was ever that of a society dominated by the One Life, walking in the One Light, obeying the One Love. The ultimate victory of redemption therefore will consist in the realization of the first Divine purpose in a race which, being composed of individuals, each of whom perfectly answers the Divine ideal, will in its entirety reveal God, and thus be His supreme medium of manifestation throughout the coming ages. Christ will only be completed in that whole race which united to Him, is to form His body.

Twice at least the apostle Paul uses the word Christ with reference to that whole race, including the Head and all the members. In writing to the Corinthians he said " for as the body is one, and hath many members, and all the members of the body, being many, are one body ; so also is

Christ." [1] Here evidently the reference is to Christ and the Church, the complete fulfillment of the Divine thought and purpose.

And again, in writing to the Ephesians, he speaks of the building up of the body of Christ, " till we all attain unto the unity of the faith, and of the knowledge of the Son of God, unto a full-grown man, unto the measure of the stature of the fullness of Christ." [2] " Christ in this passage (so full of the idea of the oneness in, and with the Lord of His mystical body) is, in effect, Christ and His Church. The Lord the Son becomes in accomplished fact all that He wills, and is willed, to be, only when He is the Head, of a perfected mystical Body, which lives by His sacred life, and is His incorporate 'limbs,' His immortal vehicle of action, if we may so speak. So He and they are guardedly and reverently spoken of here and there as One Christ with full reservation, from other Scriptures, of the truth of the undying personality of each individual 'limb' of the glorious Head, and of His Divine Personality." [3] The specific purpose of this unity is declared by the apostle in the glorious doxology with which the first part of his Ephesian letter closes. " Unto Him be the glory in the Church and in Christ Jesus unto all generations forever and ever. Amen." [4]

It is not, however, sufficient to declare that redemption's final victory is that of the realization of this primal Divine intention. While that is true, it must not be lost sight of that the peculiar and marvellous plan of the victory lies in the future, that this result is produced by Christ through victory gained over the original failure. The glory of the first ideal was great, but the glory of the realization of that ideal, out of

---

[1] I Cor. 12 : 12.

[3] Bishop Handley Moule.

[2] Eph. 4 : 13.

[4] Eph. 3 : 21.

all the awful results of human sin, is infinitely greater. Perhaps the note that now wakes the profoundest wonder in the mind of unfallen intelligences concerning the issue of redemption is that suggested when in speaking of the glories of Christ in his Colossian epistle, the apostle refers to Him as "the First-born from the dead." [1]   As to all creation Christ is the First-born, but the added wonder with regard to the new creation is that it has been created by the emergence of the last Adam from the death which resulted from the failure of the first Adam, and His having brought out of that death, members of the new race.   Thus redemption's greatest victory lies, not merely in the fact that through the new race the glory of God is to be manifest, but that the profounder truth will be revealed that His greatest glory lies in the mighty working of His wondrous grace.   The sublimest and profoundest song of all will be that ascription of praise, which occurring in the first chapter of the Apocalypse, prepares for, and includes within itself all the subsequent numbers of that majestic oratorio, the subject of which is the movement to finality of the dispensations of God.   "Unto Him that loveth us, and loosed us from our sins by His blood; and He made us to be a kingdom, to be priests unto His God and Father; to Him be the glory and the dominion forever and ever.   Amen." [2]

[1] Col. 1 : 18.   [2] Rev. 1 : 5, 6.

" Crown Him with many crowns,
   The Lamb upon His throne ;
Hark ! how the heavenly anthem drowns
   All music but its own.
Awake, my soul, and sing
   Of Him Who died for thee,
And hail Him as thy chosen King
   Through all eternity.

" Crown Him, the Lord of Love !
   Behold His Hands and Side
Rich Wounds, yet visible above
   In beauty glorified :
No angel in the sky
   Can fully bear that sight,
But downward bends his burning eye
   At mysteries so bright.

" Crown Him, the Lord of Peace :
   Whose power a sceptre sways
From pole to pole—that wars may cease
   Absorbed in prayer and praise :
His reign shall know no end,
   And round His piercèd Feet
Fair flowers of paradise extend
   Their fragrance ever sweet.

" Crown Him, the Lord of Years,
   The Potentate of time ;
Creator of all rolling spheres,
   Ineffably sublime :
All hail ! Redeemer, hail !
   For Thou hast died for me :
Thy praise shall never, never fail
   Throughout eternity."
               —M. BRIDGES

INDEXES

Compiled by Winifred M. Howells

Scriptures Referred To

Indicates passages more fully dealt with.
f indicates that the subject is also dealt with on following (f) page.

Genesis:	PAGE
i, 1,	54
26,	393
26, 27,	24
iii,	21 f
5,*	57
9,	401
24,*	34, 48
v, 1,	24
ix, 6,	24
xxii, 7,	145

Numbers:	
xxiv, 17,	99

Deuteronomy:	
vi, 4,	88, 132
13,	201
16,	201
viii, 3,	201
xxix, 29,	69

1 Samuel:	
ix, 6,	137
9,	137

1 Kings:	
xxi, 19,	239

2 Kings:	
xvii, 33,	236

Job:	
i, 9,	166
xi, 7,	40
xxvi, 7,	54

Psalm:	
ii,	320 f
6, 7,	190

Psalm:	PAGE
ii, 7,	121
8, 9,	190
12,	121
viii, 4–8,	125
xvi. 8–11,*	352
xxiv, 7, 8, 10,	394
xxv, 14 (mar.),	130
xlviii, 2,	176
xci, 1,	180
ciii, 20,	439
cxv, 4–8,	48
cxxii, 4,	176
cxxv, 2,	176
cxxxvii, 5,	176

Proverbs:	
xviii, 14,	399

Canticles:	
ii, 17,	222

Isaiah:	
vii, 14,	96, 100
ix, 6,*	16
xxv, 9,	437
xxx, 21,	256
xxxii, 15,	409
xliv, 3–5,	409
l, 6,	399
liii, 2,	133
3,	100
4, 5,	400
7,	296

Jeremiah:	
ix, 1,	220
xxxi, 15,	100

Hosea: PAGE
   ix, 7 (A. V. mar.), . . . 137
   xi, 1, ... 100
   xiii, 2, ... 43, 49

Joel:
   ii, 28–32, ... 410

Micah:
   v, 2, ... 100

Habakkuk:
   iii, 4, ... 225

Matthew:
   i, 1,* 14
     20, ... 99
     20–23, ... 70
     21, ... 397
     23, ... 100
   ii, 1, 2, ... 97
     1–12, ... 65
     2, ... 99
     6, ... 100
     13–15, ... 108
     15, ... 100
     17, ... 100
     19–23, ... 108
     23, ... 100
   iii, 7, ... 140
     11, 12, ... 142
     13–17, ... 105
     14, ... 124
     15, ... 288
     17, ... 123, 167, 190
   iv, 1, ... 155 f
     1–11, ... 151
     3, ... 162, 167, 179
     4, ... 170, 200
     5, ... 174
     5, 6, ... 175
     6, ... 178 f
     7, ... 181 f, 201
     8, ... 188
     9, ... 189
     10, ... 192 f, 201
     10, 11, ... 162
     11, ... 207 f
     17, ... 307
     v, 8, ... 132

Matthew: PAGE
   v, 46, ... 56
   vi, 24, ... 45
     33, ... 202
   viii, 31, 32, ... 208
     33, ... 308
     34, ... 309
   ix, 6, ... 278
     15, ... 279
   x, 38, ... 284
     38, 39, ... 279
   xi, 28–30, ... 91
   xii, 38, ... 378
     40, ... 280, 378
   xiii, 44–46,* 280
   xvi, 13–16, ... 252
     14–19, ... 247
     17, ... 220
     21, ... 288
     21–23, ... 247
     22, ... 217
     23, ... 251
   xvii, 1, ... 215
     1, 2, ... 215
     1–9, ... 213
     2, ... 219, 225, 246
     4, ... 217, 251
     5, . . . 123, 221, 254, 256
     7, ... 258
     8, ... 258
     9, ... 260
     17, 18, ... 263
     24–27, ... 264
   xviii, 12, ... 282
   xix, 14, ... 92
   xx, 18, 19, ... 285
     22, ... 285
     28,* 58, 286
   xxi, 37–44, ... 287
   xxvi, 2, ... 287
     12, ... 286
     18, ... 287
     21, ... 287
     53, ... 209
     56, ... 293
   xxvii, 32–56, ... 271 f
     37, ... 306
     42, ... 341
     54 (mar.), . . . 331, 337
     56, ... 330
   xxviii, 1–8, ... 347
     6, ... 375

Mark:

	PAGE
i, 9–11,	105
12,	155 *f*
12, 13,	151
13,	126, 157, 160
ii, 10,	278
19, 20,	279
v, 37–41,	248
41,	249
vi, 2,	128
3,	113
viii, 36,	204
ix, 2,	215, 248
2, 3,	225
2–10,	213
6,	250
x, 33, 34,	285
35–40,	248
38,	285
45,	286
xii, 6–10,	287
xiv, 8,	286
33, 34,	249
34,	250
xv, 22–41,	272
34,*	294 *f*
39, 40,	330 *f*
xvi, 1–11,	347
12,*	76
19,	387

Luke:

	PAGE
i, 11,	99
26,	99
28,	336
35,	71
75,	442
ii, 6–17,	65 *f*
7,	71
10–12,	99
18,	100
21, 22,	108
40,*	109
41–51,*	110
52,*	112, 292
iii, 1, 2,	138
7, 8,	139 *f*
9,	141
13, 14,	141
21, 22,	105
22,*	121
iv. 1,*	155 *f*, 206

Luke:

	PAGE
iv, 1, 2,	160
1–13,	151 *f*
2,	156 *f*
5,	188
13,	207
14,*	206
16–21,	115
v, 24,	278
34, 35,	279
vii, 8,	337
ix, 28,	215
28, 29,	219
28–36,	213 *f*
29,	226
30,	243
30, 31,*	317
31,	240, 288
32,	242
33,	250
38,	262
x, 18,	283
xi, 30,	280
xii, 50,	284
xiii, 32,	284
xiv, 27,	284
xv, 4, 5,	284
xvii, 25,	285
xviii, 31–33,	285
xx, 13–18,	287
xxii, 39–44,	289
xxiii, 27,	330
27–49,	272 *f*
xxiii, 34,	294
38,	325
42,	327
43,	294, 327
44, 45,	325 *f*
46,	294, 324
47,	331, 338
xxiv, 1–12,	347 *f*
21,	342
50, 51,	387

John:

	PAGE
i, ix,	72 *f*
1–4,	37
11,	95
14,*	66, 72 *f*, 255
15,	143
18,	391, 429
26,	143

John:	PAGE
i, 26–28,	143
27,	143
29,*	143*f*, 298
29–34,	143
34,	147
35, 36,	143
36,	148
47,	277
51,	277
ii, 4,	277
18,	378
19,	278, 378
25,	131
iii, 13,	229
14, 15,	278
16,	437
18,	81
29, 30,	148
iv, 34,	278
v, 17,	443
21,	279
25,	81
vi, 35,	119
51–56,	281
vii, 6–8,	282
15,	129
16, 17,	130
33, 34,	282
viii, 12,	119
28,	282
29,	133
58,	119
ix, 4,*	283
35,	81
x, 7,	119
11,	119, 283
17, 18,	283, 361
36,	81
xi, 4,	81
9,	285
25,	119
xii, 7,	286
28,	123, 289
31,	189
34,	82
xiv, 6,	119, 239
8,	428
9,	429
16, 17,	407
26,	407, 429
30,	168

John:	PAGE
xv, 1,	119
26,	407, 429
xvi, 8–11,	420
9,	403
11,	412
13, 14,	429
xix, 17–37,	273*f*
25,	330
26, 27,	294
28,	294*f*
30,	294, 302, 314, 324, 376
xx, 1–18,	348*f*
29,	265

Acts:	
i, 1,	115
4,	407
9–11,	387
ii, 22, 23,	304
22–24,	352
25,	356
24–28,	351
25–28,	353
26,	357
28,	357
33,	405
vi, 15,	227
viii, 32,	146
x, 38,*	115
43,	239
xvii, 22–28,	51
xxiv, 24,	417
xxvi, 24,	129

Romans:	
iii, 23,	232
26,	422
v, 10,	94, 427
12,	22, 395
20,	316
vii, 21,	323
viii, 34,	371
37,	185
x, 9,	372
xii, 1,	27, 134
xvi, 10,	417

1 Corinthians:	
ii, 2,*	371
9, 10,	428
10,	290, 411, 429

1 Corinthians: PAGE
xi, 7, ... 24
xii, 3,* 403
12, ... 447
xiii, ... 437
xv, 14–17, ... 372
24, ... 322
45, ... 156

2 Corinthians:
ii, 14, ... 417
iv, 4, ... 24
v, 19,* 84, 417
21,* 298
x, 5 (mar.), ... 426
xii, 2, ... 417

Ephesians:
i, 3, ... 417
18–20, ... 362
19,* 367
ii, 1, ... 420
12, ... 49
iii, 21, ... 447
iv, 13, ... 447
18, ... 421
30, ... 400

Philippians:
ii, 5, ... 93
6, 7, ... 75
9, ... 396
13, ... 426
iv, 8, ... 445
13, ... 424

Colossians:
i, 15, ... 24
18, ... 448
19, ... 424
21, 22, ... 85
24–ii, 5, ... 424
ii, 2, ... 67
10, ... 424
iii, 10, ... 24

1 Thessalonians:
iv, 14, ... 384
16, ... 417

2 Timothy: PAGE
i, 7,* 393

Hebrews:
i, 1, 2, ... 255
3,* 24
14, ... 439
ii, 6–9, ... 125
ix, 14, ... 406
x, 7, ... 228
xi, 13, ... 235
22, ... 318
xii, 2, ... 240

1 Peter:
i, 12, ... 392
18, 19, ... 281
19, ... 146
ii, 24, ... 279, 299, 302

2 Peter:
i, 15, ... 250, 318
16, ... 227, 373
16–18, ... 256

1 John:
i, 5, ... 436
ii, 17, ... 196
iii, 2, ... 441
2, 3, ... 440
iv, 8, ... 401
19, ... 38

Jude:
6,* 355

Revelation:
i, 5, 6, ... 448
10, ... 432
17, 18, ... 394
v, 1–10, ... 387
6, ... 399
xi, 15,* 197
xxii, 21,* 14

Poetry

		PAGE
" AND as the load immense, intolerable," *E. H. Bickersteth* . . .		270
"Yesterday, To-day, and Forever."		
"Bars and riven, Foes are driven," . . *Anon*		328
"Crown Him with many crowns," . . *M. Bridges*		449
"From death to life," . . . . . *B. M.*		386
"Ezekiel and other Poems."		
"Grace is flowing like a river," . . . *Anon*		315
"Hath it been ever granted those, who have pass'd," . . . . *E. H. Bickersteth* . . .		245
"Yesterday, To-day and Forever."		
"He found me the lost and the wandering," . . . . *V. M. C.*		415
"Hymns of Ter Steegen, Suso."		
"He hell in hell laid low," . . . . . *Anon*		208
"He saw me ruined in the fall," . . . *S. Medley*		61
"I stand upon the mount of God," . . *G. B. Bubier*		221
"I take O Cross, thy shadow,". . . . *E. C. Clephane* . . .		344
"Jesus shall reign where'er the sun,". . *I. Watts* ·		315
"Light after darkness," . . . . . . *F. R. Havergal* . . .		221
"Under The Surface."		
"My Lord at home," . . . . *F. W. H. Myers* . . .		104
"St. John the Baptist."		
"O Jesus, Lord, 'tis joy to know," . . *Anon*		302
"Our Lord is now rejected," . . . . *Maj. Whittle*		403
"Our wills are ours, we know not how," *A. Tennyson*		32
"In Memoriam."		
"Rock of Ages, cleft for me," . . . . *A. M. Toplady* . . .		396
"See the conquering hero comes," . . *T. Morell*		58
"The foe behind, the deep before," . . *Dr. Neale*		346
"The Transfiguration," . . . . . . *G. Rawson*		212
"Songs of Spiritual Thought."		

" There is a fountain filled with blood,"   *W. Cowper* 341

" There is no place where earth's sorrows," . . . . *F. W. Faber* 244

" Where He displays His healing power," *I. Watts* 423

" With glory wrapped around," . . . *Mrs. Alexander* 236

" Yet I doubt not through the ages," . *A. Tennyson* 132
           " Locksley Hall."

Writers Quoted or Referred to

		PAGE
BAYNE, PETER, . .	"Testimony of Christ to Christianity," . .	12
BURTON, HENRY, .	"The Gospel of Luke," Expositors' Series.	150
BUSHNELL, HORACE,	"The New Life,"	20
DARWIN, ...		40
HUXLEY, ...		40
JOSEPHUS, ...		178
KANT, ...		27
MOULE, HANDLEY, ... Cambridge Bible . .		68, 427, 447
PARKER, JOSEPH, ...		30
ROBERTS, RICHARD, ...		98
RUSKIN, JOHN, . . "Modern Painters,"		64
	"St. Mark's Rest,"	7
SPENCER, ...		40, 41
STRAUSS, ...		373
TYNDALL, ...		40
WESTCOTT, ...		129

Subject Index

ABEL,   PAGE
  the basis of his acceptance, 392
  in heaven, ... 392
Acceptance,
  The basis of Abel's, . . 392
Acquaintance,
  of Jesus at the Cross, The, 343
Act,
  of crucifixion, The hu-
    man, ... 305 *f*
  of love, God's rejection of
    man an, ... 368
  The resurrection a Divine, 364
Action,
  The fall the result of in-
    dependent, ... 33
Activity,
  of redeemed man, The, . 443
Adam,
  The first, ... 156
  The last, ... 156
Administrator,
  The Lamb the active, . . 404
Affection,
  Jesus perfect in, . . 131 *f*
  of man restored, The, . . 444
Afters,
  God's, ... 221
Agent,
  of temptation, The devil
    the, ... 157 *f*
Agony,
  The cry of physical, . . 295
Alienation,
  a Divine act, ... 34
  of man the result of dis-
    obedience, The, . . . 34
  Man a ruin through, . . 35

Anchorage,   PAGE
  The resurrection faith's, 373 *f*
Angelic,
  ministry, The purpose of, . 439
Angels,
  The fall of Satan and the,
              158, 355
Anguish,
  The cry of spiritual, . 297 *f*
Annunciations,
  of the birth of Jesus, The, 70 *f*
Apostles,
  their attitude towards death,
    The, ... 247
  associated specially with
    Jesus, The, ... 247
  The three, ... 218
Appearances,
  after resurrection, The, . 382
Apprehension,
  of Christ, The individual, 433
Approach,
  The sense of hunger, the
    avenue of, ... 165
Approval,
  of Jesus, God's continual, 363
Argument,
  of the devil, The, 167, 178, 189
  for resurrection, Paul's, . 378
Ascension,
  The fact of the, ... 389
  of Jesus, The, ... 397
  the link between resurrec-
    tion and Pentecost, . . 389
  of the Man of Nazareth,
    The, ... 392

Aspect, PAGE
  of Christ's coming, The
    constructive, ... 142
  of Christ's coming, The
    destructive, ... 142
Assumed,
  Jesus' victory over sin, 356 f
Atonement,
  Incarnation not, ... 74
  A theory of the, . 297, 301
Atoning,
  sufferings, The, ... 303
Attitude,
  of the apostles towards
    death, The, ... 247
Authority,
  over evil, Jesus', . . 207 f
  The Lamb the final, . . 403
  of the Mosaic economy,
    The Divine, ... 205
  of the New Testament,
    The, ... 382
  won in victory, Jesus', . 192

BAAL,
  The worship of, ... 44
Baptism,
  Jesus' consciousness of the
    Cross at, ... 288
  of Jesus, The, ... 120
Baptist,
  John the, ... 137 f
Basis,
  of Abel's acceptance, The, 392
Beasts,
  Jesus and the wild, . . 157
Beginning,
  In the, ... 72
Being,
  Man restored to the possi-
    bility of his own, . . 443
Benefactor,
  Jesus a, ... 116
Bible,
  Christ the Subject of the, 13
Birth,
  of Jesus, The annuncia-
    tions of the, ... 70 f

Birth, PAGE
  of Jesus, The declarations
    of the . . . . . . 71 f
Blundering,
  of Peter, The, . . 233, 250 f
Body,
  the expression of the spirit,
    The, ... 27

CAPACITY,
  for joy and sorrow, Love
    the, ... 401
  Man's original, ... 36
  Revelation according to, . 222
Carpenter,
  Jesus a, ... 113
Carpentry,
  of Jesus, The perfect, . . 134
Centurion,
  at the Cross, The, 331, 337 f
Character,
  of Christ, The, ... 393
  and conduct, ... 441
  and conduct of Christ, Man
    like God in realizing the, 443
χαρακτήρ,
  25
Childhood,
  of Jesus, The, . . . 110
Choirs,
  The heavenly, ... 394
Christ,
  The individual apprehen-
    sion of, ... 433
  God's approbation of, . . 123
  The atoning sufferings of, 303
  His challenge to the devil
    as Man, ... 169
  The character of, . · 393
  and the Church, . . . 446
  The constructive aspect of
    the coming of, . . . 142
  the engraved copy of God, 26
  The destructive aspect of
    the coming of, . . . 142
  the Creator of history, . 259
  The crises in the life of, . 17

Christt, PAGE
His delight in the will of
God, ... 175
The expiatory sufferings
of, ... 303
The forsaking of, . . 297 *f*
the Fulfiller of history . 259
the Fulfiller of past proph-
ecy, ... 87
The gift of, ... 61
His glory hidden, . . 224 *f*
The growing isolation in
the life of, ... 292
The issue of His work, . 425
Life, The, ... 423
His life a Divine work, . 16
The Lord Jesus, . . . 14
His loyalty to God's will
attacked, ... 163
Man like God in realizing
the character and con-
duct of, ... 443
The magnifying of the
Man Jesus, ... 436
The mind of, ... 93
The mission of, ... 14
His mission attacked, . . 186
the mystery of God, . 67 *f*
the Object presented, . . 434
The perfection of the
Church in, ... 424
The promise of the Spirit
made by, ... 407
is restored to God, Man
joined to, ... 422
His resurrection, God's
seal upon His work, 361 *f*
is God's Medium of Self-
revelation, ... 428
received the Spirit for
others, . . . 408, 410
to man, The Spirit reveals, 430
The Spirit unveils, . . 433 *f*
Why the Spirit was given
to, ... 411
the Subject of the Bible, . 13
His sufferings impossible
of final statement, . . 293
and the temple, ... 177
His trust in God attacked, 174 *f*
The vicarious sufferings
of, ... 303

Christt, PAGE
His perfect victory over
evil, ... 198 *f*
Church,
Christ and the, ... 446
in Christ, The perfection
of the, ... 424
The heresies of the, . . 18*?*
the supreme proof of the
resurrection, The, . . 383
Circumcision,
of Jesus, The, ... 109
City,
of Jerusalem, The, . . 175 *f*
Claim,
of the devil to the king-
doms, The, ... 189
Cloud,
The bright, ... 253 *f*
Colossians,
The threefold mystery in, 424
Coming,
The constructive aspect of
Christ's, ... 142
The destructive aspect of
Christ's, ... 142
of the Greeks, Jesus' consciousness of the Cross
at the, ... 289
Communion,
issues in transfiguration, . 222
Completion,
of every temptation, The, 207
Conduct,
Character and, ... 441
of Christ, Man like God
in realization of the
character and, . . . 443
possible? Is righteousness
of, ... 291
Confession,
of defeat, The devil's, . 202
of Peter, Jesus' consciousness of the Cross at the, 288
of Peter, The transfiguration after the, ... 215
Confirmation,
of Jesus, The, . . . 110 *f*

Conflict, PAGE
  Love and sin in, . . . 305
  Jesus' supreme, ... 154
  Thirty years of, ... 153
Consciousness,
  of lack, Sorrow the, . . 299
Consummation,
  The transfiguration a, . . 228
Continuity,
  of existence after death,
    The, ... 243
Conversation,
  of the exodus, The, . . 216
Conviction,
  The work of the Spirit
    that of, ... 419
Cost,
  of possessing the kingdoms,
    The, ... 192
Creation,
  Jesus Master of, ... 126
  Jesus a new, ... 354
  Man, master of, ... 125
  Man's cultivation of, and
    dominion over, . . . 30
  The purpose of man's, . 439
  The Word in, ... 37
Creator,
  of history, Christ the, . . 259
Crises,
  in the life of Christ, The, 17
Crisis,
  God's method of process
    and, ... 16
  John's sense of a coming, 141
Cross,
  His acquaintance at the, . 343
  at baptism, Jesus' con-
    sciousness of the, . . 288
  The centurion at the, 331, 337f
  at the coming of the
    Greeks, Jesus' con-
    sciousness of the, . . 289
  The shepherdless crowd at
    the, ... 342
  His disciples at the, 332, 343
  The facts preceding the, 295f
  Earth's religious failure at
    the, ... 340

Cross, PAGE
  The Divine foreknowl-
    edge of the, ... 304
  in the Garden, Jesus' con-
    sciousness of the, . . 289
  Worldly government at
    the, ... 337f
  The revelation of grace
    in the, ... 311f
  Jesus always conscious of
    the, ... 275
  The revelation of love in
    the, ... 312f
  The malefactors at the,
    331, 339
  Mary Magdalene at the, . 330
  Mary His mother at the, . 330
  the meaning of Messiah-
    ship, The, ... 215
  The multitude at the, 332, 342
  at Peter's confession, Jesus'
    consciousness of the, . 288
  The chief priests at the,
    332, 340
  solves two problems, The, 290
  Salome at the, . . . 330
  The Sanhedrin at the, 332, 340
  The soldiers at the, 331, 338
  Sorrow at the, . . . 333
  The superscription of the, 325
  at transfiguration, Jesus'
    consciousness of the, . 288
  The seven utterances of
    the, ... 294
  The revelation of wisdom
    in the, ... 313f
  The women at the, . . 330
  The world's folly at the, . 341
Crowd,
  at the Cross, The shep-
    herdless, ... 342
Crucifixion,
  The human act of, . . 305f
  Human degradation in the, 306
Cry,
  of physical agony, The, 295f
  of spiritual anguish, The, 297f
Culture,
  Greek, ... 96

DARING, PAGE
of the devil, The, . . . 186

Days,
of Incarnation, The, . . 390

Death,
Continuity of existence
after, ... 243
The disciples' attitude to-
wards, ... 247
The Master bowing to, . 249
The Master Lord over, . 249
The Master superior to, . 249
why a necessity to man, . 395
Reconciliation only through, 94
The resurrection of Jesus
proves the value of His, 377
Spiritual and material, . 49
The transfiguration the
prelude to, ... 231
The transfiguration the
preparation for, . . . 233
The moral value created
in Jesus', ... 359

Declarations,
of the birth of Jesus, The, 71 f

Deeds,
of Jesus, The, ... 91

Defeat,
The devil's confession of, 202
of the devil, The utter, . 199

Degradation,
in the Cross, Human, . . 306

Deities,
Man's creation of false, . 42 f

Destruction,
of swine, The, . . . 308 f

Devil,
the agent of temptation,
The, ... 157 f
The argument of the, . .
167, 178, 189
His claim to the king-
doms, ... 189
His confession of defeat, . 202
The daring of the, . . . 186
The utter defeat of the, . 199
His estimate of humanity, 166
His estimate of Jesus, . 203

Devil, PAGE
His estimate of Divine
Sonship, ... 167
His inversion of Divine
order, ... 201
Job and the, ... 166
The method of the, . . 32
The personality of the, . 158
The repulse of the, . .
168, 181, 192
The subtlety of the, . . 154
The use of the Word by
the, ... 180

Disciples,
at the Cross, The, . 332, 343
The dazed, ... 250
The influence of the trans-
figuration on the, . . 255
specially associated with
Jesus, The, ... 247
Their misunderstanding of
Messiahship, ... 217
Their speech interrupted, 254
The transfiguration for the
sake of the, . . 219, 246
The transfiguration for the
strengthening of the faith
of the, ... 218

Disease,
in Jesus, No, ... 135

Divine,
act, The resurrection a, . 364
foreknowledge of the
Cross, The, ... 304
Kingship, . . . 319 f
Kingship acknowledged,
The, ... 327
purpose, Jesus the perfection of the, ... 393
satisfaction of Jesus, The, 254

Doing,
and teaching of Jesus,
The, ... 115

Dominion,
over creation, Man's, . . 30

Dove,
The descending, . . . 121

EARTH, PAGE
   Its religious failure at the
      Cross, ... 340
   The interest of heaven in, 244

Economy,
   The Divine authority of
      the Mosaic, ... 205

Egypt,
   The flight of Jesus into, 108 f

Εἰκὼν,
   25

Elijah,
   and Moses still men, . . 243
   the prophet and reformer,
              236 f, 390

Enoch,
   390

Estimate,
   of the devil of humanity,
      The, ... 166
   of the devil of Jesus, The, 203
   of the devil of Divine
      Sonship, The, ... 167
   of the Master of one soul,
      The, ... 204

Evil,
   The authority of Jesus
      over, ... 207 f
   Christ's thirty years' con-
      flict with, ... 153
   Christ's perfect victory
      over, ... 198 f
   in man, The genesis of, . 57

Existence,
   after death, Continuity of, 243

Εξοδον,
   . . . . . . 240, 318

Exodus,
   The children of Israel,
      and their, ... 240 f
   The completed, ... 326
   The conversation of the, . 216
   The Kingly, ... 317 f
   The unfinished, ... 326

Expiatory,
   sufferings of Christ, The, 303

Expositor,
   of the Word, The Spirit
      the, ... 430

FACT, PAGE
   of ascension, The, . . . 389
   The value of the resurrec-
      tion granted by the, . 377

Facts,
   preceding the Cross, The, 295 f

Failure,
   at the Cross, Earth's relig-
      ious, ... 340

Faith,
   The resurrection the an-
      chorage for, . . . 373 f
   The transfiguration for the
      strengthening of the
      disciples', ... 218

Fall,
   The ignorance resulting
      from the, ... 40
   of man, The, ... 158
   the result of independent
      action, The, ... 33
   of Satan and the angels,
      The, ... 158, 355

Familiarity,
   with the Word, The Mas-
      ter's, ... 205

Father,
   Jesus a full Revelation of
      the, ... 391

Favourite,
   Jesus a, ... 113

Fellowship,
   of the shekel, The, . 263 f

First,
   Adam, The, ... 156

Flight,
   of Jesus into Egypt, The, 108 f

Floral,
   culture, ... 30

Folly,
   in the Cross, The world's, 341

Food,
   Spiritual food more than
      material, ... 171

Forces,
   The three world, . . 306 f

Foreknowledge,
   of the Cross, the Divine, . 304

Forerunner,   PAGE
    John the, ... 137 *f*

Forsaking,
    of Christ, The, . . . 297 *f*

Fulfiller,
    of history, The Christ the, 259
    of past prophecy, The
      Christ the, ... 87

GARDEN,
    The consciousness of the
      Cross in the, ... 289

Genesis,
    of evil in man, The, . . 57

Gift,
    of Christ, The, . , . . 61

Gifts,
    of the Magi, The, . . . 100

Glorification,
    the third fact in redemp-
      tion, ... 440

Glory,
    hidden, Christ's, . . 224 *f*
    inherent, The transfigura-
      tion, ... 227

God,
    His " afters," 221
    His approbation of Christ, 123
    His continual approval of
      Jesus, ... 363
    The attack on Christ's
      loyalty to the will of, . 163
    The attack on Christ's
      trust in, ... 174 *f*
    Christ's delight in the will
      of. 175
    Christ the Mystery of, . . 67 *f*
    Human conception of, . . 41
    Development of the reve-
      lation of, ... 16 *f*
    The God-man the meeting
      place between man and, 426
    Jesus the Gateway of man
      to, ... 90
    Jesus the purpose of, . . 87
    Jesus not smitten of, . . 400
    Jesus identified as Son of, 254
    His knowledge infinite, . 54 *f*
    The Lamb of God the
      Son of, ... 148

God,   PAGE
    Human life sustained in, . 51
    The infinite love of, . . 437
    His love the necessity of
      His Being, ... 61
    His love the reason of
      redemption, ... 61
    Man's anthropomorphic
      ideas of, ... 86
    Man joined to Christ is re-
      stored to, ... 422
    known to man, . . . 435 *f*
    Man a revelation of, . . 443
    Man the shadow of, . . 25
    His methods of process
      and crisis, ... 16
    expressed in Nature . 50, 86
    The pain of, ... 400
    in realization of the char-
      acter and conduct of
      Christ, Man like, . . 443
    His rejection of imperfec-
      tion, ... 365
    His rejection of man an
      act of love, ... 368
    Restoration to the image
      of, ... 439
    Satan a servant of, . . . 354
    His seal upon Christ's
      work the resurrection, 361 *f*
    The Self-revelation of, . 87
    The severity and judg-
      ment of, ... 312
    The Son of, ... 81
    capable of sorrow, . . . 401
    The unity of, ... 88
    The value of the approba-
      tion of, ... 123 *f*
    The way back to, . . . 411
    His will simple, . . . 57
    The work of, ... 283
    The alone worship of, . . 194

God-Man,
    No explanation of the, . 79
    unknown in history, The, 80
    human and Divine, The, 78
    the meeting-place between
      man and God, The, . 426

Gods,
    of Rome and Greece, The, 87

Government, PAGE
at the Cross, Worldly, . 337 f
of Rome, The, ... 96
Grace,
abounded more exceed-
ingly, ... 316
at the Cross, The revela-
tion of, ... 311 f
Γράμματα,
. . . . 129
Greece,
The culture of, ... 96
The gods of, ... 87
Greeks,
Jesus' consciousness of the
Cross at the coming of
the, ... 289
Growth,
of Jesus, The, . . . 110 f

HAPPEN,
If no resurrection, what
did, ... 380
Head,
of a new race, Jesus the, . 369
Heaven,
Abel in, ... 392
in earth, The interest of, . 244
Heavens,
The opened, ... 120
Hebrew,
nation a theocracy, The, . 177
prophets, The, ... 137
religion, The, ... 196
Heresies,
of the Church, The, . . 182
Herod,
and the innocents, . . . 100
History,
Christ the Creator of, . . 259
Christ the Fulfiller of, . . 259
Humanity,
The devil's estimate of, . 166
The solidarity of, . . . 446
in transfiguration, Perfect, 229
Hunger,
the avenue of approach,
The sense of, ... 165

Hunger, PAGE
natural and sinless, The
sense of, ... 165
I,
am's of Jesus, The, . . 119
Ideal,
The realization of the
ideal greater than the
original, ... 447
Ideas,
The Incarnation corrects
false, ... 85
Identification,
of Jesus with sinners, The, 120
If,
Christ be not risen, . 378 f
Image,
Man's restoration to God's, 439
Imperfection,
God's rejection of, . . . 365
Importance,
of the resurrection, The, . 371
In,
the beginning, ... 72 f
Incarnation,
not atonement, The, . . 74
The days of the, . . . 390
corrects false ideas, The, . 85
initial and fundamental,
The, ... 67
The purpose of the, . . 84
not reconciliation, The, . 94
The testimony of Scripture
to the, ... 67
Individual,
apprehension of Christ,
The, ... 433 f
Induction,
of Jesus to office, The, . 115
Infancy,
of Jesus, The, . . . 108 f
Influence,
of the transfiguration on
the disciples, The, . . 255
Innocents,
The slaughter of the, . . 100

Intelligence,   PAGE
  Human wisdom limits hu-
    man, ... 68
Interest,
  of heaven in earth, The, . 244
Introduction,
  of John the Baptist, The, 138
Inversion,
  of the Divine order, The
    devil's, ... 201
Investiture,
  with a name, Jesus', . 396*f*
Isolation,
  in Christ's life, The grow-
    ing, ... 292
Issue,
  of Christ's work, The, . 425
  The seed and its, . . . 230
  of sin, The final, . . . 297

JERUSALEM,
  The city of, . . . 175*f*
  Jesus and, ... 176
  The temple at, ... 177

Jesus,
  perfect in affection, . 131*f*
  God's continual approval
    of, ... 363
  The ascension of, . . . 397
  His authority over evil, 207*f*
  The baptism of, ... 120
  and the wild beasts, . . 157
  a Benefactor, ... 116
  a Carpenter, ... 113
  His carpentry perfect, . 134
  The childhood of, . . . 110
  The circumcision of, . . 109
  The confirmation of, . 110*f*
  a new creation, ... 354
  always conscious of the
    Cross, ... 275
  His death valuable because
    of His perfect life, . . 231
  The deeds of, ... 91
  The devil's estimate of, . 203
  The three disciples asso-
    ciated with, ... 247
  No disease in, ... 135
  His doing and teaching, . 115

Jesus,   PAGE
  a favourite, ... 113
  The flight into Egypt of, 108*f*
  The Fulfiller of prophecy, 221
  The Gateway of God to
    man, ... 90
  The Gateway of man to
    God, ... 90
  not smitten of God, . . 400
  The growth of, . . . 110*f*
  the Head of a new race, . 369
  The "I am's" of, . . . 119
  His identification with
    sinners, ... 120
  His induction to office, . 115
  The infancy of, . . . 108*f*
  His investiture with a
    Name, ... 396*f*
  and Jerusalem, ... 176
  and John, ... 142
  the Lamb of God, . . . 143
  The Manhood of, . . 112*f*
  Man's unpreparedness for, 95
  Master of creation, . . 126
  Master of learning, . 129*f*
  conscious of His whole
    mission, ... 275
  only, ... 265
  His perfection, ... 120
  His physical perfection, 133*f*
  the perfection of the Di-
    vine purpose, ... 393
  His perfection of Spirit, 126*f*
  a perfect human Personal-
    ity, ... 89
  in the temple, The presen-
    tation of, ... 108*f*
  God's purpose for human-
    ity, ... 87
  a thought reader, . . . 130
  His relation to unfallen
    powers, ... 208*f*
  His return to Nazareth, 108*f*
  the full Revelation of the
    Father, ... 391
  the final Sacrifice for sin, 145
  The Divine satisfaction of, 254
  All secrets apparent to, . 131
  the Self-revelation of God, 87
  the Shepherd of the sheep, 370
  identified as the Son of
    God, ... 254

Jesus, PAGE
  led by the Spirit in temp-
    tation, ... 159
  His teaching, ... 90
  His teaching in John,. . 118
  His teaching in Luke, 117 f
  His teaching in Mark, . 117
  His teaching in Matthew, 116f
  perfect in spite of tempta-
    tion, ... 136
  The transfiguration unnec-
    essary to, ... 228
  The moral value created
    in the death of, . . . 359
  His victory over sin as-
    sumed, ... 356 f
  His victory over sin as
    origin, ... 354
  His victory over sin from
    without, ... 356
  The youth of, . . . 112 f

Jewish,
  nation, The, ... 326

Jews,
  Their misunderstanding of
    Scripture, ... 95

Job,
  and the devil, ... 166

John,
  the Baptist, ... 137 f
  His congregations in Ju-
    dæa,. 139
  His consciousness of sin, 139
  the forerunner, . . . 137 f
  His minute introduction, . 138
  and Jesus, ... 142
  Jesus' teaching in the
    Gospel of, ... 118
  the last of the prophets, . 137
  and the publicans, . . 140
  His sense of a crisis, . . 141
  and the soldiers, . . . 141
  His preliminary vision, . 139
  His supreme vision of love, 142

Joy,
  and sorrow, Love the ca-
    pacity for, ... 401

Judæa,
  John's congregations in, . 139

Judaism, PAGE
  238

Judgment,
  of God, The severity and, 312

Justification,
  . . . . 291, 422
  the first fact in redemp-
    tion,. 440

KING,
  The resurrection the vic-
    tory of the, ... 364
  The Son the anointed, . . 190

Kingdom,
  The perfect, ... 196 f

Kingdoms,
  The claim of the devil to
    the, ... 189
  The cost of possessing the, 192
  The imperfect, ... 195
  The vision of the, . . . 188

Kingship,
  acknowledged, The Di-
    vine, ... 327

Knowledge,
  God's infinite, ... 54 f
  of man restored, The, . . 443

LACK,
  Sorrow the consciousness
    of, ... 299

Lamb,
  the active Administrator,
    The, ... 404
  the final authority, The, . 403
  the Bearer of sin as a
    principle, The, ... 147
  of God, Jesus the, . . . 143
  slain, A, ... 402
  the Son of God, The, . . 148
  in the Old and New Testa-
    ments, The, ... 145
  on the throne of power,
    The, ... 403

Last,
  Adam, The, ... 156

Lawgiver,
  Moses the, ... 236

Learning,
  Jesus Master of, . . . 129 f

Life,   PAGE
  The Christ, ... 423
  all sustained in God, . . 51
  The growing isolation in
    Christ's, ... 292
  Jesus' death valuable be-
    cause of His perfect, . 231

Link,
  between resurrection and
    pentecost, The ascension
    the, ... 389

Lord,
  over death, The Master, . 249

Love,
  the capacity for joy or sor-
    row, ... 401
  of God, the infinite, . . . 437
  God's rejection of man an
    act of, ... 368
  John's supreme vision of, 142
  the necessity of God's Be-
    ing, ... 56, 61
  The revelation of, . . 312 f
  and sin in conflict, . . . 305

Loyalty,
  to God's will attacked,
    Christ's, ... 163

Luke,
  Jesus' teaching in the
    Gospel of, ... 117 f

Lunatic,
  in the valley, The, . . 262 f

MAGI,
  The, ... 98
  The gifts of the, ... 100

Malefactor,
  The story of the, ... 325

Malefactors,
  at the Cross, The, . 331, 339

Mammon,
  worship, ... 45 f

Man,
  The activity of redeemed, 443
  The original capacity of, 36
  Christ's challenge as, . . 169
  Christ Jesus, The magni-
    fying of the, ... 436

Man,   PAGE
  joined to Christ is restored
    to God, ... 422
  made for communion with
    God, ... 28
  His conception of God, . 42
  His cultivation of creation, 30
  Death why a necessity to, 395
  and false deities, ... 42 f
  His dominion over crea-
    tion, ... 30
  The fall of, ... 158
  His fall independent ac-
    tion, ... 33
  His fall and ignorance re-
    sulting, ... 40
  The free will of, . . . 32, 38
  The genesis of evil in, . 57
  demands a god, ... 41
  fallen unlike God, . . . 59
  like the God he creates, . 48
  like God in realization of
    the character and con-
    duct of Christ, ... 443
  God known to, ... 435 f
  The God-man the meet-
    ing-place between God
    and, ... 426
  His ideas of God anthro-
    pomorphic, ... 86
  the image of Deity in
    spirit, ... 27
  a ruined instrument, . . 41
  Jesus the Gateway of God
    to, ... 90
  know thyself, ... 52
  His knowledge, affection,
    and will restored, . . 443 f
  His knowledge restored
    in redemption, ... 37 f
  fallen a lie, ... 60
  master of creation, . . . 125
  of Nazareth, The ascen-
    sion of the, ... 392
  restored to the possibility
    of his own being, . . 443
  The preparation of the
    spirit of, ... 433
  The purpose of the crea-
    tion of, ... 439
  The resurrection of the
    perfect, ... 364

Man, PAGE
a revelation of God, . . 443
a ruin through alienation, 35
his ruin and redemption, 17
a shadow of God, . . 25
The Son of, ... 81
essentially spirit, . . 26 *f*, 52
The Spirit reveals Christ
to, ... 430
responding by submission
is saved, ... 420
The transfigured, . . . 225
His unpreparedness for
Jesus, ... 95
created for work, . . . 198
Manhood,
of Jesus, The, . . . 112 *f*
The perfection of, . . . 392
Mark,
Jesus' teaching in the
Gospel of, · 117
Mary,
Magdalene at the Cross, . 330
Magdalene, The sorrow
of, ... 333 *f*
His mother at the Cross, 330
The sorrow of His
mother, ... 335 *f*
Master,
bowing to death, The, . 249
Lord over death, The, . 249
superior to death, The . 249
His estimate of one soul, 204
His familiarity with the
Word, ... 205
His temptation in relation
to His ministry, . . 205 *f*
His use of the Word, . . 205
Matthew,
Jesus' teaching in the
Gospel of, ... 116 *f*
Meaning,
of Messiahship, The Cross
the, ... 215
Mediation,
perfect in resurrection,
The Saviour's, ... 364
Medium,
of Divine expression, The
Word, ... 73

Medium, PAGE
of Self-Revelation, Christ
God's, ... 428
Men,
Moses and Elijah still, . 243
Messiahship,
The Cross the meaning of, 215
The disciples' misunder-
standing of, ... 217
Methods,
of God in process and
crisis, The, ... 16
of the devil, The, . . . 32
Mind,
of Christ, The, ... 93
Ministry,
Angelic, ... 99
The Master's temptation
in relation to His, . 205 *f*
The purpose of angelic, . 439
Mission,
The attack on Christ's . 186
of Christ, The, ... 14
Jesus conscious of His
whole, ... 275
Misunderstanding,
of Messiahship, The dis-
ciples', ... 217
Moloch,
The worship of, ... 44
Μορφή,
. . . . 76
Moses,
and Elijah still men, . . 243
the Lawgiver, ... 236
Mother,
at the Cross, His, . . . 330
The sorrow of His, . . . 335
Mountain,
The temptation on the, . 188
Multitudes,
at the Cross, The, . 332, 342
Mystery,
in Colossians, The three-
fold, ... 424
revealed, The, ... 68
of silence, The, ... 301
The secret things a, . . 69

NAME, PAGE
 Jesus' investiture with a, 396
 above every name, The, 396 f

Nation,
 The Jewish, ... 326

Nature,
 God expressed in, . . 50, 86
 of sin, The true, . . . 304 f

Nazareth,
 The ascension of the Man
  of, ... 392
 and its inhabitants, . . . 127
 Jesus' return to, . . . 108 f

Necessity,
 to man, Death why a, . 395
 The resurrection a, . . . 352

New,
 Testament, The authority
  of the, ... 382

OBEDIENCE,
 to revelation demanded, . 434

Object,
 presented, Christ the, . . 434

Occasion,
 of the transfiguration,
  The, ... 215 f

Order,
 The devil's inversion of
  Divine, ... 201
 of the temptations, The, 162

Origin,
 of sin, The primal, . . . 355
 Jesus' victory over sin as, 354

PAIN,
 of God, The, ... 400

Parable,
 The threefold, ... 280

Paralysis,
 of sin borne and broken,
  The, ... 324

Parliament,
 of religions, The, . . . 253

Passing,
 of Moses and Elijah, The
  significance of the, . . 241

Paul, PAGE
 His argument for resurrection, ... 378

Penalty,
 of sin borne and broken,
  The, ... 324
 borne, A value in the, . 299

Pentecost,
 The ascension a link be-
  tween resurrection and, 389

Perfection,
 of the Church in Christ,
  The, ... 424
 of Divine purpose, Jesus
  the, ... 393
 of Jesus physically, The, 133 f
 of Jesus in spite of temptation, The, ... 136
 of Manhood, The, . . . 392
 The resurrection the Man's, 364
 of Saviourhood, The, . . 394

Personality,
 of the devil, The, . . . 158
 Jesus a perfect human, . 89
 unlimited, Perfect, . . . 28

Peter,
 The blundering of, 233, 250 f
 Jesus' consciousness of the
  Cross at the confession
  of, ... 288
 His Pentecostal sermon, . 351
 The transfiguration after
  his confession, ... 215

Pharisees,
 the ritualists, The, . . . 140

Place,
 of the temptation, The . 156

Plan,
 Temptation in the Divine, 159

Plentitude,
 and power of the Spirit,
  The, ... 206

Possessing,
 the kingdoms, The cost of, 192

Possibility,
 of his own being, Man restored to the, ... 443

Power, PAGE
The Lamb on the throne
of, ... 403
and plentitude of the
Spirit, The, ... 206

Powers,
Jesus' relation to un-
fallen, ... 208 f

Preparation,
for death, The transfiguration the, . . . 233
of man's spirit, The, . 433
of a written record, The, 430 f

Presence,
of Moses and Elijah, The
significance of the, . . 237

Presentation,
in the temple of Jesus,
The, ... 108 f

Priestism,
destroyed in resurrection, 367

Priests,
at the Cross, The chief,
332, 340

Principle,
governing will, The, . . 38

Privacy,
of the thirty years, The, 107 f

Problems,
The Cross solves two, . . 290

Process,
God's method of crisis and, 16

Promise,
made by Christ of the
Spirit, The, ... 407
of the Spirit, The, . . . 408
of the Spirit through the
prophets, The, . . . 408 f

Proof,
of resurrection, The Church
the supreme, ... 383

Prophecy,
Jesus the Fulfiller of, . . 221
The voices of, ... 99

Prophet,
and reformer, Elijah the,
236 f, 390

Prophets, PAGE
The Hebrew, ... 137
John the last of the, . . 137
The promise of the Spirit
through the, . . . 408 f

Publicans,
and John, The, ... 140

Publicity,
of the three years, The, 115 f

Purpose,
of angelic ministry, The, 439
of Incarnation, The, . . 84
Jesus the perfection of the
Divine, ... 393
for humanity, Jesus God's, 87
of man's creation, The, . 439
of the transfiguration,
The, ... 219 f

RACE,
Jesus the Head of a new, 369

Rationalists,
The Sadducees the, . . . 140

Realization,
of the ideal greater than
the original ideal, The, 447

Reconciliation,
Incarnation not, ... 94
only through death, . . . 94

Reconstruction,
impossible within destruction, ... 60

Record,
The Spirit the Expositor
of the, ... 432
The Spirit the Preparer
of a, ... 430 f

Redemption,
Glorification the third fact
in, ... 440
Justification the first fact
in, ... 440
Knowledge restored to
man in, ... 37 f
God's love the reason of, 61
Man's ruin and, ... 17
Sanctification the second
fact in, ... 440
the work of the Spirit,
The experience of, . . 420

Reformer,   PAGE
    ah the prophet and, .
                        236 f, 390
Regeneration,
      420
Rejection,
    of imperfection, God's, . 365
    of man an act of love,
        God's, ... 368
Relation,
    to unfallen powers, Jesus',
                            208 f
Religion,
    The Hebrew, ...   96
Religions,
    The Parliament of, . . . 253
Repulse,
    of the devil, The, 168, 181, 192
Responsibility,
    Revelation creates, . . . 222
Restoration,
    Governmental, ... 425
    Judicial, ... 421
    of man to God's image,
        The, ... 439
    Vital, ... 423
Result,
    of the vision, The, . . 260 f
Resurrection,
    a Divine act, The, . . . 364
    Faith's anchorage in the, 373 f
    The appearances after the, 382
    Paul's argument for the, . 378
    The Church the supreme
        proof of the, ... 383
    granted by the fact, The
        value of the, ... 377
    What did happen if no,   380
    The importance of the, . 371
    The Saviour's mediation
        perfect in, ... 364
    a necessity, The, ... 352
    and Pentecost, The ascen-
        sion the link between, 389
    the Man's perfection, The, 364
    Priestism destroyed in,   367
    God's seal upon Christ's
        work, The, ... 361 f

Resurrection,   PAGE
    proves the value of the
        death of Jesus, The, . 377
    the King's victory, The, . 364
    a perfect victory, The, . . 351
    a threefold victory, The, 353 f
    The world powers over-
        thrown in, ... 367
Return,
    of Jesus to Nazareth, The,
                            108 f
Revealed,
    The mystery, ... 68
Revelation,
    according to capacity, . . 222
    Christ God's Medium of
        Self-, ... 428
    The development of God's, 16 f
    of the Father, Jesus the full, 391
    of God, Man a, ... 443
    of grace in the Cross, The,
                            311 f
    of love in the Cross, The, 312 f
    demanded, The obedience
        to, ... 434
    creates responsibility, . . 222
    of wisdom in the Cross,
        The, ... 313 f
Righteousness,
    of conduct possible ? Is, . 291
Risen,
    If Christ be not, . . . 378 f
Ritualists,
    The Pharisees the, . . . 140
Rome,
    The gods of, ... 87
    The government of, . . . 96
SACRIFICE,
    for sin, Jesus the final, . 145
Sadducees,
    The rationalists the, . . 140
Salome,
    at the Cross, ... 330
    The sorrow of, ... 335
Sanctification,
    the second fact in redemp-
        tion, ... 410

Sanhedrim, PAGE
at the Cross, The, . 332, 340
Satan,
and the angels, The fall
of, ... 158, 355
a servant of God, . . . 354
Satisfaction,
of Jesus, The Divine, . . 254
Saul,
of Tarsus, ... 383
Saviour,
The resurrection the medi-
ation of the, ... 364
Saviourhood,
The perfection of, . . 394
Scientific,
discovery, ... 31
investigation, ... 53
Scripture,
The Jews' misunderstand-
ing of, ... 95
to Incarnation, The testi-
mony of, ... 67
Seal,
upon Christ's work, The
resurrection God's, . 361 f
Secrets,
to Jesus, No, ... 131
Seed,
and its issue, The, . . . 230
Sermon,
Peter's Pentecostal, . . . 351
Servant,
of God, Satan a, ... 354
The suffering, ... 95
Service,
Worship is, ... 194
Severity,
and judgment of God,
The, ... 312
Shadow,
of God, Man a, ... 25
Sheep,
Jesus the Shepherd of the, 370
Shekel,
The fellowship of the, 263 f

Shepherd, PAGE
of the sheep, Jesus the, . 370
Shepherds,
of Bethlehem, The, . . . 100
Significance,
of Moses' and Elijah's
passing, ... 241
of Moses' and Elijah's
presence, ... 237
of the temptation, The, . 159
Silence,
The mystery of, ... 301
Sin,
The initial act and result
of, ... 33 f
assumed, Jesus Victor over,
356 f
John's consciousness of, . 139
at the Cross, ... 339
on the intellect, The effect
of, ... 53
The final issue of, . . . 297
Jesus the final sacrifice for, 145
in conflict with love, . . 305
The true nature of, . . 304 f
The primal origin of, . . 355
as origin, Jesus Victor
over, ... 354
borne and broken, The
penalty and paralysis
of, ... 324
as principle, The Lamb
the Bearer of, ... 147
The relative result of, . . 43
The slavery of, ... 317
from without, Jesus Victor
over, ... 356
Slain,
A Lamb, ... 402
Slaughter,
of the innocents, The, . 100
Slavery,
of sin, The, ... 317
Soldiers,
at the Cross, The, . 331, 338
and John, The, ... 141
Solidarity,
of humanity, The, . . . 446

Son,   PAGE
  The, ...   82
  of God, The, ...   81
  of God, Jesus identified as
    the, ...   254
  The anointed King the, . 190
  of God, The Lamb the, . 148
  of Man, The, ... 81 f

Sonship,
  The devil's estimate of
    Divine, ... 167

Σοφία,
  128

Sorrow,
  the consciousness of lack, 299
  at the Cross, ... 333 f
  God capable of, .   . . 401
  Love the capacity for joy
    and, ...   401
  of Mary Magdalene, The,
                           333 f
  of Mary His mother,
    The, ... 335 f
  of Salome, The, ... 335

Soul,
  The Master's estimate of
    one, ...   204

Speech,
  of the disciples interrupted,
    The, ...   254

Spirit,
  The body the expression
    of the, ...   27
  A broken, ... 399
  made by Christ, The prom-
    ise of the, ... 407
  for others, Christ received
    the, ... 408, 410
  reveals Christ to man,
    The, ...   430
  unveils Christ, The, . . 433 f
  why given to Christ, The, 411
  Conviction the work of
    the, ...   419
  the Expositor of the Rec-
    ord, The, ... 430
  The perfection of Jesus
    in, ...   126 f
  The plentitude and power
    of the, ... 206

Spirit,   PAGE
  The preparation of Man's, 433
  the Preparer of a written
    Record, The, .   . . 430 f
  The promise of the, . . 408
  through the prophets, The
    promise of the, .   . 408 f
  The experience of redemp-
    tion the work of the, . 420
  Atoning suffering in the
    wounding of Jesus', . 400
  in temptation, Jesus led
    by the, ... 159

Star,
  in the east, The, . . .   97

Statement,
  The sufferings of Christ
    impossible of final, . . 293

Story,
  of the malefactor, The, 325 f

Strength,
  of manhood is in submis-
    sion, The, ... 170

Submission,
  is saved, Man responding
    by, ... 420
  The strength of manhood
    is in, ...   170

Subtlety,
  of the devil, The, . . . 154

Suffering,
  in the wounding of Jesus'
    Spirit, Atoning, . . . 400

Sufferings,
  Atoning, ... 303
  of Christ impossible of
    final statement, The, . 293
  Expiatory, ... 303
  Vicarious, ... 303

Superscription,
  of the Cross, The, . . . 325

Swine,
  The destruction of, . . 308 f

Symbols,
  The sacramental, . . .   31

Tarsus,
  Saul of, ... 383

Teaching, PAGE
of Jesus, The doing and, 115
Jesus', ... 90

Τέχτων,
. . . . 114

Telepathy,
. . . . 131

Temple,
Christ and the, ... 177
at Jerusalem, The, . . . 177
The temptation on the
wing of the, ... 175 f
The wing of the, ... 178

Temptation,
Completion of every, . . 207
Forty days of, ... 162
The devil the agent of, 157 f
Jesus led by the Spirit in, 159
Jesus perfect in spite of, 136
of the Master in relation
to His ministry, The, 205 f
on the mountain, The, . 188
The place of the, ... 156
in the Divine plan, . . . 159
The significance of the, . 159
The time of the, . . . 155 f
in the wilderness, The, 163 f
on the wing of the temple,
The, ... 175 f

Temptations,
The order of the, ... 162

Testament,
The authority of the New, 382

Testaments,
The Lamb in the Old and
New, ... 145

Testing,
of trust, The, ... 183

Theocracy,
The Hebrew nation a, . 177

Theory,
of Atonement, A, . 297, 301

Things,
The mystery of secret, . 69
Secret and revealed, . . 69

Thought,
Reader, Jesus a, ... 130

Throne, PAGE
of power, The Lamb on
the, ... 403

Time,
of the temptation, The, 155 f

Transfiguration,
Communion issues in, . . 222
The consciousness of the
Cross at, ... 288
a consummation, The, . . 228
The conversation of the
exodus at the, ... 216
for the disciples' sake,
The, ... 219, 246
glory inherent, ... 227
Perfect humanity in, . . 229
Its influence on the dis-
ciples, ... 255
unnecessary to Jesus, The, 228
its occasion, The, . . 215 f
after Peter's confession,
The, ... 215
the prelude to death, The, 231
the preparation for death,
The, ... 233
its purpose, The, . . . 219 f
for the strengthening of
the disciples' faith, The, 218
and its witnesses, The, . 218

Trust,
in God attacked, Christ's, 174 f
never tempts, Perfect, . 183 f
The testing of, . . . 183

Unity,
of God, The, ... 88

Utterances,
of the Cross, The seven, 294

Valley,
The lunatic in the, . . 262 f

Value,
of God's approbation of
Jesus, The, ... 123 f
created in the death of
Jesus, The moral, . 359
of Jesus' death, The resurrection proves the, . . 377
in the penalty borne, A, . 299

Value,   PAGE
    of resurrection granted by
        the fact, The,   . . . 377
Vicarious,
    sufferings, ... 303
Victory,
    The authority of, ... 207
    Christ's perfect, . . . 198 f
    The resurrection the
        King's, ... 364
    The resurrection a perfect, 351
    The resurrection a three-
        fold, ... 353 f
    over sin assumed, Jesus', 356 f
    over sin as origin, Jesus', 354
    over sin from without,
        Jesus', ... 356
Vision,
    of the kingdoms, The, . 188
    John's preliminary, . . . 139
    of love, John's supreme, . 142
    The result of the, . . 260 f
Visions,
    The worth of, ... 261
Voice,
    The living, ... 121

WAY,
    back to God, The, . . . 411
Weapon,
    The Word the Master's,
                            169, 181, 193
Wilderness,
    The temptation in the, 163 f
Will,
    Christ's delight in God's, 175
    of God attacked, Christ's
        loyalty to the, ... 163
    of God simple and benefi-
        cent, The, ... 57
    of God under authority,
        The, ... 39
    The governing principle
        of, ... 38
    Jesus perfect in, . . 132 f
    Man's free, ... 32, 38
    restored, Man's knowl-
        edge, affection, and, 443 /
Wing,
    of the temple, The, . . 178

Wisdom,   PAGE
    The Cross the revelation
        of Divine, ... 313 f
    limits human intelligence,
        Human, ... 68
Without,
    Jesus' victory over sin
        from, ... 356
Witnesses,
    of the transfiguration, The, 218
Women,
    at the Cross, The, . . . 330
Word,
    The devil's use of the, . 180
    of God in creation, The, 37
    The Master's familiarity
        with the, ... 205
    The Master's use of the, . 205
    the Master's weapon, The,
                            169, 181, 193
    the Medium of Divine ex-
        pression, The, ... 73
Work,
    of God, The, ... 283
    The issue of Christ's, . . 425
    Man created for, . . . 198
    The resurrection God's
        seal upon Christ's, . 361 f
    of the Spirit, Conviction the, 419
    of the Spirit, The experi-
        ence of redemption the, 420
World,
    at the Cross, The folly of the, 341
    forces, The three,   306 f
    powers overthrown in res-
        urrection, The, ... 367
Worship,
    of Baal, The, ... 44
    of God alone, The, . . . 194
    of Mammon, The, . . 45 /
    of Moloch, The, . . . 44
    is service, ... 194
    Spiritual, ... 27
Worth,
    of visions, The, ... 261
Years,
    of conflict with evil, Thirty, 153
    The thirty private, . . 107 f
    The three public, . . 115 f
Youth,
    of Jesus, The, ... 112 f